PHOENIX ROCK II

CENTRAL ARIZONA GRANITE

GREG OPLAND

CHOCKSTONE PRESS
EVERGREEN COLORADO

DEDICATION

This guide is dedicated to my first climbing partner, Tim Schneider, for all the good times and great summits we've experienced together. From forty foot sport routes, up the snow covered slopes of Mt. Humphreys and onto the walls of Yosemite. And for those climbs still to come. Keep 'em comin' Toolman!

And to my other climbing partners, who've put up with my grouchy moods, notetaking, photo sessions, and other guidebook related pursuits. Good partners make all the difference in the world and I've been luckier than anyone.

Felicia Terry	Mike Kaczocha
Scott Aldinger	Dean Wade Vincent
Lisa Schmitz	Pam Metzger
Al Muto	and Fred the Wünderhünd

Thanks!

PHOENIX ROCK II

Front cover: Climbers on the summit of the Praying Monk at Camelback Mountain. The McDowell Mountains are in the distant background. Photo by the author.

Back cover: Felicia Terry on the second pitch of Don't Bug Me at Jacuzzi Spires. Photo by the author.

ISBN 1-57540-023-5

Published and distributed by:
Chockstone Press, Inc.
P.O. Box 3505
Evergreen, Colorado 80437-3505

WARNING: CLIMBING IS A SPORT WHERE YOU MAY BE SERIOUSLY INJURED OR DIE.
READ THIS BEFORE YOU USE THIS BOOK.

This guidebook is a compilation of unverified information gathered from many different climbers. The author cannot assure the accuracy of any of the information in this book, including the topos and route descriptions, the difficulty ratings, and the protection ratings. These may be incorrect or misleading and it is impossible for any one author to climb all the routes to confirm the information about each route. Also, ratings of climbing difficulty and danger are always subjective and depend on the physical characteristics (for example, height), experience, technical ability, confidence and physical fitness of the climber who supplied the rating. Additionally, climbers who achieve first ascents sometimes underrate the difficulty or danger of the climbing route out of fear of being ridiculed if a climb is later down-rated by subsequent ascents. Therefore, be warned that you must exercise your own judgment on where a climbing route goes, its difficulty and your ability to safely protect yourself from the risks of rock climbing. Examples of some of these risks are: falling due to technical difficulty or due to natural hazards such as holds breaking, falling rock, climbing equipment dropped by other climbers, hazards of weather and lightning, your own equipment failure, and failure or absence of fixed protection.

You should not depend on any information gleaned from this book for your personal safety; your safety depends on your own good judgment, based on experience and a realistic assessment of your climbing ability. If you have any doubt as to your ability to safely climb a route described in this book, do not attempt it.

The following are some ways to make your use of this book safer:

1. **CONSULTATION:** You should consult with other climbers about the difficulty and danger of a particular climb prior to attempting it. Most local climbers are glad to give advice on routes in their area and we suggest that you contact locals to confirm ratings and safety of particular routes and to obtain first-hand information about a route chosen from this book.

2. **INSTRUCTION:** Most climbing areas have local climbing instructors and guides available. We recommend that you engage an instructor or guide to learn safety techniques and to become familiar with the routes and hazards of the areas described in this book. Even after you are proficient in climbing safely, occasional use of a guide is a safe way to raise your climbing standard and learn advanced techniques.

3. **FIXED PROTECTION:** Many of the routes in this book use bolts and pitons which are permanently placed in the rock. Because of variances in the manner of placement, weathering, metal fatigue, the quality of the metal used, and many other factors, these fixed protection pieces should always be considered suspect and should always be backed up by equipment that you place yourself. Never depend for your safety on a single piece of fixed protection because you never can tell whether it will hold weight, and in some cases, fixed protection may have been removed or is now absent.

Be aware of the following specific potential hazards which could arise in using this book:

1. **MISDESCRIPTIONS OF ROUTES:** If you climb a route and you have a doubt as to where the route may go, you should not go on unless you are sure that you can go that way safely. Route descriptions and topos in this book may be inaccurate or misleading.

2. **INCORRECT DIFFICULTY RATING:** A route may, in fact, be more difficult than the rating indicates. Do not be lulled into a false sense of security by the difficulty rating.

3. **INCORRECT PROTECTION RATING:** If you climb a route and you are unable to arrange adequate protection from the risk of falling through the use of fixed pitons or bolts and by placing your own protection devices, do not assume that there is adequate protection available higher just because the route protection rating indicates the route is not an "X" or an "R" rating. Every route is potentially an "X" (a fall may be deadly), due to the inherent hazards of climbing – including, for example, failure or absence of fixed protection, your own equipment's failure, or improper use of climbing equipment.

THERE ARE NO WARRANTIES, WHETHER EXPRESS OR IMPLIED, THAT THIS GUIDEBOOK IS ACCURATE OR THAT THE INFORMATION CONTAINED IN IT IS RELIABLE. THERE ARE NO WARRANTIES OF FITNESS FOR A PARTICULAR PURPOSE OR THAT THIS GUIDE IS MERCHANTABLE. YOUR USE OF THIS BOOK INDICATES YOUR ASSUMPTION OF THE RISK THAT IT MAY CONTAIN ERRORS AND IS AN ACKNOWLEDGMENT OF YOUR OWN SOLE RESPONSIBILITY FOR YOUR CLIMBING SAFETY.

PREFACE

Well climbers, here we go again! Fifteen years ago, three of the Phoenix area's most promi-nent climbers, Jim Waugh, Larry Treiber, and Bruce Grubbs teamed up to produce A Climber's Guide to Central Arizona, the first area guide that detailed the local rock climbing scene and the numerous routes that had been established up to that time. In those days, one of the most popular climbing spots was the Carefree Rockpile, an unspoiled desert climbing area in the desert north of Carefree.

Nearly ten years ago, in a massive solo effort, Jim Waugh produced Phoenix Rock, a 422 page dictionary of Central Arizona climbing that set a standard for guidebook quality and detail. The hot spots for climbing at that time included Pinnacle Peak, Troon Mountain and the McDowell Mountains. Little Granite Mountain was undergoing additional route develop-ment at that time, and climbers were starting to check out the "leftovers" over on Cholla Mountain.

Finally a new and updated edition of Phoenix Rock! The scene has changed drastically since the days of 1987. The burgeoning sub-culture of sport climbing has brought new climbers into the sport by the thousands while dragging it kicking and screaming into the cultural mainstream. Indoor climbing has become the hot ticket and new climbing gyms are sprout-ing up in cities from coast to coast. On the local front, the years have produced some set-backs that are grim reminders of the days of the Carefree Boulderpile. The good news is that it looks like Pinnacle Peak is (eventually) going to end up as a Scottsdale City Park, preserv-ing the climbing for future generations. On the flip side, development of "master-planned communities" in the northeastern metro threaten many of the other granite climbing areas in this guide, including Troon Mountain, Little Granite Mountain, Cholla Mountain and all of the areas along the northern side of the McDowells. Some headway has been made to pre-serve the climbing in these areas, but not nearly enough! The writing is on the table! It's time for the climbers to get involved or these areas will be history! Apathy means we'll end up climbing in the gym! Join the Access Fund, contribute to the McDowell-Sonoron Land Trust, vote...do whatever it takes! Forever is a long time.

In the mean time...Happy Climbing!

Greg Opland
September 1996

ACKNOWLEDGMENTS

How did I get into this mess? Trying to finish this thing has been like trying to stack BBs on a windy day in Kansas. Along the way, I began to refer to this as "Guidezilla." When I finally got serious about finishing it up and getting it to the publisher, I sat down and listed all the things I had to do before it was finished. Three full pages later, I knew I had missed plenty, and still wondered how I would ever see the door finally closed on this project. Since you're reading this now, I must have reached the end of the third page and the pages that came after.

This all started innocently enough in the fall of 1991. Four-and-a-half years later and hundreds of hours spent crouched over a computer terminal, the first part of the monster is finally complete. Somewhere in the middle, I signed up for the entire job. It has been an uphill climb (so to speak) all the way. It's also taken a lot more work to complete than I ever would have guessed. I suppose I wouldn't be the first guidebook author to feel that way. My sincere thanks go to various partners I've had while working on this book, for being patient with me while I was running off to take photos, or make sketches and notes. Also for putting up with my repetition of the words "I've got to finish the guidebook" over and over again. Anyway, enough said. I wouldn't have missed it for the world, and I hope you will find the final product to be worth the time it's taken.

It would take a serious bunch of pages to properly thank all the people who provided the groundwork for this guide. Instead of making the book longer, I'd just like to offer my sincere thanks to all those who contributed to the previous area guidebooks. Also thanks to everyone who ever told me about, or let me copy information, or suggested where the new routes were. It was a big job that I couldn't have done alone. I offer my sincere thanks!

The one person that absolutely needs to be mentioned is Jim Waugh, long time Phoenix climber and guidebook author, who provided significant foundation material from the previous edition of *Phoenix Rock*. I can't say enough about the help this gave me. Many thanks, Jim. After Jim set the standard with the original *Phoenix Rock*, I hope this guide lives up to expectations. Also, special thanks should also go to Rick Donnelly, Jan Holdeman, Paul Paonessa, and Marty Karabin, who all provided additional information and corrections on the information contained within these pages.

Thanks also, to the Phoenix climbing community. Without the climbers, there would be no need for a guide.

THE TAO OF THE GUIDEBOOK

In the beginning, there were no guidebooks. Adventure was the name of the game, and the game was practiced by all climbers who dared venture to the rock. The secrets of the routes the climbers did were often jealously guarded and only available to those willing to partake of the adventure. The price was high and these rugged explorers sometimes paid dearly for their hard-won knowledge. But the rewards were high as well, for those who sought the path of the unknown.

As time passed, more and more information became available to climbers, through the ever evolving art of the guidebook. Climbers could learn everything they ever wanted to know about routes without even setting boot to stone. This evolution has continued, and is propagated in this guide as well. All the information is at your very fingertips at the turn of a page. Has the adventure been lost to some degree?

I'd like to offer this simple advice: Don't give up the adventure. Branch out for new things. Stretch the envelope. Leave the beaten path for something new and inviting. Try that route that nobody's done for the last five years, just to see what it's like. Explore for new rock and new unclimbed routes. Get onto the path of the unknown. Once there, you will find that it was worth the effort and the adrenaline.

> Two roads diverged in the forest and,
> I took the one less traveled by.
> And it has made all the difference.
>
> Robert Frost

Table of Contents

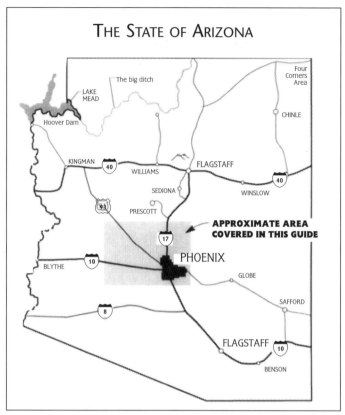

THE STATE OF ARIZONA

The big ditch

LAKE MEAD

Hoover Dam

Four Corners Area

CHINLE

KINGMAN

WILLIAMS

FLAGSTAFF

WINSLOW

SEDIONA

PRESCOTT

BLYTHE

PHOENIX

APPROXIMATE AREA COVERED IN THIS GUIDE

GLOBE

SAFFORD

FLAGSTAFF

BENSON

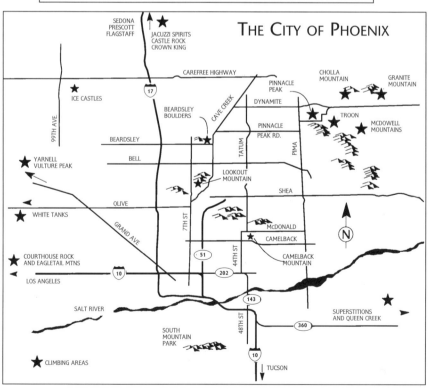

THE CITY OF PHOENIX

SEDONA PRESCOTT FLAGSTAFF

JACUZZI SPIRITS CASTLE ROCK CROWN KING

CAREFREE HIGHWAY

ICE CASTLES

99TH AVE

BEARDSLEY BOULDERS

CAVE CREEK

CHOLLA MOUNTAIN

GRANITE MOUNTAIN

PINNACLE PEAK

DYNAMITE

TROON

McDOWELL MOUNTAINS

PINNACLE PEAK RD.

TATUM

PIMA

BEARDSLEY

YARNELL VULTURE PEAK

BELL

LOOKOUT MOUNTAIN

WHITE TANKS

OLIVE

GRAND AVE

7TH ST

SHEA

McDONALD

CAMELBACK

N

COURTHOUSE ROCK AND EAGLETAIL MTNS

LOS ANGELES

51

44TH ST

202

CAMELBACK MOUNTAIN

SALT RIVER

143

48TH ST

360

SUPERSTITIONS AND QUEEN CREEK

SOUTH MOUNTAIN PARK

10

TUCSON

★ CLIMBING AREAS

INTRODUCTION

Welcome to the wonderful world of central Arizona granite! Phoenix is probably better known for its professional basketball team or its flaming, egg-frying, summertime weather than it is for quality climbing areas, but the fact is that some very enjoyable and challenging climbing can be found only a short drive from the city in any one of several areas. The local granite crags range from about 30 to nearly 300 feet in height. Of the areas included in this guide, climbing in the northeastern areas is found on relatively clean, thoroughly featured desert granite, while more "adventurous" geological phenomena can be found at such areas as Camelback Mountain, Courthouse Rock, and the White Tank Mountains.

Having a metro area in the neighborhood of two million people right on the edge of the climbing area (and overlapping in some cases) might be disconcerting to climbers looking for a wilderness experience, but it also insures that you have a good selection of bars, restaurants, and other amenities to head for when the gear and ropes are heaved into the trunk at the end of another great day of climbing. If you're in need of a climbing partner, the closest thing we have to a centralized climber's hangout is the local climbing gym. If you're in need of some quick beta, someone at the local climbing shops or in the rock gym will be more than happy to help. Some of the friendliest climbers in the country live and climb here in central Arizona.

Climbing

Climbing in the desert is a unique experience. It's an acquired taste in some respects, but if you spend some time listening and looking while you're out there, you will be rewarded. There's nothing like climbing here in the spring when the cactus and the wildflowers are sending off vibrant colors and smells. The peace and quiet only disrupted by the occasional lizard, snake or javalina making its way through the underbrush while hawks circle in the sky above.

Virtually all of the areas described in this guide are of the traditional type. The desert granite with minimal crystal holds and fractured crack systems generally doesn't lend itself to the practice of sport climbing. That is to say that, while there are well protected and even thoroughly bolted routes detailed here, the majority of these climbs are the result of traditional, sometimes fairly bold, ground-up route development that reached its peak in the early 1980s. The climbers doing first ascents during this period, when faced with the choice between trying to put in a bolt with a minimal stance, or running it out to a good stance, often chose the latter, if the fall was clean and the protection was good. While you will find some face routes that seem to be a little stretchy between bolts, in most cases, you'll find that the bolts provide perfectly adequate protection for leaders solid at the grade, with little possibility for groundfall.

Bear in mind that I said MOST cases. It is up to you to inspect the possibility of bad falls on any route you attempt. To help identify these, most of the routes in this book that have runout sections of climbing have been noted with an "R" following the rating (i.e., 5.9 R). Routes that have the potential for severe injury or death in event of a fall have been marked with an "X" similarly (i.e. 5.10X). These indications are only meant to aid you in selecting a route to climb. By no means should you assume that every route with the possibility of runout or dangerous protection has been duly noted in this book. Check your routes out before climbing them. Inspect the bolts you're about to clip, some of them have been there for quite a while. Check that flake you're about to put a cam behind. And then back it up! Safe climbing is YOUR responsibility!

Climbing Season and the Weather

The basic climbing season in central Arizona lasts from the last gasp of summer, sometime in September or early October, until the beast of solar energy descends once again, sometime in May to early June when the temperatures climb into the three-digit range again. The heat controls the climbing. Phoenix sees around 300+ days of sun per year. We also get an average of about seven inches of rain per annum, so you can pretty much bank on being able to climb nearly all the days you have plans.

Average Temperatures By Month

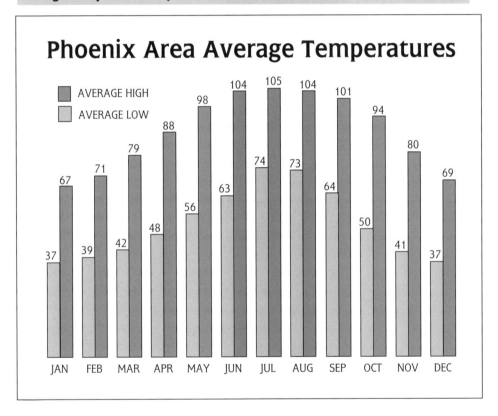

How hot does it get? The hottest day in the last five years was on June 26, 1990, when the mercury finally creaked to a halt next to a record 122 degrees F (that's 50 degrees C for you retro types). Either way, it was like being a pie in an oven. During the summer, when the heat makes it uncomfortable and nearly impossible to climb, most locals make the drive either north to the Flagstaff climbing areas, south to the top of Mt. Lemmon near Tucson, or west to the alpine elevations of Tahquitz and Suicide Rocks near Idyllwild, California. As with climbing at Joshua Tree, it is possible to climb here during the summer, if you cower to the shady side of the rock during the early part of the day, but you'll probably be heading for the air conditioning by lunch.

If you're out climbing during the hotter parts of the year, be sure to take plenty of water and try to stay on the shady side of the rocks. Heat exhaustion and heat stroke are very real possibilities, so be careful out there. The heat is a funny thing. It will sap you of moisture while you're not looking. About two years ago, a group was hiking in the Grand Canyon when a girl in the party keeled over and died of dehydration. Up until she collapsed, they had no indication that she was even thirsty. Water, water, water! Sunscreen is also a definite addition to the list of essential gear, no matter what time of the year you're climbing.

Desert Nasties

The desert can be an inhospitable place for us soft cushy human types. Nearly every plant and animal that resides in the desert has some kind of pointy weapon to use against unwarranted, unprotected intruders bent on climbing rocks. There are several kinds of cactus, including saguaro, ocotillo, prickly pear, barrel, catclaw (my personal favorite, I seem to have a soft spot in my head for making catclaw infested approaches) and the king of the nasties, cholla, that are waiting to crisscross and puncture any and all exposed areas of skin you might provide. Your best bet against these, obviously, is total avoidance. This can be done by following game trails (keep an eye out, you'll find them), climber trails (easier to find), or sticking to areas where you can scramble on boulders and rock slabs. Normally, it is not a good idea to foray down into washes, as the nasty plant life tends to congregate heavily where water tends to flow during the few rainstorms a year. Catclaw loves washes.

Saguaro Cactus in bloom and in the wild!

Barring the option of evading punctures altogether, your next best weapon is to wear protective layers of clothing. Long pants constructed of rugged material and possibly a long-sleeved shirt (less essential, but sometimes a good idea) are the primary approach armor for some of the more plant-filled climbing areas. A good, sturdy pair of hiking shoes can go a long way, too. Wearing Tevas (or other "river runner" style sandals) is best left for the post-climbing party. The last thing you want is "jumping" cholla embedded in your foot! Trust me on this one.

So much for the flora (stickies), now for the fauna (creepy crawlies). As with the plants, the various forms of bugs and animals that reside in the desert are better left alone. Avoidance remains the best policy here. These include rattlesnakes, bees, scorpions, black widows, gila monsters, coral snakes and just about any other weird looking creatures you might run across. Many of these, while not a guaranteed trip to the morgue for most adults, can put a real kink in a good day out climbing. You'll probably never even see more than a couple of the beasties on this list. Of the creepies listed above, the ones you're most likely to see are the rattlesnake, bees, and the scorpion.

For the most part, scorps will be out of sight behind that flake you're using as a handhold, or under a rock. This means that as long as you don't yard the flake off, or pick up the rock, you may never even see them. I've learned that it's good to get in the habit of checking under rocks if you pick any up.

Rattlesnakes are a different matter. You're basically invading their habitat, so they will be very sensitive if given cause. The good news is that they aren't hiding under every bush, and they're also defensive in nature. If you don't back one into a corner, you probably won't have a problem. Your best bet if confronting a snake, especially one that's making a lot of noise, is to back slowly away and then take a different route. During the more "snake friendly" times of the year in spring and fall, tread softly, and make dang sure you don't step on a snake on the trail. This inevitably leads to a bite unless you're lucky. If you're nighted on a climb and have to hike out in the dark, watch for snakes laying on sun-warmed boulders and rock slabs. In the last five years, I've seen two snakes while out climbing, both of which were easily avoided.

Normal, basic honey bees in general aren't a problem. They kind of stick to their own business and let the rest of the world go on by. Enter the Africanized "Killer Bees," which infiltrated the Phoenix area in the early 1990s. These babies don't mess around. If you've entered their safety zone, you're gonna get shelled and this can be deadly. As some of the local rocks seem to be preferred hive sites for bees, it is worth a word of caution to climbers. Keep an eye out for bees flying in and out of crack systems, this is a good indication that there is a hive inside. Watch out for routes with the word "bee" in their names (i.e., **Beeline, Bee Direct, Beegee, Beehive**). These names were given for a reason. This is not to say that every hive of bees, or every bee that you see will be of the "killer" variety (that takes a genetic test of the bees), but it is best to avoid them if you can.

The last nasty, can be the rock itself. If you head out to climb on the granite around Phoenix, you better bring a healthy set of pads (on the fingers), and a spare set of shoes. The desert granite here is of the "cheesegrater" variety, and is well known for its ability to leave your skin raw and your shoes worn. The rock is sharp, but provides amazing holds, and some really nice crystal and friction climbing on steep clean faces and cracks. Many local climbers use tape gloves or Spider Mitts™ to protect the tender skin on the back of their hands from rough crystalline jams. Athletic tape and/or Band-Aids™ are also handy to have around in case a wild crystal rips a nasty flapper in your finger.

Recommended Protection and Rack

A standard "cragging" rack for one- to two-pitch climbs is sufficient for pretty much all the climbs included in this guide. This might include eight to ten Quickdraws, a set of nuts/stoppers, a set of hexes, and a set of SLCDs (cams: Friends, Aliens, Quadcams, Camalots, etc.) up to four inches or so. Your mileage may vary (i.e., you decide how much gear you like to take with you). Individual pro recommendations may be found in the route descriptions. It's always a good idea to take too much pro with you on a route than trying to cut corners and skimp on it.

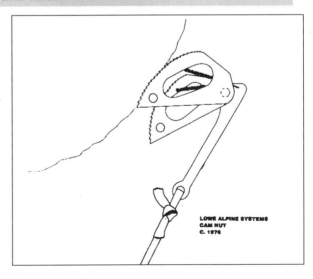

LOWE ALPINE SYSTEMS
CAM NUT
c. 1976

Camping

Camping is an interesting proposition in the Phoenix area. With a city so close, it's possible to get a hotel to fit just about anyone's budget. The selection of available camping is fairly sparse, as might be expected this close to suburbia. For traveling climbers on a shoestring budget, the nearest convenient campground can be found out at the McDowell Mountain Regional Park, about 15 miles northeast of Scottsdale.

This campground would apply for nearly all the climbing areas in this book, with the exception of some of the outlying areas. The park is accessed from Fountain Hills Boulevard (see map below). This is an RV-style campground complete with hookups, water and toilets, so you can probably expect some company from the urban masses. The cost is $8 per day. The telephone number is (602)471-0173.

Other options might be found out in the open desert as well by inventive and fairly low-profile climbers, but this is NOT recommended by this guide. The best option would be to get a cheap hotel or arrange to stay with local climbers.

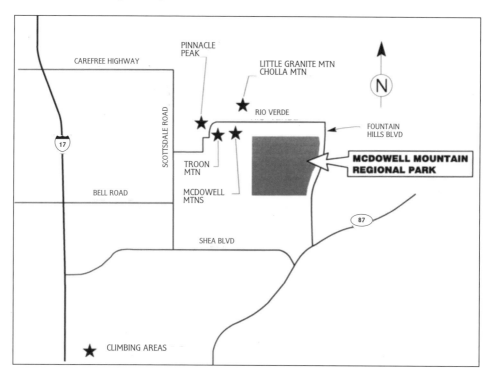

Climbing Gear and Guide Services

You can get climbing gear at any one of the following shops, as well as local beta, guidebooks, and camping gear. If you're in need of a guide, they can steer you in the right direction or provide guides as needed.

Desert Mountain Sports (DMS)
2824 E. Indian School Rd.
(northeast corner: 28th St. at Indian School)
Phoenix, AZ 85016
(602)955-2875

Recreational Equipment, Inc. (REI)
1405 W. Southern
Tempe, AZ 85282-4446
(602)967-5494

Arizona Hiking Shack
11649 Cave Creek Rd.
(¼ mile south of Cactus at Cave Creek)
Phoenix, AZ 85028
(602)944-7723

Ascend Arizona
680 S. Mill Ave.
Tempe, AZ 85282
(602)495-9428

Recreational Equipment, Inc. (REI)
Located on Paradise Village Parkway west of
Paradise Valley Mall, next to Target
Paradise Valley, AZ
(602) 996-5400

Local Climbing Clubs

A climbing club can be a good way to meet local climbers of all abilities. Some clubs offer
other activities as well, such as mountain biking, hiking, camping, mountaineering, trail
maintenance and other outdoor pursuits. For climbers that are new to the area, this can be
a good way to "get into" the local scene.

Arizona Mountaineering Club (AMC)
PO Box 1695
Phoenix, AZ 85001-1695

(602) 817-0271

Southwest Outdoor Club
c/o Wayne Thomas
1109 W. Pebble Beach Drive
Tempe, AZ 85282
(602 894-2629

Rescue and Emergency Facilities

Technical rock rescue in the Phoenix area is possible but difficult to initiate if proper proce-
dures are not followed. The easiest way to get a rescue started is to call the statewide
emergency number, 9-1-1. At this point, the dispatcher determines who has legal authority
over your locale.

For example, if you are within the Phoenix city limits (Camelback Mountain), then the
Phoenix Fire Department will most likely be dispatched. A problem is that the Phoenix Fire
Department is limited in their technical rock rescue abilities. In the event that the Phoenix
Fire Department determines that they need more technical assistance, then the Central
Arizona Mountain Rescue Association (CAMRA, an official posse for Maricopa County Sheriff's
Department) will be summoned. Fortunately, this rescue team is more experienced in moun-
tain rescue than other governmental teams. If you are outside of Phoenix, but within
Maricopa County (Little Granite Mountain, McDowell Mountains, Pinnacle Peak, Troon
Mountain, and the White Tanks), then most likely CAMRA will be dispatched first. If you are
within Pinal County (Queen Creek Canyon, Santans, Superstitions), then most likely the Pinal
County Sheriff's Department will dispatch their appropriate team, which again is limited in
technical rock rescue.

Essentially, aid the dispatcher by specifying what type of team is needed and be aware of
which county you are in when climbing. Also, supply sufficient information such as location,
number of injured, nature of injuries, number of party able to assist, equipment at scene,
kind of terrain, and any other pertinent information.

(Note: CAMRA, associated with Mountain Rescue Association, will go outside of Maricopa
County.)

The best advice is to climb safely and be knowledgeable in self-rescue techniques.
Nevertheless, to further aid, a chart (listing addresses and telephones) and map (for loca-

tions) are provided of the closest emergency centers near the climbing areas. These emergency rooms are to be utilized only if the victim is transporting him/herself and has a "Level 2" or less (serious but not life-threatening) injury.

Emergency Medical Facilities

NORTHERN AREAS: Little Granite Mountain, Pinnacle Peak, McDowell Mountains, Troon Mountain, Four Peaks

Phoenix General Hospital
19829 N. 27th Ave
Phoenix, AZ 85027
879-5353

Scottsdale Memorial Hospital North
10450 North 92nd Street
Scottsdale, AZ 85260
860-3000

Humana Hospital (Desert Valley)
3929 East Bell Road
Phoenix, AZ 85032
867-1881

CENTRAL AREAS: Camelback Mountain

Humana Hospital (Phoenix)
1947 East Thomas Road
Phoenix, AZ 85016
241-7600

Scottsdale Memorial Hospital
7400 East Osborn Road
Scottsdale, AZ 85025
994-9616

WESTERN AREAS: White Tanks, Courthouse Rock, Eagletail Mountains

Samaritan West Valley Health Center
488 North Litchfield Rd.
Goodyear, AZ
932-5701

Boswell Memorial Hospital
10401 Thunderbird Boulevard
Sun City, AZ 85351
876-5351

Valley View Community Hospital
12207 North 113th Avenue
Youngtown, AZ 85363
933-0155

Maryvale Samaritan Hospital
5102 West Campbell Avenue
Phoenix, AZ 85031
848-5000

Access

The subject of access is a tender one in the Phoenix climbing community. A lot of the climbing detailed in this guide resides on privately held land. Traditionally, that has not proven to be an access problem, as the land in question was more or less in the middle of nowhere in the open desert. As the city and the golf courses encroach on these areas, we may continue to deal with more and more access issues as they arise. Older local climbers will remember the story of the Carefree Rockpile, one of the most popular climbing areas near Phoenix a few years back. Then came the Boulders Resort. Houses went up, the golf course was laid out and the landscaping was done. And when the dust cleared and it was all over, the climbers had lost one of their dearest areas forever.

Don't look now, but we're in the same boat for some of the areas shown in this guide (those in the neighborhood of the McDowell and Little Granite Mountain areas). The sights and sounds of desert climbing are part of our desert heritage. More and more, those sounds are more likely to be that of a bulldozer or dumptruck as construction projects invade the desert, intent on installing another set of condensed houses or another 18 holes of retirement golf that our meager water supplies cannot hope to support.

We have had some successes with access in recent months. Some, if not all, of the climbing on Pinnacle Peak should be available to us by the creation of a City of Scottsdale Park encompassing the area and scheduled to be "created" sometime in 1996. Scottsdale voters, in April of 1995, voted nearly two-to-one in favor of a small tax hike in order to raise the funds necessary to expand the McDowell Mountain Regional Park and create a wildlife and recreation area. Some local climbers and climbing groups have helped with this effort and we are hopeful that the climbing will be available for future generations to enjoy, even if we gotta look down on another (arguably unnecessary) golf course.

As climbers, we all have to get together to do our part for the cause of access. Some of the things you can do (and this list is definitely not limited to these few items):

Contribute time and money to access causes (either the Access Fund or a local group). Get involved in the fight for access. The climbing areas you save may be your own!

Don't litter while out climbing. Even better, take a trash bag or two with you when you climb and bring out any trash you find along the way. If smoking is your thing, take your butts with you and get rid of them properly. A little help goes a long way.

Minimize our impact to the areas. Stay on established trails (braided trails are a significant source of climber impact). Be nice to indigenous plant life. Use environmental colors (no neons!) if you leave a sling at a rap station. If possible, use colored bolt hangers on new routes.

If you're climbing near residential areas, try to keep any yelling and unnecessary noise down to a minimum. Be polite to homeowners (and anyone else you see while climbing).

Climb safe. Back up your anchors, tie your belayer in. Every climber that craters draws negative attention to the climbing community. Accidents happen, but the less we have, the better.

We have some potentially rough years ahead with some of the climbing areas outlined in this book. Please, please, please get involved with access issues as they arise. We have to stick together if we are to continue climbing on Phoenix granite. Apathy will only leave us with nowhere left to climb. Remember the Carefree Boulderpile!

> *Everybody knows the dice are loaded,*
> *everybody rolls with their fingers crossed.*
> *Everybody knows that the war is over,*
> *everybody knows that the good guys lost.*

Concrete Blonde

Ethics

Well, I had to bring it up, didn't I? The notion of ethics in today's vertical world seems to be the most confusing climbing topic most of us will deal with. I would probably be better off staying away from the topic of ethics altogether, but there are a few things well worth mentioning here, if for no other reason than to give beginning climbers some kind of background in such issues and other climbers an opportunity to contemplate. While I spew on in the following paragraphs, I will say that I wholeheartedly agree with what Jim Waugh said in his short article on this subject in the first edition of *Phoenix Rock*: "Under no circumstances should anyone take this essay too seriously as enough seriousness occurs on the end of a rope. So read, ponder, argue, and laugh as you will."

When Jim wrote on this subject in *Phoenix Rock*, the gist of his essay dealt with style as it applied to first ascents. Did someone hang on the first ascent? Did they use hooks to put in the bolts? The world of climbing has changed quite a bit in the last nine years, as sport climbing has taken the climbing world by storm. The concerns of ascent style have reached complexities far beyond the simple arguments of yesterday. Most of the style issues have been redefined by a developing majority of the climbing community, most of whom are climbing on relatively short, bolted climbs in newly developed sport climbing areas. The practices of rap bolting, previewing and the redpoint ascent have now been established and accepted by most climbers as they relate to bolted climbs in sport areas. More and more, they have been used and accepted in the more traditional areas as well. Luckily (except for recent developments in a certain newly "created" sport area of northern Arizona) the abhorrent practices of glueing, chipping and other rock modification for the purpose of "creating" first ascents seems to remain unanimously rejected by virtually all climbers. One can only hope that this remains true in the future. There can be no justification for bringing the rock down to our level, eliminating challenges for coming generations of climbers. In the not-so-distant-past, "how" you climbed something was just as important as the climb itself. Food for thought.

As I have worked on this guide, I have seen a disturbing trend. Over the course of the last five years, as I returned to areas to map and gather data on the climbs, I have seen bolts magically appear here and there, even appearing on established routes periodically. Why would someone presume to add protection to existing climbs that have been climbed by so many people before? I heard rumors of a bolt that had been added to **Shalaly Direct**, a fine three-star face climb on Pinnacle Peak. Even more amazing, was that the bolt had been placed next to a perfectly good nut placement. Although I'm happy to report that this bolt met the business end of a crowbar, I still wonder at the audacity it took to place it at all. For those who would copy this kind of action, I can only say that these bolts will most likely meet with a similar fate. If you feel an established route is too "dangerous" for you to attempt as it is, maybe you should leave it for a time when you feel your skills are up to the challenge?

Since there is no one out there policing the climbing community. It is up to the climbers themselves. Toward that end, please don't add bolts to established routes. What you may consider runout or unsafe may not seem so to others. There are those who consider climbing as much a mental game as it is a physical one. If you think something is too dangerous, climb something else. You may return someday and see the route in a whole new light. Respect others (and their routes) as you would want to be respected yourself.

History

The history of modern rock climbing in the Phoenix area began during WWII. The Boy Scouts of Troop #9 at Creighton school had been introduced to rock climbing through a class and several outings taught by pilot, cinematographer and ex-Teton guide Ray Garner. Following the war, Garner teamed with the two scouts who had shown the strongest interest, Ben Pedrick and Ed George. They reformed the scout troop into a mountaineering oriented club and thus was born the Kachinas. By 1947, more members had joined the group and the Kachinas became Senior Scout Outfit #1. For the next five years members of the Kachinas would push new routes up many of the probable lines on Camelback's conglomerate rock. Classics like **Suicide** (direct), **The Ridge Route**, **The Hart Route**, and **Pedrick's Chimney** were climbed in this period. Ralph Pateman would push local free standards with his ascent of **Pateman's Cave** (5.7) and Gary Driggs would forge the first line (still very popular today!) up The Monk with questionable pins for protection (it was later that bolts appeared). The Kachinas also expanded their attention to other nearby formations and in 1947, Ed George with Bill McMorris would make the first of many ascents of Pinnacle Peak via the **South Crack.** McMorris had spied a slender formation on the ridge of the McDowells and later returned with Dick Hart to bag the first ascent of The Dork (known today as Tom's Thumb). The Kachinas were also very active statewide completing ascents in the Superstitions, Eagletail Mountains, Kofa Mountains, and the Navajo Reservation as well as in Wyoming's Tetons and the Canadian Rockies. Perhaps the crowning Arizona ascent for the Kachina's was of the second major volcanic summit of the Four Corners area, the 1000-foot Agathlan Peak in late May of 1949. In an epic 24-hour ascent, Ray Garner accompanied by Lee Pedrick (Ben's brother) and South Dakota's Herb Conn, climbed over miles of poor rock and remarkably placed only a single bolt to gain the summit. The desert icon, Shiprock (at 1800 feet), saw it's first ascent by Californians in 1939, but the Kachina's Agathlan climb came a full three years before the second ascent of Shiprock.

By the mid-1950s, many of the active Kachinas had moved on and new climbing activity was concentrated in other parts of the state. It was not until 1962, when ASU student Bill Forrest (of later Forrest Mountaineering fame) joined forces with Kachina-trained Doug Black to offer climbing instruction to increase the pool of partners. As the local interest in climbing grew, Forrest and Black accompanied by Wally Vegors and Dick Greenwood formed the Arizona Mountaineering Club. The AMC has since become the oldest climbing club in Arizona and has seasoned many generations of Phoenix climbers. Together, the team of Forrest and Black along with other club members would establish several routes at Camelback including **Doug's Dandy** and the notoriously devious **Suicide**. Bill Forrest would also link up with new AMC member Gary Garbert to climb many of the hardest aid and long mixed routes in central Arizona. Moving on to form a climbing business, Forrest and Garbert left Phoenix in the mid-1960s as a number of up and coming AMCers took the reigns in climbing development. Members began to frequent the Precambrian granite of the Carefree Boulderpile, Pinnacle Peak and the McDowell Mountains. Bill Sewrey and Larry Treiber would also take this opportunity to explore the climbing potential of The Outback with their first ascent of Vulture Peak's 600-foot east face (5.5 A4) in 1966.

Two brothers had joined the AMC early on and began to truly develop the potential of the Phoenix area. Lance and Dane Daugherty devoured the rock, free climbing many of the existing lines like **Suicide** (direct) (5.8) at Camelback, **Lizard Lip** (5.8) at Pinnacle Peak, and the ultra classic **Treiber's Deception** (5.7) at Tom's Thumb. They also broke into the 5.9 realm with first ascents of **Kneexit** (Lance's very last route) at Carefree and the thin **Redemption** on the Wedge at Pinnacle Peak. Tragically, before the peak of his climbing career, Lance Daugherty was killed in a motorcycle accident in 1968. Only a short time later, his brother Dane would also be lost in a car accident. The Daugherty's motivation and influence was not lost as it continued by sparking a desire for the "free" ascent in many of their fellow climbers.

The Arizona Mountaineering Club celebrated its 30th anniversary with a climb of Tom's Thumb.

One of those climbers was Larry Treiber. He often accompanied the Daugherty's and after their passing, Treiber emerged as the area's finest free climber. Honing his skills at Tahquitz Rock in California and tenacity at Granite Basin in Prescott, Treiber teamed up with Pete Noebels, Chuck Parker, Dennis Abbink and others to climb the fingercrack of **Hangovers** (5.9), the thin faces of **White Warlock** (5.10c) and **The Naked Edge** (5.9), and the difficult and wide **Hades** (5.10b), all at Pinnacle Peak. In the McDowells, the obvious lines of **Sacred Datura** (5.9), **Succubus** (5.10a), **Renaissance** (5.7), and the grand traverse **Gobs of Knobs** (5.8) were all bagged by Treiber and his compadres. Treiber's climbing ability and motivation also allowed him to expand beyond the Phoenix valley and become a prolific statewide climber. He arrived at Prescott's Granite Mountain to pluck more than a dozen choice routes and develop classics in the Grand Canyon, the Superstitions, and southern Arizona.

As a part owner and founder of Desert Mountain Sports with Bill Sewrey, Treiber influenced many of the local climbers for more than a decade. The times were different as chalk use was frowned upon and state of the art protection consisted of primitive Stoppers, hexes, and Forrest T-tons. Despite these limitations, climbers Dana Hollister, Pete Noebels, Rick Fritz, Dennis Abbink, and Chuck Parker persisted and managed to free many high standard routes well into the '70s. Early in 1979, Pete Noebels smoothly fired his first free ascent of **Sidewinder** (5.11a) elevating the Phoenix free climbing standards to 5.11.

The close of the decade ushered in a new generation along with the introduction of Friends, the RP micronut and a general acceptance of gymnastic chalk. The emergence of this new protection and the adoption of alternative ethics allowed many previously overlooked lines to be climbed free. Leading this new wave was a brash young Harley owner and iconoclast named Stan Mish. Uniting with climbers Dave Black and Jim Waugh, Mish astonished the locals with dramatic ascents. While on lead, Mish coolly found precarious stances to hand drill on **Fear of Flying** (5.10c) and **Powder Puff** (5.11a), and led free the six-inch offwidth **Beelzebub** (5.11a) and intimidating 160-foot **Deep Freeze** (5.11a). Mish also pushed the 5.12 barrier with his difficult to protect first free ascent of **Lost Nut's** (5.12a/b). This storm of free climbing activity would have a profound effect on Mish's contemporaries.

Jim Waugh seized this new philosophy and began a string of significant first ascents. Hailing from Nebraska, this ex-rock-and-roll drummer found the time to train religiously in the gym and on the rock to become one of Arizona's most important climbers. With various partners, Waugh showed his command of different techniques as he climbed the amazing handcrack of **Rhythm and Blues** (5.10b), the airy and thin faces **Pussyfoot** (5.10b) and **Never Never Land** (5.11a), and the insecure lichen lieback of **Jungle Jim** (5.11b). When Waugh teamed with bandanna-clad John Ficker, the duo produced the finest route on Phoenix granite, **Shalayly Direct** (5.11b/c) at Pinnacle Peak. Waugh's training would pay off as he would go on to free climb 5.12s throughout the state and bring the rating of 5.13 to Granite Mountain in Prescott with his first free ascent of **The Nose** route, which he renamed **A Bridge Across Forever**.

When a Phoenix climber thinks of a local, one name comes to mind, John Ficker. Always tempering his ratings and working from the ground up, Ficker focused his eye on the numerous outcrops at Little Granite Mountain, the McDowell Mountains, Windy Walks (aka Troon Mountain) and Pinnacle Peak. Climbing with Glen Dickenson, Jim Zahn, Mike Long and Jason Sands, Ficker methodically ticked off hundreds of routes including the deluxe classics **Sweet Surprise** (5.7), **Fist Grease** (5.11b), **Space Cadets** (5.10a), **Hard Drivin'** (5.11a), **Only the Strong Survive** (5.11a), and **Loafer's Choice** (5.10a R) to mention only a few. Always active, John added to his impressive first ascent tally with yet a couple of new lines, **Happy Hooker** and **By Hook or By Crook** on the Summit Boulder on Toon Mountain in 1988. One only has to scan the first ascent list in this guide to see the impact that John Ficker has had on Phoenix rock.

Unfortunately, it would be impossible to list here all the great contributions made by so many of those who have come before. The rich legacy of the pioneers of Phoenix climbing must be envisioned by leading the heroic routes that they left.

By Rick Donnelly
May 1996

Organization

This guide is organized into nine chapters covering the main climbing areas surrounding the Phoenix metro area and some of the outlying crags to the north and west. The chapters, in order of presentation will include: General Information, Beardsley Boulderpile, Camelback Mountain, Cholla Mountain, Jacuzzi Spires, Little Granite Mountain, McDowell Mountains, Pinnacle Peak, Troon Mountain, White Tank Mountains, and The Outback.

Those that own the original edition of *Phoenix Rock* will notice some differences with this guide. Most notably, the Santan Mountains, Queen Creek Area and Superstition Mountains are absent. Due to massive new route activity in these areas (except the Santans), the guide would have had to have been over twice as large. These will hopefully be presented in another guidebook, as a companion to this one.

Another difference with this guide is the inclusion of some of the more remote crags within the central Arizona area. A few of these areas were included in the predecessor to the original *Phoenix Rock (Climber's Guide to Central Arizona)*, but were excluded from the *Phoenix Rock* guide. It is my hope to re-introduce some of these worthwhile (and sometimes adventurous) climbing areas to the new generations of climbers before the information is lost.

For each area, there will be a short introduction to the area, the type of climbing to be found there, and a text description of how to get to the area. This will be followed by a map showing how to get to the area (and where to park). The guts of each chapter will be the route information. This will be presented using topos and textual route descriptions. It is hoped that this will give the climber enough information to locate and climb their desired route. (Some would say too much beta, but you're still on the hook to do your own climbing!) The drawing format used in this guide is an attempt to make the route topos more three-dimensional in nature, hopefully helping climbers to "visualize" the routes easier. I have made every attempt at including pertinent information to climbers on each topo, such as crag height, descent information, and individual route notes when applicable. Text descent information will also accompany the route descriptions where it is useful. The topo key (below) will help to "explain" some of the notations used in the topos for this guide.

The route descriptions following the topos will start where the topos leave off. The information given in the descriptions will help you find the route path when the drawing is unable to represent enough detail. Many of the route descriptions are from the previous edition of *Phoenix Rock*, and were written originally by Jim Waugh. I have left most of these intact in an attempt to retain some of the historical tidbits and first ascent anecdotes included in the descriptions.

Key to Reading Route Topos

The last section of this book will contain the route first ascent information and the route indices. There is a real trend in the guidebook community to leave first ascent information out of new guides. I feel to leave this information out is simply giving up the history of the climbing areas. I can understand this practice in areas where the first ascents were all done with a power drill within a short period of time, but for some of the older, more traditional areas, you can retain a flavor and a unique perspective of the area's route development by preserving this information. Therefore, I'm keeping it. Following the first ascent info will be the route indices, both by name and by rating. These should allow you to locate climbs easily.

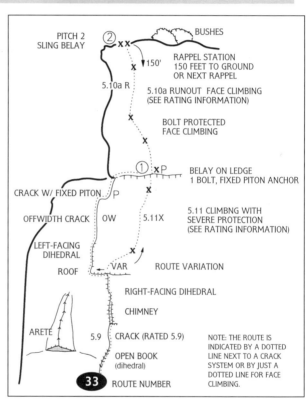

Rating System

The rating system used in this book is the Yosemite Decimal System (YDS), commonly used throughout the United States. I have included the ratings chart below, to give visiting off-shore climbers an idea of the relationship between the YDS and various difficulty rating systems around the world. Bear in mind, that the difficulty comparisons are very general and subjective in nature. It is always best to sample a few climbs several levels below your ability, to get an idea of an area's difficulty level. This is a good rule of thumb no matter where you're climbing. I'll say it one time, and one time only: Phoenix ratings tend to be quite conservative at times.

Ratings Comparison Chart

West Germany	Yosemite Decimal	N.C.C.S.	British		Australian	Dresden	French	Sweden
3	5.0				4			
3+	5.1				5			
4−	5.2		3a	VD	6			
4	5.3		3b		7			
4+	5.4		3c		8,9	IV	3	
5−	5.5		4a	S	10,11	V	4	4+
5	5.6		4b	HS	12,13	VI	4c	5−
5+	5.7	F7			14,15	VIIa	5a	5
6−	5.8	F8	4c	VS	16	VIIb	5b	5+
6	5.9	F9	5a	HVS	17		5c	6−
6+	5.10a	F10	5b	E1	18	VIIc	6a	6
7−	5.10b			E2	19	VIIIa		6
7	5.10c	F11	5c		20	VIIIb	6b	6+
7+	5.10d				21	VIIIc		
	5.11a	F12		E3	22	IXa	6c	7−
8−	5.11b		6a		23	IXb		7
8	5.11c	F13		E4	24		7a	7+
	5.11d				25	IXc		8−
8+	5.12a	F14	6b	E5	26	Xa	7b	
9−	5.12b				27	Xb		8
9	5.12c	F15		E6			7c	8+
	5.12d		6c		28	Xc		9−
9+	5.13a	F16		E7	29	N/A	8a	9
10−	5.13b		7a		30			
	5.13c						8b	
10	5.13d			E8	31			
10+	5.14a		7b		32		8c	
11−	5.14b							
11	5.14c		7c	E9	33		9a	

Ratings Comparison Chart

The development of the current "Class" system to grade various levels of rock climbing started in 1937 with the Walzenbach rating system. This system, with its subsequent modern technical climbing modifications, is defined and used in this guide as follows:

Class 1	Scrambling on rocky terrain, generally upright, not requiring the use of hands.
Class 2	Scrambling on sloping rocky terrain, sometimes requiring the use of hands for balance. Rope generally not needed.
Class 3	Scrambling over rocks, using the hands frequently for balance and some upward progress. Exposure may be encountered. A rope might be a good idea.
Class 4	Some intermediate level of climbing is required. Exposure will be encountered and most climbers will desire the use of a rope. A fall could cause serious injury or possibly death. Also can be defined at the point where most beginners and average climbers begin to want a belay for safety.
Class 5	Technical Rock climbing. Includes the use of a rope and artificial or fixed anchors (protection) for safety in case of a fall. Can be subdivided as such:
5.0–5.5	Beginning climbs which usually can be climbed by beginning climbers with a reasonable fitness level, often with only snug footwear or tennis shoes.

5.6–5.9	Intermediate climbs, requiring climbing shoes, some knowledge of climbing techniques (jams, chimneying, etc.), and strength.
5.10 and up	Advanced climbing. Shoes, techniques, advanced strength, and knowledge will be required.
Class 6	Artificial or "Aid" Climbing. The use of artificial or fixed anchors are used by the climber to make upward progress. This class is further defined by the use of A0 to A5 ratings, much as in free climbing. The exact definition of these levels is cause for some debate in the climbing community, so these are general indications of the requirements.
A0	Fixed aid, either bolts or pins. May include pendulums or rappels.
A1	Solid aid placements that are easy to get and bomber.
A2	Solid aid placements, but may require a bit of tinkering by the leader to get them set.
A3	Fairly solid aid placements, which would hold only a short fall. May require a reasonable amount of skill to set.
A4	Body weight only aid placements. Would not hold any fall.
A5	Enough A4 placements so that the leader will experience a significant fall, hopefully to a placement that will hold.

Another notation which may be used in conjunction with technical ratings can be the time required to complete the indicated climb (also known as the "commitment rating"). These are divided into six "Grades" as follows:

Grade I	Short in length, up to a few hours
Grade II	Slightly longer, perhaps half a day
Grade III	Slightly longer, three quarters of a day
Grade IV	A full day's climbing
Grade V	A day-and-a-half worth of climbing
Grade VI	Multiple days of climbing

The use of this time rating assumes an average climbing team, moving steadily on the approach, climb and on the way back to the car. The use of the grading system in this book will be done on a "car-to-car" basis (i.e., from the car to the climb, up the climb and back to the car). If no grade is shown for a climb, you can assume that it is of the Grade I variety.

Finally, in addition to the technical YDS rating of the climb, a "star" rating system has been used to indicate the overall quality of a given route. The quality ratings may make it easier for visiting climbers with limited time to select the best of the local climbs to sample, or for local climbers with little knowledge of the area's routes to start out on the best ones. Factors used in the selection of stars for the routes include the quality of the rock, protection, quality of the climbing, and the consensus opinion of climbers who have done the route. In the case of some of the routes, the quality rating may be selected purely on my opinion, or on the opinion of the previous guidebook author for any one of several subjective reasons. The star system is as follows :

★★★	One of the areas best routes. A classic route that should not be missed.
★★	An excellent route. Nearly a classic.
★	A good quality enjoyable route.

If a route has no stars, it might be bad, good, just ok, or the actual quality may not be known to the author. As an author and experienced in the way of the guidebook, I can only say that you should only use the star ratings to get you started on the area climbs, but unless it is specifically stated that the climb is better avoided, don't let a star get in the way of climbing a route. If you are near a climb that has no stars in the book, and it looks good, go ahead and try it. You might be trying one of the "missing classics." No guarantees, but at the very least, you might get to experience something new and different.

Bouldering

Bouldering in the Phoenix area is fairly limited, but there are some good possibilities here and there. At the current time, the two best areas within the metro area are at Camelback Mountain and the Beardsley Boulderpile. If you want to drive a little further, you can also find some decent problems in the McDowell Mountains (near the Morrell's Wall and Gardener's Wall parking areas) as well as on the boulders just east of the south end of Little Granite Mountain. For concentrated fields of boulders and boulder problems, head out of town to the boulders near Oak Flat Campground, just east of the tunnel up the hill from Superior.

Bouldering Ratings

Camelback Mountain – Some decent bouldering can be found a short hike up the summit trail out of the Echo Canyon parking lot (see the Camelback chapter). The Triangle Boulder is just off the left side of the trail (can't miss it). There are also several boulders in the area immediately to the northeast of the Triangle Boulder that have colorful names and can provide a few hours of entertainment or workout, whichever you're after. The rock is the same as that on the rest of Camelback (petrified mud), so it's always a good idea to boulder somewhat conservatively or use a spotter. Holds have been known to blow at the most inconvenient times.

At the print time The Bolus is closed! While The Bolus has historically provided some of the best hard bouldering in the Phoenix area and been the site of a previous Phoenix Bouldering Contest, it also sits on private property. The owner does not want climbers in there and you will be ejected, either by the owner or by the authorities. If you decide to go anyway and risk getting thrown out, you're simply helping cause more potential access problems and giving the public a negative perception of climbers. Please respect the owner's wishes and boulder elsewhere until (unlikely) access is restored.

Beardsley Boulders – Another site of the Phoenix Bouldering Contest (back in the dark ages), Beardsley still provides some decent problems on finger-ripping granite boulders strewn about the east side of the hills by Cave Creek and Beardsley Roads (see map). The original access to the bouldering, from Cave Creek Road on Lone Cactus, has been barricaded. Please respect the barricade and come in from the Deer Valley Road access (dirt road along fence).

The Beardsley Boulders area sits on BLM land, and consequently has taken more than its fair share of abuse at the hands of bored high school students seeking a secluded spot for weekend parties. This abuse has included fire

Bouldering Scale	
Vermin Scale	**Yosemite Decimal**
V0–	5.7
V0	5.8/5.9
V0+	5.10
V1	5.11a
V2	5.11b/c
V3	5.11d/12a

next to boulders, broken beer and booze bottles, and the use of spray paint on the faces of boulders. The east face of the Pencil Thin boulder has been rendered nearly unclimbable because of the layers of paint covering the rock, although Bob Blair told me recently that he has cleaned the paint off of many of the critical holds. While climbers have staged several clean-up days at Beardsley, the clean-ups do not maintain pace with the destruction. The area has also been systematically denuded of plant life, as the partiers attempt to burn anything within reach. It's a crying shame when a generation has no more respect for a place than that shown for the Beardsley Boulders. Please do your part if you can. If you go there to do some bouldering, fill up a trash bag and take it out with you. Every little bit helps. A cardboard box and some gloves might even be better to take out a bit of the shattered glass laying around.

Introductory information for the bouldering at Beardsley may be found in the chapter dedicated to that area in this book. There are many more established and potential boulder problems than those listed, so feel free to explore and create your own.

Queen Creek Bouldering – Site of the last several Phoenix Bouldering Contests, the area of boulders near Oak Flat Campground, east of Superior, can provide a full lifetime of entertaining bouldering on volcanic tuff. All you need is a pair of shoes, a chalk bag and your imagination to guide you. Bring your tape too, this stuff is rough.

Phoenix Rock Geology

AUTHOR'S NOTE: The following essay was originally compiled by George B. Allen. Jim Waugh did some editing and revisions for inclusion in the first edition of *Phoenix Rock* to simplify the text and apply it specifically to climbing. Following these modifications, George Allen no longer wished authorship for professional reasons. Nevertheless, very special thanks are extended to him. Most of the text included is his phrasing and word choice. I have included the entire text of the essay, even though the Superstition Mountains, Santan Mountains and Queen Creek areas are not included in this guide, to give climbers a feel for the geologic formation of all of the area's rock climbing venues.

The processes responsible for the present expression of rocks are complex. As climbers we are normally less concerned with probing the abyss of time than exploring the beauty and facility of rocks. Even so, to better appreciate Phoenix's rock, we must consider the total history as well as the immediate environmental circumstance. To geologists this is the field of geomorphology; for climbers, with their subtle and unique observations, this is climbing geomorphology.

The majority of Phoenix rock climbs (excluding the White Tanks) can be discussed in terms of three geological terranes: first, the mud flow breccias and fluvial sediments of Camelback Mountain, that constitute the youngest and most easily interpreted terrane; second, the extensive Superstition Mountains' volcanic field that requires reference to older and more obscure events; third, the 1.4 billion year old Ruin Granite of the Phoenix Valley which is the most difficult to interpret.

As one reads the following text, notice that those unique characteristics, that make it possible to climb rock, are highlighted. This essay offers a geologic explanation for those characteristics and intends to offer climbers not only an explanation for the rock's present condition but also knowledge that can be applied when looking for "new" rock to climb around Phoenix.

Ruin Granite of the Phoenix Valley
(Little Granite Mountain, Cholla Mountain, McDowell Mountains, Pinnacle Peak, and Troon Mountain):

Perhaps the most striking, even cutting, feature of the Ruin Granite is its abrasiveness. Visitors to the desert have long been told that the climate is responsible for the crumbly slopes and knobby, abrasive climbs. However, a visit to the Pikes Peak Granite near Colorado Springs, Colorado and the Vedauwoo climbing area, hosting Sherman Granite, near Laramie, Wyoming, avails the same gravelly slopes and abrasive climbs even though the rocks are in climates markedly different from Phoenix's. A look even closer to home, at Granite Mountain (Prescott) and at the Wilderness Granite atop Mt. Lemmon, show that even within the desert not all granites weather like the Ruin. Instead of climate alone, a better explanation of the Ruin Granite's coarseness can be found in its petrology (structure).

The Ruin Granite, Pikes Peak Granite, and the Sherman Granite are almost all rapakivi granites. The term rapakivi refers to the chemistry of some of the feldspar crystals in granite. In most granites the feldspar crystals have a core rich in sodium and a rim rich in potassium; however, rapakivi granites have feldspar crystals that are core-rich in potassium and rim-rich in sodium. The significance is that sodium rich rim is less stable at surface conditions than potassium rich rim (Erickson, 1968). Consequently, rapakivi granites weather more quickly than non-rapakivi granites: thereby leaving abrasive gobie-spawning (lumpy and/or irregular) surfaces.

Another texture producing phenomena occurs during the situating or positioning of a magma body when pieces of wall rock break off into the magma. These inclusions may melt or remain intact. Intact pieces are called zenoliths and frequently look like spoiled black potatoes drowned in a sea of granite. Zenoliths are frequently finer-grained than the encompassing granite; consequently, they are more resistant to weathering and form welcome "thank God" holds.

Offering an explanation for the hazardous, gravelly slopes and the knobby faces only partially accounts for Ruin Granite climbs. One must also account for the orderly crack systems as seen on the North Face of Tom's Thumb and the flat-edged, straight faces like **Shalayly Direct** at Pinnacle Peak. The igneous rock fracturing present at the Lower East Wall at Pinnacle Peak, North Face of Tom's Thumb, etc., occurs as magma cools over a long period of time. As this cooling takes place, the interplay of compression and relaxation with unevenly distributed liquid and solid fractions produces a type of fracturing known as disrupture and accounts for many of the orderly crack systems in Phoenix. On the other hand some fractures show displacement as well as disrupture. These are called faults. The flat planar character of the Wedge's East Face and the **Shalayly Direct** face along with the platform nature of their holds is a marked contrast to the majority of the face climbs which have knobby holds. (Note: Look for the section that fell away at the base of The Wedge and at the base of Hidden Chimneys at the Lower East Wall for examples.)

Concluding the processes responsible for Ruin Granite morphology is difficult because of the great age of the granite itself. In contrast, the Superstition Mountains volcanic field's geomorphology can be more confidently interpreted owing to their relative youth and the numerous modern environments.

Superstition Field
(Queen Creek Canyon, Santans and Superstition Mountains):

The Superstition field is east of Apache Junction and formed 15 to 24 million years ago (Sheridan, 1978). Its original extent may have exceeded two thousand square miles (Peterson, 1968). Superstition climbs are of two types. First, the classic spire and ridge climbs, like **Weaver's Needle** and **The Hand**, are found on intrusive necks and dikes respectively. Second, steep face and crack climbs, such as on Barks Canyon Wall, Queen Creek Canyon and The Acropolis, are on ash flow tuff canyon walls.

In hand, a tuff is punky white grey and can be scratched with a fingernail. Lithics, pieces of rocks other than tuff and pumice pieces, are randomly oriented in a non-welded tuff. Vapor cavities may also be of random orientation. Increasing degrees of welding show progressive flattening of all these features and progressive hardening of the tuff. The ability to discern degrees of welding can aid a climber in the discovery of rock that is worthwhile for climbing (see figure 3). For example, severely fractured walls or the spires of Chiricahua National Monument are welded tuffs that are uninviting at best. All told, the ash flow environment sounds inhospitable to climbers. Indeed, an appreciation for the diversification of ash flow terranes is evidenced by such worthy climbing areas as Smith Rock in Oregon, Dead Man's Summit in California, and portions of the Superstitions. The steep, firm face and crack climbs that exist in these areas are probably the result of case hardening (outer hardened covering) of well exposed zones of partial welding. The majority of holds are the result of weathering of soft pumice from the tuff. (Peterson 1968) attributes the cracks to the same processes as offered for the cracks in the Ruin Granite section.

While understanding the geology of ash flows may help climbers to find safe passage over its walls and cracks, describing the geology of small intrusives may provoke second thoughts before deciding to cap the Superstition's summits. Four characteristics of small intrusion formation contribute to their high fracture density and consequent looseness. One, as small bodies, they cool rapidly, thereby resulting in glassier, more easily fractured rock than had it cooled slowly. Two, the liquid composition as opposed to solid composition of certain minerals in the rock results in a larger volume when cooling, thus producing fracturing. Three, the presence of fluids in the late stages of cooling releases vapor. As pressure builds from the vapor, fracturing can result. Fourth, when intrusives occur in fault systems or at fault junctures, movement can easily fracture dikes like The Hand (faults are commonly subject to multiple episodes of movement). Close inspection should display those spires that are less fractured than others consequently providing safer climbing.

In contrast to the explanations for the Superstition field, the processes that formed Camelback Mountain's climbs are easily tangible.

Camelback Mountain

Most of the climbing on Camelback Mountain is on the mountain's western third, the Camel's Head region, in a 15 million year old, 300 to 600 foot alluvial fan and mud slide sequence formed by deposits of sand and mud which lies on granite. The area is further complicated by minor faulting: the East Wall of the Praying Monk buttress is exemplary.

Cordy (1968) described the Camel Head's formation by dividing it into four members, each of which hosts some climbing. The Dromedary member or first member is a red, well-bedded, pebbly sandstone. The walls to the east of The Praying Monk (most visible when hiking Echo Canyon Trail to the top of the Camel's Head) are the best examples of this member. Most climbers avoid this member because of poor cementation, silt layers, and limited outcrops.

The Echo Canyon member or second member receives much attention from climbers as the medium range of climbing from the Headwall area to the Camel's Ear and beyond. Ranging from 200 to 300 feet, this member is the thickest of all the members. Bold, steep, featureless walls produce unnerving exposure such as witnessed on the climb **Suicide**.

The Papago Park member or third member lies above the Echo Canyon member and hosts the Praying Monk and Gargoyle Wall climbs. This member is a tan to red, well-hardened, well-layered sandstone comprised of interbedded silty, sandy, cobble and boulder beds. It is thought to have been deposited as water laid sediments in an alluvial fan. Flake and cobble-related holds make passage easier for climbers through the Papago member.

Essentially, there are two types of flake-related holds. One, exfoliation holds occur as the rock's response to released compression from weathering. The wall to the right of Pedrick's Chimney displays several exfoliation flakes. Two, companion holds are the flat steps that remain from broken exfoliation holds.

Cobble-related holds include the protruding cobbles imbedded in the member or the incut casts they leave when broken from the member. Observing these types of holds can help a climber to realistically predict the nature of certain upcoming holds before using them.

Occasionally, one other type of hold appears. Hollowed pockets which appear as holes in the rock are known as tafoni. The Papago Park member is well endowed with tafoni as the Gargoyle Wall exemplifies.

The Camel's Ear member or fourth member caps the Camel's Head formation and nearly all of the area's summits. This member is a dark red brown sandstone with occasional non-granitic rocks. The sediments are debris flow and water laid deposits of an alluvial fan. The bizarre boulder problem atop the Camel's Head, the last pitch of the Hart Route, and some unpleasant cracks on the south side of the Camel's Head are exceptions to the notion that the Camel's Ear member is not a source of climbs. The lack of climbing in this member seems to be attributed to a muddier, more poorly sorted breccia as opposed to its underlying member, Papago Park.

Geology adds another dimension to the world of climbing. The three climbing terranes of the Phoenix Rock area exemplify vast and diverse geologic processes. Fostering this understanding can ultimately aid route finding skills and the search for new climbs.

Bibliography

Anderson, J. L. "Proterozoic anorogenic granite plutonism of North America," Geologic Society of America Memoir. No. 161, 1983, pp. 133-154.

Cordy, G. E. "Environmental Geology of the Paradise Valley Quadrangle, Maricopa County, Arizona, Part II", Arizona State University M.S. Thesis. 1978, pp. 1-89.

Erickson, R.C. "Petrology and Geochemistry of the Dos Cabezas Mountains, Cochise County, Arizona", University of Arizona PhD Thesis. 1969, pp. 66-112.

Flint, R.F. and Skinner, B.J. Physical Geology. New York: John Wiley & Sons, 1977, pp. 114-115.

Krauskopf, K.B. Introduction to Geochemistry. New York: McGraw-Hill Book Company, 1979, pp. 91-93.

Lipman, P.W. "The Roots of Ash Flow Calderas in Western North America: Windows Into the Tops of Granitic Batholiths," Journal of Geophysical Research. Vol. 89, No. B10, 1984, pp. 8801-8841.

Peterson, D.W. "Zoned ash-flow sheet in the region around Superior, Arizona", Arizona Geological Society Southern Arizona Guidebook III. 1968, pp. 215-222.

Sheridan, M.F. "The Superstition Cauldron Complex: in Burt, D.M. and Pewe, T.S., eds," Guidebook to the Geology of Central Arizona. 1978, pp. 85-96.

Smith, R.L. "Zones and Zonal Variations in Welded Ash Flows," U.S.G.S. Professional Paper 354-F. 1960, pp. 149-159.

Summary

Well...that's about it. Not much left to say, except "Have a Great Time!"

Climb Safe!
G. Opland, 1996

> The clock of life is wound but once
> And no man has the power
> To tell just when the hands will stop
> On what day–or what hour.
> Now is the only time you have
> So live it with a will
> Don't wait until tomorrow
> The hands may then be still.
>
> H. Endler

BEARDSLEY BOULDERS AREA MAP

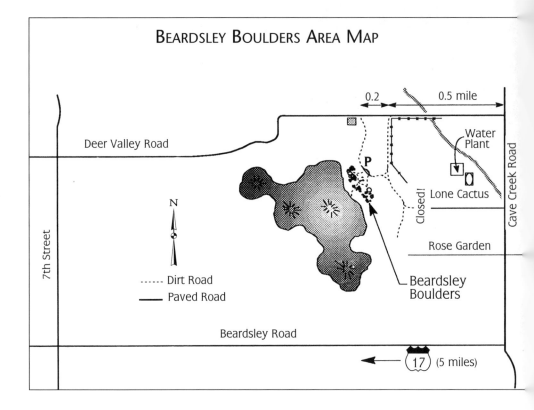

Chapter 1

BEARDSLEY BOULDERS

Located in the north part of the Phoenix metro area, Beardsley Boulders has been a traditional bouldering spot for many years, even serving as the showcase for the 3rd Phoenix Bouldering Contest in 1985. The area is named for it's proximity to Beardsley Road, found to the south. Beardsley offers some quality boulders that will leave your fingers shredded and your tendons pounding. Obviously, as a bouldering area, Beardsley is most rewarding as a weekday workout spot for local climbers. Climbers, visiting or otherwise, short on time may also find a "quick-fix" lead climbing experience here as well.

For low-energy days, bouldering on finger-rending granite can be found only a quick stroll from the parking area. For those with a bit more achievement in mind, leadable (albeit short) routes may be found on the larger unbroken formations up the hill and behind the bouldering area.

Be forewarned before you come to Beardsley. Some of the area has the distinct appearance of "ground-zero" of a nuclear explosion. The Beardsley Boulders area sits on BLM land, and consequently has taken more than it's fair share of abuse at the hands of bored high school students seeking a secluded spot for the weekend parties. This abuse has included bonfires next to boulders, broken beer and booze bottles, and the use of spray paint on the faces of boulders. The east face of the Pencil Thin Boulder has been rendered nearly unclimbable because of the layers of paint covering the rock. Possible manufactured V14 boulder problems? While climbers have staged (and continue to hold) clean-up days at Beardsley, the clean-ups do not nearly maintain pace with the destruction. The area has also been systematically denuded of plant life, as the partiers attempt to burn anything within reach. It's a crying shame when a generation has no more respect for a place than that shown for the Beardsley Boulders. Please do your part if you

Pencil Thin Boulder, with many quailty problems, has taken the brunt of damage by high schoolers for the last five years.

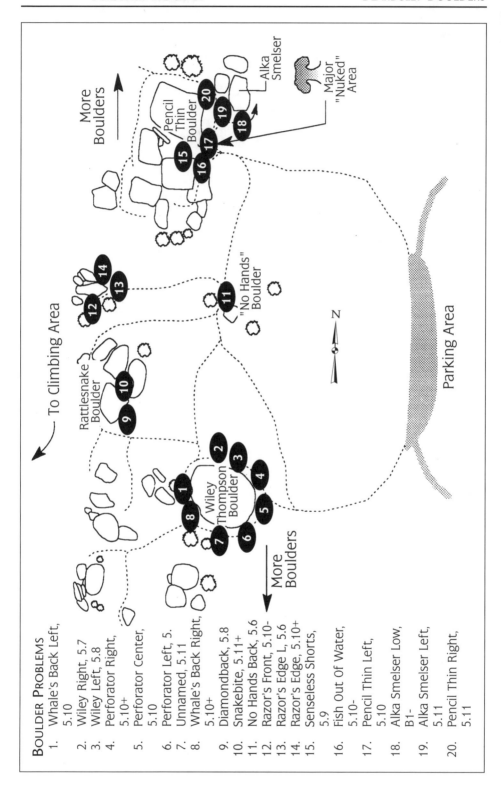

Boulder Problems

1. Whale's Back Left, 5.10
2. Wiley Right, 5.7
3. Wiley Left, 5.8
4. Perforator Right, 5.10+
5. Perforator Center, 5.10
6. Perforator Left, 5.
7. Unnamed, 5.11
8. Whale's Back Right, 5.10+
9. Diamondback, 5.8
10. Snakebite, 5.11+
11. No Hands Back, 5.6
12. Razor's Front, 5.10-
13. Razor's Edge L, 5.6
14. Razor's Edge, 5.10+
15. Senseless Shorts, 5.9
16. Fish Out Of Water, 5.10-
17. Pencil Thin Left, 5.10
18. Alka Smelser Low, B1-
19. Alka Smelser Left, 5.11
20. Pencil Thin Right, 5.11

can to help keep damage to a minimum and access open. If you go there to do some bouldering, fill up a trash bag and take it out with you. A cardboard box and a pair of gloves might even be better to take out a bit of the shattered glass laying around. Every little bit helps.

Warning! Some of the routes at Beardsley have ¼" bolts on them. There's nothing warm and wonderful about an old rusty "quarter-incher." Please take the time to inspect the bolts if you're going to trust them to possible lead falls.

Approach: From the metro area, there are a couple of ways to get to Beardsley. The easiest way is probably to head north on I-17 to the Union Hills/Yorkshire exit. Continue north on the frontage road past Yorkshire to Beardsley Road (1 mile). Go right (east) on Beardsley and drive to Cave Creek Road (5 miles). Head left on Cave Creek and drive north to Deer Valley (traffic lights). Go left (west) on Deer Valley and drive 0.7 mile to a dirt road that can be found just on the other side of the water plant (see map). Another dirt road can be found 0.2 mile past that which also goes to the parking area. If it's easier to drive in using Cave Creek Road, these directions may also be followed when Deer Valley Road is reached. Once on the dirt road, follow it back south and west to the parking area. The climbing areas may be seen on the hillside to the southwest. Currently, both dirt roads are navigable with a normal passenger car.

Access: Beardsley Boulders resides on BLM land. No access problems exist at the current time, but the access via Lone Cactus road has been closed! Please respect this closure and use the dirt access roads described above. Any access problems with the area would probably arise in response to the damage done by high schoolers (see comments above), but the BLM doesn't seem too excited about this at the current time.

Bouldering

The bouldering at Beardsley is a good reason to visit. Many quality boulders are spread along the base of the mountain, providing some worthwhile bouldering. The nature of bouldering is such that a detailed map will only serve to limit the imagination of climbers who practice it's unique challenges. As bouldering should not be limited, I will only provide a starting point, indicating some of the older established problems (see map).

Note: Some of the problems indicated may be rendered nearly impossible by some of the grafitti described above! You could consider it a challenge.

Beardsley Boulder Problems

1. **Whale's Back Left, 5.10**   Top of flake, step left and then up face.
2. **Wiley Right, 5.7**   Gain arête on far right via good holds, continue up arête.
3. **Wiley Left, 5.8**   Climb face on positive edge holds.
4. **Perforator Right, 5.10+**   Start on overhanging holds, follow seam up and left.
5. **Perforator Center, 5.10**   Start in scoop, gain good edge above, straight up.
6. **Perforator Left, 5.**   Hard smack on arête, thin holds up face.
7. **Unnamed, 5.11**   Straight up the south face on thin edges.
8. **Whale's Back Right, 5.10+**   From flake, friction up rounded arête.
9. **Diamondback, 5.8**   Undercling "pistol" grip, up and over.
10. **Snakebite, 5.11+**   Static face using the two obvious edges.
11. **No Hands Back, 5.6**   Up face, no hands. Tricky balance problem.
12. **Razor's Front, 5.10-**   Vertical face up center.
13. **Razor's Edge L, 5.6**   Lieback/Vertical up blunt arête.
14. **Razor's Edge, 5.10+**   Thin seam left of "knob."
15. **Senseless Shorts, 5.9**   Climb shelf, get feet high, reach over top.

16. **Fish Out Of Water, 5.10-**   Mantle problem on corner of boulder.
17. **Pencil Thin Left, 5.10**   Up left arête, lieback, traverse, move up and over top.
18. **Alka Smelser Low, B1-**   Sit-down start, traverse entire boulder. Either direction.
19. **Alka Smelser Left, 5.11**   Sit-down start, climb up and out of cave to top.
20. **Pencil Thin Right, 5.11**   Vertical right, up corner arête. Slightly right at top.

Climbing

The routes at Beardsley offer an alternative to the bouldering. The leadable routes are found on the larger formations distributed amongst the rubble on the hillside above the bouldering area. The routes are generally short in nature with the longest (approximately. 70 feet) being found on Fear Rock, just below the crest of the mountain. While not a destination spot for lead climbing, there are some worthwhile and enjoyable routes here. It should be noted that many of the longer faces found among the formations on the hillside have been toproped by Beardsley regulars at one time or another, including routes from about 5.9 to 5.12. Be sparing if you decide to get the bolt kit out.

Fear Rock

Fear Rock is provides the longest routes (70 feet) at Beardsley. Routes are described from left to right. The formation is easily spotted from the bouldering area as the largest unbroken piece of rock near the top of the slope and on the left.

21. **Black And Decker Pecker Wrecker, 5.6**   Approximately 100 feet uphill and left from Fear Rock, climb a smooth face for 15 feet to a vertical crack. Climb crack to top. Pro: Small to large nuts.
22. **Naked Bimbos From Mars, 5.7**   This route is located on the left side of Fear Rock at a short dihedral. Climb dihedral to an overhang. Turn the overhang on it's right side and continue in crack to top. Pro: Stoppers and cams.
23. **Brown Sugar, 5.7 (R)**   Start 15 feet right of **Naked Bimbos**. Step right off a spike and climb face past three bolts. Continue out right to clip fourth bolt of **Grandma Got Run Over**. Climb runout (but easy) face to top. Pro: Four bolts.
24. **Grandma Got Run Over By A Reindeer, 5.9 (R)** ★   15 feet to the right of **Brown Sugar**, climb face straight to top past four bolts. A bit of runout is encountered past the last bolt (easier climbing). Pro: Four bolts.
25. **The Fear Of Having Sex With Dead People, 5.7 (R)** ★   One can only wonder about Bob's rather inventive route names! This one is located about 20 feet to the right of **Grandma Got Run Over** on the lower right corner of Fear Rock. Step off a rock, climb left and up face past two bolts. When possible, climb straight up to thin crack (TCU). Climb crack to its end, then continue on easy, but runout, face to top. Pro: Two bolts, small to large nuts.
26. **The Flake, 5.8 (TR)**   Climb "ripper" detached flake to the right of **Dead People**. Pro: TR. The following two routes are located on a 30-foot formation approximately 150 feet uphill and right from Fear Rock.
27. **Teenage Enema Nurses In Bondage, 5.9** ★★   On left-hand side of rock, climb crack to top using a variety of techniques. Pro: Small to large nuts.
28. **Wait Until Dark, 5.10a** ★   Just to the right of **Teenage Nurses**, climb face past three bolts to top. Pro: Three bolts.

Tombstone Area

This area includes those boulders found slightly down and 150 feet to the right of Fear Rock. The hardest lead route at Beardsley, **Sad But Sweet,** is found here.

29. **Sad But Sweet, 5.11b** ★   This climb is located on a large boulder formation with a huge overhang on its south (left) face. The route is on the right side of the boulder.

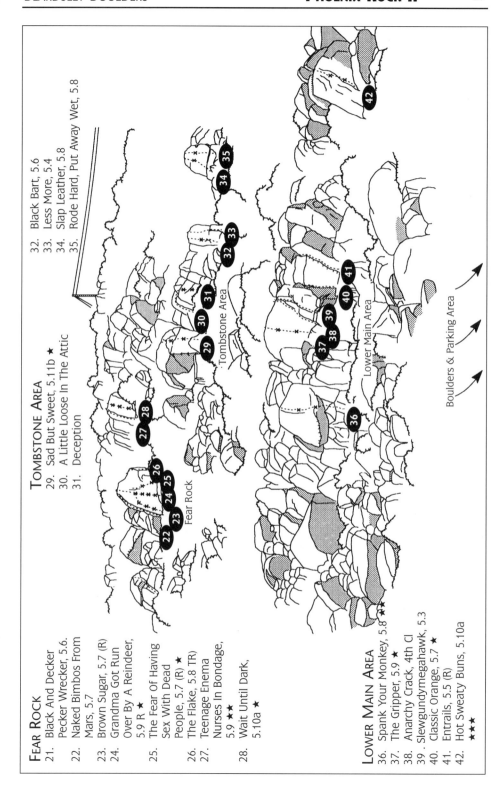

FEAR ROCK

21. Black And Decker
    Pecker Wrecker, 5.6.
22. Naked Bimbos From
    Mars, 5.7
23. Brown Sugar, 5.7 (R)
24. Grandma Got Run
    Over By A Reindeer,
    5.9 R ★
25. The Fear Of Having
    Sex With Dead
    People, 5.7 (R) ★
26. The Flake, 5.8 TR)
27. Teenage Enema
    Nurses In Bondage,
    5.9 ★★
28. Wait Until Dark,
    5.10a ★

LOWER MAIN AREA

36. Spank Your Monkey, 5.8 ★★
37. The Gripper, 5.9 ★
38. Anarchy Crack, 4th Cl
39. Slewgundymegahawk, 5.3
40. Classic Orange, 5.7 ★
41. Entrails, 5.5 (R)
42. Hot Sweaty Buns, 5.10a
    ★★★

TOMBSTONE AREA

29. Sad But Sweet, 5.11b ★
30. A Little Loose In The Attic
31. Deception

32. Black Bart, 5.6
33. Less More, 5.4
34. Slap Leather, 5.8
35. Rode Hard, Put Away Wet, 5.8

Fear Rock

Tombstone Area

Lower Main Area

Boulders & Parking Area

Climb overhanging face past a bolt to a handrail. Climb easy ground past another bolt to top. Pro: Two bolts.

30. **A Little Loose In The Attic**   Bush start, continuous handcrack. Loose at top. Pro: Small to medium nuts.

31. **Deception**   Scramble to top of boulder to access two-bolt face above. Pro: Two bolts.

32. **Black Bart, 5.6**   Starts on a boulder 150 feet to the right of **Sad But Sweet**. Climb flake and face to bolt. Continue on face (TCU's and stoppers) to top. Pro: One bolt, small to medium nuts.

33. **Less More, 5.4**   Starts 15 feet to the right of **Black Bart**. Climb a crack over a small overhang. Climb easy rock to the top. Pro: Small to medium nuts.

34. **Slap Leather, 5.8**   This is the left-hand route on the Tombstone. Climb past a small overhang (medium crack) to a bolt. Continue past bolt to two-bolt belay. Pro: Small to medium nuts, one bolt.

35. **Rode Hard, Put Away Wet, 5.8**   Right-hand route on the Tombstone. Climb up to large flake/block. Continue up past bolt and on to top and two-bolt belay. Pro: Small to medium nuts, 1 bolt.

Note: The face on the left-hand side of the Tombstone, just left of **Slap Leather** has been toproped (5.10).

Lower Main Area

The Lower Main Area includes several large boulder formations running along the lower part of the mountain. This area has a short approach and some decent moderate climbs.

36. **Spank Your Monkey, 5.8**
★★   Start 40 feet to the left of **The Gripper** near an overhang. Climb 15 feet to a large triangular block. Grapple onto the block and clip first bolt. Continue up face to ledge, past another bolt and on to the top. Pro: Two bolts, cams.

37. **The Gripper, 5.9** ★   Climb easy rock in corner to a ledge. Move slightly right, then continue up past two bolts to the top of the rock. This route displays a machine-gun blast to the left of the line and goes through some grafitti at below the first bolt.

Note: The large unbolted boulder about 100 feet left of **The Gripper** has been toproped by several variations from approximately 5.10+ to 5.12.

38. **Anarchy Crack, (Cl. 4)**
Start same as **The Gripper**.

Wayne Schroeter cranks his way up a variation of **Spank Your Monkey** (5.8), Lower Main Area, Beardsley Boulders.

Avoid the face, climbing up and right following an easy crack to top. Pro: Small to medium.

39. **Slewgundymegahawk, 5.3**   Starts 20 feet to the right of **The Gripper**. Step off a spike and climb up 15 feet to an overhang. Climb overhang to a thin crack which is followed to the top. Pro: Small to medium.

40. **Classic Orange, 5.7 ★**   Climb nice short handcrack in left-facing dihedral to ledge. Pro: Medium.

41. **Entrails, 5.5 (R)**   Climb the crusty squeeze chimney just to the right of **Classic Orange.** Watch out for loose junk! Pro: None.

42. **Hot Sweaty Buns, 5.10a ★★★**   Maybe the area's best route! Rumored to have originally been led (date unknown) using stoppers! Definitely bold. Climb right-leaning seam and steep face past two bolts to top. Pro: Two bolts.

Rogil Schroeter liebacks up **Classic Orange** (5.7), Lower Main Area, Beardsley Boulders.

CAMELBACK ROAD MAP

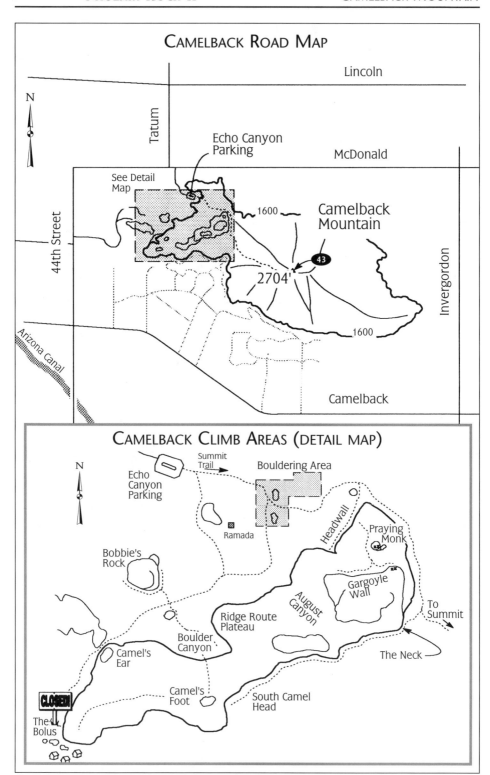

Lincoln

N

Tatum

Echo Canyon Parking

McDonald

See Detail Map

1600

Camelback Mountain

44th Street

43

2704'

Invergordon

1600

Arizona Canal

Camelback

CAMELBACK CLIMB AREAS (DETAIL MAP)

N

Summit Trail

Bouldering Area

Echo Canyon Parking

Ramada

Headwall

Praying Monk

Bobbie's Rock

Gargoyle Wall

August Canyon

To Summit

Ridge Route Plateau

Boulder Canyon

Camel's Ear

The Neck

CLOSED

Camel's Foot

South Camel Head

The Bolus

CHAPTER 2

CAMELBACK MOUNTAIN

Camelback Mountain, smack dab in the middle of the Phoenix metro area, has the shortest drive of any area detailed in this guide. It's pretty hard to miss the mountain, it's the big one that looks like a kneeling camel. The rock on which most of the climbing is found (see Geology section) is best described as "petrified mud", a factor you will have to deal with if you plan on climbing here. Care must be taken on routes (with a few exceptions) as there are lots of rocks here just waiting to experience the effects of gravity.

The mountain has two summits. The eastern, known as the Camel's Hump, is the higher of the two, at an elevation of 2704 feet. The Hump is composed of granite, but offers very little

climbing. It does provide an excellent hike that begins at the Echo Canyon Parking Lot and culminates with a spectacular view of the Phoenix metro area. Camelback is part of the Phoenix Mountains. In the last couple of years, the Phoenix Parks and Recreation department has been establishing localized trails to minimize wear and tear on the area. At this point, it is believed that none of the climbing areas are inaccessible at this time, but stay on established trails as much as possible. If you are stopped by a ranger concerning access trails, please be polite. There may be an initial "breaking in" period while the trail process is worked out.

Nearly all of the climbing at Camelback is done on the northern side of the lower western summit, on and near what is commonly referred to as the "head" of the camel. The climbs range from fairly short (40-foot), simple routes, to somewhat longer (200+ foot), more involved multi-pitch routes. The face climbing found at Camelback is somewhat unique, involving moves over embedded knobs and pebbles in a petrified mixture of lava and stone. Add this to the historical nature of the Camelback climbs, and it comes out to a pretty cool experience. Although most of the more traveled routes are largely free of loose rock, it might be a good idea to check the solidity of the next hold before

Lisa Schmitz attempts the Chipmonk Boulder while Tim Schneider spots.

you grab and launch on it. The air-time you save may be your own!

As a positive note, the climbing environment at Camelback Mountain is a convenient and pleasurable escape. You can get into your car after work, climb in a seemingly remote desert terrain, and be home by dark. It is stimulating to wander through the many minor canyons on top of the Head massif. You can get away and feel alone, while still within a metropolitan area. No doubt, there is certainly better rock to climb around Phoenix, but none of the areas offer these unique features.

The climbing history of Camelback is the oldest of the Phoenix areas, starting with the original Kachinas (see History section) in the 1940's and continuing to the present day. As you climb on some of the older routes, and wonder about the sanity of it all, it is interesting to consider that some of them were done by climbers wearing hiking books and tied into hemp ropes!

A note about fixed protection: The lack of crack systems and other naturally protectable features at Camelback has prompted the use of expansion bolts on many routes. Many have quite a few years under their hangers and should be checked before trusted to hold a leader fall of any significance!

Approach: Camelback is that big camel-shaped rock in the center of Phoenix, sticking up near the intersection of 44th Street and Camelback Road. See the map. The parking area is accessed from McDonald Street. The Echo Canyon parking lot is accessed from the north side just to the east of the McDonald/Tatum intersection (see map). Parking is fairly limited here due to the popularity of the Camelback summit trail! If you pick the wrong parking place assuming you won't get a ticket, you may get a big surprise. Most of the time, a little patience will pay off as the turnover rate (hikers leaving for home) in the parking lot is fairly high and constant depending on the time of day.

Access: Camelback Mountain is one of the official Phoenix mountain parks. Housing development has enclosed the mountain on all sides and eliminated most of the possible parking,

Lisa Schmitz climbing Hard Times (5.7), on the Gargoyle Wall.

except for the lot in Echo Canyon on the north side (see map). While the battle goes on for housing to be stopped on the southern slopes, most of the climbing areas lie within the park and should be available to future generations of climbers. One area that has been lost to development is the Bolus. While this has long been a popular local spot for hard bouldering (and home to at least one Phoenix Bouldering Contest), the owners of this land have taken a stand and will not allow climbing any longer. Please respect this closure and climb elsewhere!

Neck

This small area has received little attention in the past because of the approach and small number of routes. However, most that have climbed here have enjoyed both the exposure (the Head drops off steeply both south and north) and scenery. It is advised to carry your packs with you as the easiest descent is nowhere near the start. Standard Descent for Neck Routes: Same as Standard Descent for Head.

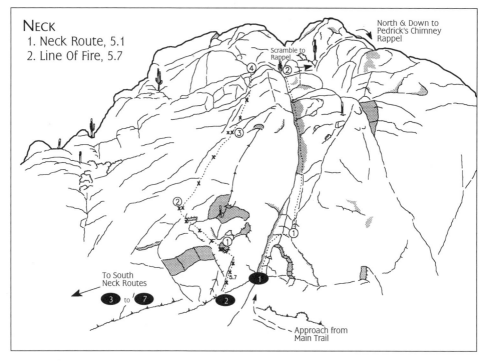

NECK
1. Neck Route, 5.1
2. Line Of Fire, 5.7

1. **Neck Route, 5.1**   Start at saddle between Head and Hump at base of gully. First Pitch: Climb loose gully with small overhangs until a traverse right leads to small belay ledge (5.1 with bolt). Second Pitch: Traverse right onto exposed face and climb straight up water chute to belay bolt in gully. Easy scrambling up gully (Cl. 2) leads to summit of Head. Pro: Two bolts, medium nuts.
2. **Line Of Fire, 5.7**   Start down and left of **Neck Route** and just right of big overhang formed by cave. First Pitch: Climb face (5.7) up, slightly right, and then back left to belay alcove with bolted anchor. Second Pitch: Exit alcove on left. Continue on face up a short distance, traverse left (5.3) several feet up and left, past bolt and then up to four-bolt belay. Third Pitch: Continue up to second bolt (5.4). At this point traverse right and slightly up past bolt, then back left and up to three bolt belay. Fourth Pitch: Climb up and right passing a couple of bolts (5.6) and then back left to top. Pro: Several bolts, medium to large nuts.

South Camel's Head

The following rather obscure routes are located along the south wall of the Camel's Head and may involve a bit of an approach or inventive solutions on getting to the bottom of these climbs. To give an alignment of the routes as they relate to other routes on the mountain, the top of the first pitch of the **Yellow Wall route** (#35) overlooks the **Open Book** (route 4). No route topos are shown.

3. **South Route, 5.2** This might be more of a mountaineering adventure than anything, but an interesting way to reach the summit. Start in gully several hundred feet to the right (east) of **Open Book** at base of deep gully. First Pitch: Climb in gully until belay is convenient (Cl. 4) Second Pitch: Continue in gully to reach head of August Canyon (Cl.3). Third Pitch: From head of August Canyon, traverse right (east) to huge ledge (Cl. 4). Fourth Pitch: Climb crack in dihedral to top (5.2). Easy scrambling to the north leads to summit of the Head. Pro: Small to medium nuts, bolts.

4. **Open Book, 5.9** As mentioned in the introduction to this section, this route is directly off the top of the first pitch of the **Yellow Wall** (route 35) that starts at the head of Boulder Canyon. It is easily identified as a huge right-facing open book that can be seen for miles. First Pitch: Climb corner about 150' to large alcove with bolt (Cl. 4). Second Pitch: Up and right, a gymnastic move is required to surmount an overhang (5.9), then climb through crack to reach large ledge with bolt. Third Pitch: Join second pitch of **Yellow Wall** (Cl. 4). Pro: Six bolts, large nuts.

5. **Anguish, 5.6 (A3)**   First Pitch: Starts as for **Open Book**. Second Pitch: Traverse left to top of large white flake (**Birdshit Flake**), climbing out around horn or up behind it, then continue until bolt is reached. Lower to bottom of flake and pendulum to horizontal crack, then go free left to belay bolt inside bottom of bomb bay chimney. Third Pitch: Climb chimney, then aid around flake and up 30 feet to belay ledge. Fourth Pitch: Traverse off ledge right and climb steep ramp to large ledge and top. Descend via scrambling left off ledge, then down gully to short rappel. Staying left of large ridge, walk on down passing **Sewery's Roof** on left. Pro: Seven bolts, pitons, small to large nuts.

The following two routes can be accessed via approaching up a ramp along the right side of Boulder Canyon as for the Camel's Foot area.

6. **Sewery's Roof, 5.4 (A1)**   The famous Bill Sewery photo route! Starts to the right of the wall where talus rises to the top. A tiny roof can be seen on upper right (east) of talus. Aid out and over roof via bolts, then step left to groove and climb free up and past overhang (bolt) to top. Pro: Twelve bolts.

7. **June Bug Crack, 5.5**   Located about 200 feet east (right) of **Sewery's Roof** at obvious left-facing chimney. Climb chimney, then finish in short crack on right side. Descend via north side of ridge, going left and down east slope. Pro: Large nuts and way-large nuts (tube chocks).

Headwall

This small wall is used primarily as an approach to the Praying Monk and the Gargoyle Wall. It offers a good warm-up for the routes in those areas. Standard Descent for Headwall: Descend **Rappel Gully** or **Headwall Route** for routes on and above the Headwall (single line rappel, large eyebolt anchor). This includes routes which descend using routes on **The Praying Monk** and the **Pedrick's Chimney** rappel. Overview photo on page 36.

8. **Class Three Gully, Cl. 3**   Start at ridge that turns into gully at left (north) end of Headwall. Climb ridge and gully up and drastically right (south) crossing **The Walk Up** and ending at top of **Rappel Gully**.

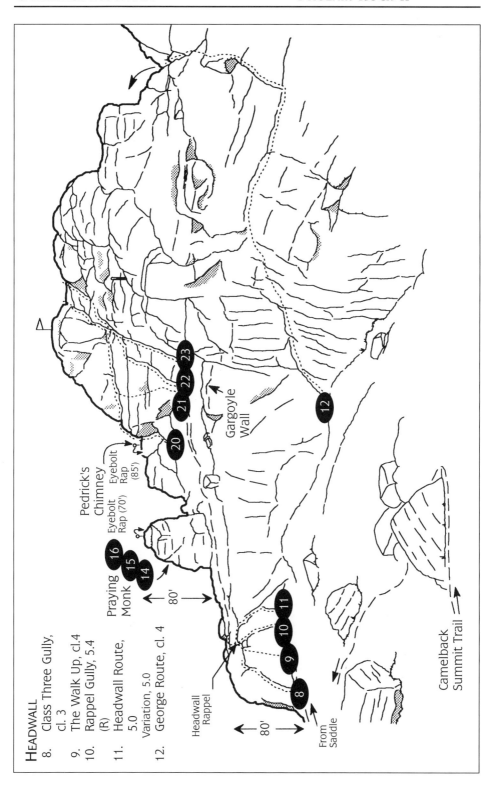

Headwall

8. Class Three Gully, cl. 3
9. The Walk Up, cl.4
10. Rappel Gully, 5.4 (R)
11. Headwall Route, 5.0
    Variation, 5.0
12. George Route, cl. 4

Praying Monk

Pedrick's Chimney

Eyebolt Rap (70')

Eyebolt Rap (85')

Gargoyle Wall

Headwall Rappel

From Saddle

Camelback Summit Trail

Headwall Area, Camelback Mountain

9. **The Walk Up, Cl. 4**   Start 70 feet right of **Class Three Gully** at steeper gully. Climb gully up and slightly right to top of **Rappel Gully**.
10. **Rappel Gully, 5.4 (R)**   Start 50 feet right of **The Walk Up** around a very recessed corner in a gully. Climb gully to top and belay from large eyebolt. Pro: Small nuts, Friends.
11. **Headwall Route, 5.0**   Start 20 feet right of **Rappel Gully** at shallow water chute. Climb face past three bolts to shallow alcove with a single bolt (can be backed up with additional pro). Pro: Three bolts, belay bolt, medium nuts.
    Variation, 5.0. Start 40 feet right of **Headwall Route**. Diagonal left on ramp system that finishes directly above normal end of **Headwall Route** Pro: None.
12. **George Route, Cl. 4**   Named after Kachina Ed George. Start approximately 400 feet right (300 feet southwest and 80 feet west-northwest of deep recessed corner) at ledge system. Traverse several hundred feet up and right into August Canyon. Continue to Head's summit via **Rotten Chimney** (Cl. 4), **Doug's Dandy** (5.6), or **Fixed Line Traverse** (5.6). Descend via Standard Descent for Head. Pro: Runners (numerous bolts will be encountered due to rescue team practice.).

Praying Monk

Although only one pitch in length, this pinnacle offers superb exposure coupled with its exciting (but comfortable) summit. A stunted saguaro cactus perched on the south side of the Monk makes it look like someone is climbing there when viewed from the Echo Canyon parking area. Don't be fooled! Standard Descent for The Praying Monk: Descend (southeast) via single line rappel from eyebolt (installed 1994) just southeast of summit belay bolts.

13. **Unnamed, 5.10**   Just to the left of the start for the **Southeast Corner** and **East Face** is a short face with two bolts. This is an old toprope problem that now has bolts–Living proof that some people will bolt anything. Climb face past bolts to top of large blob. Pro: Two bolts, assortment of pro for anchor.
14. **Southeast Corner, 5.7** ★   Bill Forrest wanted a more difficult line up the east face of the Monk. The result was a moderately fine climb that unfortunately receives very few ascents. Start is same as **East Face**. Instead of scrambling up into cave, climb face

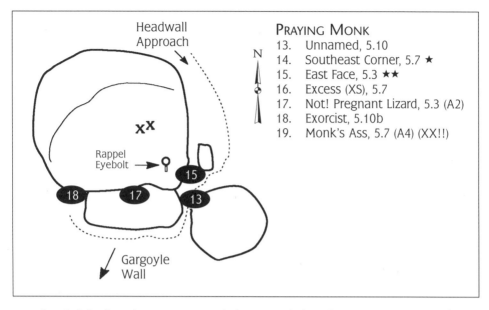

Headwall
Approach

N

XX

Rappel
Eyebolt →

15

18   17   13

Gargoyle
Wall

PRAYING MONK
13. Unnamed, 5.10
14. Southeast Corner, 5.7 ★
15. East Face, 5.3 ★★
16. Excess (XS), 5.7
17. Not! Pregnant Lizard, 5.3 (A2)
18. Exorcist, 5.10b
19. Monk's Ass, 5.7 (A4) (XX!!)

directly left of southeast corner past bolt to same ledge where **East Face** route gains access to the east face. Continue up corner staying left of **East Face** to top. Pro: Four bolts, three belay bolts.

15. **East Face, 5.3 ★★** This ancient classic has spectacular exposure and a quite aesthetic summit. Start at southeast corner. Scramble up (west) into cave and then traverse back right to gain east face. Wander up face to top. Pro: Several bolts, three belay bolts.

16. **Excess (XS), 5.7** Start is the same as **Southeast Corner.** After moving up to same ledge where **East Face** route gains access to the east face of the Monk, traverse down and right several feet above overhang to the right section of the east face and bolt. At this point wander up loose rock past another bolt to top. Pro: Three bolts, three belay bolts.

17. **Not! Pregnant Lizard, 5.3 (A2)** In the middle of the south face, climb past two bolts (these have been replaced) to sloping shelf. Aid past bolts up into the overhang and to the summit. The age of the bolts and the relative security of

Bill Wright lookin' good on the 5.7 start to the East face of the Praying Monk.

Camelback petrified mud-rock should keep your pulse up and your mind in an uproar!! Pro: Twelve bolts (bring a couple of 3/8-inch hangers and capscrews just for karmas sake). Note: This route was incorrectly identified as **Pregnant Lizard** in a recent mini-guide to Camelback. That route is actually located over by **Pedrick's Chimney** but is not included here.

18. **Exorcist, 5.10b**   Start at south face. Climb up and diagonal left toward southwest corner. Just before corner follow a line of bolts directly to top. Pro: Several bolts, three belay bolts.

    Next Time Variation, 5.7   Start is same as regular route. First Pitch: Climb up to fourth bolt , then traverse right under overhang past three bolts to small stance on the Southeast Corner (5.7). Second Pitch: From stance, continue up Southeast Corner to top (5.7). Pro: Three bolts, four belay bolts.

19. **Monk's Ass, 5.7 (A4) (XX!!)**   This route is located on the northwest face. It is included here just for historical purposes, for those that ever wondered why there weren't any routes on the "other" side of the Monk. It's history included a sheared bolt from a 30-foot screamer taken near the summit. This one has way more than its share of rotten rock. Definitely NOT RECOMMENDED! Thus, no route description.

Gargoyle Wall

Undoubtedly, this is the best wall to climb on at Camelback Mountain. Be sure to look for the tafoni (see Geology section). Standard Descent for Gargoyle Wall: Same as Standard Descent for Head. Scramble west and south down Cl. 2 gullies to top of **Pedrick's Chimney**. Rappel **Pedrick's Chimney** (90 feet) to upper talus from large eyebolt. Continue down to Headwall and use Standard Descent.

20. **Pedrick's Chimney, 5.1**   Named after Kachina Ben Pedrick, start at highest point of upper talus (see Camel's Head map). Climb wide easy dihedral up and left to base of chimney, then up chimney past bolt to broad ledge with large eyebolt (installed 1994–backup bolt 1995). Scramble south and west up Cl. 2 gullies to reach summit of Head. Pro: Medium to large nuts, one bolt, large eyebolt belay.

21. **Misgivings, 5.8 ★**   Start 130 feet right of **Pedrick's Chimney** or 20 feet left of **Hart Route**. First Pitch: Climb thin crack and face up to bolt, then move left and up to a pair of bolts (one loose). Continue up steep face until possible to move left and up to ledge (5.8) and two-bolt belay. Second Pitch: Traverse left 25 feet over small lip to another ledge (5.7). Third Pitch: Step right a few feet and climb directly up face to large ledge. Fourth Pitch: Climb face above, then traverse left (Cl. 3) to top of **Pedrick's Chimney** (beware of tricky downclimb) or right to last pitch of the **Hart Route** for approach to summit. Pro: Several bolts, several belay bolts.

22. **Hart Route, 5.2 ★**   Perhaps one of the more commonly climbed routes at Camelback. Start 20 feet right of **Misgivings** or 150 feet right of **Pedrick's Chimney** in trough at left edge of giant flake-mass. First Pitch: Climb trough past bolt to ledge (5.0) and two-bolt belay. Second Pitch: Continue up cracks and dihedral to small overhang. Pass overhang on left and climb chimney to ledge (5.1) with tree. Third Pitch: Walk right into Cl. 3 gully and up to base of 60-foot "friction pitch" on right. Belay at two-bolt anchor. Fourth Pitch: Climb face past two bolts to top (5.2). Summit of Head may be reached by scrambling south and east. Pro: Small to large nuts, several bolts.

    North Central Variation, 5.2   Begin 50 feet right of usual start. Climb deep gully-chimney dihedral system joining regular route at base of "friction pitch.".Pro: Two bolts, medium to large nuts.

23. **Cholla Traverse, 5.5 ★**   Never fear, you probably will not encounter any cholla on this route, but you still may get quite a sting. Start is same as **North Central Variation**. First Pitch: Traverse right to two bolt hanging belay (5.5). Second Pitch: Continue straight up for 60 feet past three bolts to reach good ledge (5.4). Third Pitch: Traverse right into

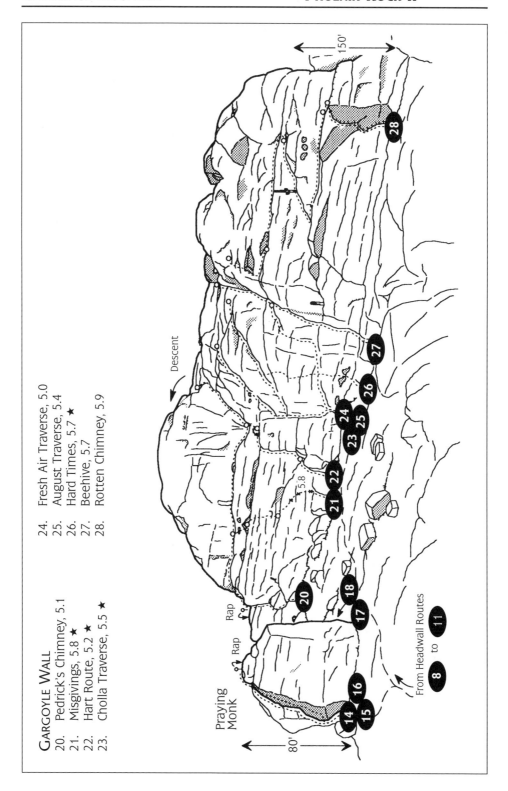

GARGOYLE WALL
20. Pedrick's Chimney, 5.1
21. Misgivings, 5.8 ★
22. Hart Route, 5.2 ★
23. Cholla Traverse, 5.5 ★

24. Fresh Air Traverse, 5.0
25. August Traverse, 5.4
26. Hard Times, 5.7 ★
27. Beehive, 5.7
28. Rotten Chimney, 5.9

Cl. 3 gully (Beehive), then follow to top. Scramble south and east to reach summit of Head. Pro: Several bolts.

24. **Fresh Air Traverse, 5.0**   Start is same as **North Central Variation**. First Pitch: Climb approximately 50 feet of **North Central Variation** until broken ledge system is visible on right (Cl. 4). This is slightly below where **August Traverse** starts. Second Pitch: Traverse right and occasionally up, about 100 feet, along broken ledge system to top (5.0). Scramble southwest and back east to reach summit of Head. Pro: Medium to large nuts, five or six bolts.

25. **August Traverse, 5.4**   Start is same as **North Central Variation**. First Pitch: Climb up North Central Variation to just below small lip (Cl. 4). This is slightly above Fresh Air Traverse. Second Pitch: Traverse right and up, along ramp on face, to top (5.4). Scramble southwest and back east to reach summit of Head. Pro: Medium to large nuts, three bolts.

26. **Hard Times, 5.7 ★**   The quality rating is for the first two pitches only. Start 20 feet right of **North Central Variation**. First Pitch: Climb 20 feet up to two large holes separated by a thin column of rocks (Cl. 4). Belay in left hole. Second Pitch: Climb up thin column of rock to second bolt, then up and slightly right past third bolt to fourth bolt. Continue up and left past bolt to good stance, then up and right to small ledge (5.7). Third Pitch: Move right, then up, until a traverse left to bolt can be made. Continue right and up to join **Fresh Air Traverse** and to top (5.5). Scramble southwest and back east to reach summit of Head. Pro: Several bolts.

27. **Beehive, 5.7**   Start 55 feet right of **Hard Times** at base of vertical crack on face between **North Central Variation** and **Rotten Chimney**. (Approach vertical crack from west to east, Cl. 3.). First Pitch: Climb 50 feet up crack to bolt below the beehive. If bees are active, it is best to traverse right, then up (5.7) and back left into crack. Continue up crack to belay at base of Cl. 3 gully. Second Pitch: Continue to top via Cl. 3 gully. Scramble south and east to reach summit of Head. Pro: Three bolts, three pitons, medium to large nuts.

28. **Rotten Chimney, 5.9**   Believe it or not, this climb has very little chimneying as far as distance is concerned. Start at far right end of wall at base of chimney. First Pitch: Climb chimney to good ledge (5.2). Second Pitch: Climb short overhanging bulge on north-facing wall to ledge (5.9). Third Pitch: Traverse left (southeast) to end of ledge (Cl. 1), then make an easy move to gain second ledge system. Traverse right until possible to climb up to third ledge system. Fourth Pitch: Move onto third ledge system and traverse left to reach tree in shallow cave (Cl. 4). Fifth Pitch: From tree scramble left a short distance, then climb up to reach Cl. 2 terrain which leads to top (Cl. 4). Scramble southwest to gully, then back east to summit of Head. Pro: Several bolts, medium to large nuts.
Variation, Cl.3 (A0)   From top of chimney, rappel southwest from two bolts into deep gully (50 feet). Walk a few feet south and climb up steep groove to left (east) to reach top of 5.9 pitch. Continue on regular route. Pro: Two rappel bolts.
Variation, Cl.2 (A0)   From top of chimney, rappel southwest from two bolts into deep gully (50 feet). Walk up right-handed gully (south) into August Canyon. Continue to summit via **Doug's Dandy** (Number 21, 5.6),or **Fixed Line Traverse** (Number 22, 5.6). Pro: Two rappel bolts.
Variation, Cl. 4   From tree at top of fourth pitch, traverse left to gully at top of **Beehive** (Number 19). Follow gully to top. Scramble south and east to reach summit of Head. Pro: Two bolts.
Variation, 5.4   Near end of last pitch, it is possible to continue straight up about 35 feet past black streak. Pro: 1 bolt.

August Canyon

This beautiful, small canyon nestled on top of the Head is well worth seeing. Approach August Canyon via **Rotten Chimney** (5.3), **Suicide** (5.5), **Suicide Direct** (5.8), or any Boulder Canyon Route. Standard Descent for Routes Originating In August Canyon: Same as Standard Descent for Head.

29. **Doug's Dandy, 5.6** ★   Start at granite outcrop about midway along east wall of August Canyon. First Pitch: Scramble up granite outcrop to large ledge under overhang (Cl.3). Second Pitch: Traverse a few feet south and climb overhang (5.6), then scramble (Cl. 2) straight up to belay bolt. Third Pitch: Walk north to large saguaro cactus (Cl.2). Fourth Pitch: Traverse north past bolt, then climb overhang (second bolt) and continue to traverse to buttress and third bolt. Climb buttress to belay (5.5). A short downclimb and Cl. 2 gullies lead east to summit of Head. Pro: Several bolts.

30. **Fixed Line Traverse, 5.6**   Start is same as **Doug's Dandy**. First Pitch: Same as **Doug's Dandy**. Second Pitch: Traverse a few feet south and climb overhang (5.6), then scramble up right until narrow ledge leading south is found. Third Pitch: Traverse past bolt and climb any of several variations to summit area (5.2). Scramble east to reach summit of Head. Pro: Three bolts.

WESTERN HEADWALL
31. Suicide, 5.5 ★
32. Suicide Direct, 5.8 ★

AUGUST CANYON
29. Doug's Dandy, 5.6
30. Fixed Line Traverse, 5.6

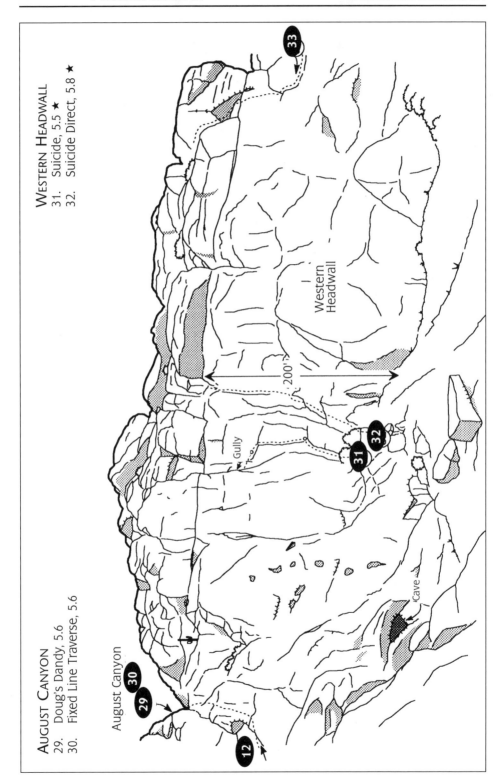

Western Headwall

This southwestern portion of the Headwall offers two good routes that allow climbers to enter an almost maze of mini-canyons that lead to August Canyon or Ridge Route Plateau. Approach from Echo Canyon Parking Lot.

31. **Suicide, 5.5** ★   Some notorious falls have added to the mystique surrounding the name of this route. Just be competent at 5.5 before attempting this one. Start at base of deep recessed gully several hundred feet right of the **George Route** or about 200 feet right of caves. First Pitch: Climb up steep flared chimney past two bolts, then up and right to large ledge (5.4). Second Pitch: From ledge climb up and traverse left along ramp past two bolts to horn. Continue left, then up to ledge (two bolts). Finish by traversing left to protruding granite boulder (5.5). Third Pitch: Traverse left into Cl. 4 gully that leads to top. Scramble east into August Canyon, where one can continue to summit via **Rotten Chimney** (Cl.4), **Doug's Dandy** (5.6), or **Fixed Line Traverse** (5.6). A way may be found to the **Ridge Route** rappel (See Standard Descent for Boulder Canyon, p. 213), if so desired. Pro: Several bolts, One fixed piton.
    Variation, 5.6   From ledge (two bolts) on second pitch, climb directly up face to another belay (5.6). Another short pitch leads to easy terrain (Cl. 4). Pro: Two bolts.
32. **Suicide Direct, 5.8** ★   A testimonial to Lance and Dane Daugherty's early free-climbing abilities. Start 100 feet right of Suicide. First Pitch: Climb Cl. 4 buttress to ledge. Second Pitch: Continue up face, then surmount difficult overhang (5.8) where a shallow groove leads to belay and top. Descend route via two double line rappels, or scramble southwest until a short easy downclimb leads to the Ridge Route Plateau. From the plateau follow Standard Descent for Boulder Canyon. One may also scramble into August Canyon where other routes lead to the summit of the Head (see **Suicide**). Pro: Five bolts.
    Variation, 5.6   From overhang traverse right, then up over slightly overhanging face, and finally back left to join regular route. Pro: None.
32b. **Black Direct, 5.10d**   This is a bolted line that goes up to the left of Suicide Direct. Pro: 6 bolts.

Boulder Canyon

For those who desire routes that will allow them to travel the Head's entire length, Boulder Canyon is their ticket. Although the routes are relatively small, if so desired, they can lead to a variety of scrambling, climbing, and more scrambling all the way to the summit of the Camel's Head. Standard Descent for Boulder Canyon: From top of Ridge Route Plateau, scramble west to **Ridge Route** rappel or scramble east to a series of tricky downclimbs that lead to Once in , continue to summit via **Rotten Chimney** (Cl. 4), **Doug's Dandy** (5.6), or **Fixed Line Traverse** (5.6). From summit the Standard Descent for the will lead to ground.

33. **Ridge Route, 5.7**   First done free in 1948, it was several years before other climbers did free ascents instead of aid. A remarkable achievement! Start at base of easy looking ridge southeast of **Bobbie's Rock**. First Pitch: Climb up ridge to belay in cave (bolt, Cl. 3). Second Pitch: Traverse left (Cl. 4) and climb to good ledge. Third Pitch: Finish up strenuous 40-foot–left-leaning crack (5.7). To descend scramble east until a short climb on right leads to Ridge Route Plateau. From the plateau follow the Standard Descent for Boulder Canyon. Pro: Five bolts.
    Tarantula Variation, 5.2   **Tarantula** may be considered a direct start to **Ridge Route**. On wall to the left of **Ridge Route** is a small tilted grey slab. Start 30 to 40 feet left of a point directly below slab. First Pitch: Climb Cl.4 20 feet to ledge, then traverse right to belay. Second Pitch: Continue right and climb steep wall to another ledge. Climb up and pass the gray slab on right, joining the Ridge Route at belay cave at top of regular first pitch (5.2). Pro: One bolt.

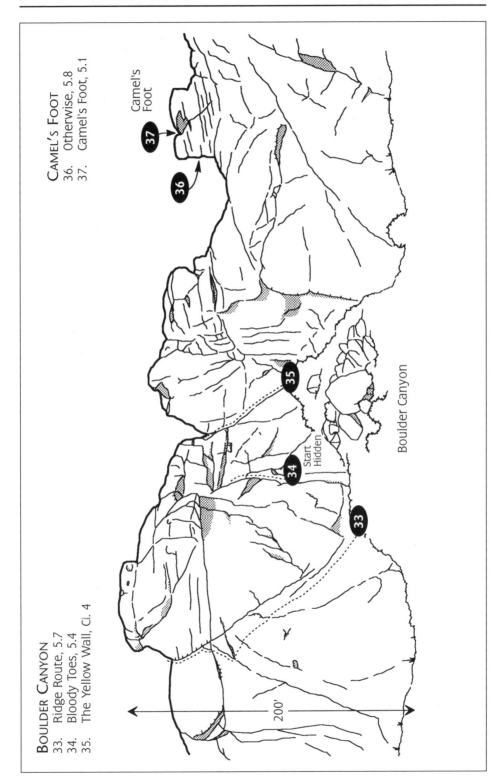

CAMEL'S FOOT
36. Otherwise, 5.8
37. Camel's Foot, 5.1

Camel's Foot

37

36

35

Start
Hidden

34

33

Boulder Canyon

200'

BOULDER CANYON
33. Ridge Route, 5.7
34. Bloody Toes, 5.4
35. The Yellow Wall, Cl. 4

34. **Bloody Toes, 5.4**   To approach walk up until several large fallen boulders are encountered. Just beyond these boulders, a steep wide shallow groove can be seen on the south-facing wall left (west) of a large cave. Start at left end of cave. First Pitch: Traverse left into groove, then climb up past overhang (two bolts) to large ledge (5.4). Second Pitch: Traverse left on wide ledge and climb into large hole. Climb overhang and diagonal right on easier ground to tree belay and top of Ridge Route Plateau (5.4). Pro: Four bolts, small to large nuts.

35. **The Yellow Wall, Cl. 4**   Start at head of Boulder Canyon. First Pitch: Scramble up gully to notch overlooking south side of (Cl. 3). Second Pitch: Traverse left, then climb up to saguaro belay (Cl. 4) and top of Ridge Route Plateau. Pro: One bolt.

Camel's Foot

This small pinnacle is located high on a ridge southwest of Boulder Canyon. How did it ever get its name? You got me! Standard Descent for Camel's Foot: Descend via single line rappel off north side.

36. **Otherwise, 5.8**   Start on east side. Climb face past two bolts to top. Pro: Two bolts.

37. **Camel's Foot, 5.1**   Start on south side. Climb south side to top. Pro: One bolt.

Bobbie's Rock

This small block of rock is probably the closest climbing to Echo Canyon Parking Lot (although it might not be the easiest to reach). It is suspected that this area is named after Bob Owens (Kachinas), but there is no evidence to back this idea. Standard Descent for **Bobbie's Rock**: Descend **Pedrick's Split** via single line rappel. **Fry Babies** and **The Flute** do not require a rappel.

38. **Pedrick's Split, 5.3**   Start at right side of large detached blocky pinnacle in middle of upper south face. Climb up to notch, then finish via short chimney and face to top. Pro: Six bolts (⅜-inch capscrews and hangers may not be in place!).

39. **Pateman's Cave, 5.7**   Start at highest cave on west face (belay bolt). Step left (north) out of cave and climb directly to top. Pro: Four bolts (⅜-inch' capscrews and hangers may not be in place!).
    FA 1950 Ralph Pateman, Stan Lerch, Gene Lefebvre
    Variation, 5.5   After stepping left out of cave, continue traversing left past piton to two bolts, which are used to protect short vertical face above. Pro: Two bolts.

40. **Fry Babies (Formerly The Bolt Ladder), 5.11a**   Start at east end of lower south face (look for old bolt hanger 10 feet up). Directly face climb old bolt ladder up and slightly right past five bolts to large ledge. Pro: Five bolts (3rd bolt suspect).

41. **The Flute, 5.10a**   This route was originally rated 5.7 as little was known about its first ascent and still is. On one ascent the climbing party thought that they were doing **The Bolt Ladder** (**Fry Babies**). Well, to their surprise, the route was neither 5.7nor **The Bolt Ladder**. Start just right of **Fry Babies**. Climb face past three bolts exiting just left of overhang to top. Pro: Three bolts, Friends.

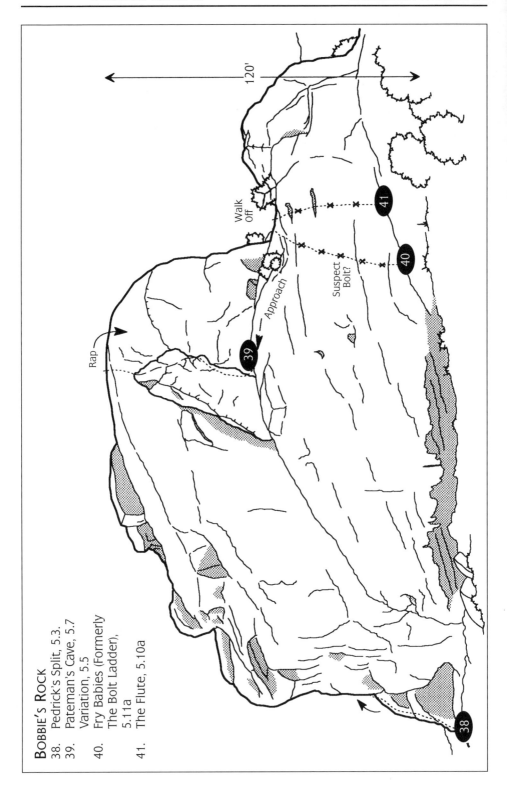

120'

Walk
Off

41

Suspect
Bolt?

40

Approach

39

Rap

38

BOBBIE'S ROCK
38. Pedrick's Split, 5.3.
39. Pateman's Cave, 5.7
     Variation, 5.5
40. Fry Babies (Formerly
     The Bolt Ladder),
     5.11a
41. The Flute, 5.10a

Camel's Ear

This formation of rock is located at the western extreme boundary of Echo Canyon Park (due southwest from **Bobbie's Rock**). Standard Descent for Camel's Ear: Descend via Cl. 3 gully to the southwest.

42. **Chase The Dragon, III 5.8 (A3)**   Start at middle of north face of Camel's Ear. First Pitch: Aid-obvious crack up past aid bolts to small ledge just above overhang (A3). Second Pitch: Continue up obvious crack free and aid past four bolts to sling belay (5.8 (A2+)). Third Pitch: Traverse right along ledge past bolt to belay stance (5.1). Fourth Pitch: Climb ramp up and right to summit (5.0). Pro: Several bolts, small to large nuts, pitons (blades to 4-inch bongs), hooks. (Take 3/8-inch capscrews and hangers for bolts.)
    Dragon Variation, 5.1   One can exit from sling belay by traversing left and up to side of buttress. Pro: One belay bolt.

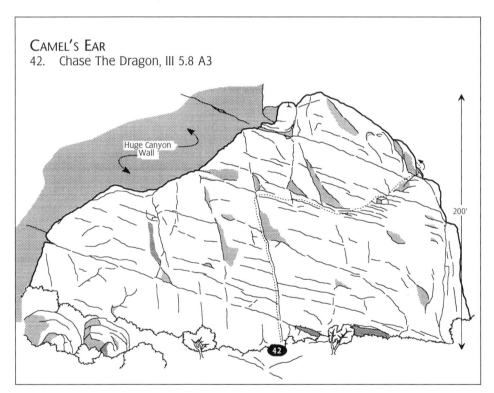

CAMEL'S EAR
42.   Chase The Dragon, III 5.8 A3

Huge Canyon Wall

200'

The Hump

This is the only route I know of on the eastern summit of Camelback. The approach is fairly obvious.–just follow the multitude of hikers. Rappel anchors can be found off the east side near the summit. The downclimb to the anchors is exposed and can be dangerous. Proceed at your own risk.

43. **Humpty Pumpty, 5.11a**   Little is actually known about the quality of this route. From a ledge off the east side of Camelback's summit rappel down the east face to the base of the wall. Climb bolts back to summit. See chapter introduction. Pro: 8 bolts.

Cholla Mountain from the southeast.

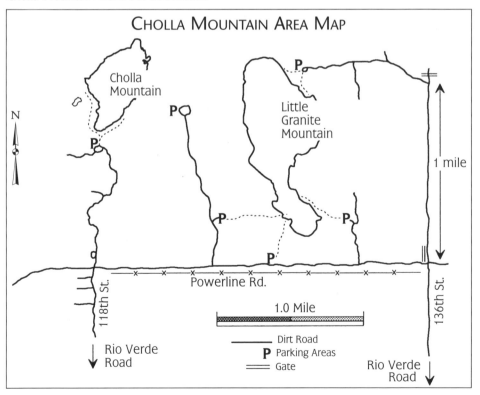

CHAPTER 3

CHOLLA MOUNTAIN

Cholla Mountain is the boulder covered mountain just west of Little Granite Mountain (northeast of Scottsdale). One can only wonder how many climbers gazed to the west from the Lost Bandana Area and Pasta Pinnacle before someone finally decided to go see if there was anything worth climbing over there. Eventually, some of the more curious climbers headed over to check it out. The rock found on Cholla Mountain ranges from pretty good to typical "desert junkoid granite." Many of the routes that have been done so far, are located on the larger boulders and obvious buttresses that have the better rock. Additional climber traffic will help make the existing routes more solid and enjoyable as the leftover temporary holds slough off. For those with an eye to do first ascents, there are a few lines left to be eeked out among the larger boulders.

Development of the climbing potential on Cholla has taken place, for the most part, since the publication of the first edition of Phoenix Rock in 1987. Local climber Jan Holdeman has been the most voracious of the first ascenders and is included in the first ascent party for many of the routes here. The activity that has taken place has produced some nice climbing on granite formations similar to those found at Little Granite. The routes tend to be fairly short for the most part and distributed among the many outcrops found on the mountain, but some enjoyable climbing in a fairly uncrowded location makes for a pleasant climbing experience.

If heading out for a day of climbing at Cholla Mountain, it's a good idea to wear a solid pair of hiking shoes and long pants. A fair amount of brush covers the mountain and the low climber traffic has not been enough to establish trails to the climbs. The mountain's namesake cactus will also be found in most areas and will inevitably end up attached to boots, legs and other body parts. Watch out for the jumping cactus!

Approach: There are two possible ways to reach Cholla Mountain. Both start with the standard drive to Pinnacle Peak/Troon Mountain (see page 175). Continue through Reata Pass until you hit Dynamite/Rio Verde Drive. Make a right (east) turn and go until you get to 118th Street. Make a left (north) turn and follow 118th Street (don't take any side turnoffs) for approximately 2 miles until you hit Power Line Road. Continue north past Power Line Road for another .7 miles on a slightly winding dirt road to the small parking area a few hundred yards north of the southeast corner of Cholla Mountain. This spot can also be reached from the Little Granite Mountain side, by driving west on Power Line Road to 118th St. (no sign) and then going north. All roads are fairly decent, but have some ruts that won't make a passenger car very happy. High clearance vehicle recommended highly!

Access: Cholla Mountain remains fairly out of the traffic pattern at the current time. Development has not entered the area to any great extent, although more and more evidence of impending housing may be seen in the next couple of years. As with the other areas that fall into this category, please be nice to anyone you happen to run into and please practice low-impact climbing! Take it for granted that the houses and golf courses are on the way.

Cholla Mountain Route Descriptions
Routes on the mountain are described from south to north, first along the east side starting at the Saguaro Hotel Area and then along the west side starting at the routes on The Whale.

Aerial elevation maps are used to help steer climbers to the right place on the mountain, rather than using overhead maps.

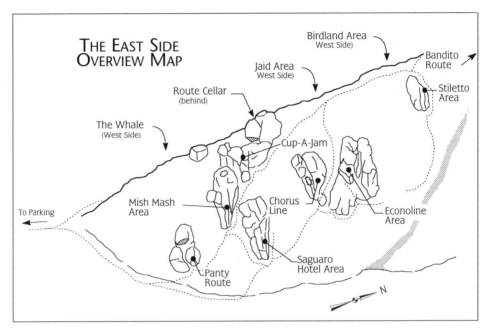

THE EAST SIDE OVERVIEW MAP

Birdland Area (West Side)

Bandito Route

Jaid Area (West Side)

Stiletto Area

Route Cellar (behind)

The Whale (West Side)

Cup-A-Jam

Mish Mash Area

Chorus Line

Econoline Area

To Parking

Saguaro Hotel Area

Panty Route

N

The East Side

The east side of Cholla Mountain has the most easily accessed routes on the mountain. The Saguaro Hotel and Mish Mash areas lie just slightly uphill from the desert floor and have several nice routes. See the aerial map for location of the eastern formations.

Saguaro Hotel Area

This area is the first one you come to when hiking in from the road to the south end of the mountain. These routes are visible from the parking area along the southeastern end of the mountain and are some of the easiest routes to approach on the mountain.

1. **Saguaro Hotel, 5.6+ ★★**   Right and down the hill from **Mish Mash.** Climb east face of formation past horizontal crack. Continue on face above past two bolts and a RURP, 60'. Pro: Medium to large (belay), two bolts, RURP.

2. **Cholla, Cholla, Cholla, 5.10b ★** Just right of **Saguaro Hotel,** climb on

Mike Stubing finds a little excitement on **Cholla, Cholla, Cholla** (5.10b), Saguaro Hotel Area.

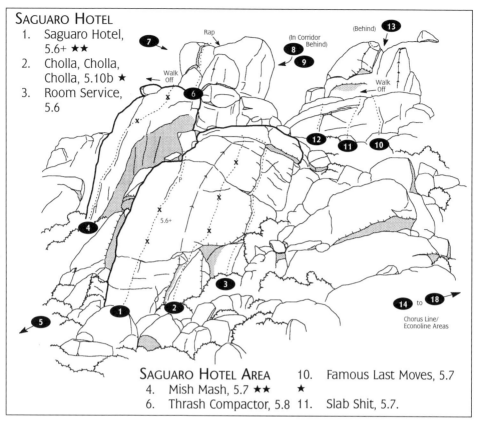

SAGUARO HOTEL
1. Saguaro Hotel, 5.6+ ★★
2. Cholla, Cholla, Cholla, 5.10b ★
3. Room Service, 5.6

SAGUARO HOTEL AREA
4. Mish Mash, 5.7 ★★ ★
6. Thrash Compactor, 5.8
10. Famous Last Moves, 5.7
11. Slab Shit, 5.7.

north face up and left to first bolt. Then work your way across face, passing two more bolts to top. Pro: Small to medium (belay), three bolts. Photo, page 52.

3. **Room Service, 5.6** Although I suspect that someone had to have climbed this route before, I didn't have any info for a previous ascent (I thought it was **Chorus Line** originally). Anyone? To the right of **Cholla, Cholla, Cholla**, climb ragged right-leaning crack system to top. Pro: Small to medium large.

About 100 yards up and left of the Saguaro Hotel area is a large formation approximately 100' high. The formation has a shallow alcove on the right hand side. You can see an exposed hanging bee hive at the top of the alcove. **Mish Mash** goes up the shallow light-colored runnel to the left of the bee-hive.

Lisa Schmitz helping out with the first ascent of **The Panty Route** (5.5) on the eastern slope of Cholla Mountain.

4. **Mish Mash, 5.7 ★★**   This nice route starts in a finger crack off a boulder. Follow the finger crack up and into a steep runnel past a couple of bolts. Continue in seam with bashies to the third bolt. Step right and continue to the top past the last bolt. Palo Verde tree belay. Pro: Small to medium, four bolts, two aluminum bashies.

5. **The Panty Route, 5.4**   This route will be found down and to the left of the start of Mish Mash on a small slab formation. Climb low angle face past one bolt to flake. Continue up and right past second bolt to top. Pro: Small to medium, 2 bolts, long sling for belay.

The following two routes are found on a small formation stacked on top of the Mish Mash buttress. Rappel off the north side of formation from sling around boulder.

6. **Thrash Compactor, 5.8**   This crack is located on the rock just behind the top of **Mish Mash**. A small barrel cactus sits below the start of the route. Climb wide crack up middle of the south face of formation. Some rotten rock in the upper section of the climb. Don't fall out at the bottom, that cactus could do a lot of damage! Pro: Medium to Large.

7. **Dado, 5.10+ ★**   Just right of **Thrash Compactor** on the southwest corner of the same formation. On the upper section, a corner forms a shallow dihedral (the "dado"). Climb up ever-overhanging corner past three bolts and fixed pin to top. Pro: 3 bolts, fixed piton.

The next two routes are found on the north side of the same formation as Thrash Compactor and Dado.

8. **Cherry Jam, 5.8 ★**   Wide crack in right-facing dihedral. Pro: Medium to large.

9. **Cup-A-Jam, 5.10d ★**   Starts in short crack to flaring bombay crack. Finish up overhanging jams to last wide crack and top. Pro: Medium to large.

Across to north of the previous two routes is a 50' slab with three routes on it. Walk off top of slab to left.

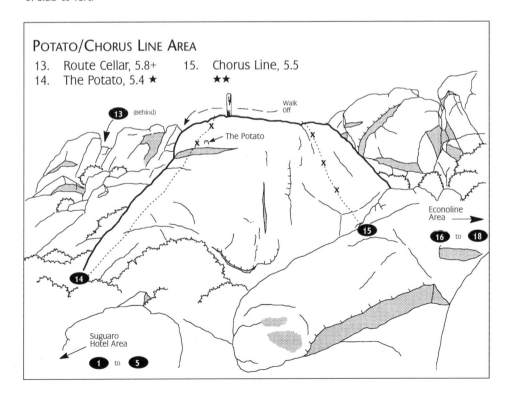

POTATO/CHORUS LINE AREA

13.   Route Cellar, 5.8+   15.   Chorus Line, 5.5
14.   The Potato, 5.4 ★   ★★

13 (Behind)

Walk Off

The Potato

Econoline Area →

15

16 to 18

Suguaro Hotel Area

14

1 to 5

10. **Famous Last Moves, 5.7 ★**   Right-hand route starts in a finger seam. Follow seam to face moves out of a "scoop" at the top past a single bolt. Pro: Small, one bolt.

11. **Slab Shit, 5.7**   Center route on the slab. Follow a seam up flaky rock to the top. Pro: not much.

12. **Sherry's First, 5.5 ★**   On the left-hand side of the slab, follow a nice crack system to final face moves. Pro: Small to Medium

13. **Route Cellar, 5.8+**   This route is found in a sunken alcove (the "cellar") within the boulders behind the top of the slab where the previous three routes are located. It can be approached by squirming through the boulders directly or from the uphill side by scrambling around the outside. Climb a crack system that goes from chimney, to offwidth, to fist, to hands and finally the top. No thrashing allowed! Pro: Medium-small to offwidth gear.

14. **The Potato, 5.4 ★**   Slightly up the hill and approximately 100 yards to the right (north) of the Saguaro Hotel Area is a large, lower-angled face with a small roof bulge in the middle of it. Climb up low-angle face to roof and first bolt, turn roof using the prominent zenolith (the "potato") just above. Continue up face above past second bolt to top. Walk off left. (120') Pro: 2 bolts, small to medium, sling for belay.

15. **Chorus Line, 5.5 ★★**   To the right of **The Potato,** on nice looking face, climb up waterstreak past three bolts to top. Pro: Medium to large.

The following routes are located on a nice looking "hooded" formation just right from **Chorus Line**. The formation can be easily identified by a tongue of rock which sticks down on the lefthand side.

16. **Econoline, 5.9 ★★**   Start on the southwest corner of formation (a bolt marks the route and is used on the way to the crack). Work your way up a thin crack in open book. From there, it gains the face on the arete where climbing past two more bolts leads to top. 70' Walk off the formation to the north. Pro: 3 bolts, small to large pro.

17. **Mainline, 5.Way Hard**   This unfinished line is a Jim Waugh creation that runs up the middle of this formation. A single bolt is seen on the lower face leading up the middle of the fomation's south side to the overlapping "hood." To the best of my knowledge the route has yet to be completed.

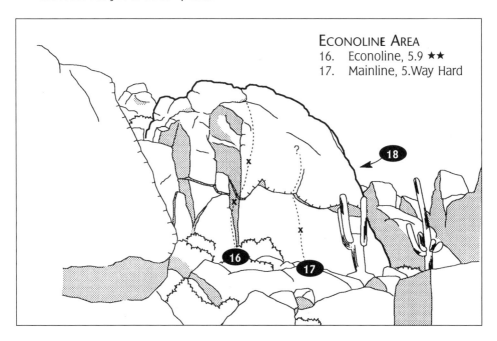

ECONOLINE AREA
16.   Econoline, 5.9 ★★
17.   Mainline, 5.Way Hard

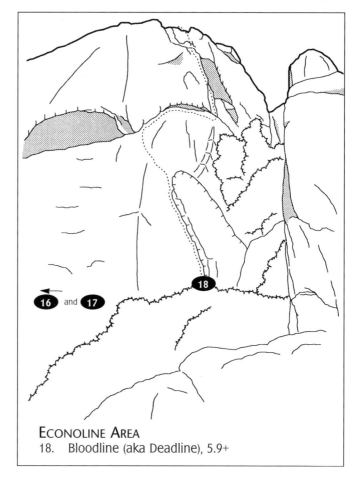

ECONOLINE AREA
18.   Bloodline (aka Deadline), 5.9+

18. **Bloodline (aka Deadline), 5.9+**   This lies on the righthand corner of the same formation as **Econoline** and **Main-line**. Climb up to corner of "hood" to wide crack (#4 Camelot). Traverse wide crack right to vertical crack up right side of hanging pillar. Keep an eye on the block at the top, although it seems solid.

Stiletto Area

Further right along the eastern side of the mountain (a few gullies over from the Econoline area) is the Stiletto formation. The crack climbs are found on the north-facing portion of the rock and described from left to right.

19. **Meander, 5.8 R ★**   A tribute to no-drill ethics! Around on the east-facing part of the rock (left and around corner from **Blockwatch**). Climb the face past horizontal cracks to top, "meandering" back and forth as needed to get protection. Pro: Small to medium.
20. **Blockwatch, 5.6**   Although the "blocks" found on this route turned out to be relatively solid, the leader had to keep his eyes peeled for possible incoming bombs. Probably still a good idea. On the north part of the formation, climb lefthand bird-stained crack system past a block in the middle. Continue up crack past loose capstone at the top. Pro: Small to large.
21. **Stiletto, 5.9 ★★**   A nice finger crack. To the right of **Blockwatch** is a finger crack with two bushes and a tiny roof. Climb this to top. Pro: Small to medium.

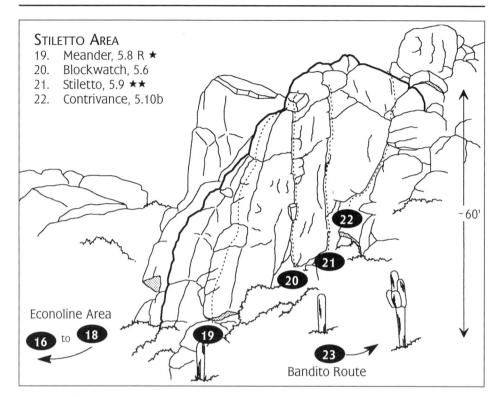

STILETTO AREA
19. Meander, 5.8 R ★
20. Blockwatch, 5.6
21. Stiletto, 5.9 ★★
22. Contrivance, 5.10b

Econoline Area
16 to 18

~60'

Bandito Route

22. **Contrivance, 5.10b** This route is best described as a "gully avoidance" route. To the left of **Stiletto**, climb crack to left-leaning horizontal. Traverse left and head up right-leaning fingers crack for a ways, then up slightly face on left to top. Pro: Very small to medium-large.

If you work your way north and west (uphill) from the Stiletto area, to a point near the very top of Cholla Mountain, there is a large rock formation with a seam running up the east end. A single bolt marks this route.

23. **Bandito's Route, Rating Unknown** This route is simply known as the "Bandito Route". It is not known at this time if this route is complete as is, or if it is an unfinished route. Either way, tread lightly. On the northeastern corner of the formation, climb groove to face past bolt. Your guess from here... Pro: Small to medium, 1 bolt.

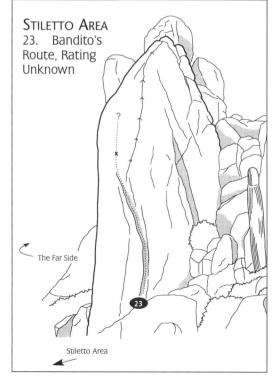

STILETTO AREA
23. Bandito's Route, Rating Unknown

The Far Side

Stiletto Area

THE WEST SIDE

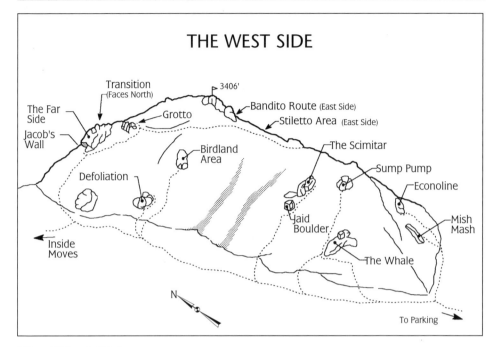

The Far Side
Jacob's Wall
Transition (Faces North)
Grotto
3406'
Bandito Route (East Side)
Stiletto Area (East Side)
The Scimitar
Birdland Area
Defoliation
Sump Pump
Econoline
Jaid Boulder
Mish Mash
Inside Moves
The Whale
To Parking
N

The West Side

The west side of Cholla Mountain consists of a vertiable maze of granite boulders and buttresses which must be negotiated in order to reach the climbing. Although most of the areas on the west side are a bit more work to get to, a pretty decent assortment of climbing can be found on several formations. The best of these is the Far Side, which offers the longest climbs on the mountain.

The Whale

The Whale is the first formation that is encountered on the hike along the west side. This is one of the larger granite blobs on the mountain, although it's contributions to the available climbing are rather small. There are three aid climbs located on the northern facing portion of the crag, as well as two free routes up the western facing slab.

24. **Save Your Desert, A2, 5.9+ ★**　Left-most (most uphill) crack system. There's a small cactus in the crack near the top that should probably be avoided if one wants to evade epidermal damage. Pro: Small to medium-large.
25. **Watch Your Wait, A2, 5.7**　Middle discontinuous cracks... Pro: Small to medium.
26. **Twat Me One Time, A2, 5.8**　Face climb up to a thin crack leading to the top. Pro: Small to medium.
27. **Unknown, 5.6?**　Around the corner to the right from **Twat Me One Time**, climb short angled face on the west side of the Whale to crack system running up left side. Finish on face above. Pro: Small to medium
28. **Unknown, 5.7?**　On the west face of the Whale, climb past two bolts and discontinuous cracks to top. Pro: Bolts, small to medium.
29. **Sump Pump, 5.6 ★**　By working up and slightly north from the north face of the Whale, a nice looking 50-foot buttress will be seen with a crack running up it's right side. The crack starts in a recessed alcove at the bottom of the wall just behind a bird-shit stained boulder. Climb the wide crack on the right side leading to the top. A cactus stands guard at the top of the crack. Potential for a hard face route exists on the rock to the left of this crack. Pro: Medium-small to way large (offwidth gear). Topo, page 58.

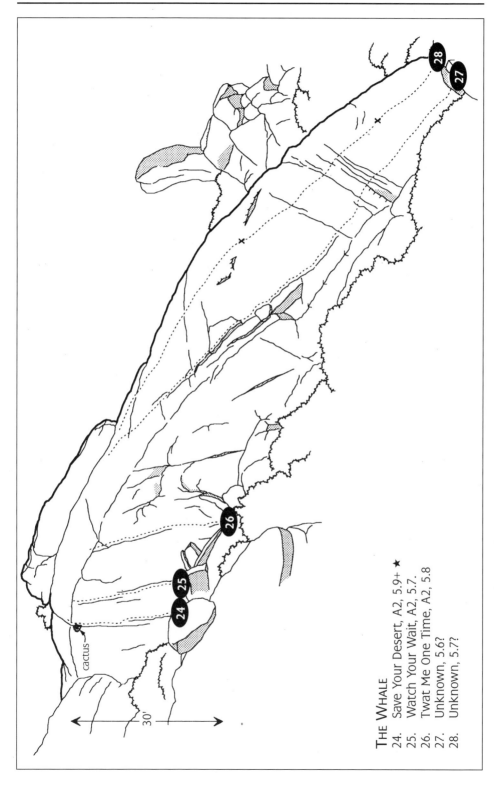

THE WHALE
24. Save Your Desert, A2, 5.9+ ★
25. Watch Your Wait, A2, 5.7.
26. Twat Me One Time, A2, 5.8
27. Unknown, 5.6?
28. Unknown, 5.7?

cactus

30'

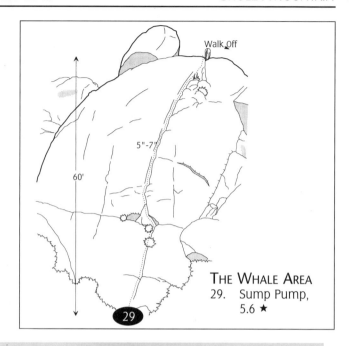

THE WHALE AREA
29.   Sump Pump,
      5.6 ★

J-Aid Boulder Area

Working to the north, the next routes are located in the next drainage running down the mountain to the north of the Whale. The routes can be easily seen from that formation looking to the north. Barring that, look for the boulder with the big reverse "J" crack in it.

30. **J-Aid, 5.6, A2+ ★**   Climb and aid the obvious reverse "J" shaped crack on south face of this large boulder. Exit from the top via tandem rappel. Pro: Small to medium-large.

31. **Carborundum**   This line awaits a first ascent! Around the corner left of Jaid, climb squiggly connected crack systems up west face of that boulder to the top. Possible bad fall if you don't get that first piece of gear in before falling. Tandem rappel from the top. Pro: Small to medium.

The Scimitar

The following three routes are located on the cool looking formation just up the hill from the J-Aid boulder, past a huge chunk of granite laying on it's side. A "scimitar" flake of rock arching up and right over a buttress of rock. The descent is to rappel from a two-bolt anchor on the east end of the "scimitar" back down **Trial Separation**. Although the rock can be a bit flaky here, the climbs on this formation are all fairly good.

32. **Trial Separation, 5.6 ★**   This is the fairly clean wide chimney formed by the "scimitar" and the buttress to it's right. The bolts for **Chips Ahoy** were placed in order to allow then to be used for this route as well. Pro: 2 bolts, 2-bolt anchor.

33. **Chips Ahoy, 5.7+ R ★**   This face climb goes up the multi-edged face to the left of the **Trial Separation** chimney. Face climb up flakes and edges past 2 bolts on the right, working right to the top of the Trial Separation chimney and two-bolt anchor. Slightly runout to get to the first bolt. When climbing this route, it's a good idea to pull down on the holds instead of pulling out! Pro: 2 bolts, 2-bolt anchor.

34. **Border Crossing, 5.8 ★**   Although the original vision for this route was to go straight up the face, the first ascent party settled for a move to the left onto the west face (thus the "border crossing") to finish this nice climb. Start just below and left of **Chips Ahoy**. Climb flakes and edges past a bolt to the white scar. Continue up to edge

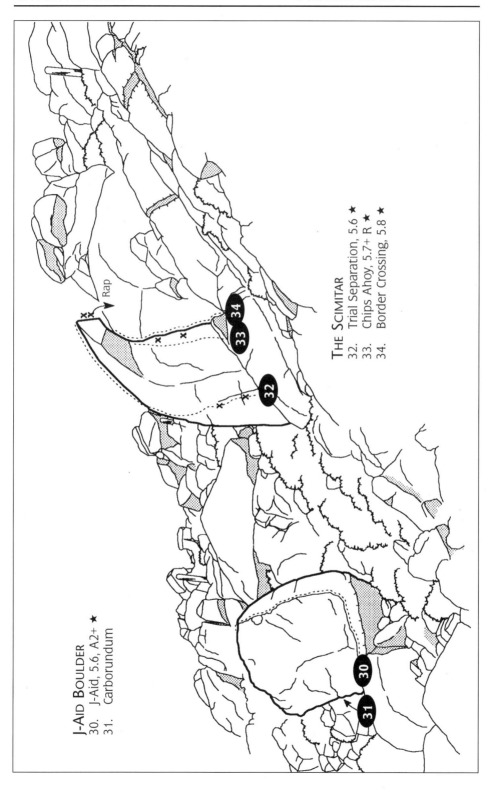

J-AID BOULDER
30.   J-Aid, 5.6, A2+ ★
31.   Carborundum

THE SCIMITAR
32.   Trial Separation, 5.6 ★
33.   Chips Ahoy, 5.7+ R ★
34.   Border Crossing, 5.8 ★

of scar to another bolt (WATCH IT! This bolt is borderline (sorry for the pun) groundfall if you miss the clip!). Then step left to arete and continue past two more bolts to top. The 2-bolt anchor can be flipped up to belay with. Then rap off. Pro: 4 bolts, 2-bolt anchor.

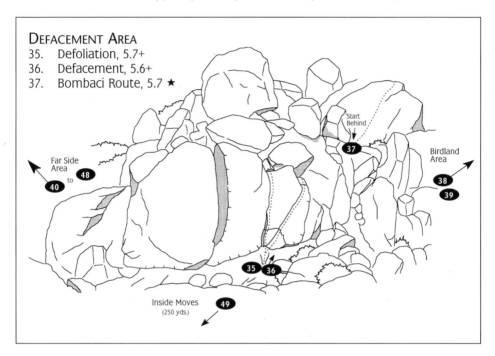

DEFACEMENT AREA
35.   Defoliation, 5.7+
36.   Defacement, 5.6+
37.   Bombaci Route, 5.7 ★

Defacement Area

The next few routes are found in the next large drainage over from the Jaid Boulder Area. An obvious south-facing formation with a wide crack running up it's left side will be seen. Described from bottom of the drainage to top.

35. **Defoliation, 5.7+**   This climb is found on an obvious buttress near the bottom of the drainage. A large crack (nearly chimney) will be seen splitting the left side of the buttress. This route goes up the crack to the right of the large split past a couple of bushes. Pro: Small to large.

36. **Defacement, 5.6+**   Climb the crack system to the right of **Defoliation.** Pro: Small to large.
FA: Tim Bombaci, Rick Forbes and Jan Holdeman, 2/91

37. **Bombaci Route, 5.7 ★**   Behind and right (slightly up hill) from the Defoliation Buttress is a slab of nice looking rock. Face climb this slab past bolts to top. Pro: Bolts

The following two routes are located on a large formation uphill on the same gully side as **Defoliation** and **Defacement.** The identifying feature of this crag is the two large flakes that are detached and standing out away from the face on the south side of the main rock. The tip of each of the flakes shows evidence of being a very popular roosting location for local aviary wildlife.

38. **Birdland, 5.8**   On the lefthand flake with "white" birdshit tip, climb up south face of flake past bolts to top. Scramble down and right to get off.

39. **Gullet, 5.5**   Behind the righthand flake with "white" birdshit tip, climb face past bolts to top. Pro: Bolts.

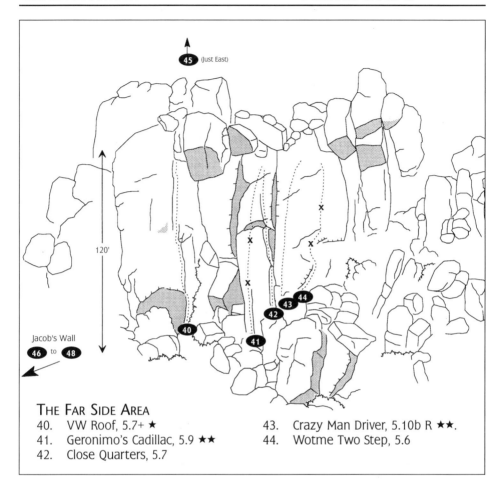

THE FAR SIDE AREA

40. VW Roof, 5.7+ ★
41. Geronimo's Cadillac, 5.9 ★★
42. Close Quarters, 5.7

43. Crazy Man Driver, 5.10b R ★★.
44. Wotme Two Step, 5.6

The Far Side

This area contains the longest routes on the mountain, with several lines up to 80' in length. It is found on the northwestern corner of the mountain, perched fairly high on the hillside. Some solid rock and interesting climbs make this one of the best places on the mountain to spend a day climbing, although the routes tend to be moderate to hard. From below the actual base of the Far Side crags are obscured by large boulders. Routes are listed left to right. The topo shown below is a semi-aerial representation of the crags.

Note: The following routes may be slightly runout at the top of the climbs where the angle of the rock lays back to make the climbing relatively easy. These runouts are not be noted in the route descriptions, but climbing in these sections should be taken seriously!

40. **VW Roof, 5.7+ ★**   This route is on the leftmost large buttress. Climb up a ramp to a roof-like flake. Continue up left side of flake, across a short face and into a widening crack system leading to the top. Pro: Small to large.

41. **Geronimo's Cadillac, 5.9 ★★**   On the center buttress to the right of **VW Roof**, climb fingers/hand crack until it peters out. Clip a bolt and continue up face to broken section. Then up face above past one more bolt to step across "chasm." Runout on easy ground at the top. Pro: Small to medium, 2 bolts.

"THE FAR SIDE" ON THE WEST SIDE OF CHOLLA MOUNTAIN.

40. VW Roof, 5.7+ ★
41. Geronimo's Cadillac, 5.9 ★★
42. Close Quarters, 5.7
43. Crazy Man Driver, 5.10b R ★★
44. Wotme Two Step, 5.6

42. **Close Quarters, 5.7**   Depending on your climbing tastes, you will either like the looks of this one, or run like mad in the opposite direction! To the right of **Geronimo's Cadillac** and just below and 10' left of **Crazy Man Driver**, climb offwidth/chimney on north side wall out of recessed alcove (behind boulders). The original ascent forbade stemming to the opposite wall of the chimney. Continue up crack until it's possible to climb face past horizontal cracks to a shallow dihedral. Climb dihedral to huge cleft. Step across and onto upper section. Climb crack and face to top. Pro: Small to WAY large (bring OW gear!).

43. **Crazy Man Driver, 5.10b R ★★**   Some discussion has taken place on this route's "R" rating. Some feel that it doesn't deserve the "R", while others do. You decide. Ten feet to the right of **Close Quarters**, on the right buttress, a crack with two rusty pitons can be seen overhead. Climb vertical section of detached flake. Make dicey step left onto face and climb past two fixed pins and a bolt to gain the upper face. Continue to top past two more bolts. 100 feet! Pro: Medium to large pro, 3 bolts and 2 pins.

44. **Wotme Two Step, 5.6**   Just right of **Crazy Man Driver**, a detached flake can be seen running up and right at the left edge of tan rock (note the huge piece of flake that has exfoliated!!!). Climb face and flake until you can step right into a "scoop." Continue up face and slightly right past two bolts to top. Pro: Medium to large, 2 bolts.

45. **Grotto, 5.9 ★**   This 35-foot climb is found east of the top of the Far Side area, past a second ridge of boulders (in a line directly east of **VW Roof**). A gully runs south/north through where **Grotto** is found. Just right of a large open book corner on the east side of the rocks, start out of an alcove within some bushes. Climb solid black rock past two bolts to top. Pro: 2 bolts, assorted pieces for belay.

Paul Paonessa leading **Wotme Two Step** (5.10b) on the west side of Cholla Mountain.

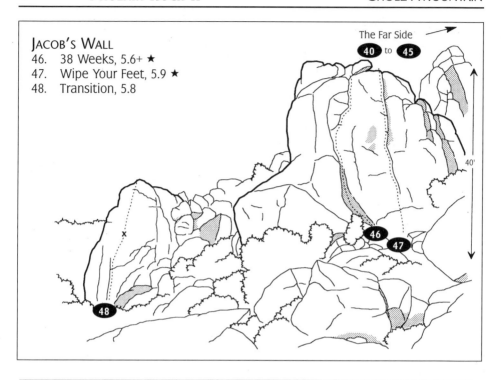

JACOB'S WALL
46.   38 Weeks, 5.6+ ★
47.   Wipe Your Feet, 5.9 ★
48.   Transition, 5.8

The Far Side →
40 to **45**

40'

46
47

48

Jacob's Wall

This small formation lies just north (left) of the Far Side group. Spot a short (40') wall with cracks running up it's face.

46.   **38 Weeks, 5.6+ ★**
Left side of wall. Hands to top. Pro: Small to medium large.

47.   **Wipe Your Feet, 5.9**
★   Right side of wall. Fingers. Pro: Small to medium.

48.   **Transition, 5.8**
East of Jacob's Wall on a north-facing formation, climb a tapering crack past one fixed piton (back it up with pro!) to face. Continue up face past 1 bolt to top. Pro: Small to medium, fixed pin, 1 bolt.

Jan Holdeman on **Watch Your Wait,** on the Whale

INDIAN ROCKS

49. Inside Moves, 5.9 ★★   50. Hallowed Ground, 5.7

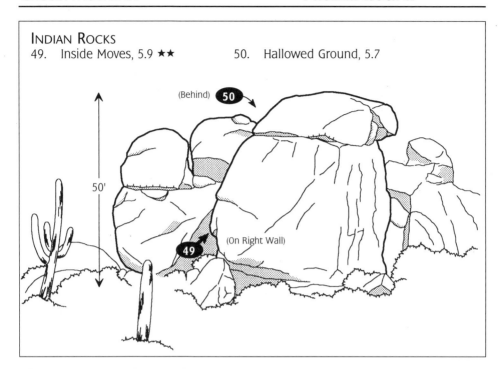

Indian Rocks

The following two climbs are found within a pile of large boulders off the western side of the mountain (see map).

49. **Inside Moves, 5.9 ★★**   Another Holdeman clean climbing effort. Inside the boulder pile, climb right facing wall of boulder past horizontal cracks (pro) to top. Although this is inside a large, wide chimney stemming to the wall behind is not allowed! Descent by tandem rappel. Pro: Medium-small to large.

50. **Hallowed Ground, 5.7**   On a 30' face in the boulders just to the west of Inside Moves, climb past horizontals to top. Walk off. Pro: Medium to large.

JACUZZI SPIRES – APPROACH MAP

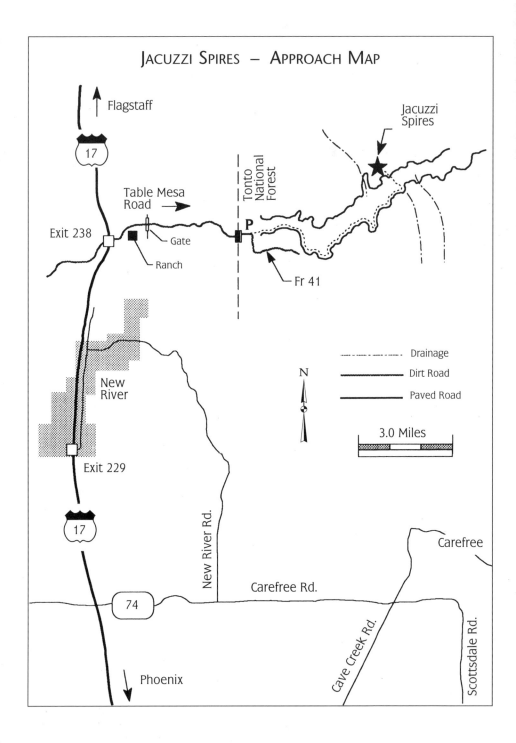

Flagstaff

17

Table Mesa Road →

Exit 238

Gate

Ranch

Tonto National Forest

P

Fr 41

Jacuzzi Spires

New River

Exit 229

17

N

Drainage
Dirt Road
Paved Road

3.0 Miles

New River Rd.

Carefree

74

Carefree Rd.

Cave Creek Rd.

Scottsdale Rd.

Phoenix

Chapter 4

Jacuzzi Spires

Jacuzzi Spires is a relatively obscure set of crags found north of the Phoenix metro area. The first spire presents the best quality climbing, but other enjoyable routes can be found on the third spire as well. The area is named for the pools of running water located in the bottom of the canyon, which have created "jacuzzis" over years of erosion. These can be enjoyed by visiting climbers when the running water coincides with the warmer months of the year. Swimsuit optional, no lifeguard on duty!

The area was originally discovered by local climber Bob Blair. He related his discovery to Paul Deifenderfer and the two, along with Andy Linkner made the first climbing foray into Jacuzzi Spires. The result of that outing (**Don't Bug Me**) followed the most obvious natural path up the spire in May of 1984. Following the ascent of **Don't Bug Me**, casual development and ascents of routes continued with contributions by John Ficker, Bob Blair andy Marquardt and various partners. This area continues to be an enjoyable destination away from the crowds of the city crags. Getting to the climbing takea a bit more work, but some fun, high-quality climbing can be found in this remote spot.

I have heard some resistance to the idea of publishing the information to this area by a few local climbers who felt that turning info to this crag over to the general climbing community would only lead to it's demise. In the end, I didn't feel it was my place to withhold submitted route info and keep this area private. I hope that this decision will not be regretted at a future time. I implore climbers who visit the Jacuzzi Spires to exercise a little more respect and care while climbing here than they would show for other more-traveled areas. The area

(Right to Left) First Jacuzzi Spire, Second Jacuzzi Spire and Third Jacuzzi Spire.

is remote and shows very little damage evidence of climber's passage. Please do all you can to maintain this precedant!

Approach: Jacuzzi Spires can be reached in one of two ways. The best way to approach the Spires is to drive north out of Pheonix on Interstate 17 to the exit for Table Mesa Road (Exit 236). This is approximately 19 miles from Deer Valley Road. Take the exit and drive east on the dirt road past a ranch house, continue around a couple of bends in the road until you run into a gate (1.1 mi. from the interstate). Another ranch house will be seen down a dirt road running off to the right (south). The road you want to take is straight ahead through the gate. The gate has been posted with a State Trust Land notification stating that trespassing is prohibited without a valid hunting or fishing license (it is your responsibility to either comply with this or face the consequences if caught within the State Trust boundaries). Once through the gate (CLOSE IT BEHIND YOU, DAMMIT!!!), continue on dirt road (stick to main artery) for 3.25 miles, where a gate/cattle guard is passed. A National Forest boundary marker sign is posted just past the gate. Continue on road until a three-way split in the road is found. Take the middle road. This leads to a deeper rock strewn gully just short of a rock knob sticking up beyond. Unless you have a 4WD vehicle, you should park before this gully. The road ends at the rock knob. Be forewarned that during some times of the year, some seriously heavy water flow will be encountered in some of the gullies on this road. It is dangerous to enter a highly flowing wash and drivers are encouraged to use good common sense during these times!

To get to the climbing area, hike over the rise and down the road until you reach a trail that goes down the side of the canyon. This is a good trail and should be fairly obvious. This trail is followed down the side of the canyon around a few bends until you can see the Jacuzzi Spires on the other (north) side of the canyon, about two-thirds of the way up the hillside. Once you're below the spires, it becomes your challenge to find the best way to the bottom of the routes. See the map for suggested lines of attack.

The second way to approach the Jacuzzi Spires area is to take a backcountry 4WD road out from the Seven Springs area north of Carefree. I leave the research of this road and it's location as an exercise for the reader. This route may become necessary if access to the area is denied through the Sate Trust land buffer zone.

Access: Jacuzzi Spires resides within the boundaries of Tonto National Forest (see comments above concerning access to the area via State Trust Land to the west). Good to know we have one crag that won't get run over by someone's golf course! I can't say enough about the responsibility of climbers who visit this area to clean up after themselves and treat this area with respect. This means you!!!!

Jacuzzi Spires Route Descriptions

First Jacuzzi Spire

The fractured, angular form of the first spire faces south towards the approach side of the canyon. This is the largest of the three spires and offers the best climbing as well. The first route in this area (**Don't Bug Me**) ascends the complete length of this spire from it's lower left section all the way to the blocky summit on it's upper right side. Several routes exist on this spire, most of which are worth an ascent. The most famous screamer story for the area occured on the first spire a few years back, when a local climber took a lead fall while pulling rope to clip a bolt on **Bugati Cafe**. Instead of screaming, she bit down on the rope and lost several teeth when she bottomed out on the fall. Moral of the story: It's better to scream when you fall, just in case the rope is in your mouth!

1. **Four Flakes (aka Three Turks), 5.9 ★**   This route is located on the lower lefthand face of the spire, 40 feet to the left of the start of **Don't Bug Me**. Climb face past four bolts to belay on the shoulder above. Walk off (probably 3rd Cl.). Pro: 4 bolts

Jacuzzi Spires

1. Four Flakes (aka Three Turks), 5.9 ★
3. Don't Bug Me, 5.6 ★★★
4. Up Tempo And Dynamic, 5.7 ★★★
5. Bugati Cafe, 5.10 R ★★★
6. Harcourt Fenton Mudd, 5.4 ★★
7. Alice's Restaurant, 5.10 R
8. Red Tail Diner, 5.9+/5.10a ★★★
9. Four Star Daydream, 5.11 ★
10. 5.12 Face, 5.12 ★
11. Second Pitch Of Something, 5.9 R
12. Play Dough Bugs, 5.9
13. Ficker-Braten, 5.9
14. Braten-Ficker, 5.9
15. John Ficker's Radically Overhung Crack, 5.11 ★★★
16. Penetration, 5.8+ ★
17. Top Out, 5.11 R
18. Maybe Whitey, 5.6 R
19. Easy You Fucking Wino, 5.7 ★
20. Where's My Whitey, 5.7 R
21. Bug Shit, 5.6 ★
22. Tom's Wonderful Thing, 5.10 R ★★
23. Okay Whitey, 5.8 ★

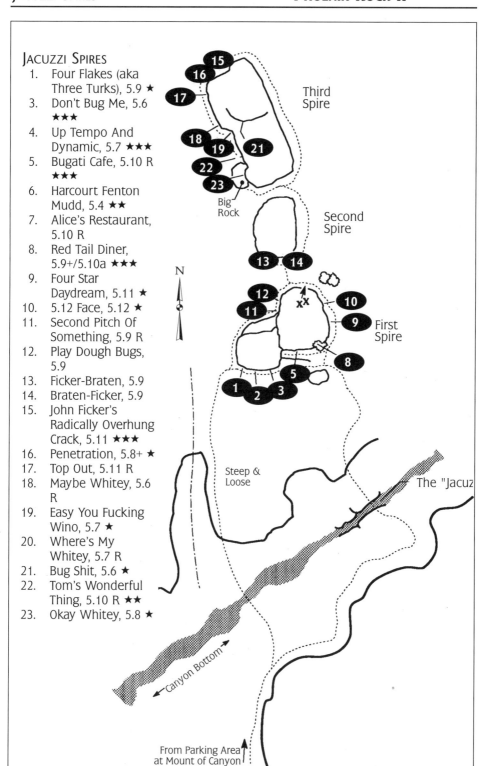

Third Spire

Big Rock

Second Spire

First Spire

N

Steep & Loose

The "Jacuz

Canyon Bottom

From Parking Area at Mount of Canyon

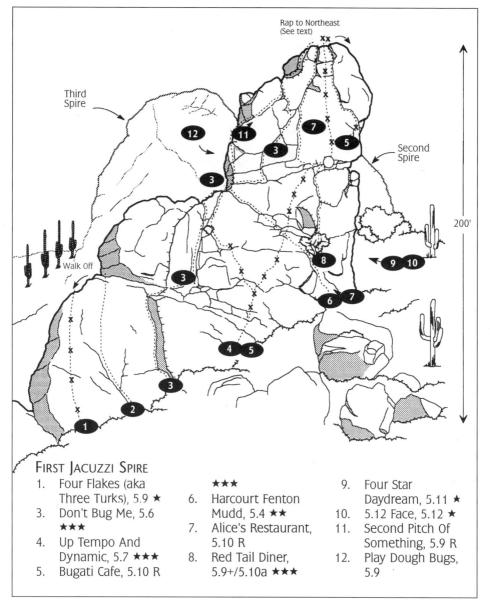

FIRST JACUZZI SPIRE

1. Four Flakes (aka Three Turks), 5.9 ★
3. Don't Bug Me, 5.6 ★★★
4. Up Tempo And Dynamic, 5.7 ★★★
5. Bugati Cafe, 5.10 R
6. Harcourt Fenton Mudd, 5.4 ★★
7. Alice's Restaurant, 5.10 R
8. Red Tail Diner, 5.9+/5.10a ★★★
9. Four Star Daydream, 5.11 ★
10. 5.12 Face, 5.12 ★
11. Second Pitch Of Something, 5.9 R
12. Play Dough Bugs, 5.9

2. **Jason's Route, 5.8 ?**   Just to the right of **Four Flakes**, climb face to gain crack system leading to the shoulder. Walk off. Pro: Unknown
3. **Don't Bug Me, 5.6 ★★★**   This classic three-pitch route was the first one done at Jacuzzi Spires. It starts on the lower left face of the spire, just to the left of a huge dihedral. Watch for the namesake stinkbugs while climbing and don't upset them! First Pitch: Climb the obvious crack until it ends on the ledge above. Traverse around to the right and belay on ledge at the base of the huge dihedral. Second Pitch: Climb the dihedral and belay on a ledge at the top. Third Pitch: Traverse out right to gain a nice crack system that heads up and right. Climb crack system (out right and then straight up) to the summit area. 4th Cl. scrambling to the east leads to the summit. Belay from bolt anchor on top. Pro: Small to large.

4. **Up Tempo And Dynamic, 5.7** ★★★ This "five-fun" 100' route ascends a steep face to a nice hand crack in the center of the main south face of the 1st Jacuzzi. Start about 40' to the right of the huge dihedral. Climb face past two bolts. At the second bolt, traverse to the left about 10 feet to a third. From there, climb straight up to a small ledge and a fourth bolt. Traverse left to gain a crack, which is followed to the notch (belay). To descend: Climb 3rd Class down the back of the notch and walk off. Pro: 4 bolts, assortment of nuts and cams.

5. **Bugati Cafe, 5.10 R** ★★★ This line goes up from the center of the south face, working to the right and finishing up the right side of the hugely exposed upper face near the arete. The second pitch of this route will definitely get your attention! First Pitch: Start as for **Up Tempo and Dynamic**, climbing the face past the first two bolts. Continue straight up the face to a third bolt, then crossing the **Harcourt Fenton** route. Working up and right past

John Ficker climbing **Four Flakes (aka Three Turks),** 5.9+, one of his first ascents at the Jacuzzi Spires.

two more bolts will put you at a small ledge belay (pro req'd) above a tree (and the crack first pitch of **Red Tail Diner**). Second Pitch: Climb from the ledge up the face to a bolt. Traverse to the right and then up (not the line of bolts straight up!) to another bolt just in from the righthand arete. Climb the face above this bolt (R) to a left-leaning crack system and on to the summit. Pro: Several bolts, small to medium large.

6. **Harcourt Fenton Mudd, 5.4** ★★ On the right side of the south face is a tree growing out of a crack about 50' off the ground. If one looks down from the tree and 20' to the left, a crack is visible. This 100' route starts there. Climb crack past a large loose-looking block until it becomes possible to hand-traverse to the left. Climb left and look for an overhang. Mount the overhang to gain a large easy crack leading off to the left. This crack leads to the notch (belay). Pro: Small to large.

7. **Alice's Restaurant, 5.10 R** This climb starts just right of **Harcourt Fenton**'s starting crack and left of the alcove with the tree in it. First Pitch: Climb face to bolt (R). Continue above to clip the last bolt on the first pitch of **Bugati Cafe** (R). Continue to the small ledge belay as for **Bugati Cafe**. Second Pitch: Continue on face above the belay (pretty much straight up) past a line of four bolts leading to the summit. Pro: Several bolts, small to medium.

8. **Red Tail Diner, 5.9+/5.10a** ★★★ If you take the time to look around while in this area, you might see the hawks that this climb is named for. The second pitch on this climb is a classic! This climb starts from the tree noted in the description for **Harcourt Fenton Mudd**. Scramble up to the tree from the right side. First Pitch: Directly behind the tree, climb the awkward handcrack to a small ledge and belay. Second Pitch: From the ledge traverse out to the left to gain a thin crack heading to the summit. Crux moves are protected with micro-nuts and feverish dedication to the friction properties

of sticky climbing rubber. Tread lightly! Pro: Micronuts (RP's) to medium large.

9. **Four Star Daydream, 5.11** ★   Around the corner of the spire, on the east side (to the left of the bolts of 5.12 Face), there is a thin right-leaning (somewhat) crack running towards the summit. Climb this crack. Pro: Small to medium.

10. **5.12 Face, 5.12** ★   This mind-blowing line is found on the east side of spire just to the right of **Four Star Daydream** (you can also get a nice closeup, birds-eye view of it when rappelling from the summit). Way tough climbing on overhanging rock past a line of bolts leads to the summit. Pro: Buncha Bolts.

11. **Second Pitch Of Something, 5.9 R**   This hair-raising pitch starts at the notch and ascends the left-hand edge of the upper south face. On the first ascent, the leader guessed at a difficulty of 5.6, taking only a few TCUs and nuts along for pro. Big surprise!

Felicia Terry leads the third pitch of **Don't Bug Me**, a 5.6 classic route on the First Jacuzzi Spire.

Long runouts and thin climbing are guaranteed to get your attention as you climb to the summit. This is a serious route! Pro: Small to large (TCUs helpful).

12. **Play Dough Bugs, 5.9**   This is the overhanging hand crack on the west face of the upper spire, to the left of Second Pitch of Something. Climb two pitches: An overhanging hand crack to a small belay ledge and then easy face to the summit. Pro: Small to medium large.

Standard Descent for the First Jacuzzi: For routes ending on the lower left shoulder, it is possible to scramble (3rd Class) off the back of the spire. For routes ending on the summit, there are two options, both which involve rappelling off the back (north) side of the Spire from bolt anchor. A single rope rappel (80') can be done which puts you at the top of a steep and loose scramble-down. One may also perform, a 2-rope rappel that will deposit you on firmer ground below the other rappel's end (120'). My recommendation is to take two ropes.

Second Jacuzzi Spire

This spire offers the least amount of climbing opportunity due to it's uncanny resemblance to a junk pile. Rumor has it that John Ficker and Larry Braten did a pair of 5.9 routes up the south side of the pile. See map for approximate location. Route information on this spire was rather sketchy, but there seem to have been a couple of 5.9 climbs that were done by John Ficker and Larry Braten on the south face of the spire.

13. **Ficker-Braten, 5.9**
14. **Braten-Ficker, 5.9**

Third Jacuzzi Spire

The third Jacuzzi has seen some development over the last few years by local route-hunter Bob Blair and various partners. Most of the routes on it's western face reach nearly 100 feet in length and present some interesting climbing problems.

15. **John Ficker's Radically Overhung Crack, 5.11** ★★★   This route starts in a over-hanging crack located to the left of Penetration on the north side of the spire. "It looks somewhat like a cleaner, longer verson of the second overhang on **BeeGee** at Pinnacle Peak." Climb the crack to reach a tree belay on top of the wall. (40') Pro: Small to large cams.

16. **Penetration, 5.8+** ★   This route was the first one done on the third spire. The start is located on the right hand side of the north face. The route description, as given by one of the first ascent team: "Climb an obvious phallic-like column to a vagina-like crack." Hmmm...anyway, climb the "phallus" (column) for 25 feet until it ends in the "vagina" (crack). Jam the overhanging crack until easy ground is reached. Finish to summit on easier climbing. (70') Pro: Small to large.

The west face of the third Spire has some interesting moderate climbs on it. Described left to right.

17. **Top Out, 5.11 R**   This rather exciting adventure may be found on the far left side of the 3rd Jacuzzi Spire. Pro: 1 bolt, TCUs.

18. **Maybe Whitey, 5.6 R**   The start of this route is located about 30 feet to the right of **Top Out**. Pro is described as "marginal." Climb up and right on poor protection, following a line of blocky shelves to reach an overhang with a crack. Turn the overhang and then continue up and right to reach a belay ledge (100'). Pro: Micronuts to Friends.

19. **Easy You Fucking Wino, 5.7** ★   This route starts just to the right of **Maybe Whitey** in a vertical broken dihedral system. Layback, stem and jam up the dihedral until it ends. Climb easy rock above to the belay ledge (100'). Pro: Small to medium large.

20. **Where's My Whitey, 5.7 R**   This one starts just to the right of the broken dihedral for **Easy You Wino**. If one moves from right to left along the base of the wall, there's a spot where the base of the wall jumps about 10'. Just left of this is the start of the route. Climb up and right over a bulge. Stay left of a black stain and climb up to the belay ledge. Pro: Small to medium large.

21. **Bug Shit, 5.6** ★   This route starts at the north side of the belay ledge for the Whitey climbs. The start can be reached either by climbing one of those routes, or by reversing the walk-off up the south ridge. Climb the left-leaning steep dihedral to the top of the crag (40'). Pro: Small to medium.

22. **Tom's Wonderful Thing, 5.10 R** ★★   This route, originally planned as a sport route, ended up as a rather sporty lead. The start is located to the right of **Where's My Whitey** and left of a large block that sits against the right side of the wall. A line of bolts should help identify the route. Climb a short crack to a bolt. Continue above to another bolt. Climb up and left over steep rock for about 15 feet where a hard move leads to the third bolt. Easy ground leads up and left into a groove (pro). After climbing the groove, continue right onto a steep slab and past three more bolts to an overhanging wall. Grapple the overhang past one last bolt to the belay ledge (100+'). Pro: 7 bolts, small to medium.

23. **Okay Whitey, 5.8** ★   This route starts on the large block leaning against the right end of the west face. Climb up to a small vertical dihedral which takes you to to an overhang. Continue up and left, passing the overhang. Horizontal cracks and sparse (tricky!) protection lead to the belay ledge (80'). Pro: Small to medium large.

Standard Descent for the Third Jacuzzi: Walk off the south ridge.

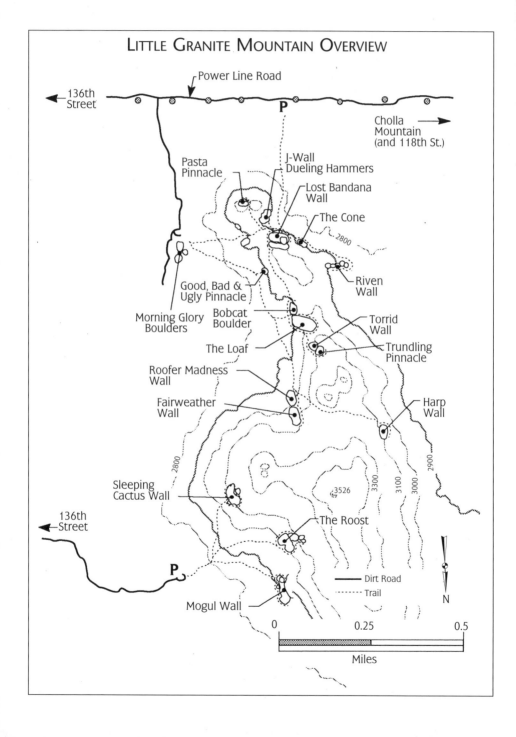

LITTLE GRANITE MOUNTAIN OVERVIEW

Power Line Road

136th Street

Cholla Mountain (and 118th St.)

P

Pasta Pinnacle

J-Wall
Dueling Hammers

Lost Bandana Wall

The Cone

2800

Riven Wall

Good, Bad & Ugly Pinnacle

Morning Glory Boulders

Bobcat Boulder

Torrid Wall

The Loaf

Trundling Pinnacle

Roofer Madness Wall

Fairweather Wall

Harp Wall

2800

3300
3100
3000
2900

Sleeping Cactus Wall

3526

136th Street

The Roost

P

Dirt Road
Trail

N

Mogul Wall

0   0.25   0.5

Miles

Chapter 5

LITTLE GRANITE MOUNTAIN

Originally called "little" because of it's bigger brother (Granite Mountain) found in Prescott, Little Granite Mountain is denoted on the USGS topographic map as "granite mountain." The climbing found on Little Granite Mountain is located on several fairly sizable crags scattered across the mountain. Most of the areas described in this chapter have routes from easy to moderately hard, providing a solid day of climbing for a good range of abilities. Crags range in size from fairly short to nearly a pitch in length. The rock here tends to be fairly solid desert granite, with lots of gnarly cracks and unique crystal face holds to test your skills and skin. Bear in mind that some of the newer areas (Mogul Wall, The Roost, Sleeping Cactus Wall and The Cone) will have some temporary holds (loose rock) until climber traffic helps clean them off.

Route development at the Little Granite areas has continued over the past few years, mainly on three new crags "discovered" on the northeastern end of the mountain. A lot of this development occurred shortly after the publication of the previous guide. Some new lines have also been climbed on the established formations. Climbing at Little Granite Mountain continues to be very enjoyable and mostly out-of-the-way. Local development may change this experience in future years, but for now, you can still have an enjoyable, quiet day of climbing on some really nice routes.

Approach: Little Granite is accessed from Rio Verde Drive via 136th Street (see map). Drive past Pinnacle Peak through Reata Pass and turn right (east) on Dynamite/Rio Verde Drive. Continue east and make a left turn (north) on 136th street (sign). Continue north to Power Line Road. Turn left to access to all areas from Lost Bandanna to Fairweather Wall/Roofer Madness Wall. Incidentally, in case it's not obvious, Power Line Road is easily identified by the line of high tension power lines running straight east-west along it. To access the north-eastern crags, continue north on 136th Street for another mile past Power Line Road to a gate on the left where another gate closes the road. Go through the gate on the left. Close the gate behind you! Additional instructions for approaching these areas are given below.

Access: Access is currently not a hot issue at Little Granite Mountain, although it may be more of a problem in coming years. According to the best information I could find, Little Granite Mountain is kind of a checkerboard of land ownership. Some state trust land is mixed in with private land. The mountain is somewhat outside the "development zone" right now, but access problems may eventually surface as development encroaches. Big money seems to talk loudest in this area and the desert is losing the fight, so watch for changes The recent fire in the McDowells might make this "pristine" area more attractive to land buyers, pressuring the access situation prematurely. Keep an eye out at the local climbing shops and/or local climbing gym for updates on the situation. According to recent rumors, the governor has proposed the preservation of some of the land in this area. Cross your fingers and lend your support for this kind of environmental stewardship!

Little Granite Mountain route descriptions will be given in three sections which correspond with the Southern, Middle and Northern sections of Little Granite Mountain. The map shows the approximate lines of division.

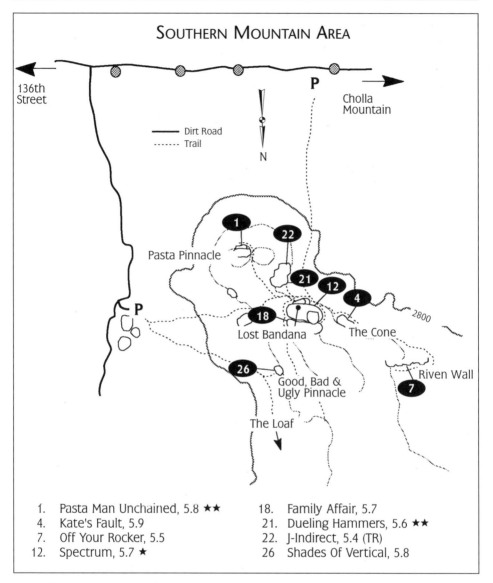

SOUTHERN MOUNTAIN AREA

136th
Street

—— Dirt Road
------ Trail

N

P

Cholla
Mountain

Pasta Pinnacle

P

Lost Bandana

The Cone

2800

Good, Bad &
Ugly Pinnacle

Riven Wall

The Loaf

1. Pasta Man Unchained, 5.8 ★★	18. Family Affair, 5.7
4. Kate's Fault, 5.9	21. Dueling Hammers, 5.6 ★★
7. Off Your Rocker, 5.5	22. J-Indirect, 5.4 (TR)
12. Spectrum, 5.7 ★	26 Shades Of Vertical, 5.8

Southern Mountain Areas

The Southern Mountain Areas include Pasta Pinnacle, The Cone, Riven Wall, Lost Bandanna Wall, J-Wall and the Good, Bad and Ugly Pinnacle. The south end of the mountain yields some fine climbs, which may be reached with a fairly short approach hike from a small parking pullout along Power Line Road directly south of the mountain. It may also be reached from the recommended parking area along the east side of the southern end of the mountain (see map above for parking areas).

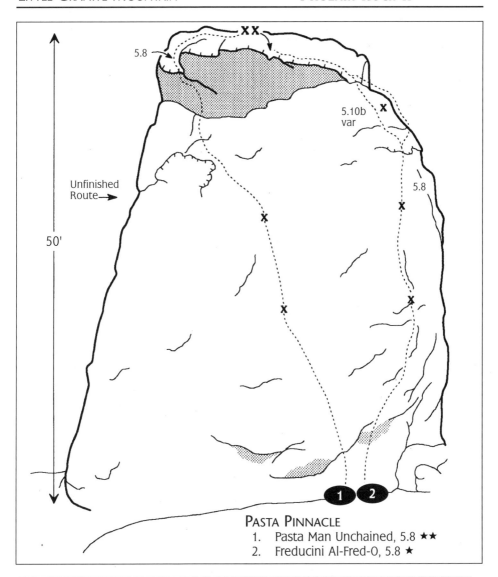

PASTA PINNACLE
1. Pasta Man Unchained, 5.8 ★★
2. Freducini Al-Fred-O, 5.8 ★

Pasta Pinnacle

This small, south-facing pinnacle is located at the extreme southern end of Little Granite Mountain near the ridgecrest. A two-bolt anchor is located on top.

1. **Pasta Man Unchained, 5.8 ★★**   Start at right side of south face. Climb face veering left past two bolts to left end of roof. A very memorable move over the roof and onto the two-bolt belay. Descend via single line rappel to south over roof. Pro: Two bolts, small to medium nuts.

2. **Freducini Al-Fred-O, 5.8 ★**   Start is just right of **Pasta Man Unchained**. Instead of going left, climb up right side of face passing three bolts. At the third bolt go right to arête and up to the two-bolt belay. A harder (5.10b) variation can be done by climbing directly up from the third bolt, avoiding the easier arête. This route may have some loose rock until it receives a bit of traffic. Pro: Three bolts.

Note: Just left of **Pasta Man Unchained** is an unfinished route.

Jan Holdeman, shown here climbing at Sleeping Cactus Wall, is responsible for many new routes at both Little Granite and Cholla mountains.

The Cone

This formation lies just downhill and to the left (west) of the Lost Bandanna area. The rock quality can be suspect in spots on this wall, but seems to be improving with a bit of traffic. Routes are described from left to right. Standard descent: Walk off the wall to the left or right and back to base.

3. **Unknown, 5.8-5.10 (TR)**   Not much is known about this route. The climb follows a smooth face up the black water chute on the far left-hand side of the wall. Depending on where you climb, it can range from about 5.8 to 5.10 Pro: Toprope

4. **Kate's Fault, 5.9**   Starting slightly right of center, climb up and left to face in center of wall past two bolts and several zenoliths to top. Natural pro required for belay anchor. Watch out for those temporary holds! Pro: Two bolts, medium to large for belay.

5. **Sideshow, 5.6 ★**   Climb the arête just right of the main wall and **Kate's Fault** past two bolts to top. Pro required for belay. Pro: Two bolts.

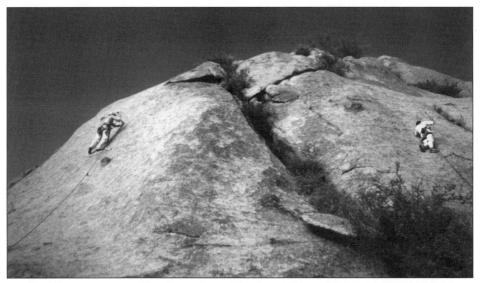

Dueling first ascents on The Cone: Doug Fletcher (left) and Chew McHugh (right). Photo by Jan Holdeman.

The Cone

3. Unknown, 5.8-5.10 (TR)
4. Kate's Fault, 5.9
5. Sideshow, 5.6 ★
6. Three Dopes On A Rope, 5.4

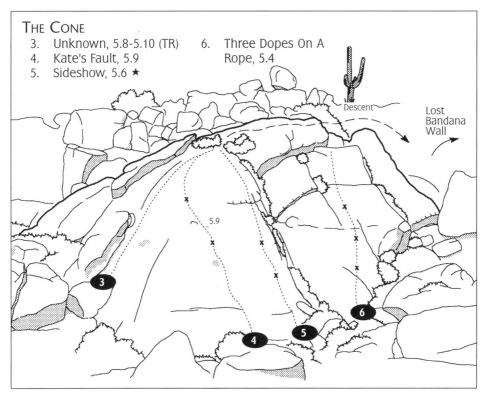

6. **Three Dopes On A Rope, 5.4**   Low angle slab on right side of The Cone. Climb up two seams past three bolts and a small tree to top. Natural pro required for belay. Good beginner lead experience. Pro: Small to medium nuts, two bolts, sling.

Riven Wall

This north-facing wall has been known by a few names (Mystery Crag, West Pinnacles). The severely fractured features give the wall it's name. Located just west and a bit north of The Cone, there are two established routes. No topo is shown.

7. **Off Your Rocker, 5.5**   Prominent left facing dihedral in center of wall. Pro: Medium to large nuts.
8. **Codgers, 5.5**   Start 25 feet right of **Off Your Rocker**. Finger/handcrack which jogs left just below top. Finish up the face. Pro: Small to large nuts.

Lost Bandana Wall

This south-facing wall is one of the more popular areas at Little Granite Mountain. The area was given its name after the mysterious disappearance of several bandannas.

9. **Slot, 5.6 ★**   Start at left end of wall in left-facing corner. Climb short crack to ledge. Continue in open book up and on right. Clear roof at top of open book on right to large ledge. One may scramble off at this point or join the second pitch of **Limbo** (5.6) if desired. Pro: Small to large nuts.
10. **Climb At First Sting (5.11b)**   Climb the steep face in between **Slot** and **Limbo**. The climb was named for a pair of frisky scorpions found behind a loose flake. The first two bolts on this climb were put in by an unknown party. Pro: Three bolts, assorted small to large.

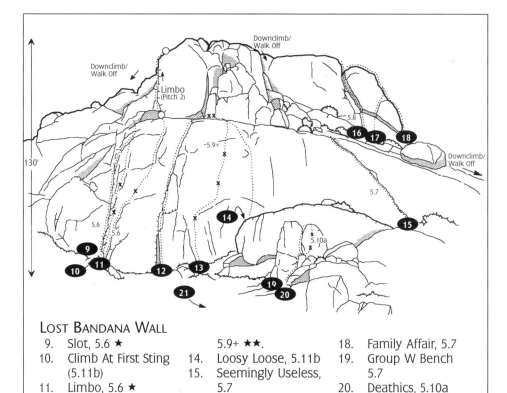

LOST BANDANA WALL

9.	Slot, 5.6 ★		5.9+ ★★.	18.	Family Affair, 5.7
10.	Climb At First Sting	14.	Loosy Loose, 5.11b	19.	Group W Bench
	(5.11b)	15.	Seemingly Useless,		5.7
11.	Limbo, 5.6 ★		5.7	20.	Deathics, 5.10a
12.	Spectrum, 5.7 e	16.	Owl Out, 5.8 ★	21.	Dueling Hammers,
13.	Lawless And Free,	17.	Footloose, 5.8		5.6

11. **Limbo, 5.6** ★   Start just right of **Slot** (3) at right-veering crack. First Pitch: Follow crack until it disappears, then climb face past bolt to horizontal crack (5.6). Continue on face to large ledge. Second Pitch: Move left into left-facing corner. Climb corner (5.6) to top. Pro: Small to large nuts, one bolt.

Standard descent for **Slot**, **Climb At First Sting** and **Limbo**: Walk off to the left (west) side of the formation, down brushy ledges.

12. **Spectrum, 5.7** ★   Start 20 feet right of **Limbo** around corner at brown-stained crack. Climb crack to ledge and two bolt belay. Scramble off right. Pro: Small to large nuts, two-bolt anchor.

Note: the hangers on the bolts at the top of **Spectrum/Lawless and Free** seem to periodically come and go. If they're missing, an assortment of medium to large cams will be needed for the anchor.

13. **Lawless And Free, 5.9+** ★★ This popular face climb is located about ten feet' to the right of **Spectrum**. Climb steep lower face to first bolt. Continue on sculpted face above past two more bolts to top (5.9+). Pro: Three bolts, two-bolt anchor.

14. **Loosy Loose, 5.11b**   Just right of **Lawless and Free**, climb slightly crumbly face past five bolts to top. Pro: Five bolts, two-bolt anchor.

15. **Seemingly Useless, 5.7**   Start at the right end of wall. Climb left-leaning seam and crack to top. Pro: Small to medium nuts.

16. **Owl Out, 5.8** ★   On the second ascent the climbers found some postcards at the base. Rather unusual. Start up from the top of **Seeminly Useless** in large chimney/gully system. Climb south-facing, left-leaning hand-and-finger crack to top. (Look out for a loose block!) Pro: Small to medium nuts.

17. **Footloose, 5.8**   Start 5 feet right of **Owl Out**. Climb left-leaning, disjointed crack system to top. Pro: Small to medium nuts and Friends.

Scott Aldinger on **Lawless and Free** (5.9+), Lost Bandana Wall, Little Granite Mountain.

18. **Family Affair, 5.7**   Start at east-facing slab to right around corner from **Owl Out.** Climb face past two bolts to top. Pro: Two bolts, medium nuts and Friends.

Standard descent for the left-side Lost Bandanna routes: Walk off and downclimb the east end of the formation. A rappel can be done from the bolts at the top of **Spectrum/Lawless and Free**, but hanger-thieves sometime swipe the hangers off these bolts.

The following two routes are located on a small outcrop just below and to the right of the **Spectrum** area (see topo). .

19. **Group W Bench 5.7**   Large fissure up the middle. Undercling flake and left-facing dihedral. Walk off. I never understood the name of the route until one day when I hap-

pened to hear the entire Alice's Restaurant on the radio. Pro: Medium to large nuts and Friends.

20. **Deathics, 5.10a**   Death to ethics? Follow **Group W Bench** until you can traverse right in the crack. Follow face above past two bolts to top. Walk off. Pro: Two bolts, medium to large nuts and Friends.

21. **Dueling Hammers, 5.6 ★★**   An appropriate name as the first ascent party and another climbing party were placing bolts on their respective routes at the same time. This northwest-facing formation (100 yards southeast of Lost Bandanna Wall) faces the east end of Lost Bandanna Wall. Climb face past two horizontal cracks and two bolts to top. Pro: Small to medium nuts, two bolts.

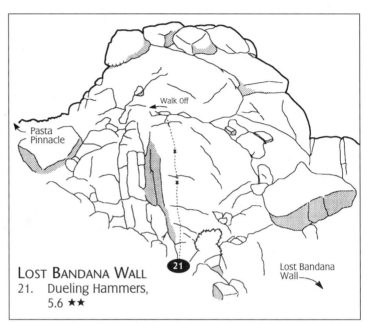

Walk Off

Pasta Pinnacle

LOST BANDANA WALL
21.   Dueling Hammers,
        5.6 ★★

21

Lost Bandana Wall

The J-Wall

This small south-facing area will be seen to the left on the approach from the pullout parking to the south of Lost Bandanna Wall (see map). The lines are somewhat indistinct, but can be located with a bit of looking. No topo is shown.

22. **J-Indirect, 5.4 (TR)**   Route goes up and to the right (35 feet). Pro: TR
23. **J-For Play, 5.7 (TR)**   This route goes straight up the end of the slab (35 feet). Pro: TR

The following two routes are located on the east-facing side of the mountain, east and a little south of the **Dueling Hammers** area.

24. **Bee Careful, 5.8**   A wide south-facing crack on the large loaf-like formation just east over the saddle from the Lost Bandanna Wall area. Pro: Medium to large.
25. **Cricket Patrol, 5.6**   Located on an east-facing slab approximately 30 yards south of **Bee Careful** (across the wash). Pro: Unknown.

Good, Bad and Ugly Pinnacle

This pinnacle is located north and east of Lost Bandanna Wall, along the trail to The Loaf from the parking area (see map). On the walk in, summit rappel slings can be seen. The following two routes are located on the east face of the pinnacle. At first glance, the rock looks too crumbly to withstand any climbing, but several ascents have proven that looks can be deceiving. Standard descent: Rappel from two-bolt anchor on top.

26 **Shades Of Vertical, 5.8** This route is located on the left side of the featured east face. Pro: Three bolts, rappel station.

27 **Grim Ripper, 5.11a** ★ Climb overhanging face just right of **Shades of Vertical** (up and right) past three bolts. Pro: Three bolts, rappel station.

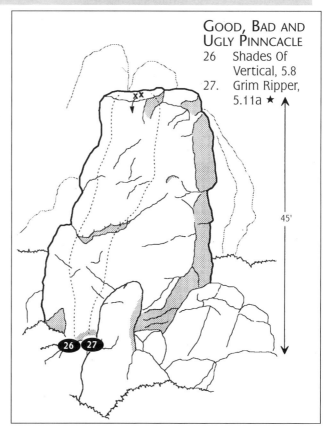

GOOD, BAD AND UGLY PINNCACLE
26 Shades Of Vertical, 5.8
27. Grim Ripper, 5.11a ★

45'

Morning Glory Boulder Area

This is a small group of large boulders on the east side of the south end of Little Granite Mountain and about 50 yards north of Power Line Road. This area is sometimes used for parking to hike to The Loaf and other crags along the southern and middle parts of the mountain. Standard Descent for Morning Glory Boulder: Rappel (sling) from south side.

28. **Flim Flam, 5.8** Climb east face of Morning Glory Boulder past bolt and horizontal crack. Pro: One bolt, small to medium tri-cams.

29. **On A Nice Windy Day, 5.6** Climb south face of Morning Glory Boulder. Pro: Unknown

30. **Seem Dream, 5.5** Climb the seam to the right of **On a Nice Windy Day**. Pro: Small nuts.

The following two climbs are located in another boulder pile, about 150 yards. south of Morning Glory Boulder.

31. **Groove Tube, 5.10b (R)** This route is on a south-facing boulder on the south side of the pile. Pro: One bolt

32. **Kadywompus, 5.8** Located 20 yards east of **Groove Tube**. Climb short hand-and-finger crack up and left. Pro: Medium

33. **Overhung Thing, 5.11b**   Obvious overhung west-facing slab located approximately 50 yards east of **Groove Tube**. Pro: One bolt
34. **Hallucination, 5.9**   The route is the northeast edge of prominent boulder. Left of large catclaw, move right onto arête. Pro: One bolt

Middle Mountain Area

The Middle Mountain Areas include Bobcat Boulder, The Loaf, Trundling Pinnacle, Torrid Wall, Roofer Madness Wall, Fairweather Wall and Harp Wall. Although a longer walk is involved in getting to this area, there is some great climbing found here. Approach from the parking area just north of Power Line Road near the Morning Glory boulders.

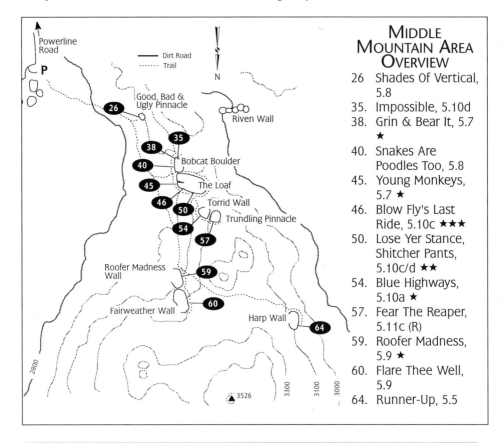

MIDDLE MOUNTAIN AREA OVERVIEW

26 Shades Of Vertical, 5.8
35. Impossible, 5.10d
38. Grin & Bear It, 5.7 ★
40. Snakes Are Poodles Too, 5.8
45. Young Monkeys, 5.7 ★
46. Blow Fly's Last Ride, 5.10c ★★★
50. Lose Yer Stance, Shitcher Pants, 5.10c/d ★★
54. Blue Highways, 5.10a ★
57. Fear The Reaper, 5.11c (R)
59. Roofer Madness, 5.9 ★
60. Flare Thee Well, 5.9
64. Runner-Up, 5.5

Bobcat Boulder

This small, south and east-facing outcrop is located just off the southeastern corner of The Loaf. Some fine short climbs can be found here. Standard descent for the Bobcat Boulder routes: Walk off towards The Loaf, passing between the two formations on the way down. Tread lightly and watch out for bees in this area!

35. **Impossible, 5.10d**   This route is located on the south wall of Bobcat Boulder to the left of **Loosinda**. Climb thin face to zenoliths. Finish via grungy crack or by traversing right. Pro: Two bolts, Friends
36. **Next To Impossible, 5.9+**   Just left of **Impossible**, climb the right-leaning finger crack to join **Impossible** at it's second bolt. Pro: Small nuts, Friends

37. **Loosinda, 5.6**   Start at right side of south face. Climb left-leaning cracks (loose rock) to top. Pro: Small to large nuts.

38. **Grin & Bear It, 5.7 ★**   Start at southeast face. Climb face past two bolts to roof. Continue over roof past bolt to top. Pro: Three bolts, large nuts. FA 1986 Doug Fletcher, Chew McHugh

39. **Crystaline Grin, 5.10c**   Just to the right of **Grin & Bear It**, climb the razor-thin face on crystals past two bolts. Work right at horizontal and con-

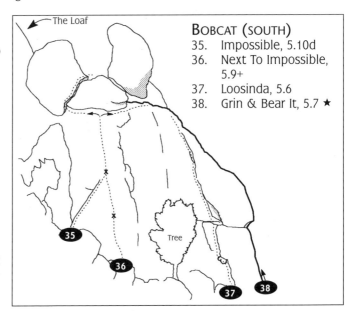

BOBCAT (SOUTH)
35. Impossible, 5.10d
36. Next To Impossible, 5.9+
37. Loosinda, 5.6
38. Grin & Bear It, 5.7 ★

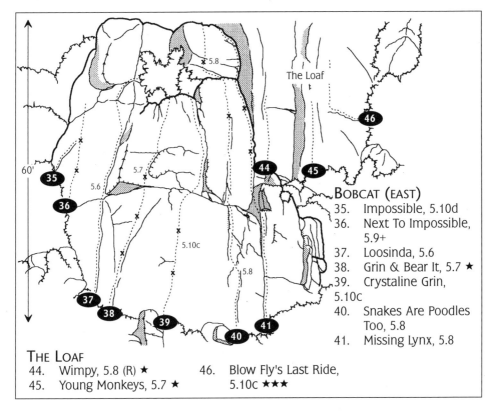

BOBCAT (EAST)
35. Impossible, 5.10d
36. Next To Impossible, 5.9+
37. Loosinda, 5.6
38. Grin & Bear It, 5.7 ★
39. Crystaline Grin, 5.10c
40. Snakes Are Poodles Too, 5.8
41. Missing Lynx, 5.8

THE LOAF
44. Wimpy, 5.8 (R) ★
45. Young Monkeys, 5.7 ★
46. Blow Fly's Last Ride, 5.10c ★★★

Chew McHugh on **Snakes Are Poodles Too** (5.8), Bobcat Boulder. Photo by Jan Holdeman.

tinue in vertical crack to same belay as **Grin and Bear It**.. Pro: Bolts, medium to large nuts, slings.

40. **Snakes Are Poodles Too, 5.8** Start at right side of east face. Climb thin crack system to ledge. Continue in crack above ledge onto face, then past bolt to another ledge. Continue on face over boulder past bolt to top. Pro: Small to large nuts, two bolts.

41. **Missing Lynx, 5.8** Start just right of wide crack to the right of **Snakes Are Poodles Too**. Up the thin seam and face to a ledge. Move up face past two bolts to the top. Pro: Two bolts and nuts.

The Loaf

Possible the best crag at Little Granite Mountain, this east-facing 170+-foot slab hosts a variety of starred routes, including a three-star route, **Blow Fly's Last Ride**. Standard descent: for routes on The Loaf: It is possible to scramble off the formation either in the gully between The Loaf and Bobcat Boulder, or by working your way down rocks and slopes to the right of **Gender Blender**. Keep an eye out for bees if you head down the gully.

42. **Shake 'n Bake, 5.6 ★** Start up at south face just left of arête. Climb left-most crack system to top. Pro: Medium to large nuts.

43. **Shake 'n Flake, 5.6 (R)** Start is same as **Shake N' Bake**. Climb right-most crack system around corner onto east face. Continue on face (5.6 R) to top. Pro: Small to medium nuts.

44. **Wimpy, 5.8 (R) ★** Start at extreme left end of east face (left of wide crack). Climb face off boulder (5.8 R) to thin horizontal and vertical cracks. Follow cracks and face past one bolt to top. Pro: Small to medium nuts, one bolt.

45. **Young Monkeys, 5.7 ★** Start just right of **Wimpy** and wide crack. Climb face on small prow past three bolts, then continue on face past another bolt to top. Pro: Small to medium nuts, four bolts.

46. **Blow Fly's Last Ride, 5.10c ★★★** Probably the finest route at Little Granite Mountain, start right and up around corner from **Young Monkeys**. Traverse horizontal crack left to just right of prow. Climb face up and right past three bolts to fourth bolt. Continue right on face to fifth bolt, then up and left to sixth bolt. Finish on face up and right past seventh bolt to top. Pro: Seven bolts.

47. **"A" Crack, 5.10c (X)** Start up and right from **Blow Fly's Last Ride**. Climb thin crack past piton to bolt on face. Continue on face up and slightly left (X) to fourth bolt of **Blow Fly's Last Ride**. Finish on **Blow Fly**. Pro: One piton, five bolts.

48. **Dike Walk, 5.10b (R) ★** Start up and right from **"A" Crack**. Traverse face left to bolt, then up to second bolt. Continue up and slightly left (R) to join **Blow Fly's Last Ride** at seventh bolt. Note: The "R" section is not very difficult climbing, but if so desired, one can traverse left to the sixth bolt of **Blow Fly**. Pro: Three bolts.

THE LOAF

42. Shake 'n Bake, 5.6 ★
43. Shake 'n Flake, 5.6 (R)
44. Wimpy, 5.8 (R) ★
45. Young Monkeys, 5.7 ★
46. Blow Fly's Last Ride, 5.10c ★★★
47. "A" Crack, 5.10c (X)
48. Dike Walk, 5.10b (R) ★
49. Sweet Surprise, 5.7 ★★
50. Lose Yer Stance, Shitcher Pants, 5.10c/d ★★
51. Gender Blender, 5.10b

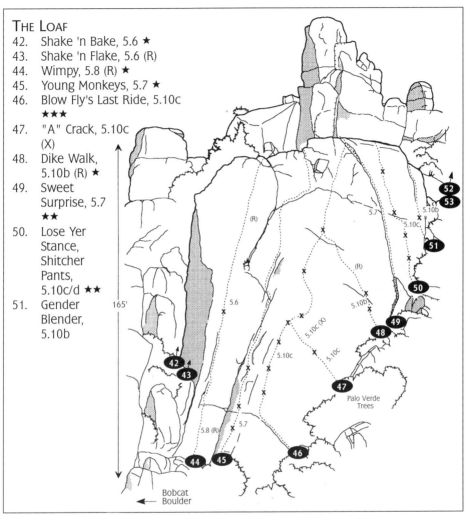

49. **Sweet Surprise, 5.7 ★★**   Start up and right of **Dike Walk**. Climb hand and finger crack to top. Pro: Small to medium nuts.
50. **Lose Yer Stance, Shitcher Pants, 5.10c/d ★★** Just to the right of the block at the base of **Sweet Surprise**, climb the face past bolts to top. The moves past the second bolt will get your attention! Natural pro required for the belay. Pro: Four bolts, medium to large nuts.
51. **Gender Blender, 5.10b**   Start up and right from **Sweet Surprise** and **Shitcher Pants**. Climb short face past bolt (5.10b) to small ledge and wide vertical crack. Continue in crack to top. Pro: One bolt, medium to large nuts.

The following two routes are located on small buttresses to the right and up from The Loaf.

52. **Arm And Hammer, 5.9**   Start 50 feet up and right of The Loaf at short buttress. Climb face past bolt and horizontal crack. Pro: One bolt, medium pro
53. **Old & Slow, 5.7**   Climb obvious two-tiered dike. Watch for rope drag between tiers. Pro: Small to medium nuts.

Torrid Wall

This east-facing wall is located approximately 60 yards slightly up and right from the top of The Loaf. It is also just below Trundling Pinnacle. Standard Descent for Torrid Wall: Scramble down Cl. 3 on north side.

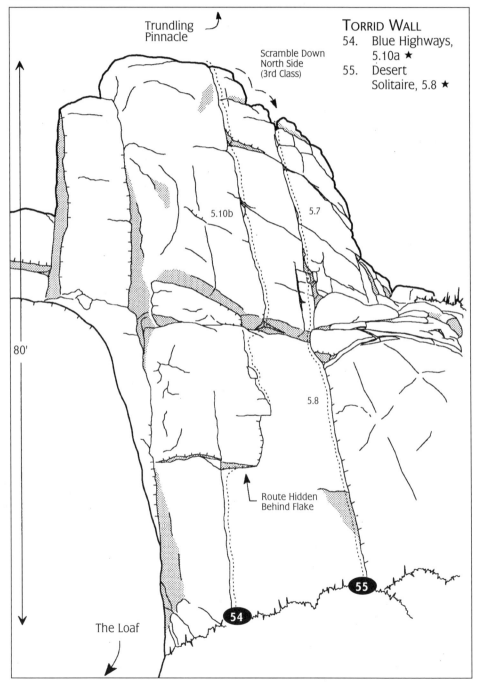

Trundling Pinnacle

Scramble Down North Side (3rd Class)

TORRID WALL
54. Blue Highways, 5.10a ★
55. Desert Solitaire, 5.8 ★

5.10b

5.7

80'

5.8

Route Hidden Behind Flake

54

55

The Loaf

54. **Blue Highways, 5.10a** ★   Start just left of left-facing dihedral at right-facing flake. Climb flake (look out for white owl) tol horizontal crack, then move right into thin crack. Follow thin crack (5.10a) to top. Pro: Small to large nuts, Friends.

55. **Desert Solitaire, 5.8** ★   Start in left-facing corner at right side of east face (just left of **Blue Highways**). Climb wide (but thinning) crack onto ledge (5.8), then continue in vertical crack to top. Pro: Medium to large nuts, Friends.

Trundling Pinnacle

Named because the first ascent party trundled some massive loose boulders off the top; this disguised pinnacle is located approximately 75 yards up and right from the top of The Loaf. Descent from the formation requires a (single line) tandem rappel off east and west sides.

56. **Some Like It Hot, 5.7** ★   One must do this route in the middle of summer to appreciate its name. Start at right side of east face. Climb onto flake at base of wall. Climb up discontinuous, thin crack, then climb face to bolt (just left of arête). Continue on face past bolt (5.7) to horizontal crack, then continue to top via slightly overhanging, wide crack (5.7). Pro: Friends, one bolt.

57. **Fear The Reaper, 5.11c (R)**   Start at center of east face of Trundling Pinnacle. Face climb directly up center of face past three bolts (second bolt may be questionable) to small roof. Turn roof and continue on easy face to top. Pro: Three bolts, medium to large pro.

58. **Auger Refusal, 5.9**   Start directly behind Trundling Pinnacle at base of short slab. Face climb past bolt and undercling. Pro: One bolt

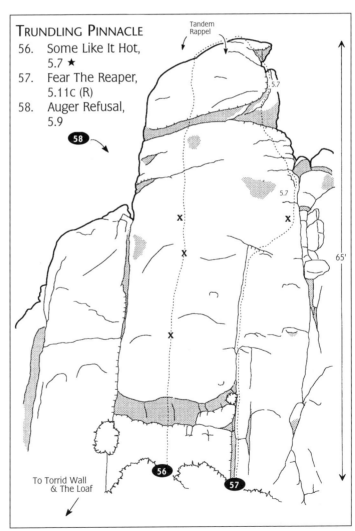

TRUNDLING PINNACLE
56. Some Like It Hot, 5.7 ★
57. Fear The Reaper, 5.11c (R)
58. Auger Refusal, 5.9

Tandem Rappel

To Torrid Wall & The Loaf

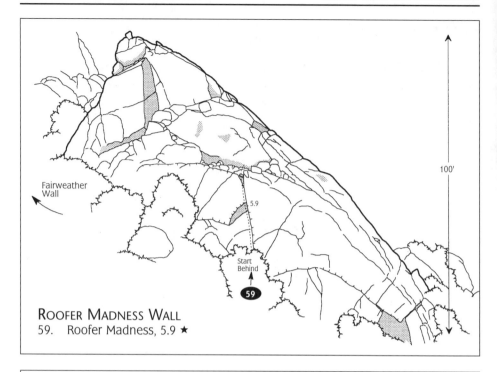

ROOFER MADNESS WALL
59. Roofer Madness, 5.9 ★

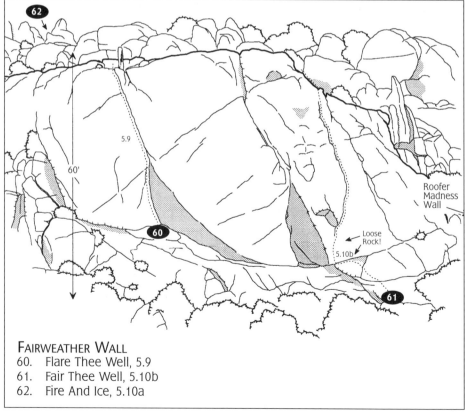

FAIRWEATHER WALL
60. Flare Thee Well, 5.9
61. Fair Thee Well, 5.10b
62. Fire And Ice, 5.10a

Roofer Madness Wall

This small, southwest-facing wall is located far to the right (northeast) from The Loaf. It can be recognized by a large, horizontal crack splitting its right side.

59. **Roofer Madness, 5.9** ★   Start at left side at slightly left-leaning crack system. Climb thin crack to roof, then clear roof via handcrack. Continue in crack to top. Pro: Small to medium nuts.

Fairweather Wall

This, like Roofer Madness Wall, is southwest-facing and located far to the right (northeast) of The Loaf. It is also above (north of) Roofer Madness Wall.

60. **Flare Thee Well, 5.9**   Start at left side. Climb overhanging open book, then continue in strenuous crack (5.9) to top. Pro: Medium to large nuts, Friends.
61. **Fair Thee Well, 5.10b**   Start approximately 40 feet right of **Flare Thee Well** at small roof. Climb incredibly rotten rock to roof, then move out right and up via rotten crack. Continue up and right past rotten bulge and follow crack to top. Get the picture about this route? Pro: Medium to large nuts, Friends.
62. **Fire And Ice, 5.10a**   Start at west-facing boulder approximately 100 yards east of the top of **Flare Thee Well**. Climb short, overhanging handcrack. Pro: Small to medium-large nuts.

Harp Wall

Although this west-facing wall is difficult to approach, the unique nature (lots of zenoliths) is worth the visit.

63. **Walkaway, 5.10b** ★   As one approaches Harp Wall along the ridge, **Walkaway** will be located on the north face of a crag, just above the fourth saddle. (This saddle is where one starts traversing west and north to Harp Wall.) Start off of slab at overhanging handcrack. Climb short crack to top. Pro: Medium nuts, Friends.

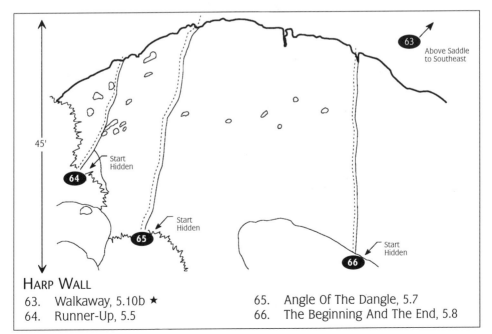

Harp Wall

63. Walkaway, 5.10b ★   65. Angle Of The Dangle, 5.7
64. Runner-Up, 5.5   66. The Beginning And The End, 5.8

64. **Runner-Up, 5.5**   Start at left side at wide crack. Climb crack via zenoliths to top. Pro: Runners.
65. **Angle Of The Dangle, 5.7**   Start six feet right of **Runner-Up**. Climb zenoliths into hand-and-finger crack. Follow crack to top. Pro: Medium to large nuts, Friends.
66. **The Beginning And The End, 5.8**   Guess where the cruxes are? Start 20 feet right of **Angle of the Dangle**. Climb thinning crack to top. Pro: Small to medium nuts.

The following climb is located on the west side of Little Granite Mountain, over the hill from The Loaf. Not much detail is known about this route and it's location is rather vague.

67. **Endure The Elements, 5.10a**   On west-facing crag, climb thin crack system up and left to horizontal crack and roof system. Roof system has not been climbed as of yet. Pro: Micro-nuts and HBs.

Northern Mountain Areas
The northern end of Little Granite Mountain has seen most of the route activity in the Phoenix granite areas since the last guidebook was published. Three previously undeveloped

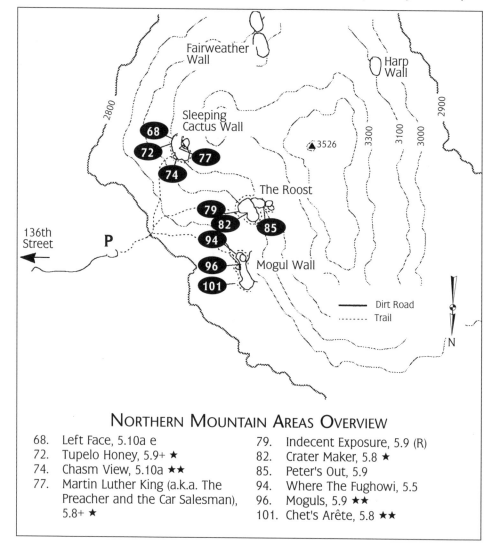

NORTHERN MOUNTAIN AREAS OVERVIEW

68. Left Face, 5.10a e
72. Tupelo Honey, 5.9+ ★
74. Chasm View, 5.10a ★★
77. Martin Luther King (a.k.a. The Preacher and the Car Salesman), 5.8+ ★

79. Indecent Exposure, 5.9 (R)
82. Crater Maker, 5.8 ★
85. Peter's Out, 5.9
94. Where The Fughowi, 5.5
96. Moguls, 5.9 ★★
101. Chet's Arête, 5.8 ★★

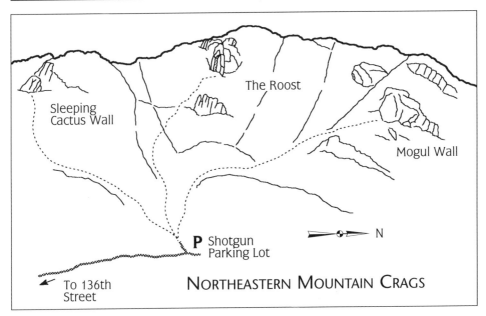

Sleeping Cactus Wall

The Roost

Mogul Wall

N

P Shotgun Parking Lot

To 136th Street

NORTHEASTERN MOUNTAIN CRAGS

areas have all received attention and have some routes that are well worth your time and attention.

The following instructions will apply to those formations on the northeastern side of the mountain: Mogul Wall, Sleeping Cactus Wall and The Roost. All of these areas are approached from what is known as the Shotgun Parking Area, situated below and left (southeast) of Mogul Wall. It is possible to hike in from 136th St. to these climbs if you don't have a high clearance vehicle.

Drive out past Pinnacle Peak and continue on past Reata Pass to the intersection of Alma School Road and Dynamite. Make a right and go east on Dynamite (Rio Verde). Make a left on 136th Street (dirt road) off of Rio Verde and go north past Power Line Road. One mile north of Power Line Road, go left through gate (Close the gate behind you!). Bear left at the "Y"; straight at the "T" and on to the end of the road (0.8 mile). If all goes well, this will put you in the parking area. This last section past the gate requires a high-clearance vehicle (Two-wheel Drive).

Sleeping Cactus Wall

This is an east-facing, 80 foot, wall on the east side of Little Granite Mountain. It has several right-leaning cracks on its right side. You can see this wall just to the south over the ridge line from The Roost on the drive in off of 136th Street. It appears as a somewhat square formation from the road. (Note: You cannot see this wall from the Shotgun Parking Area!) From the parking area, you will see a ridge line to your left (south) that runs up and to the left of The Roost. There are two "notches" in the ridge line. Hike towards the upper "notch" by whatever game trail works best. When you get to the "notch," go right (west) and you will be able to see Sleeping Cactus Wall. The rest is easy. Standard descent for Sleeping Cactus Wall: For all climbs, you can set up a rappel from a two-bolt anchor at the top of **Jibbering Seconds** or downclimb to the west and then north and around to the bottom of the wall. Rappelling is easier, but getting over to the anchor is kind of tricky.

Routes are described from left to right.

68. **Left Face, 5.10a** ★   This is the route at the far left side of the wall with one bolt about 15 feet up. Climb face past one bolt and crux to easier Cl. 4 to top. Rumor has it

that Peter Hogan put in the bolt but was unable to complete the route due to wasted arms. The route was "finished" on lead in January of 1992 with bolts to make it a safe climb. After the route had been "finished", it was found that Larry Braten may have done the route in its original "X" rated condition. Pro: Four bolts, assorted small to large pro for belay.

69. **Dublin - High Road, 5.7**   Climb right-arching off-width to a small platform; then up crack through flakes to horizontal crack. Follow this up and right to large vertical crack and on to top. Pro: Small to large stoppers, Friends.

70. **Dublin - Low Road, 5.8**   Five feet right of **High Road**, climb right-arching undercling past platform to join **High Road** just below large vertical crack. Pro: Small to large stoppers, Friends.

71. **The Bickerson's Dirty Habits, 5.9 ★★**   Thin and steep. A demanding lead. About five feet right of **Low Road**, climb parallel cracks to flake crack to horizontal crack. Step up to bolt on face and continue past second bolt to top. Exit route to the right. Pro: Small to large stoppers, Friends.

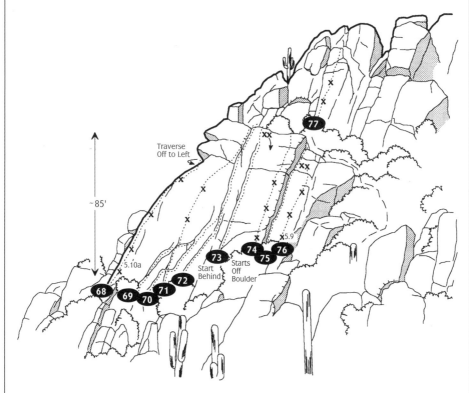

SLEEPING CACTUS WALL

68. Left Face, 5.10a ★
69. Dublin - High Road, 5.7
70. Dublin - Low Road, 5.8
71. The Bickerson's Dirty Habits, 5.9 ★★
72. Tupelo Honey, 5.9+ ★
73. Jibbering seconds, 5.7
74. Chasm View, 5.10a ★★
75. Fake Out Flake, 5.7
76. Greg And Al's Excellent Adventure, 5.9 ★
77. Martin Luther King (a.k.a. The Preacher and the Car Salesman), 5.8+ ★

SLEEPING
CACTUS
WALL

72. **Tupelo Honey, 5.9+** ★   *She's as sweet as Tupelo Honey!* This one has some really sweet moves as well. Start five feet right of **The Bickerson's Dirty Habits**, climb the thin right-leaning seam to join the **Dublins** at large vertical crack. Pro: Small to medium stoppers, Friends.

73. **Jibbering Seconds, 5.7**   15 feet right of **Tupelo Honey**, climb the prominent (wide), right-leaning crack. Some crusty rock may be encountered. Pro: Small to large stoppers, Friends.

74. **Chasm View, 5.10a** ★★   The climbing on this route will definitely keep your attention. Start fifteen feet right from **Jibbering Seconds** at right side of main wall. Step onto the face from the large boulder to clip the first bolt (or climb up from below–harder). Climb up through horizontal past two more bolts to ledge. Step right and climb past horizontal to top. Pro: Three bolts, small stoppers, tri-cam and medium Friends.

75. **Fake Out Flake, 5.7**   Just to the right of the **Chasm View** face, climb wide crack in right-facing corner to ledge, then up small crack/face to belay at small tree (or belay at **Excellent Adventure**, anchor and rappel off). Pro: Medium to large friends.

76. **Greg And Al's Excellent Adventure, 5.9** ★   Climb the face just right of **Fake Out Flake** past three bolts to a two-bolt belay. Rap the route. The route had most likely been toproped prior to being bolted. Pro: Three bolts.

77. **Martin Luther King (a.k.a. The Preacher and the Car Salesman), 5.8+** ★   On a small crag just above the top of **Fake Out Flake**, climb the face to the right of the chimney. Hard start is avoidable by stepping off the boulder to the left. Climb up past two bolts to top. Pro is tricky in the crappy rock at the top. A large stopper or medium tri-cam may be used. Take a large sling to help with the belay as well. Pro: Two bolts, large stopper/medium tri-cam

The Roost

This is an obvious east-facing, open book formation up the hill (west) and slightly left (south) of the Shotgun Parking Area. The best approach is to work your way left out of the parking lot along the upper side of the gully that heads up to The Roost. When you see a gully heading off right to the bottom of the wall, you can cut right and bushwhack/boulder hop

96

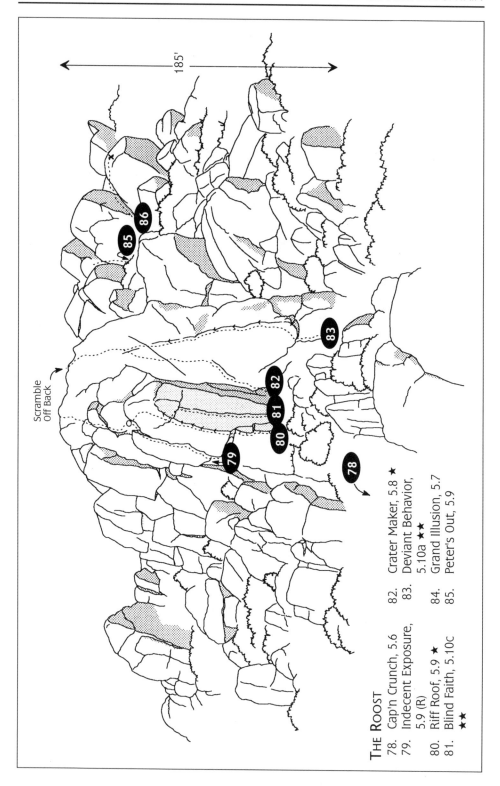

185'

Scramble
Off Back

THE ROOST

78. Cap'n Crunch, 5.6
79. Indecent Exposure,
    5.9 (R)
80. Riff Roof, 5.9 ★
81. Blind Faith, 5.10c
    ★★

82. Crater Maker, 5.8 ★
83. Deviant Behavior,
    5.10a ★★
84. Grand Illusion, 5.7
85. Peter's Out, 5.9

to the base of The Roost. There are no established climber trails but there's a pretty decent game trail along the upper side of the gully. Standard descent from The Roost: From all routes in the main dihedral, descent seems to be walking off the top to the northwest. To finish the routes on the left side, you have to ascend a short off-width section to top out and walk off.

THE ROOST

78. **Cap'n Crunch, 5.6** This route is located on outcrop approximately 100 yards down below The Roost. Start at center of face where crack/seam leads up to obvious roof. Climb crack, exiting to right side of roof. Pro Small to medium pro.

79. **Indecent Exposure, 5.9 (R)** This route climbs the left arête of the large open book. First Pitch: Face past horizontal crack to bolt. Continue on face (5.9 (R)) to ledge with horizontal crack. Second Pitch: Easy face and wide crack directly above to top. Scramble south to walk off in either direction. Pro: Three bolts, small to medium pro

80. **Riff Roof, 5.9 ★** Start 50 yards up, left of **Indecent Exposure** and at base of obvious crack with 4-foot roof. Climb face to roof, turn roof (5.9) and continue in crack to face and top (70 feet). Pro: Small to medium pro

81. **Blind Faith, 5.10c ★★** Start 25 feet right of **Indecent Exposure** at center of face forming the left wall of the large dihedral. First Pitch: Climb obvious hand-and-finger crack until it ends. Continue on face, lleft past bolt to arête and join **Indecent Exposure** at its third bolt. Second Pitch: Continue up **Indecent Exposure** to top. Pro: Small to medium stoppers, Friends, two bolts.

82. **Crater Maker, 5.8 ★** Start at center of face which forms right wall of large dihedral (opposite **Blind Faith**). Climb crack and face to bolt. Continue on face past three more bolts up and right to arête. Follow arête past horizontal crack and another bolt to top on easier ground. Additional bolts (at the suggestion of the first ascent party) were put in after the first ascent to get rid of the route's original "X" protection rating. Pro: Five bolts, small to medium pro

83. **Deviant Behavior, 5.10a ★★** Start at right side of large dihedral at base of wall. Route follows obvious arête formed by right dihedral wall. Climb face past bolt (5.10a) to gain horizontal crack and arête. Continue on arête past two more bolts to join **Crater**

Maker at the top. Belayer must climb 15 feet for leader to finish (185 feet!) Pro: Three bolts, small to medium pro

84. **Grand Illusion, 5.7**   70 feet up and right of **Deviant Behavior**, Climb obvious corner system with thin crack. Continue in corner to top. Pro: Small to large nuts.

85. **Peter's Out, 5.9**   This climb is located off the top of the right dihedral, on the northwest side of The Roost formation. The route is a 30-foot J-shaped crack that dies out to face climbing for the last ten feet. Good moves get you off the ground and into the crack from a small overhang. Pro: Small to medium pro (same for belay). FA 1987 Jan Holdeman, Peter Hogan

86. **Bumps, 5.6**   Route is located in a boulder alcove approximately 30 feet to the right of **Peter's Out**. Climb knobby face on south side (inside alcove) of the Fresh Nugs Boulder past one bolt to top. One-bolt rappel back down route. Pro: One bolt, one belay bolt.

87. **Matterhorn, 5.6**   150 yards northwest (right) and up from **Grand Illusion**. Climb double cracks in shallow chimney to large horn and belay ledge. Pro: Small to large pro.

88. **Wetterhorn, 5.7**   Start 25 feet right and around corner of **Matterhorn** at obvious handcrack. Climb crack to horn and ledge. Pro: Small to medium pro.

Mogul Wall

This is a large east-facing wall on the north end of Little Granite Mountain. The wall was named for the scoops found on the center-left portion of the wall that resemble moguls on a ski run. Mogul Wall is the biggest wall off to the northwest as you stand in the Shotgun Parking Area. From the left side, use whatever trail looks good to work your way up to the wall. This is the land of catclaw, so long pants–at the very least–are a good idea. Standard descent for Mogul Wall: You can walk down from the top of the wall by going off the top, around and down to the south (see topo). You can also do a rappel (two ropes) from the palo verde tree at the top of **Where The Fughowi**.

89. **Incognito, 5.9 ★**   >This climb is located on a 30-foot wall below Mogul Wall. Climb the crack with a large flake lodged in it. Hand to fist crack. Pro: Small to large pro.

90. **Writer's Block, 5.5+**   Two feet left of **Duckin' For Jesus** above a barrel cactus. Scramble up boulders. Climb crack at right-facing dihedral. Traverse to right under overhanging block, then continue up crack to palo verde tree (Rap station). 35 feet Pro: Large hexes, medium Friends.

91. **Buckets Of Quicksand, 5.6**   At far left end of Mogul Wall, climb face past the diagonal crack. Above the crack, traverse right to vertical crack and follow it to top. Watch out for a couple of beehives to the left of the start. (90 feet). Pro: Small to large stoppers, Friends.

92. **Duckin' For Jesus, 5.6 ★**   Dihedral above and left of gully/chimney. Climb the right-facing dihedral, then traverse right onto face to arête, then up face to top. Pro: Small to large nuts, Friends.
    Variation, 5.7   Climb chimney above, but go out on face before dihedral.
    Variation, 5.8   Start 5 feet right of and before chimney. Climb face midway between **Duckin'** and **Made In The Shade**.

93. **Made In The Shade, 5.10a**   20 feet right of **Dukin' For Jesus** and left of **We're the Fughowi**. Climb past horizontal cracks to prow past bolt, then on face past two bolts to top. Pro: Three Bolts, small nuts.

94. **Where The Fughowi, 5.5**   Just right of **Made In The Shade**. Climb shallow chimney to handcrack. Face climb to top on left side of gully. Pro: Small to large nuts, Friends.

95. **Bitches' Itch, 5.9**   Start ten feet right and around the corner from **We're the Fughowi**. Climb finger crack to roof. Turn roof on right and continue on face joining **We're the Fughowi** (see below) at handcrack. Pro: Small to large nuts, Friends.
    Variation, 5.5   Same route as above, but turn roof on left.

MOGUL WALL (AKA TEENAGE FACE)

96. **Moguls, 5.9** ★★   Start ten feet right of **Bitch's Itch**. Climb short crack past small roof to face. Continue past bolts to top. Pro: Six Bolts

97. **Rampit, 5.7**   Start 1 feet' right of Moguls. First Pitch: Climb crack in center of face to bowl. Second Pitch: Continue up ramp to right-angle flake with small roof. Pro: Small to large pieces.

98. **Manly Bulges, 5.10b**   Start ten feet right of **Rampit**. Climb finger crack to face. Face climb past bolt to crack. Pro: One bolt, small to large nuts.

99. **Tolkien Roof, 5.7**   Climb right facing, low-angle dihedral to roof. Surmount roof via handcrack. Joins **Rampit** to end. Pro: Very small wireds to medium pieces.

100. **Won't Get Fooled Again, 5.11a** ★★   Start above **Manly Bulges** at base of trough. Climb trough past cracks to ledge and bolt. Face climb past second bolt to undercling and third bolt. Continue on face directly above bolt to top. Pro: Three bolts.

101. **Chet's Arête, 5.8** ★★   50 feet right of **Rampit** (right of loose gully) climb obvious asthetic rounded-arête. First bolt is 3 feet left of the arête, then up and right 8 feet' on top of arête to large belay blocks. Pro: Four bolts.

102. **S & M, 5.9+** ★   20 yards. to the right of **Manly Bulges** at base of distinct buttress. Climb face past bolt (5.9+) to gain right-angling flake. Follow flake to end then face to the top. Pro: One bolt, small to large nuts.

103. **Fatal Attraction, 5.7** ★   50 feet to the right of **S & M** at center of low-angle slab. Climb discontinuous seam to horizontal crack. Continue on face (5.7) to the top. Pro: One bolt, small to large nuts.

The following routes are located on the short wall that sits just above the top of Mogul Wall.

104. **Okay With Gaye, 5.7+** ★   On a small, rectangular wall 200 yards south and above Mogul Wall, climb left-facing dihedral. Pro: Small to medium nuts and Friends.

105. **Fu Man Chew, 5.9** ★   Start 150 feet above **Dukin' For Jesus**. Climb right arching handcrack. Pro: Small to large nuts.

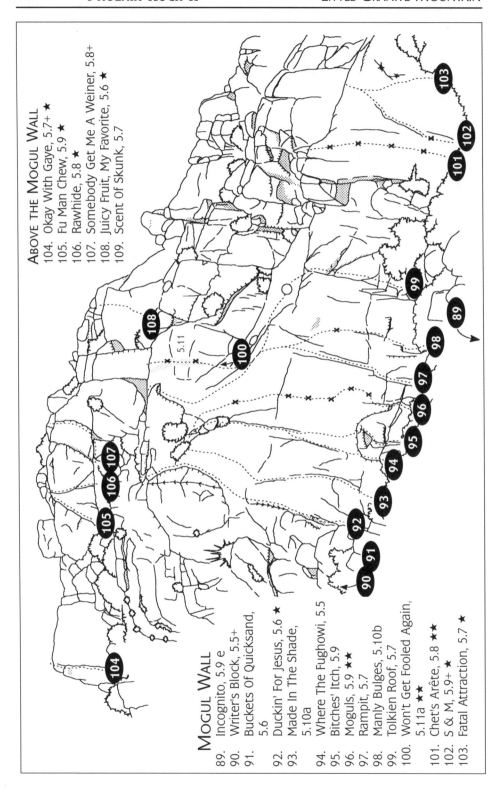

ABOVE THE MOGUL WALL
104. Okay With Gaye, 5.7+ ★
105. Fu Man Chew, 5.9
106. Rawhide, 5.8 ★
107. Somebody Get Me A Weiner, 5.8+
108. Juicy Fruit, My Favorite, 5.6 ★
109. Scent Of Skunk, 5.7

MOGUL WALL
89. Incognito, 5.9 e
90. Writer's Block, 5.5+
91. Buckets Of Quicksand, 5.6
92. Duckin' For Jesus, 5.6 ★
93. Made In The Shade, 5.10a
94. Where The Fughowi, 5.5
95. Bitches' Itch, 5.9
96. Moguls, 5.9 ★★
97. Rampit, 5.7
98. Manly Bulges, 5.10b
99. Tolkien Roof, 5.7
100. Won't Get Fooled Again, 5.11a ★★
101. Chet's Arête, 5.8 ★★
102. S & M, 5.9+ ★
103. Fatal Attraction, 5.7 ★

106. **Rawhide, 5.8 ★** Start ten feet to the right of **Fu Man Chew**. Finger/handcrack to top. Pro: Small to large nuts.

107. **Somebody Get Me A Weiner, 5.8+** Game Seven, World Series. 50 feet left of **Juicy Fruit, My Favorite**, ascend right-leaning handcrack to roof. Traverse right under roof to alcove, then go up to low-angle dihedral and on to top. Descend by walking off to north. Pro: Small to large pieces.

108. **Juicy Fruit, My Favorite, 5.6 ★** 200 feet above and north of Mogul Wall where an east-facing slab joins a very large roof. Ascend the slab, climb the vertical crack to horizontal crack, continue on face past three bolts to top (60 feet.) Pro: Three bolts, medium hex or Friends.

Some climbing has been done on a small formation that lies just north of the approach drive to the Shotgun Parking Area. It is believed that the following route is on this formation, known by the names Skunk Slab and also Knee Wall.

109. **Scent Of Skunk, 5.7** Low angle face on Skunk Slab. Pro: Three bolts.

Tim Schneider on **Silhouette** (5.8), Pinnacle Peak South; one of the newer routes on Pinnacle Peak. For route description, see page 169.

Chapter 6

McDOWELL MOUNTAINS

The McDowell Mountain climbing areas detailed in this chapter contain the largest concentration of granite routes in the Phoenix area. Most of the crags are found on the northern slopes of the mountain range and are easily visible from that side. Other formations have also been developed within the many washes and valleys that riddle the mountain range just south of the main northern areas, Most of these will require at least one of (but not limited to) the following: good pair of hiking shoes, extra water and a sharp eye.

The well established crags in the area (Sven Slab, Morrell's Wall, Gardener's Wall and Tom's Thumb) offer many types of enjoyable routes on solid, (mostly) dependable rock. The less-travelled formations (Hog Heaven, Goat Hill, Sven Towers and Granite Ballroom) will be a bit more of an adventure, both to approach and to climb, but offer some of the same quality climbing as the more accessible formations. It is a good idea to keep an eye out for loose rock and friable holds while climbing in any of the remote areas as they don't see a lot of climber traffic and consequently aren't as cleaned off as the traveled routes.

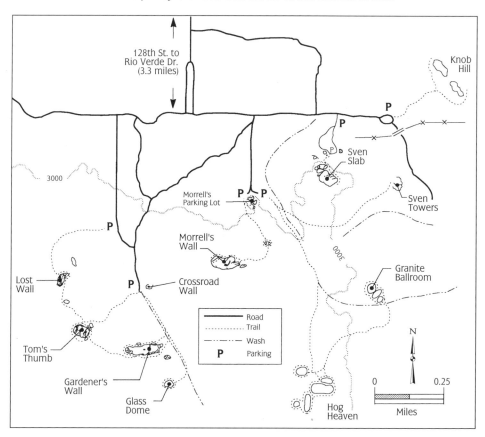

Fire Scorches McDowell Park

July 7th, 1995, a bolt of lightning set off a fire that completely wasted much of the McDowell Mountain range, from Rio Verde Drive on the north running over the mountains to the south nearly all the way to Fountain Hills. Known as the "Rio" fire, it eventually covered a 20,000 acre area and overran most of the climbing areas in this chapter. While most of the desert in this area now resembles the face of the moon, the rock made it through with little or no damage in most cases. This may help to slow the housing development of this area, but expect the construction (and it's associated access problems) to continue unabated within the next few years.

Approach: From the Scottsdale area, drive north on Scottsdale Road to Pinnacle Peak Road. Turn right (east) on this Pinnacle Peak Rd. and continue on Pima Road, Happy Valley Road and Alma School Road to reach Dynamite Road. Turn right and drive east on Dynamite until you reach 128th Street. Turn right on 128th Street and follow dirt (at least for now) road 3.3 miles to its end. At this point refer to McDowell Mountain's Aerial for more complete directions to the individual crags. For those that live on the western side of I-17, Bell Road can be taken east to Cave Creek Road. Take Cave Creek northeast until it intersects with Pinnacle Peak Road. Go east (right) on Pinnacle Peak Road for several miles until it passes Scottsdale Road. Continue on Pima as noted above. See the Map of Phoenix Crags for more detail.

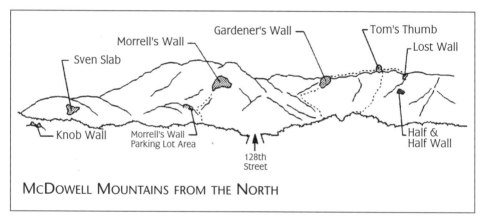

McDOWELL MOUNTAINS FROM THE NORTH

Access: The McDowell Mountains are almost totally private property. More development has been taking place in the area immediately to the north of the mountains over the last two or three years, so be forewarned that the houses and golf courses are on the way. As the development takes hold, the current access points are sure to change; and in some cases, areas might be closed off. Please stay advised and park where you will not offend land owners. Two recent developments will hopefully help to save these climbing areas for future generations of climbers. The damage due to the Rio fire (see above) should make the area somewhat less attractive to land buyers, at least in the near term and the recent passage of a tax bill by Scottsdale voters is supposed to provide money to buy up more land in the McDowells to turn it into a mountain park. It remains to be seen if the climbing areas will be included in this plan, but there's always hope! The best things climbers can do are to continue low-impact climbing practices and to get involved in the ongoing struggle for access to these historic climbing locations.

Lost Wall

This southeast-facing wall is located just below the ridge line to the northwest of Tom's Thumb, the most prominent landmark on the ridge. It features moderately difficult climbs on an almost 90' wall.

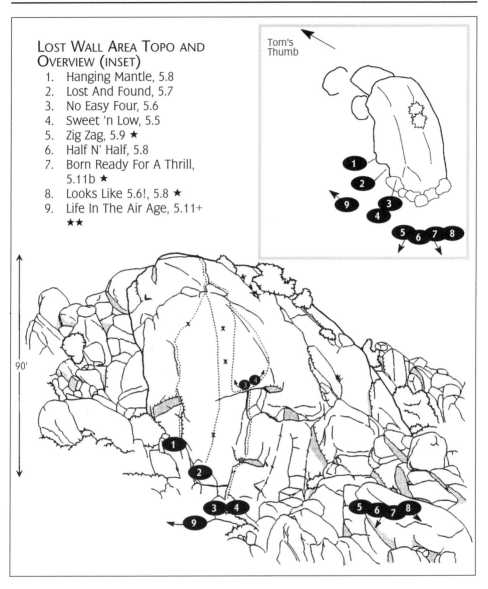

Lost Wall Area Topo and Overview (inset)

1. Hanging Mantle, 5.8
2. Lost And Found, 5.7
3. No Easy Four, 5.6
4. Sweet 'n Low, 5.5
5. Zig Zag, 5.9 ★
6. Half N' Half, 5.8
7. Born Ready For A Thrill, 5.11b ★
8. Looks Like 5.6!, 5.8 ★
9. Life In The Air Age, 5.11+ ★★

Tom's Thumb

1. **Hanging Mantle, 5.8**   Start at left (southwest) end of wall below overhang. Climb up overhang, then continue on face to flake. At top of flake, traverse right past bolt, then up face to top. Pro: Medium nuts, one bolt.

2. **Lost And Found, 5.7**   Start 10 feet down and right (northeast) of **Hanging Mantle** on top of V-shaped lip. Climb face to bolt, then continue on face to left end of horizontal crack. Move past crack and climb face left of two bolts to top. Pro: Medium nuts, three bolts.

3. **No Easy Four, 5.6**   Start 4 feet right (northeast) of **Lost and Found** on top of large standing flake in gully. Climb crack system directly above to horizontal crack. Traverse crack left until below bolt on face above. Climb face staying right of two bolts to top. Pro: Medium nuts, two bolts.

4. **Sweet 'n Low, 5.5**   Start is same as No Easy Four. Climb cracks up to their end, then continue up on face past two bolts to top. Pro: Friends, medium nuts, two bolts.

5. **Zig Zag, 5.9★** Start at rock below Sweet 'N Low on boulder at very bottom of north face. Climb face to uppermost horizontal crack, then follow crack left to base of right-arching crack. Follow arching crack up to alcove (bolt). Exit up and left to bulge where bolt allows one to rappel to ground. Pro: Small to medium nuts, Friends, one bolt, one rappel bolt.

6. **Half N' Half, 5.8** This route is located on a prominent, east-facing, white slab split by a horizontal crack approximately 100 yards below and slightly right of Lost Wall. Start on left side of slab. Climb face past two bolts and horizontal crack to top. Pro: Two bolts, small to medium nuts.

7. **Born Ready For A Thrill, 5.11b ★** Start down and right of **Half N' Half** approximately 30 feet. Climb undercling (5.11b) right into right-facing dihedral. Follow crack to top. Pro: Small to large nuts, Friends.

8. **Looks Like 5.6!, 5.8 ★** Start down and left from **Half N' Half** approximately 150 feet. Climb gully up into right-facing corner, then follow corner until possible to step left onto face to gain access to crack (5.8). Follow crack to top. Pro: Medium to large nuts, Friends.

The following route is found on a diamond-shaped face in the drainage between Tom's Thumb and Lost Wall (opposite side of drainage from Lost Wall).

9. **Life In The Air Age, 5.11+ ★★** Climb the diamond-shaped face (facing Lost Wall) past three bolts. Hard route. Pro: Three bolts

Fort McDowell

This area lies down below Lost Wall. It can be identified by a prominent stain on it's east face and a dorsal, fin-like rock above it. No topo is shown.

10. **Flipper's Testicle Stretch, 5.9** Start on the right side of the east face. Gain the left side by traversing the double crack to the vertical thin crack. Climb the crack up and left off the face towards the dorsal fin. Pro: Small nuts, Friends
Sandshark Variation, 5.7 After climbing the vertical crack, proceed straight up over two summit blocks. Pro: Small nuts, Friends

11. **Almost Whitney, 5.6** Start on southeast corner. Climb thin cracks under the stacked buttress, then short face section above. Pro: Medium nuts, Friends

Tom's Thumb

This incredible formation perches atop a ridge in the McDowell and is visible on clear days from the city. Named for one of Tom Krueser's opposable appendages, not enough can be

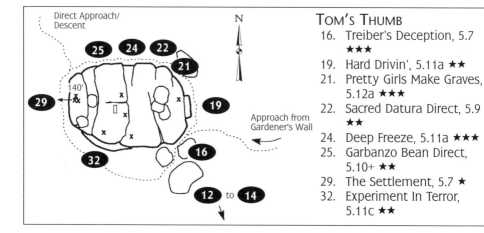

TOM'S THUMB
16. Treiber's Deception, 5.7 ★★★
19. Hard Drivin', 5.11a ★★
21. Pretty Girls Make Graves, 5.12a ★★★
22. Sacred Datura Direct, 5.9 ★★
24. Deep Freeze, 5.11a ★★★
25. Garbanzo Bean Direct, 5.10+ ★★
29. The Settlement, 5.7 ★
32. Experiment In Terror, 5.11c ★★

said about the spectacular climbs that abound in this single area. Not only that, the views of the Valley of the Sun are spectacular from the summit. Recently named "Best Climbing Area" in a Best of Phoenix publication (climbing goes mainstream?), Tom's Thumb is by far the most recommended area in the McDowells. Standard Descent for Tom's Thumb: Rappel (two ropes, 140 feet) off three-bolt anchor at west end of pinnacle.

12. **Slip 'n Slide, 5.5** ★ Start approximately 200 yards southeast of Tom's Thumb at base of southwest facing slab. Climb brown water streak past three bolts to top. Pro: Three bolts, small to medium nuts.
    Variation, 5.9 Instead of following brown water streak, climb thin crack just right and join regular route at third bolt. Pro: Small nuts.

13. **Venturi Highway, 5.6** About 40 feet to the right of **Slip 'N Slide** is a large chimney. Climb a right arching crack found on the left (north) wall of the chimney. Continue on face to climb out left using crack between chimney and chockstones. When crack runs out, move up and left to belay. Scramble off east. Pro: Medium to large nuts, slings.

14. **Barbeque Chips And Beer, 5.7** 40 feet left of Slip 'N Slide, climb over a small roof and up face past four bolts. Pro: Four bolts

15. **Water Drawn From an Ancient Well, 5.7** Start approximately 20 yards east–southeast from Tom's Thumb at east face of 30-foot boulder. From just right of triangular shaped rock, climb thin crack system to a larger left-leaning crack. Continue straight up on face, past left-leaning crack, to saddle-shaped top. Pro: Small to medium nuts.

16. **Treiber's Deception, 5.7** ★★★ This route's name is most appropriate considering that the original rating was 5.5! Start at left end of southeast face. Chimney up between large boulder and wall until possible to step across onto wall. Continue in

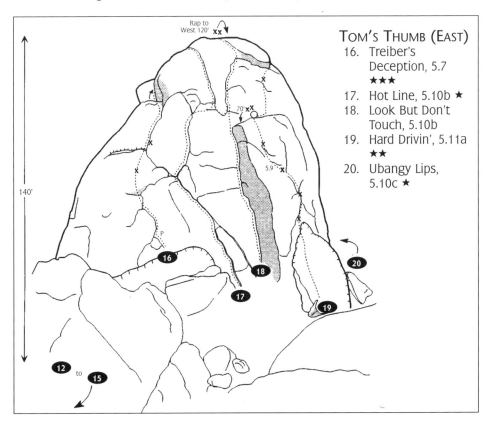

Tom's Thumb (East)

16. Treiber's Deception, 5.7 ★★★
17. Hot Line, 5.10b ★
18. Look But Don't Touch, 5.10b
19. Hard Drivin', 5.11a ★★
20. Ubangy Lips, 5.10c ★

crack past fixed piton up to short face. Climb face past bolt and up and left to base of short wide crack. Continue up crack past bolt and left to base of another wide crack. Follow crack to top. Pro: One fixed piton (may or may not be there), medium to large nuts, two bolts

Men At Work Variation, 5.11a   Instead of regular start, scramble down left between boulder and wall to start of overhanging crack. Climb crack direct until it joins regular route. Pro: Medium to large nuts (#5 Camelot may prove useful).

17. **Hot Line, 5.10b ★**   Start 20 feet right and up from Treiber's Deception. Climb lower crack of two left-leaning cracks up and left (5.9) until they join, then continue in crack (5.10a) until possible to move up past rotten rock into small alcove. Continue up crack (5.10b) until possible to traverse right into another vertical crack. Follow crack to top. Pro: Medium to large nuts, Friends, one fixed piton.

    Powell Variation, 5.8   Instead of moving up into alcove, continue traversing left to join Treiber's Deception. Pro: Medium nuts.

18. **Look But Don't Touch, 5.10b**   Aesthetic-looking climb but unaesthetic rock. This climb has the potential to be led in one pitch. Be careful under any circumstances! Start six feet right from Hot Line. First Pitch: Climb off-width and chimney to large ledge (5.9). Second Pitch: Traverse left (5.10b) into crack system that leads to top. Pro: Tube chocks, Friends, one bolt, medium to large nuts.

19. **Hard Drivin', 5.11a ★★**   It probably took five times longer to drill the bolts than to do the moves! As a interesting point, this climb was originally rated 5.9, an incredible "sandbag". Start around corner (east and north) from **Look But Don't Touch** at face that is formed by a large flake. First Pitch: Climb face on flake approximately 30 feet to a bolt. Step over chasm at top of flake onto face, where climbing up and left (5.9) past three bolts leads to large ledge with two belay bolts (this is a good pitch for 5.9 leaders!). Second Pitch: Move right on ledge, then climb face past small, discontinuous, horizontal cracks and bolt (5.11a) to horizontal crack. Follow crack right and then another crack up to top. Pro: Five bolts, two belay bolts, small nuts, Friends.

20. **Ubangy Lips, 5.10c ★**   On the first ascent bolt hangers were forgotten. The leader had to tie-off the bolt driver to finish the lead. Gulp!!!!!!! Start around corner (north and west) from **Hard Drivin'** in a chimney system. Scramble chimney until possible to step into a crack on main wall. Climb crack up and slightly right into the "lips" (5.9). Continue out right side in small crack that eventually disappears. Continue on face (5.10c) past bolt to crack system that leads to top. Pro: Small to medium nuts, one bolt.

21. **Pretty Girls Make Graves, 5.12a ★★★**   Start at indistinct aréte between **Ubangy Lips** and **Sacred Datura**. Climb face and aréte (5.12a) past four bolts. Join **Ubangy Lips** at bolt and continue on face to horizontal crack. Step right and climb face up over small roof, then continue on aréte past bolt to top. Pro: Six bolts, Friends, small nuts.

22. **Sacred Datura Direct, 5.9 ★★**   Good rock and continuous climbing characterize this route. Start 20 feet right from **Ubangy Lips.** Climb small dihedral until possible to step right onto face. Continue up face past a bolt and right into another vertical crack. Climb crack (5.8) to alcove. Climb crack and face directly above (5.9) to horizontal crack and bolt. Continue to top via small, discontinuous cracks and face directly above (5.8). Pro: Small to medium nuts, two bolts.

23. **Sucubus, 5.10a ★★**   Don't take this one lightly! Start 15 feet right from **Sacred Datura Direct**. Climb crack to small roof, then continue in small crack right around roof (5.10a) to bolt. Continue in wide crack to top (5.9). Pro: Small to large nuts, one bolt.

24. **Deep Freeze, 5.11a ★★★**   One of the best climbs in Phoenix! Start 25 feet right from **Sucubus**. Step off flake onto face to enter vertical crack. Climb crack past bolt (5.11a) where unusual climbing in "pockets" leads to a final bulge. Clear final bulge via crack (5.11a) and onto a face that leads up past two bolts and left to top. Pro: Small to large nuts, three bolts.

25. **Garbanzo Bean Direct, 5.10+ ★★**   Why skip all that beautiful rock below the upper slot of **Garbanzo Bean**? Climb steep face past five bolts to join **Garbanzo Bean**

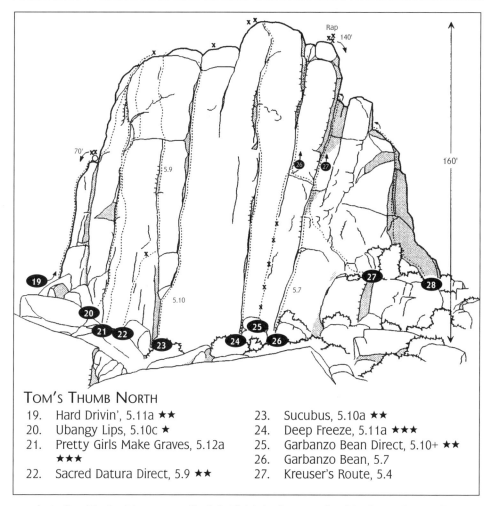

Tom's Thumb North

19. Hard Drivin', 5.11a ★★
20. Ubangy Lips, 5.10c ★
21. Pretty Girls Make Graves, 5.12a ★★★
22. Sacred Datura Direct, 5.9 ★★

23. Sucubus, 5.10a ★★
24. Deep Freeze, 5.11a ★★★
25. Garbanzo Bean Direct, 5.10+ ★★
26. Garbanzo Bean, 5.7
27. Kreuser's Route, 5.4

just after it's short traverse to the left. Finish in that route's wide slot to the top. Pro: Five bolts, medium to large pro.

26. **Garbanzo Bean, 5.7**   Start eight feet right from **Deep Freeze**. Climb crack, then continue on easy climbing (**Kreuser's Route**) to fixed piton. Step left onto pink band of rock on face and traverse left (5.7) to wide vertical crack. Continue to top via crack. Pro: Medium to large nuts, one fixed piton.

27. **Kreuser's Route, 5.4**   This route on the north corner is named after Tom Kreuser and the entire pinnacle commemorates his thumb. Start 50 feet right and up from **Garbanzo Bean**. First Pitch: Climb crack system and ramps left and then up chimney to large ledge (5.4). Second Pitch: Join **West Corner** to top (Cl. 4). Pro: Medium to large nuts, one fixed piton, belay bolts.

   Variation, 5.6   Instead of regular start, start just right of **Garbanzo Bean**. Climb short crack to join regular route. Pro: Medium nuts.

28. **Great Compromise, 5.9**   Start at left (north) end of west face. First Pitch: Climb ramp system up and right to left-leaning crack. Climb crack (5.9), then up and right to ledge. Second Pitch: Join **West Corner** to top (Cl. 4). Pro: Small to large nuts, belay bolts.

29. **The Settlement, 5.7 ★**   Start off obvious large detached flake on west face. First Pitch: Climb face to bolt, then continue right past bolt to crack and overhang. Climb

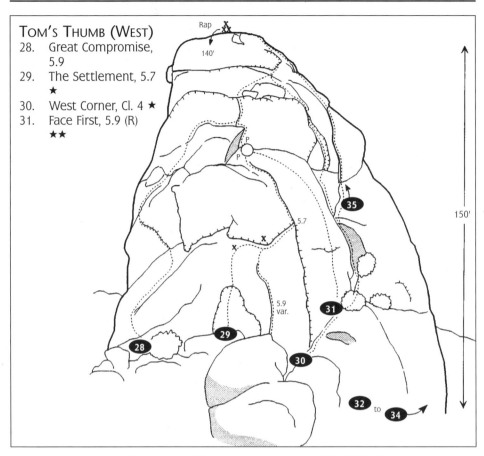

Tom's Thumb (West)
28. Great Compromise, 5.9
29. The Settlement, 5.7 ★
30. West Corner, Cl. 4 ★
31. Face First, 5.9 (R) ★★

overhang up and left (5.7) to platform. Continue up short dihedral and crack to large ledge. Second Pitch: Join **West Corner** to top (Cl. 4). Pro: Medium nuts, two fixed pitons, belay bolts.

Variation, 5.6 (R)   After climbing face to first bolt, continue straight above over bulge and face to join regular route. Pro: None.

Variation, 5.9   Instead of regular start, move right a few feet. Climb thin crack to join regular route. Pro: Small nuts.

Variation, 5.6   Instead of regular start, move right to base of chimney. Climb chimney through rotten rock to join regular route at overhang. Pro: Large nuts.

30. **West Corner, Cl. 4 ★**   Being the first route to the top of the pinnacle, Dick Hart and Bill McMorris originally named the **Thumb the Dork**. Somehow this name was lost in time until after **Tom's Thumb** became the accepted name. Start 20 feet right from **The Settlement**. First Pitch: Scramble up gully and ledge system 25 feet to tree belay. Second Pitch: Climb the left, wide-crack system up, then traverse right under overhang and up to top. Pro: Medium to large nuts, belay bolts.

31. **Face First, 5.9 (R) ★★**   Let's hope one doesn't do a "face first" on this climb. Start up and right of **The Settlement** or scramble partway up the first pitch of **West Corner** to steep south face. Climb face to horizontal crack, then continue on face past one bolt until possible to join **The Settlement** to top. Pro: One bolt, medium nuts, Friends.

32. **Experiment In Terror, 5.11c ★★**   Beware of this rating if you are under 5'10"! Originally, the rating for this climb was 5.10+. What wasn't taken into account was that the climb had been rehearsed before leading. The first ascent party now agrees with

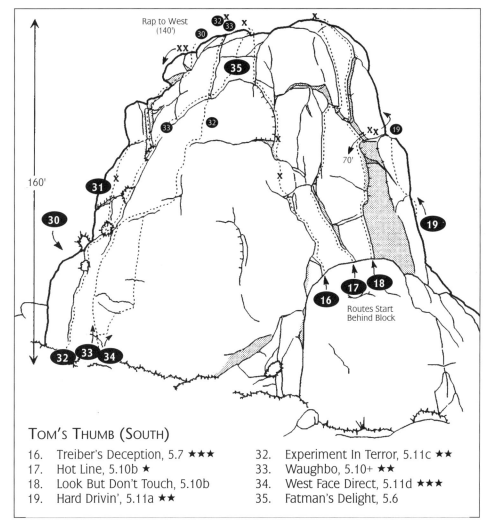

Rap to West
(140')

70'

160'

Routes Start
Behind Block

TOM'S THUMB (SOUTH)

16. Treiber's Deception, 5.7 ★★★
17. Hot Line, 5.10b ★
18. Look But Don't Touch, 5.10b
19. Hard Drivin', 5.11a ★★

32. Experiment In Terror, 5.11c ★★
33. Waughbo, 5.10+ ★★
34. West Face Direct, 5.11d ★★★
35. Fatman's Delight, 5.6

the present rating and realizes that their skills exceed 5.10+ climbing. Start near left (west) end of south face at thin, water-streaked crack. First Pitch: Climb face and crack past fixed piton to large ledge (5.11c). Second Pitch: Traverse horizontal crack right back onto south face until vertical crack. Continue up vertical crack to another horizontal crack. Cross horizontal crack and climb face above to large ledge. Third Pitch (formerly **Yurassis Dragon**): Climb finger and handcrack to top (5.8). Pro: Small to medium nuts, one fixed piton, Friends.

33. **Waughbo, 5.10+ ★★**   Start as for **West Face Direct**. Instead of going right after the first bolt of **West Face**, take the undercling flake to the left and climb past one bolt up face to ledge. Pro: Two bolts, small to medium pro.

34. **West Face Direct, 5.11d ★★★**   The last part of **Experiment in Terror** was originally conceived as the finish of this route. All in all, it makes a better line up the wall. Start 15 feet right of **Experiment in Terror**. Climb left-arching crack until able to step right onto face. Climb face to obvious ledge. Traverse ledge right to first bolt, then continue up face past two bolts, joining **Experiment in Terror**. Pro: Three bolts, small to medium nuts, Friends

35. **Fatman's Delight, 5.6** Start is same as **West Corner**. First Pitch: Scramble up gully and ledge system 25 feet to tree. Continue scrambling up and right to another tree belay. Second Pitch: Climb left-facing, short, narrow, squeeze chimney to top (5.3). Pro: Medium to large nuts, tube chocks.

The Rist

This small outcrop lies approximately 150 yards northwest of Tom's Thumb. There are three routes located on the north face. No topo shown.

36. **Yee Haa, 5.7** Climb the left crack on the north face. Pro: Unknown
37. **Last Line Of Defense, 5.9** Climb crack about 50 feet to the right of **Yee Haa**. Pro: Unknown
38. **Overtime, 5.9** Climb west end of face past diagonal crack Pro: Unknown

Parking Lot Wall

This wall is located approximately 100 yards uphill and east of the parking lot for Gardener's Wall and Tom's Thumb. See basic topo for route info.

39. **Crossroads, 5.10a ★★** Start at the left end of the wall, at crack right of low-angled–four-inch crack (two bushes). Climb thinning crack, then continue on face to next crack. Crossover crack to top. Pro: Small to medium nuts, Friends
40. **Overpass, 5.9 ★** Start ten feet to the right of Crossroads. Climb overhanging hand-crack (5.9) to easy ground. Protect in horizontal crack and climb face to top. Pro: Medium to large nuts, Friends.

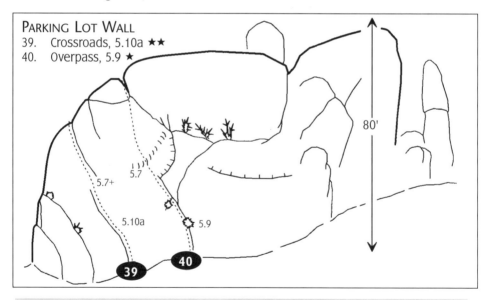

PARKING LOT WALL
39. Crossroads, 5.10a ★★
40. Overpass, 5.9 ★

Gardener's Wall

This wall was originally called Garner's Wall after Ray Garner (see history section). A good variety of crack climbs complimented by some superb face routes make this one of the best crags in the McDowells. A word of warning: since this particular wall faces north, it tends to be very cold in winter. Although it is possible to scramble off the back of the wall and back to the base, a two-bolt rappel anchor has been installed just left of the top of **Hanging Gardens**. If you take a second rope, it's a quick ride back to the ground via the three-bolt anchor at the top of **Hanging Gardens'** first pitch. Note: It is NOT possible to rappel this with only one 165-foot climbing rope.

41. **Child Of Troubled Times, 5.9 (R)** ★   This route is located on the approach to Gardener's Wall. It lies on the north face of a large boulder in a gully and becomes visible just as one crosses the rocky gully from left to right to begin the final approach to the base of the wall. Start by stepping off boulder onto face. Then make a tricky unprotected move (R) onto good foothold to reach bolt. Move on face past bolt into crack, then continue in crack past fixed piton to top. Pro: One bolt, one fixed piton.

42. **Southeast Aréte, 5.10b** ★   Start down and right below **Facer's Choice** approximately 35 feet. Climb discontinuous crack to bolt. Continue on easy face until possible to climb aréte past two bolts to top. Pro: Small to medium nuts, three bolts.

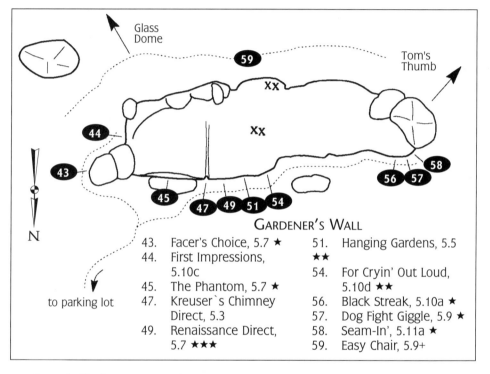

43. Facer's Choice, 5.7 ★
44. First Impressions, 5.10c
45. The Phantom, 5.7 ★
47. Kreuser`s Chimney Direct, 5.3
49. Renaissance Direct, 5.7 ★★★
51. Hanging Gardens, 5.5 ★★
54. For Cryin' Out Loud, 5.10d ★★
56. Black Streak, 5.10a ★
57. Dog Fight Giggle, 5.9 ★
58. Seam-In', 5.11a ★
59. Easy Chair, 5.9+

GARDENER'S WALL

to parking lot

43. **Facer's Choice, 5.7** ★   This route is an excellent warm-up in winter months as it faces east. Start below east end of wall at large boulder mass. Scramble right out bush-filled ledge to large crack and obvious face. Climb east face to knife-edged top. Traverse left to descend. Pro: One bolt.

44. **First Impressions, 5.10c**   Start up and slightly left from **Facer's Choice** at base of short, wide crack. Climb crack until possible to follow left-arching crack to horizontal crack. Continue in crack left (5.10c) until small ledge and then step left to larger ledge and belay. Pro: Medium to large nuts, Friends.

45. **The Phantom, 5.7** ★   Named because the first ascent party is unknown, this route offers an excellent first pitch. Start at left end (east) off large-boulder mass resting against wall. (Approach via Cl. 4, scramble from east to west.) First Pitch: Climb thin crack to large ledge (5.7). Second Pitch: Climb cracks and flakes up and left where Cl. 3 climbing leads back right to top. Pro: Small to medium nuts, one fixed piton.

Crime of the Century Variation, 5.11a   On the north face of the large-boulder mass resting against wall, climb indistinct, thin crack and face through overhang, then continue in crack systems to start of regular first pitch. Pro: Small to large nuts.

GARDENER'S WALL

42.	Southeast Aréte, 5.10b ★	49.	Renaissance Direct, 5.7 ★★★
43.	Facer's Choice, 5.7 ★	50.	Fearless Leader, 5.10a (R) ★
44.	First Impressions, 5.10c	51.	Hanging Gardens, 5.5 ★★
45.	The Phantom, 5.7 ★	52.	Brusin' And Cruisin', 5.8
46.	Gobs Of Knobs, 5.8 ★★	53.	Lickety Split, 5.7 (R) ★
47.	Kreuser`s Chimney Direct, 5.3	54.	For Cryin' Out Loud, 5.10d ★★
48.	Phantom Of The Opera, 5.10a (R) ★	55.	Gravity, 5.10a

46. **Gobs Of Knobs, 5.8 ★★**   As one traverses almost the entire face of Gardener's Wall, this girdle is guaranteed to yield "gobs of knobs". Start is same as **The Phantom**. First Pitch: Same as **The Phantom** (5.7). Second Pitch: Climb cracks and flakes until possible to traverse right and up in thin crack to vertical crack and chimney (5.8). Third Pitch: Continue traversing right across chimney and face to gully system, then continue right and slightly down to two-bolt belay (5.4). Belay is same as top of **Hanging Garden's** first pitch. Fourth Pitch: Continue traversing past two bolts and up to large ledge (5.6). Fifth Pitch: Climb crack up and over slight bulge, then continue on face and crack to top (5.6). Pro: Small to medium nuts, several bolts.

47. **Kreuser`s Chimney Direct, 5.3**   Start 15 feet right and down from **The Phantom**. First Pitch: Climb chimney to "gopher hole", then squeeze through hole and out onto face to ledge on right. Second Pitch: Move left back into chimney. Continue in chimney to top. Pro: Medium to large nuts.

48. **Phantom Of The Opera, 5.10a (R) ★**   The"R" rating should not really scare away too many climbers as it is only 5.7 and can easily be avoided if so desired. Watch out for those first moves though! Start down and right from **Kreuser's Chimney Direct** between large boulder and face at insipid crack. First Pitch: Climb face and insipid crack (5.10a) up and left. When possible, traverse left crossing **Kreuser's Chimney** into horizontal crack. Follow horizontal crack left to vertical fingercrack. Climb thin crack up to ledge and belay (same belay as top of **Phantom's** first pitch). Second Pitch: Climb face above, past two bolts to right-leaning, thin crack; cross crack and continue on face above to top (5.7 R). Pro: Small to medium nuts, Friends, two bolts.

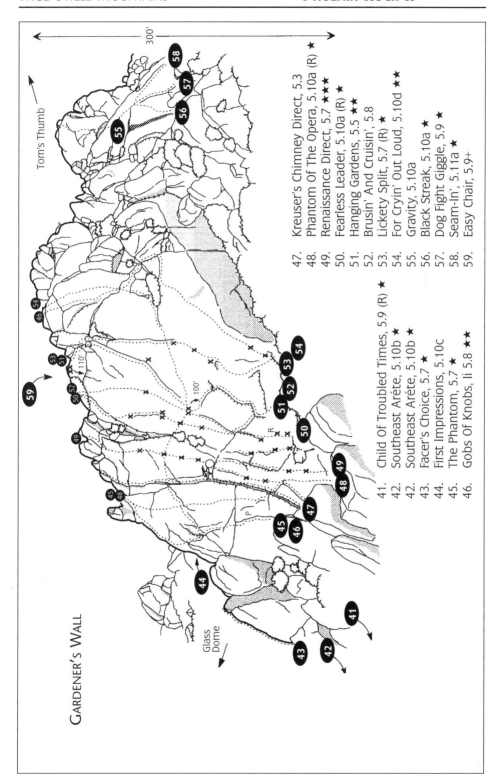

Gardener's Wall

Glass Dome

Tom's Thumb

41. Child Of Troubled Times, 5.9 (R) ★
42. Southeast Aréte, 5.10b ★
42. Southeast Aréte, 5.10b ★
43. Facer's Choice, 5.7 ★
44. First Impressions, 5.10c
45. The Phantom, 5.7 ★
46. Gobs Of Knobs, Ii 5.8 ★★

47. Kreuser's Chimney Direct, 5.3
48. Phantom Of The Opera, 5.10a (R) ★
49. Renaissance Direct, 5.7 ★★★
50. Fearless Leader, 5.10a (R) ★
51. Hanging Gardens, 5.5 ★★
52. Brusin' And Cruisin', 5.8
53. Lickety Split, 5.7 (R) ★
54. For Cryin' Out Loud, 5.10d ★★
55. Gravity, 5.10a
56. Black Streak, 5.10a ★
57. Dog Fight Giggle, 5.9 ★
58. Seam-In', 5.11a ★
59. Easy Chair, 5.9+

49. **Renaissance Direct, 5.7 ★★★**   Face climbing, crack climbing and more face climbing yield one of the more aesthetic climbs at Gardener's Wall. A must for 5.7 climbers. Start just right of **Phantom of the Opera** at face. First Pitch: Climb face past two bolts to ledge (5.7). Continue up right-facing dihedral over small roof to ledge (5.6). Move left to belay (same as **Kreuser's Chimney Direct**). Second Pitch: Climb face above past four bolts to top (5.6). Pro: Small to medium nuts, six bolts.
Parental Guidance Variation, 5.9   Instead of regular start, begin just right of **Kreuser's Chimney Direct** at base of right-leaning crack. Climb crack until left of ledge at base of dihedral on the regular first pitch. Traverse slightly left onto face. When possible, climb face (5.9) above into indistinct crack, then continue in crack to ledge. Continue on second pitch. Pro: Two bolts, small nuts to medium nuts.
Variation, 5.5   Instead of second pitch, traverse right to join **Hanging Gardens**. Continue to top via **Hanging Gardens** (5.5). Pro: None.

50. **Fearless Leader, 5.10a (R) ★**   Lots of exposure as well as a hanging belay make this an exercise in mind control. Start at a point directly underneath the left-most edge of the **Hanging Gardens** flake up on face. First Pitch: Climb face up to second bolt (5.10a), then left and up to flake and third bolt (R). Follow flake joining **Hanging Gardens**, momentarily at its extreme left, then step left and climb face up, right and then up to hanging belay. Second Pitch: Continue on face up, left and then right to top (5.6). Pro: Six bolts, two belay bolts.

51. **Hanging Gardens, 5.5 ★★**   This has traditionally been one of the all-time classics (and a really nice beginner multi-pitch climb as well). Start right and up from **Fearless Leader** below large flake situated on center of face. First Pitch: Scramble up and left to flake, then climb thin crack to small ledge. Continue in right-leaning crack to two-bolt belay on top of flake. Second Pitch: Continue up and right to vegetated crack, then follow crack to clump of trees. Traverse ten feet left; follow groove and cracks to top. Pro: Medium to large nuts.

52. **Brusin' And Cruisin', 5.8**   The question is whether to off-width (bruisin') or lieback (cruisin'). Start is same as **Hanging Gardens**. First Pitch: Scramble up and left to flake, then climb right side of flake until possible to exit left and up to two-bolt belay (5.8). Belay is same as top of **Hanging Gardens'** first pitch. Second Pitch: Climb face above up for 165' (5.2) past one bolt to top. Pro: Medium to large nuts, one bolt.

53. **Lickety Split, 5.7 (R) ★**   Originally rated 5.6, this bold lead is difficult to find because of the small number of bolts. Study the Gardener's Wall photo carefully before attempting this route. Start 25 feet right of **Hanging Gardens** at short, right-arching crack. First Pitch: Climb crack right until possible to follow indistinct, thin crack back left to large flake and crack. Then climb lichen-covered rock up past horn and right to small ledge (belay bolt) (5.7). Second Pitch: Climb face to bolt, then up and right to small down-sloping ledges and second bolt. Move left, then climb prominent water groove to reach crack. Climb crack to large clump of trees and top. Pro: Small to medium nuts, two bolts.
Variation, 5.6   Many climbers have done this variation thinking that it is the original line. When at the second bolt (second pitch), instead of moving up and right, continue up to another bolt (**Gobs of Knobs**), then continue face climbing up until possible to join **Hanging Gardens** and on to top.

54. **For Cryin' Out Loud, 5.10d ★★**   Be sure to look at the bolt hangers for a surprise! Start just right of **Lickety-Split** at short, right-arching crack. First Pitch: Follow crack to stance on flake. Climb face above to second bolt, then traverse right past two bolts into thin, right-leaning crack. Follow crack until possible to step right to bolt (5.10d), then climb face above (5.10b) to right end of ledge and horizontal crack. (Stay off of ledge as it is an owl nesting area!) Traverse horizontal crack right and up to belay. Second Pitch: Climb up and left over boulders to area under small roof. Move out left side of roof and step back right on face as soon as possible. Climb face above past three bolts to top (5.7). Pro: Small to medium nuts, eight bolts.

55. **Gravity, 5.10a**   Start at extreme right end of wall. Scramble up low-angled slab to reach roof split by crack. Climb crack out roof, then continue in thin crack on left side of flake until face climbing leads up and right to top. Pro: Small to large nuts.

56. **Black Streak, 5.10a** ★   Start directly down and left of Gravity approximately 60 feet. Climb obvious "black streak" up to bolts on right. Follow face past bolts to thin crack. Continue to top via crack. Pro: Small to medium nuts, Friends, two bolts.

57. **Dog Fight Giggle, 5.9** ★   Start 20 feet right of **Black Streak**. Climb lieback flake to ledge (5.9). Continue up right-facing corner (5.8) past one bolt, then continue in thin crack to top (5.7). Pro: Small to medium nuts, Friends, one bolt.

58. **Seam-In', 5.11a** ★   Start 30 feet right of **Dog Fight Giggle**. Climb face past one bolt to thin crack (5.11a). Climb crack left past two fixed pitons, then continue up crack until possible to join **Dog Fight Giggle**. Climb thin crack to top. Pro: one bolt, small nuts, two fixed pitons, Friends.

59. **Easy Chair, 5.9+**   Start 50 yards west of the back side of **Hanging Gardens**. Climb the east-facing slab past two bolts. Pro: Two bolts.

Glass Dome

This area yields moderate and difficult climbs. Although short in length, the rock in most areas is unusually polished and worth the extra hike. Standard Descent for the Glass Dome: Scramble down northwest (Cl. 4) or rappel (two bolts) single line south.

60. **Hand-Some, 5.8** ★   This route is located on the left side of the wash approximately 100 yards above the Gardener's Wall cut off. It is only about 40 feet east of the trail. Start on north side of boulder. Climb vertical crack to top. Pro: Small to medium nuts, Friends.

61. **Ariba-Dirt-Cheap, 5.9**   This route is located on the same boulder as **Hand-Some**. Start at south side. Climb vertical crack to top. Pro: Medium to large nuts, Friends.

61a. **Feminine Protection, 5.10** ★★   20 feet to the right of **Ariba-Dirt Cheap**, climb left-facing undercling corner to face above. Continue right on face to top. Pro: Small to large nuts, Friends.

62. **The White Line, 5.10c** ★   Start by scrambling from southwest corner to upper south face. Climb left-leaning crack to stance. Exit up face past bolt to top. Pro: Small nuts, Friends, one bolt.

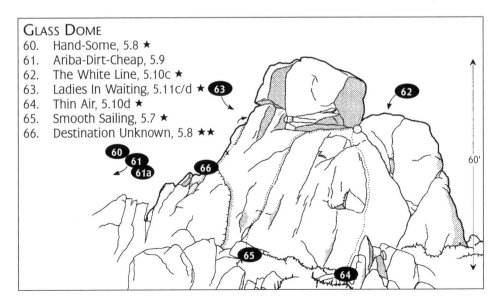

GLASS DOME
60.   Hand-Some, 5.8 ★
61.   Ariba-Dirt-Cheap, 5.9
62.   The White Line, 5.10c ★
63.   Ladies In Waiting, 5.11c/d ★
64.   Thin Air, 5.10d ★
65.   Smooth Sailing, 5.7 ★
66.   Destination Unknown, 5.8 ★★

60'

63. **Ladies In Waiting, 5.11c/d ★**   Tough route! Just right of **The White Line**, scramble (Cl. 4) up to a ledge on the south face. Climb thin, strenuous face past bolts to top. Originally climbed with three bolts, one of the bolts was sheared off in an ankle-busting whipper and may not have been replaced. Probably a good idea to verify three bolts before jumping on this one. Pro: Three bolts (see above), assorted pro for belay.

64. **Thin Air, 5.10d ★**   Start on north side of dome. Climb face to fixed piton at base of thin, shallow, fingercrack. Follow crack past another fixed piton to its end and exit via face moves to obvious belay. Pro: Small to medium nuts, Friends, two fixed pitons.

65. **Smooth Sailing, 5.7 ★**   Start about 20 feet left of **Thin Air** at open book. Climb dihedral to stance and bolt, then continue to horizontal crack. Follow horizontal crack right to obvious belay. Pro: Small nuts, Friends, one bolt.

66. **Destination Unknown, 5.8 ★★**   Start up and left of Smooth Sailing by scrambling up broken boulders to short face. Climb face past bolt to crack, then crack to ledge. Continue up to bolt on aréte, then up aréte to top. Pro: Small nuts, Friends, two bolts.

67. **Hot Shoe, 5.6**   This climb is located approximately 200 yards southwest of Glass Dome on an east-facing wall. Climb a right-facing dihedral until it ends. Continue on the face past a bolt to a horizontal crack. Finish to top. Pro: One bolt, medium to large nuts.

Goat Hill

This area is found by parking and hiking up trail that leads to Gardener's Wall. Instead of crossing the gully to head for Gardener's, continue up the gully, past Glass Dome to the saddle above. At saddle, contour up and left across a barren slope to reach Goat Hill (south side of ridge where Hog Heaven is located).

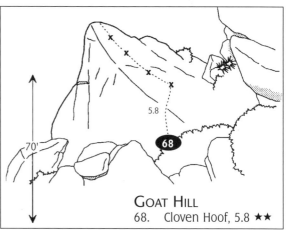

GOAT HILL
68.   Cloven Hoof, 5.8 ★★

68. **Cloven Hoof, 5.8 ★★**
Another fine line weeded out of the McDowells by Jan Holdeman! This four bolt face follows an aréte for 75 feet. Expect tricky and committed moves to get to the first bolt. Then follow the aréte for three more bolts to top. Pro: Four bolts

69. **Nice Yard, 5.10b**   This route lies on the south side of a formation that is best identified by a collection of six cracks that converge at a single point on it's west face. Climb overhanging handcrack (5.10b) to ledge alcove. Move up left and follow left-leaning book (5.7+) to belay. Pro: Medium to large.

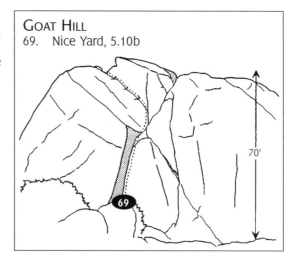

GOAT HILL
69.   Nice Yard, 5.10b

Morrell's Wall Parking Lot

Just to the northeast of the Morrell's Wall parking area is a group of large boulders and granite formations. The routes in this area are distributed on virtually all sides of the outcrop.

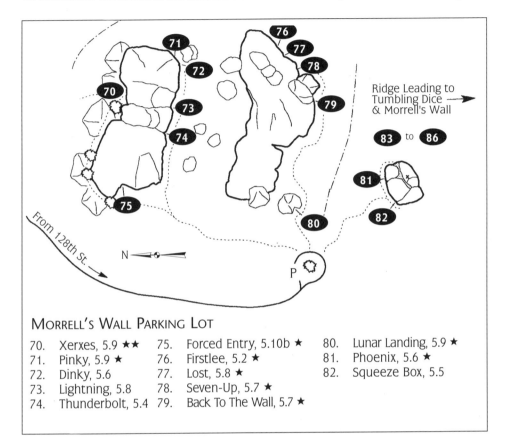

MORRELL'S WALL PARKING LOT

70.	Xerxes, 5.9 ★★	75.	Forced Entry, 5.10b ★	80.	Lunar Landing, 5.9 ★
71.	Pinky, 5.9 ★	76.	Firstlee, 5.2 ★	81.	Phoenix, 5.6 ★
72.	Dinky, 5.6	77.	Lost, 5.8 ★	82.	Squeeze Box, 5.5
73.	Lightning, 5.8	78.	Seven-Up, 5.7 ★		
74.	Thunderbolt, 5.4	79.	Back To The Wall, 5.7 ★		

70. **Xerxes, 5.9 ★★**   This route is at the north end of the rockpile on a large face split by a horizontal crack. Start at the lower left end of the face at the base of a right-leaning fist crack. Climb crack to face, traversing up and right past first bolt to horizontal crack. Pass crack and second bolt to undercling pocket. Step left and up past third bolt to top. Pro: Three bolts, small to large nuts.

71. **Pinky, 5.9 ★**   Start south and east in gully system (west side of ridge) from **Forced Entry**. Climb short, steep face to crack (south-facing), then continue in crack to top. Pro: Small to medium nuts.

72. **Dinky, 5.6**   Climb the obvious off-width ten feet to the right of **Pinky**. Avoid touching the boulder on the right at the start. Pro: Medium friends in crack on the right

73. **Lightning, 5.8**   Start 25 feet left of **Pinky**. Climb left leaning off-width to horizontal crack. Traverse crack right (5.8) and continue up chimney to top. Pro: Medium to large friends.

74. **Thunderbolt, 5.4**   Start 20 feet left of **Lightning**. Climb short zig-zagging crack. Pro: Small to medium nuts.

75. **Forced Entry, 5.10b ★**   South of the parking area, start at northwest corner of boulders. Climb thin, overhanging crack to top. Pro: Small to medium nuts.

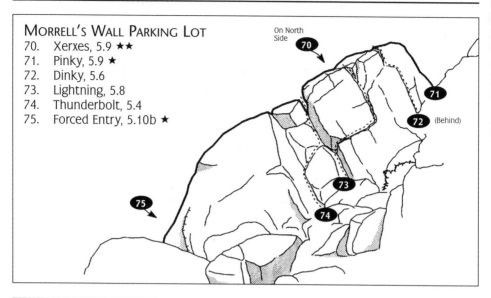

MORRELL'S WALL PARKING LOT
70. Xerxes, 5.9 ★★
71. Pinky, 5.9 ★
72. Dinky, 5.6
73. Lightning, 5.8
74. Thunderbolt, 5.4
75. Forced Entry, 5.10b ★

On North Side

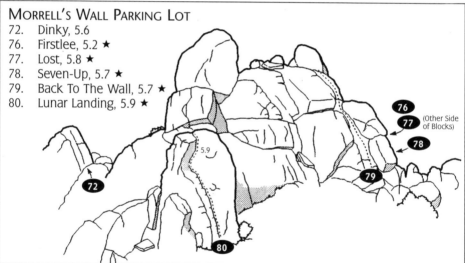

MORRELL'S WALL PARKING LOT
72. Dinky, 5.6
76. Firstlee, 5.2 ★
77. Lost, 5.8 ★
78. Seven-Up, 5.7 ★
79. Back To The Wall, 5.7 ★
80. Lunar Landing, 5.9 ★

(Other Side of Blocks)

76. **Firstlee, 5.2 ★**   Start 30 feet down and right of **Lost**. Climb face right of right-facing dihedral past horizontal crack. Join dihedral to top. Pro: Medium to large nuts.
77. **Lost, 5.8 ★**   Start 10 feet right of **Seven-Up**. Climb face up past horizontal crack to large boulder. Climb left side of boulder (forms crack) to top. Pro: Small to large nuts.
78. **Seven-Up, 5.7 ★**   Start 20 feet left of **Back To The Wall**. Climb face on right side of flake past three bolts to top. Climb is approximately 60 feet. Pro: Three bolts.
79. **Back To The Wall, 5.7 ★**   Southeast from the parking area, start at southeast corner of rockpile on left side of large, left-leaning flake that rests against the wall. Climb up face on left of flake, then from top of flake, climb face up and left past two bolts to top. Climb is approximately 60 feet. Pro: Medium to large nuts, two bolts.
80. **Lunar Landing, 5.9 ★**   This route is on the prominent pinnacle at the southwest end of the rockpile and is visible from the road end. Start at base of left facing dihedral. Climb crack in dihedral to base of thin, right-arching crack. Climb overhanging crack (5.9) to top. Pro: Small to medium nuts.

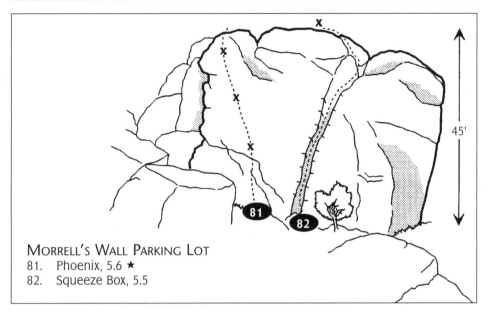

MORRELL'S WALL PARKING LOT
81. Phoenix, 5.6 ★
82. Squeeze Box, 5.5

81. **Phoenix, 5.6** ★   A post-fire route that rose from the ashes! About 15 feet to the left
     of **Squeeze Box**, climb the knobby face past three bolts to top. Step across the void at
     top to set up belay. To the right is single bolt (be sure to back up with pro) for belay.
     Descent same as **Squeeze Box**. Pro: Three bolts. Medium to large for belay (plus one
     belay bolt).
82. **Squeeze Box, 5.5**   Straight south across the gully from **Lunar Landing** climb the
     obvious off-width on a large boulder formation. The squeeze comes onto a ramp above
     with crack. At the top, move left and over onto top of boulder formation. Downclimb
     into center chimney to walk off to east. Pro: Medium to large, one belay bolt.
83. **Sphinctre Boy, 5.9**   If you head south from the parking area for Morrell's Wall, the
     first crag visible has a thin crack on it's eastern flank. Climb a right-arching fingercrack
     on the north face. Pro: Unknown
84. **Girlie Man, 5.9+**   Five feet left of **Sphinctre Boy**, climb past three bolts to top. Pro:
     Three bolts
85. **Another Piece Of Meat, 5.9**   100 yards left of **Girlie Man** and the east face. Climb
     the center right face past two bolts. Pro: Two bolts
86. **Brain Fart, 5.8**   15 feet left of **Another Piece of Meat**, climb past one bolt and
     cracks to top. Pro: One bolt, small to medium cams.
87. **Slickophobia, 5.10a**   30 feet left of three-bolt 5.7 route (**Back to the Wall???**) climb
     past two bolts to a down-facing block (gear). Continue left to a third bolt, then to a
     horn-shaped flake (sling).
     Variation, 5.10d   Instead of going up at the third bolt, move left.
88. **Fairies In Tights, 5.9**   This route is found on the first boulder grouping on the trail
     to Morrell's Wall, just before a really steep boulder. Climb the left side of the east face
     past two bolts. Pro: Two bolts
89. **Under Pressure, 5.10a**   15 feet right of **Fairies in Tights**. Climb face past two bolts.
     Pro: Two bolts.

Morrell's Wall

Another of the fine walls in the McDowells, Morrell's Wall shouldn't be missed. Many quality
climbs are found here, the two best being **Space Cadets** and **Beat Feet**. This wall gets less
traffic than the more popular (and easier to approach) Sven Slab and Gardener's Wall areas,

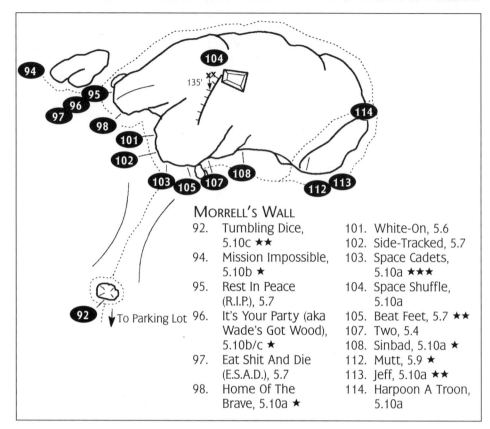

MORRELL'S WALL

92. Tumbling Dice, 5.10c ★★	101. White-On, 5.6
94. Mission Impossible, 5.10b ★	102. Side-Tracked, 5.7
95. Rest In Peace (R.I.P.), 5.7	103. Space Cadets, 5.10a ★★★
96. It's Your Party (aka Wade's Got Wood), 5.10b/c ★	104. Space Shuffle, 5.10a
97. Eat Shit And Die (E.S.A.D.), 5.7	105. Beat Feet, 5.7 ★★
98. Home Of The Brave, 5.10a ★	107. Two, 5.4
	108. Sinbad, 5.10a ★
	112. Mutt, 5.9 ★
	113. Jeff, 5.10a ★★
	114. Harpoon A Troon, 5.10a

making it a good place for a little less crowded climbing experience. A bolt/chain anchor can be found near the top of the wall where **Space Cadets** and **Beat Feet** top out. Two ropes are required to rappel from this spot (approximately. 135 feet) to the bottom of the wall.

90. **Seduction Production, 5.6**   As one looks (southeast) at the ridge that leads to Morrell's Wall, notice that the ridge has three major rises. Start at the west side of prominent pinnacle located just above first rise. This pinnacle is lower but on the same ridge as **Tumbling Dice**. Climb crack to ledge, then move left to aréte. Climb aréte past two bolts to top. Rappel (two bolts) single line off north side. Pro: Friends, two bolts, two rappel bolts.

91. **Waste Eep (Way Steep, Waist Deep), 5.8**   From the parking area, walk up towards the ridge until you see two large boulders in a gully right of the ridge. (This will be right before you cut up to the ridge to approach Morrell's Wall.) Start at second boulder back at obvious face. Step up on pedestal in hole and clip bolt. Follow face past this bolt and two more to top. One will have to drop off the back side to set up belay as there are no bolts on top. Pro: Three bolts.

92. **Tumbling Dice, 5.10c ★★**   Steep and exhilarating face climbing highlight this short route. After one has gained the ridge leading to Morrell's Wall, a small pinnacle (50-foot) will be encountered. This will be just below the third major rise on the ridge. Start at rectangular north face. Climb steep face past two bolts to top. Descend via single line rappel. Pro: Two bolts.

93. **Crack A Smile, 5.9 ★**   Although relatively hard to locate, this climb is worth the effort. Start approximately 150 yards east of Morrell's Wall at an obvious outcropping of rock with a handcrack angling left to right through the center of the outcrop. Traverse

Morrell's Wall

94. Mission Impossible, 5.10b ★
95. Rest In Peace (R.I.P.), 5.7
96. It's Your Party (aka Wade's Got Wood), 5.10b/c ★
97. Eat Shit And Die (E.S.A.D.), 5.7
98. Home Of The Brave, 5.10a ★
99. Dead On Arrival (D.O.A.), 5.11a ★
100. Halloweenie, 5.9
101. White-On, 5.6
102. Side-Tracked, 5.7
103. Space Cadets, 5.10a ★★★
104. Space Shuffle, 5.10a
105. Beat Feet, 5.7 ★★
106. Jungle Gym, 5.11b
107. Two, 5.4
108. Sinbad, 5.10a ★
109. Gargoyle, 5.9
110. Leave It To Beaver Direct, 5.10a ★
111. Epacondilitis, 5.8 ★★
112. Mutt, 5.9 ★
113. Jeff, 5.10a ★★
114. Harpoon A Troon, 5.10a

in from east side of boulder to crack, then climb crack to top. Pro: Small to medium nuts, Friends.

94. **Mission Impossible, 5.10b ★**   Start at southeast side of wall (up from main north-facing wall). Climb short face to obvious crack that arches right to left. Climb crack until possible to exit on face. Pro: Small nuts, Friends.

95. **Rest In Peace (R.I.P.), 5.7**   Start around corner at east side of wall on an obvious face with two thin cracks. Traverse in from left and climb left crack to top. Pro: Small nuts.

96. **It's Your Party (aka Wade's Got Wood), 5.10b/c ★**   The route's original line was envisioned by a climber who, when asked for guidance on a gripped lead, would advise: "It's your party, fly if you want to!" Start at the base of the main slab directly below (and between) **E.S.A.D.** and **R.I.P.** Climb slab past bolt to another bolt at overhang. Turn the overhang (5.10b/c) and continue to bolt on the **E.S.A.D.** traverse. Climb center of face between **E.S.A.D.** and **R.I.P.** past two bolts to top (5.8+) and two-bolt belay anchor. Pro: Five bolts

97. **Eat Shit And Die (E.S.A.D.), 5.7**   Start is same as **Rest In Peace**. Traverse in from left and climb face past one bolt into right crack. Continue in crack to top. Pro: One bolt, small nuts.

98. **Home Of The Brave, 5.10a ★**   The leader's first first ascent lead turns out to be a fine, bold lead. Start approximately 20 feet right of **E.S.A.D.** Climb short, right-facing corner to lieback flake on an overhang. Continue past one bolt, then climb crack and face

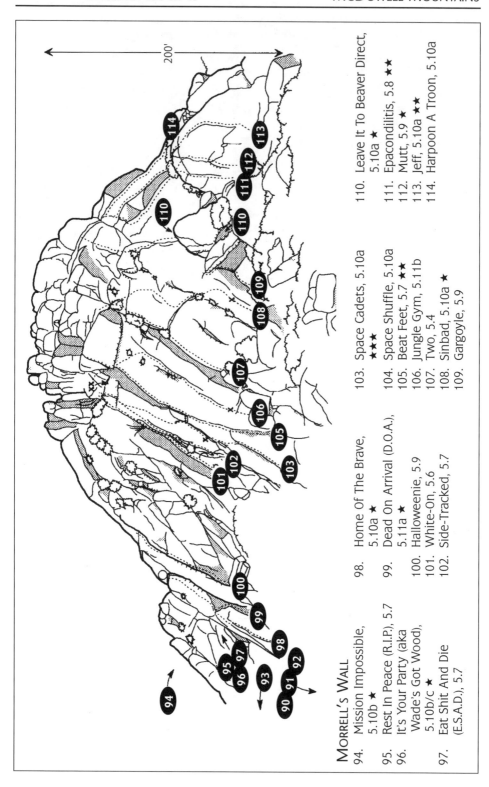

200'

MORRELL'S WALL

94. Mission Impossible, 5.10b ★
95. Rest In Peace (R.I.P.), 5.7
96. It's Your Party (aka Wade's Got Wood), 5.10b/c ★
97. Eat Shit And Die (E.S.A.D.), 5.7

98. Home Of The Brave, 5.10a ★
99. Dead On Arrival (D.O.A.), 5.11a ★
100. Halloweenie, 5.9
101. White-On, 5.6
102. Side-Tracked, 5.7

103. Space Cadets, 5.10a ★★★
104. Space Shuffle, 5.10a
105. Beat Feet, 5.7 ★★
106. Jungle Gym, 5.11b
107. Two, 5.4
108. Sinbad, 5.10a ★
109. Gargoyle, 5.9

110. Leave It To Beaver Direct, 5.10a ★
111. Epacondilitis, 5.8 ★★
112. Mutt, 5.9 ★
113. Jeff, 5.10a ★★
114. Harpoon A Troon, 5.10a

ner to lieback flake on an overhang. Continue past one bolt, then climb crack and face to top. Pro: Small to medium nuts, Friends, one bolt.

99. **Dead On Arrival (D.O.A.), 5.11a** ★   The leader took a "screamer" on his first attempt but returned later to lead it without falling or weighing the rope at any time (red point). Start 20 feet right of Home of the Brave around corner. Climb overhanging, thin crack up and right until possible to move left via overhanging, discontinuous cracks around corner. At this point, join **Home of the Brave** just below its bolt. Pro: Small to medium nuts, Friends, one bolt.

100. **Halloweenie, 5.9**   Start approximately 30 feet right of **D.O.A.** and just right of a little cave. Climb face a short ways to crack, then continue in crack to top. Pro: Small to large nuts, Friends.

101. **White-On, 5.6**   Start off boulder, 50 feet left and around corner from **Space Cadets** and 15 feet left of juniper tree on **Side-Tracked**. Climb face off boulder to gain crack system which angles up. Exit right to reach top. Pro: Small to medium nuts, Friends.

102. **Side-Tracked, 5.7**   Start 15 feet right of White-On or 35 feet left and around corner from **Space Cadets**. Scramble up gully to small juniper tree. Step right around tree and continue up crack to roof. Exit roof on right and join **Space Cadets** to top. Pro: Small to medium nuts, Friends.

103. **Space Cadets, 5.10a** ★★★   Continuous climbing and excellent rock make this route one of the best at Morrell's Wall. Start at left end of essentially north-facing wall at base of small, right-leaning seam. First Pitch: Climb seam in corner (5.9) to bolt and belay. Second Pitch: Climb past belay bolt on right of flake to right-leaning crack. Climb crack to roof and seam above. Climb face up and slightly left (5.10a) past bolt to flake and small roof belay on right side of roof. Scramble Cl. 4 to top. Pro: Small to large nuts, Friends, two bolts.

104. **Space Shuffle, 5.10a**   Climb squeeze chimney above second pitch of **Space Cadets**. Pro: Large

105. **Beat Feet, 5.7** ★★   Although this route is only rated 5.7, it has many sections that make the climbing very continuous. Start 25 feet right of **Space Cadets** at base of slightly right-leaning crack. Climb crack to small roof, then pass roof on right and continue in crack in dihedral. A small chimney problem leads to top going up and left. Be sure to properly runner protection and use a 165-foot rope to lead this climb in one pitch. Pro: Medium to large nuts.

106. **Jungle Gym, 5.11b**   Start 20 feet up and slightly right from Beat Feet. Approach by scrambling Cl. 3 to top of boulders. Climb face up and slightly right to small seam (5.11b). Continue in right-leaning seam to bush and grass-filled crack (the jungle). Climb the jungle until possible to move left on face under large roof and join **Beat Feet** for final chimney problem. Pro: One bolt, small to medium nuts, Friends.

107. **Two, 5.4**   Start at center of wall 35 feet right and slightly up from **Jungle Gym** in right-facing dihedral at base of wide crack. Climb crack past natural chockstones to ledge, then up chimney and groove to top. Pro: Medium to large nuts.

108. **Sinbad, 5.10a** ★   Start approximately 30 feet right and slightly down from **Two** below left-leaning ramp just right of vegetated crack. Climb face on ramp up past five bolts to large ledge. At this point climb face up and slightly left past two bolts (5.10a) to top. Pro: Seven bolts. Note: The first five bolts on this route were placed by another party who thought they were doing a new line. The resulting line, the **Dale Low Memorial Route**, is actually the first part of the original line for **Sinbad**.

109. **Gargoyle, 5.9**   The last moves on this route may just leave you looking like a gargoyle. Start just right of **Sinbad** at right-leaning dihedral that has a large flake lying above (almost like a chockstone). Climb right-arching crack until under flake, then step left around flake exiting to top. Pro: Small to medium nuts, Friends.

110. **Leave It To Beaver Direct, 5.10a** ★   Many styles of climbing are incorporated in this route. The first pitch may be avoided if so desired. Start near right side of wall underneath large flake. It will appear as though you are caving. First Pitch: Climb crack

in right-facing dihedral (5.10a) out of dark abyss until possible to move left to base of wide chimney (just left of lichen-covered face). Second Pitch:Climb chimney and crack until possible to move left over small overhang into shallow dihedral (5.7). Follow dihedral to small ledge. Third Pitch: Climb brown-stained crack (directly above) up and right (5.9), then up face to top. Pro: Small to large nuts, Friends.

Eddie Haskell Variation, 5.9 (R) Instead of exiting out left on second pitch, continue in crack to headwall. At this point face climb up and right to corner, then turn corner and climb up to belay. Pro: Small to medium nuts, Friends.

111. **Epacondilitis, 5.8 ★★** This climb ascends the crack and aréte on the northeast corner of the flake that forms the bottom of **Mutt**. Climb crack to horizontal ledge. Step up into shallow dihedral, then move right and up aréte to top. Pro: Medium to large, two bolts.

112. **Mutt, 5.9 ★** Who is Mutt - John Dargis or Jim Waugh? Start on lower slab down and right of main wall. The second pitch of this route was originally considered a separate line, called **Lumpy**. First Pitch: Climb left vertical crack to brushy ledge (5.7). Second Pitch: Scramble up and left to obvious left-leaning, wide crack. Climb crack (5.5), then turn lip to gain corner system. Climb thin crack in corner (5.9) to face, then continue on face to top. Pro: Small to large nuts, tube chocks, Big Bros or #5 Camelots are useful, Friends.

113. **Jeff, 5.10a ★★** Well, who is Jeff - Jim Waugh or John Dargis? Start on lower slab down and right of main wall. The second pitch of this route was originally considered a separate line, called **Time Out**. First Pitch: Climb right vertical crack to top (5.7). Second Pitch: Scramble across ledge and up to slab. Climb face up and slightly right past three bolts to top (5.10a). Pro: Small to medium nuts, three bolts.

114. **Harpoon A Troon, 5.10a** Start 20 feet right of the second pitch of **Jeff** at slab. Climb face past three bolts to top. Pro: Three bolts.

Sven Slab

This wall received its name when the original pioneers used a Sven power saw to cut a trail

HAWK BOULDER AREA
115. Energizer, 5.8 ★
116. Hawk, 5.7 ★
117. Cold Fingers, 5.9
118. Arrowhead, 5.7 ★

SVEN SLAB
119. One For The Road, 5.6 ★★★
120. Half Moon, 5.2
121. The Chute, 5.4 ★
123. Mousetracks, 5.6 ★
125. Black Death, 5.8 ★
127. Ego Trip, 5.7 (R) ★
129. Quaker Oats, 5.5 ★★★

NIT NAT AREA
130. Changes In Longitude, 5.5 ★★
131. Dark Passage, 5.10c ★★
132. Changes In Attitude, 5.10-
133. Peaches & Cream, 5.7
134. Changes In Latitude, 5.10b ★★
135. Nit Nat, 5.10a ★
136. Hippity Hop, 5.6 (R) ★

119 120
121
123
90'
125
Sven Slab 127 134
129
130
131 136
132 133 135
Nit Nat
Area
N
Hawk
Boulder
118
115
P
116 117
High Clearance
Vehicle Only!
P

to the base of the wall. Although the more difficult climbs are predominately face, there are some crack climbs in the moderate range as well. The main face climbing has become quite popular with beginner climbers in the last few years. Expect to have a bit of company if you climb here on a weekend.

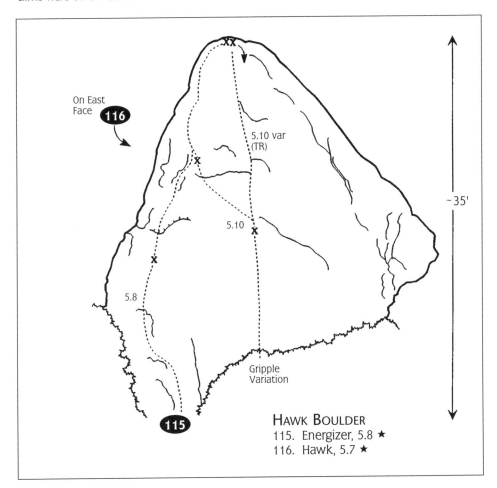

Hawk Boulder
115. Energizer, 5.8 ★
116. Hawk, 5.7 ★

115. **Energizer, 5.8 ★**   Below Sven Slab and just east of the parking area on top of the hill, a large triangular boulder may be seen sitting in a sunken area. Three bolts may be seen on the west–northwest (wnw) face. Start on the left side of this face. Climb face and aréte past two bolts to top. Descend via single line rappel. Pro: Two bolts.
     Gripple Variation, 5.10a   Start just right of original start in middle of face. Climb face to bolt, then continue on face up and left to join regular route. Pro: One bolt.

116. **Hawk, 5.7 ★**   On the opposite side (facing east) of **Energizer**, climb face past two bolts to top. Descent is the same as **Energizer**. Pro: Two bolts.

117. **Cold Fingers, 5.9**   This route is found about 50 yards west of **Energizer** on the north face of a large boulder. Climb to top past a left-angling seam and single bolt. Pro: One bolt

118. **Arrowhead, 5.7 ★**   This route is found 200 yards west and a bit south of the Hawk Boulder on a large pointed boulder shaped like an arrowhead (thus the name). Climb the northeast face to a two-bolt anchor. Pro: Two bolts, Friends, two belay bolts.

SVEN SLAB AREA

117. Cold Fingers, 5.9
118. Arrowhead, 5.7 ★
119. One For The Road, 5.6 ★★★
120. Half Moon, 5.2
121. The Chute, 5.4 ★
122. Mousetrap, 5.3
123. Mousetracks, 5.6 ★
124. Over The Hill, 5.11a
125. Black Death, 5.8 ★
126. Cakewalk, 5.8 ★

127. Ego Trip, 5.7 (R) ★
128. Sinkso, 5.8 (R)
129. Quaker Oats, 5.5 ★★★
130. Changes In Longitude, 5.5 ★★
131. Dark Passage, 5.10c ★★
132. Changes In Attitude, 5.10-
133. Peaches & Cream, 5.7
134. Changes In Latitude, 5.10b ★★
135. Nit Nat, 5.10a ★
136. Hippity Hop, 5.6 (R) ★

119. **One For The Road, 5.6 ★★★**   A sweet route! Start at far left end of wall. This route is up and left of the broken section dominated by large roofs . Look for thin, right-leaning crack on left side of gully. First Pitch: Climb crack to bush-filled ledge. Scramble down gully on right or left. Second Pitch: Above the belay, climb a short dihedral and then move right. Climb face past discontinuous RP cracks. A bolt was placed on this pitch by another party in 1988. Pro: Small to medium, RPs (second pitch), one bolt.

120. **Half Moon, 5.2**   50 feet right of **One for the Road's** second pitch, climb a left-arching crack. Pro: Unknown.

121. **The Chute, 5.4 ★**   This route was listed as **Arrowhead** in the previous edition of this guidebook. The first ascentionists have set us straight! Start right of **One For The Road** (right of gully and left of aréte). Climb face past two bolts to horizontal crack. Continue on face past bolt to ledges. Scramble down gully to left. Pro: Three bolts, large nuts.

122. **Mousetrap, 5.3**   The name is certainly appropriate! Start at broken section up and left from prominent white face where **Cakewalk** (#75) is located. This section is characterized by several large roofs. Scramble up over brush and up low-angled open book until a traverse left leads behind a tree and to a boulder enclave. Continue traversing

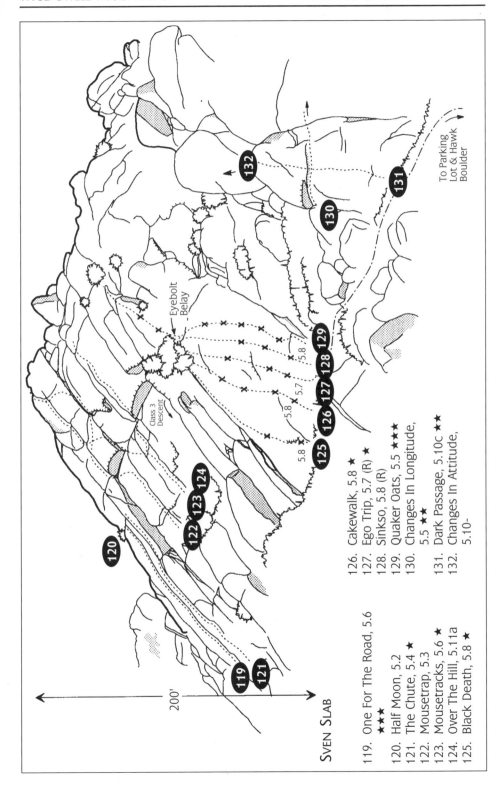

Sven Slab

119. One For The Road, 5.6 ★★★
120. Half Moon, 5.2
121. The Chute, 5.4 ★
122. Mousetrap, 5.3
123. Mousetracks, 5.6 ★
124. Over The Hill, 5.11a
125. Black Death, 5.8 ★

126. Cakewalk, 5.8 ★
127. Ego Trip, 5.7 (R) ★
128. Sinkso, 5.8 (R)
129. Quaker Oats, 5.5 ★★★
130. Changes In Longitude, 5.5 ★★
131. Dark Passage, 5.10c ★★
132. Changes In Attitude, 5.10-

up and left over boulders to a spot directly underneath the right side of the largest roof. Climb open book to right side of highest large roof, then traverse left under roof along horizontal crack passing one vertical crack (with tree) to second vertical crack. Climb this crack up until possible to traverse back right over tree and under a smaller roof. Continue traversing to wide vertical crack that leads to a left-leaning crack that leads to the top. Pro: Small to large nuts.

123. **Mousetracks, 5.6 ★**   Start and approach are the same as **Mousetrap** but stop at tree and boulder enclave. First Pitch: Follow right-leaning crack behind tree up over a small overhang (5.6) . Continue up crack until possible to traverse left to right side of large roof. Climb off-width and face on right side of roof until an indistinct ledge (horizontal crack) intersects (5.6). Traverse ledge left to spacious belay ledge. Second Pitch: Step up and right on face to base of thin, right-leaning crack. Climb thin crack until it disappears, then up and left on face to top (5.5). Pro: Small to large nuts, Friends.

124. **Over The Hill, 5.11a**   Start is the same as **Mousetracks**. Directly behind tree, climb a right-leaning crack (5.6) up to left edge of a roof. Clear roof via a right-arching crack (5.11a) until easier climbing leads to top. Pro: Small to large nuts, Friends.

125. **Black Death, 5.8 ★**   Start at left end of prominent white face at right-arching crack. Climb crack until possible to step left onto face and bolt. Follow thin lieback flake above up to a second bolt. Continue straight up to a broken area and a right-leaning handcrack. Follow this crack to a belay left of tree. Scramble Cl. 3 off left. Pro: Two bolts, Friends.

126. **Cakewalk, 5.8 ★**   Start near left end of prominent white face 20 feet right of right-arching crack. Climb face off boulder up and right to bolt, then up face to another bolt and horizontal crack (right-arching crack). Continue up face and slightly right to third bolt, then up passing fourth bolt to belay left of tree. Scramble off Cl. 3 to the left. Note: It is suspected that the fourth bolt was placed sometime after the first ascent. Care should be exercised as the buttonhead on this bolt is cracked. Pro: Four bolts.
   Variation, 5.8   From second bolt, climb large flake and face up and left to bolt. At this point, climb face up and left to crack, then up crack to same belay as regular route. Pro: One bolt, medium to large nuts.

127. **Ego Trip, 5.7 (R) ★**   Start ten feet right of **Cakewalk**. Climb face directly underneath bolt (past bolt) and slightly right to second bolt. Continue on face to undercling, then move out right and climb face straight up to third bolt. Continue on face to belay on right side of tree. Scramble off Cl. 3 to the left. Pro: Three bolts, Friends.

128. **Sinkso, 5.8 (R**)   Just right of **Ego Trip**, climb face past three bolts to belay on right side of tree. The route can be identified by it's rather elevated first bolt. Pro: Three bolts

129. **Quaker Oats, 5.5 ★★★**   This climb was originally more or less third-classed. The leader did lay a stopper on top of a flake as a joke. Following the ascent, with the permission of the first ascent party, climbers added bolts to make it a safe lead for moderate range climbers. Start 20 feet right of **Ego Trip**. Scramble up until a traverse leads left on small indistinct ledge to bolt. Climb face by easiest means past five bolts to ledge. Belay at this point or continue on small face above past two bolts to next major ledge system. Scramble off Cl. 3 left if belay is at tree; scramble off Cl.4 right if belay is at next major ledge system. Pro:Seven bolts, medium nuts.

130. **Changes In Longitude, 5.5 ★★**   An excellent girdle! Start at left side of lower crag at right (northwest) end of wall under small roof. First Pitch: Traverse horizontal crack right past fixed piton to vertical crack. Then follow vertical crack up to another horizontal crack. Traverse horizontal crack right and slightly down to large chimney. Second Pitch: Climb chimney to chockstone, then move left onto face and up to top. Pro: One fixed piton, small to medium nuts.

131. **Dark Passage, 5.10c ★★**   Thin and sustained face climbing make this a dark passage indeed. Start down and right of Changes in Longitude and 30 feet up and left of

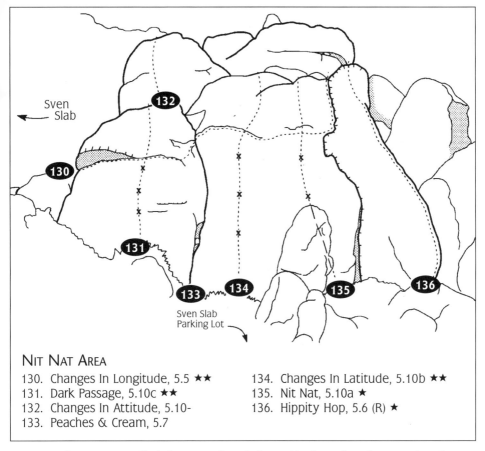

NIT NAT AREA

130. Changes In Longitude, 5.5 ★★
131. Dark Passage, 5.10c ★★
132. Changes In Attitude, 5.10-
133. Peaches & Cream, 5.7

134. Changes In Latitude, 5.10b ★★
135. Nit Nat, 5.10a ★
136. Hippity Hop, 5.6 (R) ★

Peaches & Cream. Climb face past three bolts and horizontal crack to top. Pro: Three bolts, large nuts, Friends.

132. **Changes In Attitude, 5.10-** This route is found on a boulder above **Dark Passage**. Step right off small boulder onto face. Climb past two bolts and horizontal crack to two-bolt belay. There will be some runout on easy ground (5.4) at the top. Pro: Two bolts, small stoppers, TCUs

133. **Peaches & Cream, 5.7** Start 30 feet down and right of **Dark Passage**. Climb crack passing small chockstone to top. Pro: Medium to large nuts.

134. **Changes In Latitude, 5.10b ★★** The bolts on this route were already in place, but to the first ascentionist's knowledge the route had never received a successful ascent. Start just right of **Peaches & Cream**. Climb face right of corner past three bolts and horizontal crack to top. Pro: Three bolts, medium nuts.

135. **Nit Nat, 5.10a ★** The first ascent party wondered which were harder, the moves or fighting off the gnats. Start 20 feet right from **Changes in Latitude** below small undercling. Climb face past three bolts to horizontal crack. Then continue past horizontal crack and on face above, to top. Pro: Three bolts, medium nuts.

136. **Hippity Hop, 5.6 (R) ★** One will get the feeling that they are climbing a spire with this route. Start at lower crag at right end of wall and up right from **Nit Nat**. Climb flared crack to boulder enclave. Traverse left onto face, then climb up past bolt to top. Descend via a short rappel south (take a huge runner to wrap top or plan on doing a tandem rappel) and scramble through chimney. Pro: Small to large nuts, one bolt.

Knob Hill

This set of seemingly low-slung granite formations can be seen just to the northeast of Sven Slab. For exact location, this outcrop is seen as "Rock Knob" on the McDowell Peak quadrangle topographic map. A few routes have been done here. At this time, parking can be found at the "turnaround" at the end of the road which passes Sven Slab. Expect this to change when development moves in.

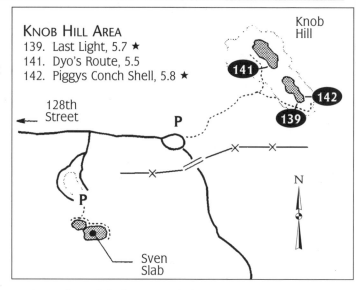

KNOB HILL AREA
139. Last Light, 5.7 ★
141. Dyo's Route, 5.5
142. Piggys Conch Shell, 5.8 ★

137. **F.C. 9797, 5.6**   Northwest face of "loaf" Pro: One bolt
138. **Freudian Slip, 5.9/10a**   A four-bolt face route in this area for which no other information was given. Pro: Four bolts

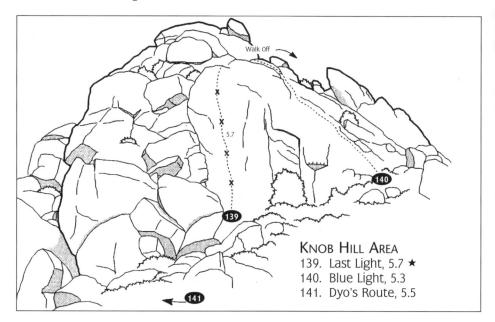

KNOB HILL AREA
139. Last Light, 5.7 ★
140. Blue Light, 5.3
141. Dyo's Route, 5.5

139. **Last Light, 5.7 ★**   This nice face climb is located on the southeast end of Knob Hill. Climb face past four bolts to top. Walk off to the east. Pro: Four bolts, few pieces of pro for anchor.
140. **Blue Light, 5.3**   Just to the right of **Last Light**, climb low-angle slab past flakes and groove to top. Pro: Small to large.

141. **Dyo's Route, 5.5** On the southwest end of Knob Hill, just west of **Last Light**, climb large crack on right margin of summit. Pro: Small to large.

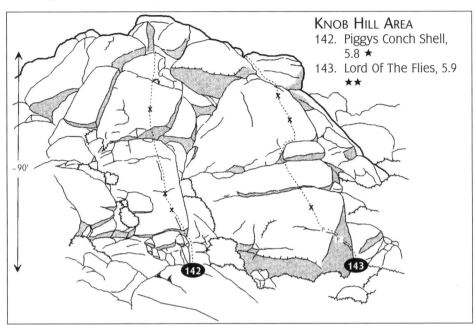

KNOB HILL AREA
142. Piggys Conch Shell, 5.8 ★
143. Lord Of The Flies, 5.9 ★★

142. **Piggys Conch Shell, 5.8 ★** This route is found on the northeast side of Knob Hill. After moving over broken rock at the base, continue up shallow, water-polished trough past two bolts to another small crack. Climbing along left side of polished trough will yield a 5.8 climb. Staying in the polished trough is much harder. Move up to sloping ledge and climb up large block past a third bolt. Finish past to top past horizontal crack and flake. Pro: Small to medium nuts, TCUs, three bolts.

143. **Lord Of The Flies, 5.9 ★★** 10 yards to the right of **Piggys Conch Shell**, climb seam up and left. Continue on face past two bolts to horizontal crack. Gain top of large boulder balanced on ledge, then continue up face (5.6+) past two more bolts to top. Pro: Four bolts, medium to large nuts.

The following two climbs are located approximately ⅓ mile south of the Knob Hill area (½ mile east of Sven Slab).

144. **Thrasher, 5.9 ★** This climb is found on a prominent granite needle. Start on the north side just right of a Crucifixion thorn tree. Climb slightly overhanging face to horizontal crack. Continue on face past bolt to horizontal handcrack (the frog crack). Hand traverse left to end of crack, then continue past horizontal OW crack, finishing on aréte up left side of summit boulder. Descend by threading rope through hole in summit boulder and simul-rapping east-west. Pro: Small to large, one bolt.

145. **Brown Nose, 5.6 (R)** 15 feet right of **Thrasher**, climb crack/trough to ledge. Step left on ledge and climb face to top of summit boulder. Pro: Small to large.

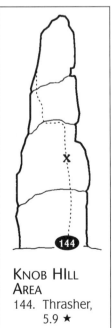

KNOB HILL AREA
144. Thrasher, 5.9 ★

Sven Towers

This group of east-facing rocks are located high up on the east side of the Sven Slab hill. The best approach is found starting from the northeastern parking area for Morrell's Wall. A boulder littered wash leads roughly east along the southern (back) side of the Sven Slab hill. Pick a route along the north edge of this wash and hang a left (north) uphill where you run into a 20-foot round boulder in the wash. This will take you into a small valley with a stand of Cholla skeletons. Turn back east and continue to the summit crest, then down the other side to the north and east. Scramble 75 feet east and downhill to the top of the crags.

One of the area developers, Jan Holdeman writes: "Unconsolidated soil and rock at the base of these crags makes hiking there generally arduous, occasionally dangerous and always damaging to the hillside. Consequently, rappel/belay anchors have been installed. You can gear up at the top, rappel to the base of the rock and then climb back to the packs." Please do your part to help mitigate the erosion damage. Until these routes have seen a few ascents, also expect some flakey or crusty rock in spots. To maintain the area's relatively remote "adventure" appeal, no topos are shown. Consider it part of the challenge. Routes are describe from north to south (right to left).

146. **Fly By, 5.8 ★**   This is the northernmost climb in the area. From the trail's end, look east and slightly down on top of a large dark brown boulder. The anchor bolts will be found there. 20 feet of easy Cl. 5 scrambling leads to the anchor. Rappel down and climb up past four bolts to the left of gully back to anchor. 60 feet. Pro: Four bolts, two-bolt anchor

147. **Just Fine, 5.6**   This route is roughly 60 feet south of **Fly By**. The anchor can be reached by heading south across slabs from near the top of **Fly By**, ending with a 5.2 downclimb and step across to the anchor. Rappel down and climb back up via face and/or resonant flake/crack past two horizontals and two bolts to top. 60 feet. Pro: Small to medium, two bolts.

148. **Feel The Creep, 5.10a ★★**   Found approximately 30 feet south of **Just Fine**. Move southwest (Cl. 4) across the slab above the **Just Fine** rappel bolts to find the rappel anchor for this route. After rapping, climb thin face past four bolts to top. Expect a smearfest! Pro: Four bolts

149. **Coloring Book, 5.10a ★★**   About 100 feet south of **Feel the Creep**, a small palo verde marks the two-bolt anchor for this route. The start of this route can also easily be reached from **Cary'd Away** (see #152 below). Climb the dihedral, formed by the right side of the flake, to a ledge. Carefully climb the broken spike to the roof. Follow crack in roof out to left (5.10). At the end of the roof, either exit into the grungy gully (left) or step right and climb past two bolts to top. South-facing, 100 feet. Pro: Medium to large, two bolts (for right exit).

The following climbs are not actually part of Sven Towers, but share the first half of the approach. Instead of turning north at the 20-foot boulder mentioned above, continue along the north side of the wash to a saddle with a great view of Four Peaks.

150. **Leaping Rabbit, 5.4 ★★**   This boulder lies at the south end of the saddle. The route is on the north side. Climb a right-leaning crack until it"s possible to climb straight to top. 40 feet. Pro: Medium pro.

151. **Unknown, 5.6 (R)**   Contour east from Leaping Rabbit approximately 100 yards. Climb crack in slab up to a steep face with a small flake. Continue past horizontal cracks to top. 100 feet. Pro: Small to medium pro.

152. **Cary'd Away, 5.7 ★★**   At the northern end of the saddle stands a well varnished south-facing wall, 100-foot wide, split into three sections by two chimneys. The climb begins on the right side. Climb the face past a single bolt, along a seam, past two horizontals and a perched boulder to the base of a handcrack leading to a short face section to the top. 100 feet. Single rope rappel descent. Pro: One bolt, small to medium.

Note: To reach the base of **Coloring Book** from this route, head east. After going about 75 feet and losing some elevation, turn north. The upper part of the dihedral and roof on **Coloring Book** should be visible about 100 feet away.

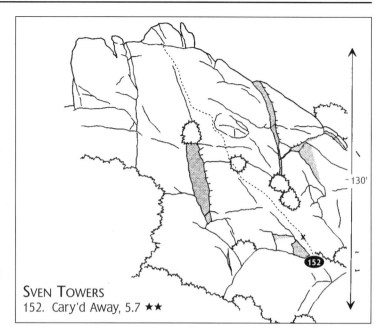

Sven Towers
152. Cary'd Away, 5.7 ★★

Granite Ballroom

For a long time this area was bypassed as climbers were more interested in the routes at Hog Heaven. Although still not many routes exist in this area, it is a remote and peaceful place to spend a day climbing. A few undiscovered gems may also be waiting for first ascent seekers.

Ballroom

This general area lies slightly south of Noah's Ark and closer to the road. The routes will be oriented to a small indistinct pinnacle that lies approximately 150 yards west of the road and north of a wash (fence heads almost directly to pinnacle).

153. **Delusions Of Grandeur, 5.11**
This route is found on the northwest corner of the main boulder pile. Climb west-facing vertical crack to ledge. Continue on face above past two bolts. Rap off. Pro: Nuts, two bolts.

154. **Uneventful, 5.8** Start at southwest side around pinnacle described above. Climb face just right of massive boulder chockstone past two bolts to top. Descend down west-facing ramp where scrambling will lead to base of the climb. Pro: Two bolts.

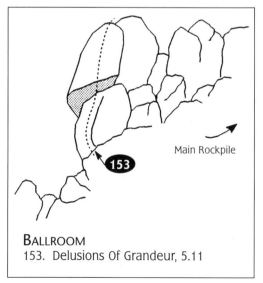

Main Rockpile

Ballroom
153. Delusions Of Grandeur, 5.11

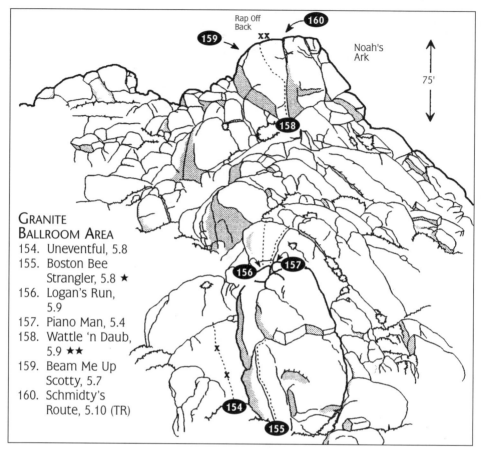

Rap Off
Back

Noah's
Ark

75'

**GRANITE
BALLROOM AREA**
154. Uneventful, 5.8
155. Boston Bee
     Strangler, 5.8 ★
156. Logan's Run,
     5.9
157. Piano Man, 5.4
158. Wattle 'n Daub,
     5.9 ★★
159. Beam Me Up
     Scotty, 5.7
160. Schmidty's
     Route, 5.10 (TR)

155. **Boston Bee Strangler, 5.8 ★**   Start just right and down from Uneventful at south-west-facing, left-leaning crack. Climb gradually narrowing off-width past large bee's nest to ledge. Scramble down and left. Pro: Medium to large nuts.
156. **Logan's Run, 5.9**   Start at slab located up and back of **Uneventful**. This slab is just right and below an overhanging face with prominent horizontal crack. Approach slab by passing the Uneventful pinnacle on right, heading up a bush-filled gully and travers-ing base of slab from right. Just left of crack (**Piano Man**), climb face past three bolts to belay. Pro: Three bolts, Friends (for belay).
157. **Piano Man, 5.4**   Start just right of **Logan's Run** at crack. Climb crack to top. Pro: Friends.

Noah's Ark

Two routes, one on the south and one on the north, surmount this impressive formation which is located up and slightly north from the Ballroom. Look for large chimney which splits the ark. A toprope ascent has also been done below the rap anchor. Standard Descent for Noah's Ark (west summit): Rappel (two bolts) single line off north side.

158. **Wattle 'n Daub, 5.9 ★★**   Start on south side at base of chimney that splits Noah's Ark. Climb chimney past one bolt, then move left onto face and climb past three more bolts to top. Pro: Friends, four bolts.
159. **Beam Me Up Scotty, 5.7**   Start at smaller chimney on north side approximately 40 feet right of main chimney. Climb chimney to ledge, then follow a diagonaling crack (first left, then right) to summit. Pro: Friends

160. **Schmidty's Route, 5.10 (TR)**   This is found on the steep face around the corner to the left of **Beam Me Up Scotty**. Step across a small gap, just right of the large chimney that splits the Ark and climb up sharp edges to the rappel bolts. Pro: Toprope

The following two routes are located just southwest (behind) of Noah's Ark, across a small saddle.

161. **Keen, 5.8+**   Climb a short (20-foot), steep, fingercrack in the short wall southwest of Noah's Ark. Pro: Small to medium.

162. **Burnt Offerings, 5.7**   This is located around the corner and a bit downhill from **Keen**. A nice looking route that starts with a handcrack. Follow handcrack up to where it starts to flare (some bad rock) but then goes back to a nice one-inch crack for a few feet. Then continue on easy but runout (5.3) face to top. 50 feet. Pro: Small to medium.

The Rosetta Stone

This formation can be found approximately 100 yards north and west of Noah's Ark. The crag faces north–northeast and averages about 80 feet in height. A remote day of out-of-the-way easy climbs are found here. Routes are described from left to right.

163. **Face Value, 5.6**   Climb face past two bolts. 40 feet. Pro: Two bolts

164. **Obscure Origin, 5.4**   To the right of **Face Value**, climb handcrack. Pro: Medium to large pro.

165. **Brazilian Tenant Farmers, 5.5 ★**   This was the first route on the crag, as well as the longest. To the right of **Obscure Origin**, climb face past horizontal cracks. At the top of a lower-angled section, step up and left over large crack and continue on slab to top. 130 feet. Pro: Small to medium pro.

166. **The Cipher, 5.5**   Right of **Brazilian Tenant Farmers**, exit roof to left, step across crack and continue on face to top. Pro: Small to large pro.

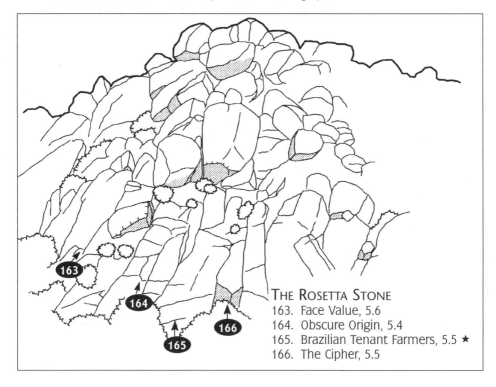

THE ROSETTA STONE
163. Face Value, 5.6
164. Obscure Origin, 5.4
165. Brazilian Tenant Farmers, 5.5 ★
166. The Cipher, 5.5

Hog Heaven

This area, named after witnessing hordes of javelina, encompasses climbing from three major crags. Although a fairly strenuous hike, the remoteness and novelty of the area make for a refreshing day.

Hog Heaven – Main Wall South

The routes on this section of the Main Wall are short but powerful. They were originally rated much lower which accounts for the "bag" in some of the route names.

167. **John's Bag, 5.10a** Originally rated 5.8++, the name makes much more sense. Start at thin crack near left end of south wall. Climb thin crack left to platform. Step left off platform under roof and traverse left off the wall. Pro: Small to medium nuts, Friends.

168. **Sand's Bag, 5.10a** Start ten feet right of **John's Bag**. Climb left-arching finger-crack to top. Pro: Small to medium nuts, Friends.

169. **Chalk Bag, 5.6** Start right of **Sand's Bag** or at right side of south wall. Climb crack staying left past bulge to hand-crack. Continue in crack to top. Pro: Medium nuts, Friends.

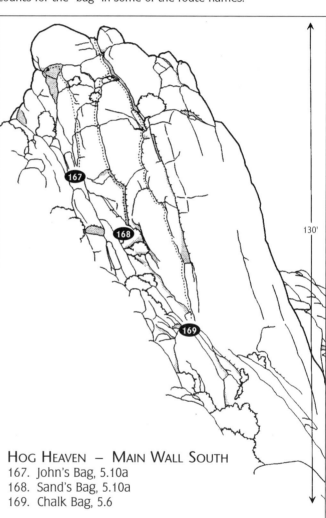

130'

HOG HEAVEN – MAIN WALL SOUTH
167. John's Bag, 5.10a
168. Sand's Bag, 5.10a
169. Chalk Bag, 5.6

Hog Heaven – Main Wall East

The climbs on this section of the Main Wall are surprisingly almost 200-foot long. A large ledge splits the routes into two pitches and conveniently allows climbers the option of traversing off or in after the first pitch.

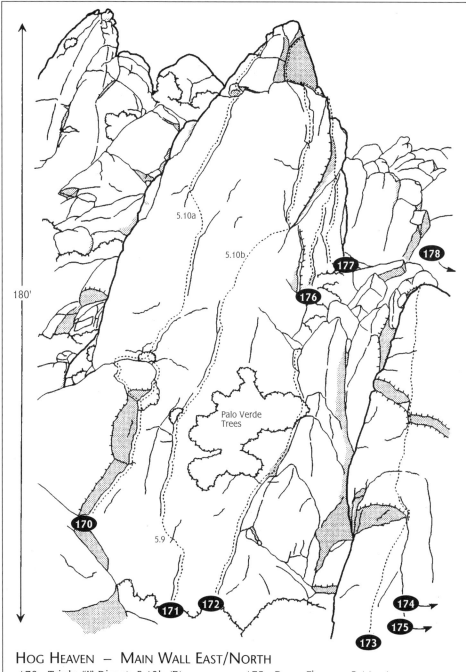

Hog Heaven – Main Wall East/North

170. Triple "J" Direct, 5.10b (R)
171. Static Cling, 5.10b (R) ★★
172. George Of The Jungle, 5.6
173. Pissed Off, 5.8 ★★
174. High On The Hog, 5.11b ★

175. Bony Fingers, 5.11a ★
176. Sudden Impact, 5.10b ★
177. Shiver Me Timbers, 5.10c ★
178. Slime Slit, 5.9 ★

170. **Triple "J" Direct, 5.10b (R)**   Guaranteed to raise the hair somewhere on your body when leading! Start on east side at base of twin handcracks. First Pitch: Climb twin handcracks to small roof, then exit either left or right. Continue to horizontal crack and belay. Second Pitch: Climb thin, right-arching crack to thin, vertical, insipid crack. Continue in vertical crack until it disappears, then traverse face left to finger-crack (5.10a). Follow this crack to top. Pro: Small to medium nuts, Friends.

171. **Static Cling, 5.10b (R) ★★**   A variety of free-climbing moves highlight this fine climb. Start 15 feet right of **Triple "J" Direct**. First Pitch: Climb small crack until possible to traverse left to bolt (5.9). Continue up past catclaw tree to crack and belay. Second Pitch: Climb up crack to its end and face climb up and right to ramp and crack (5.10b) Follow ramp to horn, then step left and climb fingercrack to top (5.10a). Third Pitch: Climb right-arching crack to top. Pro: Small to medium nuts, Friends, 1 bolt.

172. **George Of The Jungle, 5.6**   Start 15 feet right of **Static Cling**. Climb wide crack to slot,then past tree to top. Pro: Medium to large nuts.

173. **Pissed Off, 5.8 ★★**   This route is the obvious direct start to **Sudden Impact** and **Shiver Me Timbers** and makes a good warm-up to boot. Start down and right of **George of the Jungle** across gully. Climb face past two bolts to roof, then continue over roof and climb face past a few cracks to top. Pro: Small to medium nuts, Friends, two bolts.

174. **High On The Hog, 5.11b ★**   This starts about 50 feet to the right of **Pissed Off**. Climb left-facing corner past two bolts to roof. Traverse under roof to third bolt and climb thin crack to top. Pro: Three bolts, small to medium nuts, TCUs.

175. **Bony Fingers, 5.11a ★**   60 feet right of **High on the Hog**, climb left-arching finger-crack. Pro: Small to medium nuts, TCUs

Hog Heaven – Main Wall North

Short but interesting thin cracks highlight this section of the Main Wall. See topo above.

176. **Sudden Impact, 5.10b ★**   A short but mighty thin crack. Start at the top of **Pissed Off** at north wall. First Pitch: Climb thin, right-arching crack on left (right of ramp on **Static Cling**) past bulge to ledge. Second Pitch: Move back left and climb **Static Cling's** third pitch. Pro: Small to medium nuts, Friends.

177. **Shiver Me Timbers, 5.10c ★**   A short but mightier thin crack. Start ten feet right of **Sudden Impact**. First Pitch: Climb thin crack in brown stain until possible to join **Sudden Impact**. Second Pitch: Same as **Sudden Impact**. Pro: Small to medium nuts, Friends.

178. **Slime Slit, 5.9 ★**   Start down and right of **Shiver Me Timbers**. Climb small crack on right corner past horizontal crack. Climb thinning crack and face to top. Pro: Small nuts, Friends.

179. **Domestic Longhair (Rating Unknown)** This is found ½ mile east (downhill) from the Hog Heaven Main Wall Area. First Pitch: Climb right side of face past three bolts to belay ledge. Second Pitch: Climb horn left of belay ledge. Continue on face above past one bolt to top. Pro: Four bolts, small to medium cams needed for belay ledge.

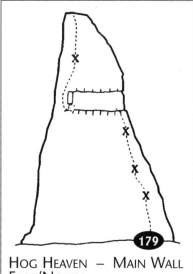

HOG HEAVEN – MAIN WALL EAST/NORTH
179. Domestic Longhair (Rating Unknown)

Hog Heaven – Upper Wall

Located up and left of the Main Wall, the Upper Wall offers a selection of moderately difficult climbs.

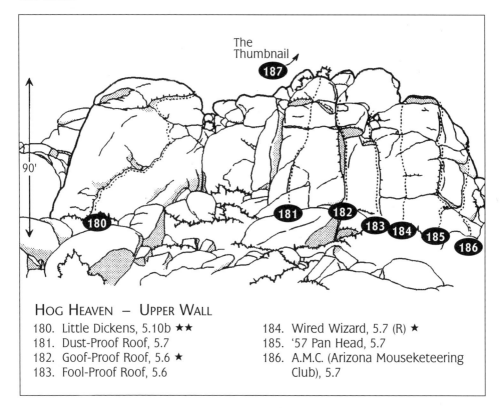

HOG HEAVEN – UPPER WALL

180. Little Dickens, 5.10b ★★
181. Dust-Proof Roof, 5.7
182. Goof-Proof Roof, 5.6 ★
183. Fool-Proof Roof, 5.6

184. Wired Wizard, 5.7 (R) ★
185. '57 Pan Head, 5.7
186. A.M.C. (Arizona Mouseketeering Club), 5.7

180. **Little Dickens, 5.10b ★★** Start at far left below long, thin, diagonaling crack. Climb crack past pin (5.10b), then continue until you can climb back left to wide crack that angles right. Finish in this crack to top. Pro: Small to large nuts, Friends.

181. **Dust-Proof Roof, 5.7** Start approximately 40 feet right of **Little Dickens**. Climb boulder against wall, then proceed up thin crack on face to roof. Climb face over roof to top. Pro: Small to medium nuts, Friends.

182. **Goof-Proof Roof, 5.6 ★** Start 15 feet right of **Dust-Proof Roof.** Climb handcrack in left corner to roof. Exit roof on left and continue to top. Pro: Medium nuts, Friends.

183. **Fool-Proof Roof, 5.6** Start ten feet right of **Goof-Proof Roof**. Climb handcrack in right corner to roof. Exit over roof to top. Pro: Medium nuts, Friends.

184. **Wired Wizard, 5.7 (R) ★** Start just right of **Fool Proof Roof**. Climb face past series of horizontal cracks and vertical cracks to top. Pro: Small to medium nuts, Friends.

185. **'57 Pan Head, 5.7** Start ten feet right of **Wired Wizard**. Traverse left into handcrack, then climb widening crack to top. Pro: Medium to large nuts, Friends.

186. **A.M.C. (Arizona Mouseketeering Club), 5.7** Start ten feet right of **'57 Pan Head**. Climb wide crack to top. Pro: Medium to large nuts, Friends.

187. **Thumbnail, 5.5** Almost directly above the Upper Wall, a prominent pinnacle can be seen. This pinnacle is easily visible from the desert floor. Start at south side. Scramble up loose rock to top. Descend via a single line tandem rappel. Pro: Friends.

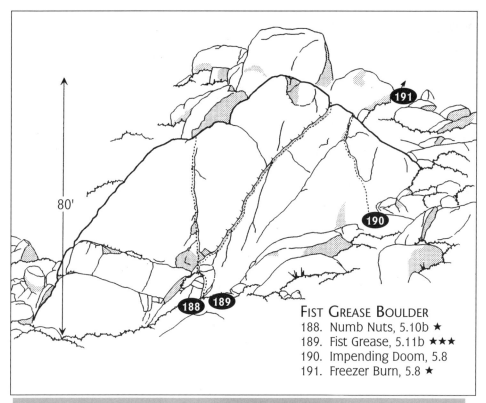

80'

FIST GREASE BOULDER
188. Numb Nuts, 5.10b ★
189. Fist Grease, 5.11b ★★★
190. Impending Doom, 5.8
191. Freezer Burn, 5.8 ★

Fist Grease Boulder

Located up and right from the Main Wall, this rock wall offers one of the best crack climbs in Phoenix.

188. **Numb Nuts, 5.10b ★**   Be awake before attempting this route. Start at crack farthest left on north face. Climb to small ledge below crack, then proceed up crack (5.10b) until it peters out to face. Finish short face past bolt to top. Pro: Small to medium nuts, Friends.

189. **Fist Grease, 5.11b ★★★**   A surprisingly sustained and difficult crack! Start is same as **Numb Nuts**. Climb to small ledge. Climb right-arching fist crack (5.11b) to alcove, then continue in crack to top. Pro: Medium to large nuts, Friends.

190. **Impending Doom, 5.8**   Start at far right under large flake. Climb face to cracks, then step left off flake to top. Pro: Small to medium nuts, Friends.

191. **Freezer Burn, 5.8 ★**   Start in gully 150 feet up and behind Fist Grease Boulder.Climb face to thin crack, then continue in crack to top. Pro: Small nuts, Friends.

Chapter 7

PINNACLE PEAK

Pinnacle Peak is a 200' granite pinnacle located at the northwest end of the McDowell Mountains, northeast of Scottsdale proper. This area has been a favorite of local climbers since the late 1960's. Most climbs at the peak are scattered over its three summits. The North Summit is the largest, but the East and West Summits are the highest. The Notch, the boulder-filled area between the summits and the Sun Deck Boulder, a large flat boulder located 100' above the talus and below the Shalayly Direct face, also serve as key landmarks when locating climbs on the Pinnacle proper. There are more starred routes (especially three-star routes) at the Peak than any other area. There area also many quality routes to be found on smaller crags surrounding the peak (see climbing area map).

Approach: From the Scottsdale area, drive north on Scottsdale Road to Pinnacle Peak Road. Turn right (east) on this road and follow (via Pima Road, Happy Valley Road and Alma School Road) around three bends until you reach a restaurant (Pinnacle Peak Patio) due east of Pinnacle Peak . For those who live on the west side of I - 17, approach Scottsdale Road via Pinnacle Peak Road or Bell Road (then north) or Carefree Highway (then south). At this point park any cars at the west end of the parking lot due west of the restaurant (traditional access has been via Pinnacle Peak Patio's parking lot).

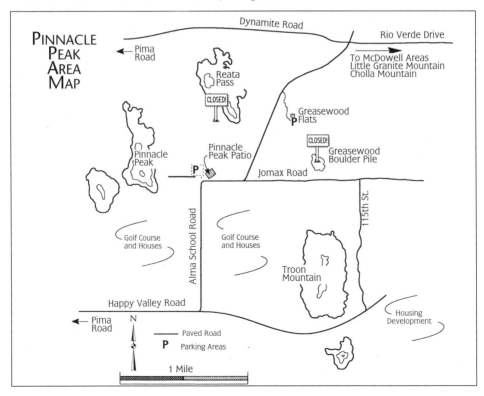

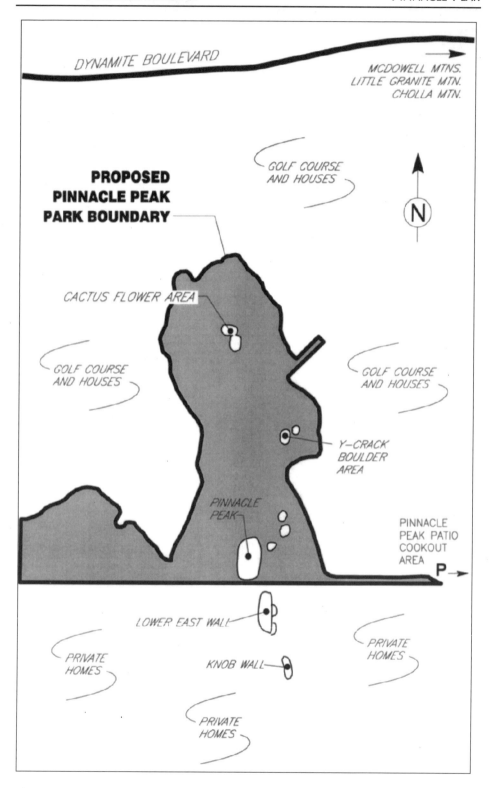

Access: For years, Pinnacle Peak has been the crown jewel of the Phoenix granite areas. Easy access, a wide variety of routes and great climbing have made it a very popular desitination for many climbers since the 1960's. As with many of the crags in northeastern Scottsdale, Pinnacle Peak is located on privately owned land. In the summer and fall of 1994, the inevitable housing development just below the Lower East Wall started. By the spring of '95, barricades had gone up between the parking lot and the crags and access denial was enforced by sherrif's deputies. The area was completely shut down at that time to all recreational activities.

At the time of publication of this guide, Pinnacle Peak may be either opened or closed. The general area surrounding the Peak (see map below) is STILL supposed to be donated as a park. The plans and layout that I have seen for this park includes all the climbing areas detailed in this chapter EXCEPT for the Knob Wall, Satan's Slab and Lower East Wall areas, which are NOT included as part of the proposed park. As these three areas will continue to reside on private land, climbing may not be allowed. At the current time, negotiations are ongoing to allow climbing at the Lower East Wall, which has been one of the most popular of the Phoenix climbing areas. It is not known what the end result of these negotiations will be. Contact local climbing shops or gyms for information on the current access situation for all areas in this chapter. We can only hope that climbing will be included as a recreational use of this wonderful landmark in the future. Cross your fingers and get involved!

The "golf-n-stuff" development the desert continues in earnest. Until things settle down and give some indication of what the climbing access will be, I can only take an optimistic guess about what is going to happen.

The map shown above is my best info guess on the eventual boundaries of the proposed Pinnacle Peak Park. This map should be taken with a grain of salt, as the eventual outcome of the park and it's boundaries (assuming it is created) will most likely undergo some change and redefinition before things are finalized.

The map above shows the layout of the Pinnacle Peak climbing areas. The trails shown are the historical approaches to the climbing areas. When Pinnacle Peak Park is finally created, there will be established park trails with access to the crags within the park. Please do your part to stay on these trails to reduce climber impact and damage.

When Pinnacle Peak reopens for climbing and other recreational activities, contact local climbing shops or local climbing gyms to get information on the current access situation. A list of these shops/gyms and their phone numbers may be found in the General Information chapter of this guide. There will probably be an increase in rules and regulations concerning climbing within the park. Please cooperate with these rules and be considerate to other park users. Practice low-impact climbing and climb safe. A good relationship between park officials and climbers can mean years of continued enjoyment of this area and it's wonderful climbing opportunities.

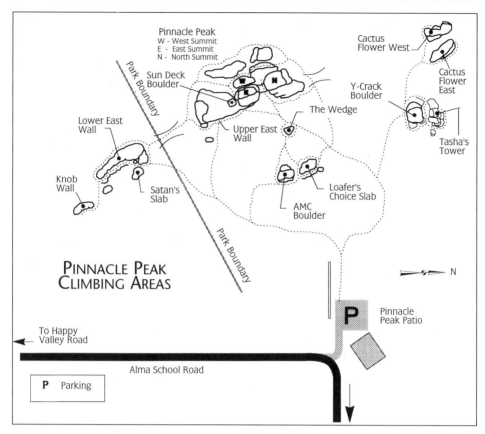

PINNACLE PEAK
W - West Summit
E - East Summit
N - North Summit

Sun Deck
Boulder

Lower East
Wall

Knob
Wall

Satan's
Slab

Upper East
Wall

Cactus
Flower West

Y-Crack
Boulder

The Wedge

Cactus
Flower
East

Tasha's
Tower

Loafer's
Choice Slab

AMC
Boulder

PINNACLE PEAK
CLIMBING AREAS

N

Pinnacle
Peak Patio

P

To Happy
Valley Road

Alma School Road

P   Parking

Pinnacle Peak Route Descriptions

Knob Wall

This small wall is located just southeast from Lower East Wall and yields a couple of fine face climbs. The access situation for this small area is rather grim at the current time and doesn't look good for future climbing here. Since miracles sometimes happen, I have optimistically included the Knob Wall information in this chapter. Please DO NOT climb here unless there is an established agreement for access between climbers and private landowners. See the Lower East Wall for an aerial map showing route location. Standard Descent from Knob Wall Routes : Walk off either side.

1. **Double Digit Dilemma, 5.10b ★★**   This name was inspired by a Reagan phrase. Start at left side of wall. Scramble up short broken section on left side of slab to first bolt Then continue up past the "knob" and three bolts to top. Pro: Four bolts, medium to large nuts (belay).

2. **Inflation, 5.9 ★** Start ten feet right of **Double Digit Dilemma**. Climb face past horizontal cracks to short vertical crack. then up crack and face (5.9) to top Pro: Medium to large nuts, two bolts.

3. **Famous Last Words, 5.10c** Climb knobby face past two bolts. Pro: Two bolts.

Lower East Wall

Until the recent access debacle, this wall was one of the busiest crags in Phoenix. Hopefully, the good old days will return if access can be worked out with the land owner. Until access

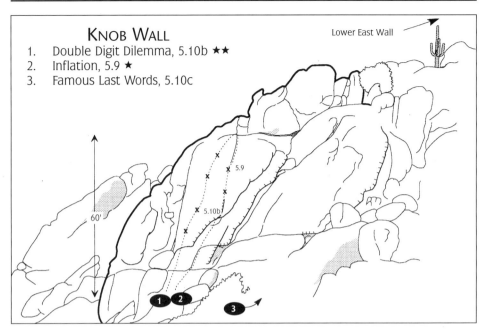

KNOB WALL
1. Double Digit Dilemma, 5.10b ★★
2. Inflation, 5.9 ★
3. Famous Last Words, 5.10c

Lower East Wall

can be restored (if and when), please **DO NOT** climb here unless there is an established agreement for access between climbers and private landowners. Access issues aside, this is an excellent training ground for aspiring climbers with a wonderful assortment of routes of all difficulties. Cracks predominate from fingers to chimney and 5.6 to 5.11a, but there are also faces ranging from 5.6 to 5.12. All this, and the fact that this wall lends itself to top-roping as well as leading, makes this a must do crag. Standard Descent for Lower East Wall routes: Walk off. Best way is to the left (south) down past Leftovers.

4. **Any Time Around, 5.10a** Just to the left of **Second Time Around**, climb short face past two bolts. Pro: Two bolts
5. **Second Time Around, 5.10d** This route is not located on the Lower East Wall but on a small east facing slab approximately 100' below the left (south) side of the Lower

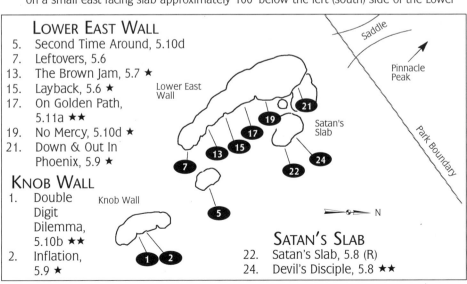

LOWER EAST WALL
5. Second Time Around, 5.10d
7. Leftovers, 5.6
13. The Brown Jam, 5.7 ★
15. Layback, 5.6 ★
17. On Golden Path, 5.11a ★★
19. No Mercy, 5.10d ★
21. Down & Out In Phoenix, 5.9 ★

KNOB WALL
1. Double Digit Dilemma, 5.10b ★★
2. Inflation, 5.9 ★

SATAN'S SLAB
22. Satan's Slab, 5.8 (R)
24. Devil's Disciple, 5.8 ★★

East Wall. Since nothing is known about the first ascent. the name is credited to Neil Sugarman who renovated the climb. and added a variation. Start underneath two parallel seams on the face. Climb left seam for 15 feet until possible to traverse right into a "dish" between the left and right seam Climb face out of "dish" (just right of left seam) to top. Pro: Small nuts (sliders may be useful), Friends. Note: Pitons were used on Neil's ascent (see following), but others claim to have lead this line on natural protection.

All the Right Moves Variation, 5.10d Start 12 feet right of regular start at right arête. Climb arête past bolt to a dished out spot". then traverse left between the two seams to the dish" as mentioned on the regular route. Finish on regular route Pro: One bolt.

6. **Bookend, 5.7** Just to the right of **Second Time Around,** climb short right-facing dihedral. Look out for crusty rock! Pro: Medium to Large

7. **Leftovers, 5.6** Start at extreme southeast end of wall at base of south-facing face Climb short. vertical crack and face to bolt Continue on face (5.6) to horizontal crack. then left and up to top. Pro: Small to medium nuts, one bolt (Hanger may not be in place)

8. **Dispute, 5.7** Start at extreme southeast end of wall just right of **Leftovers.** Climb short. vertical crack in right-facing dihedral. passing small roof to top Pro: Small to medium nuts.
   Variation, 5.6 Instead of following crack directly to top. traverse off left via short. left-veering crack. Pro: Small nuts.

9. **Lizard's Lip, 5.8 ★** Beware of the chuckwalla in the upper crack! He's still there after all these years of climber feet and hands. Start six feet right of Dispute. Climb flake and short, vertical crack in left-facing dihedral Continue in crack passing roof to top (5.8). Pro: Small to medium nuts.
   Variation, 5.6 From small ledge even with lip of roof, traverse right into the **Groin.** Continue to top via the Groin. Pro: Small to medium nuts.

10. **The Groin, 5.6 ★** All one has to do is look at the pillar of rock where the climb starts and think about falling on it to understand this route's name. Start six feet right of **Lizard's Lip.** Step off boulder against main wall and continue in crack to top. Pro: Small to medium nuts.

11. **Wheat Thin, 5.11a** Many falls were taken trying to protect the opening crux section before the leader could even think about moving through the crux. Start just right of the **Groin.** Step off boulder against main wall Climb face and thin crack over bulge Continue in crack system to top. Pro: Small to medium nuts

12. **The Last Detail. 5.10a ★★** This climb was thought to be the last conceivable line on the wall that had not been climbed Little did the first ascent party realize Start is just right and down from **Wheat Thin.** Climb right-leaning cracks to enter overhanging, broken, dihedral system. After clearing dihedral system (5.10a). join a right-facing dihedral just left until possible to step right into thin crack Continue up this crack to top Pro: Small to medium nuts.

13. **The Brown Jam, 5.7 ★** Start five feet right of the **Last Detail.** Climb brown-stained crack. as direct as possible. to top. Pro: Medium to large nuts.
    FA 1972 John Byrd. Doug Rickard

14. **Drop, Plop, Fly Or Die, 5.12** Climb face between **Brown Jam** and **Layback** past several bolts. Although originally rated at 5.13a, subsequent ascents have shown this rating to be a bit elevated. Pro: Several Bolts

15. **Layback, 5.6 ★** Except for some loose rock at the top, this is a good 5.6 climb. Start right of the **Brown Jam.** Climb shallow dihedral to top Pro: Medium to large nuts, one bolt.
    Variation, 5.7 ★ Start just right around corner. Climb steep crack (loose rock) to join regular route halfway. Pro: Small to large nuts.

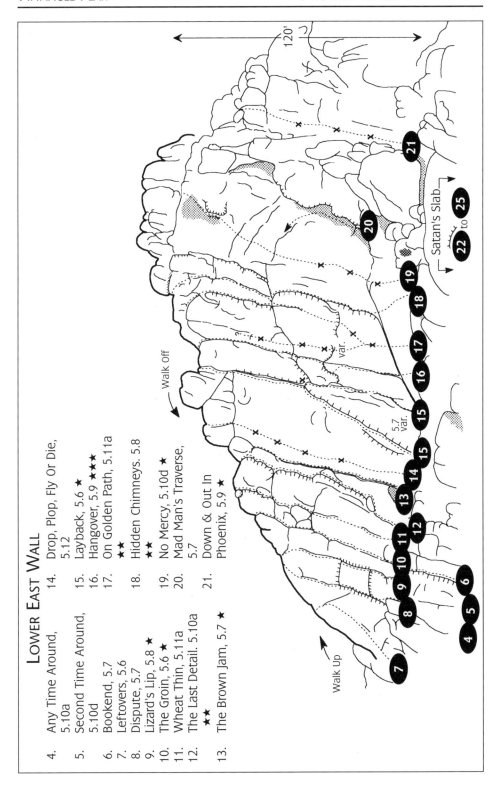

LOWER EAST WALL

4. Any Time Around, 5.10a
5. Second Time Around, 5.10d
6. Bookend, 5.7
7. Leftovers, 5.6
8. Dispute, 5.7
9. Lizard's Lip, 5.8 ★
10. The Groin, 5.6 ★
11. Wheat Thin, 5.11a
12. The Last Detail. 5.10a ★★
13. The Brown Jam, 5.7 ★
14. Drop, Plop, Fly Or Die, 5.12
15. Layback, 5.6 ★
16. Hangover, 5.9 ★★★
17. On Golden Path, 5.11a ★★
18. Hidden Chimneys. 5.8 ★★
19. No Mercy, 5.10d ★
20. Mad Man's Traverse, 5.7
21. Down & Out In Phoenix, 5.9 ★

16. **Hangover, 5.9** ★★★ There are a variety of small variations that can increase the difficulty Your imagination is the limit! Start ten feet right of **Layback**. Climb thin crack by easiest means past two small overhangs to top Pro: Small to medium nuts, one bolt.

17. **On Golden Path, 5.11a** ★★ Who says that old men can't climb? Start six feet right of Hangover. Climb face passing horizontal crack to bolt. Continue up and right past another bolt (5.11a) to a small roof. Clear roof (5.11a) into a vertical crack that leads to a ledge. At this point the route crosses **Hidden Chimneys**. Climb a short thin crack just right of a right-facing dihedral to top Pro: Small to medium nuts, two bolts. Friends.
    Variation, 5.11b/c This line appeared on the wall in 1991 or so. So far, no one has taken credit for the bolting. From the second bolt of **On Golden Path**, climb slightly left to another bolt. Continue straight up past another couple of bolts to top. Pro: Five bolts

18. **Hidden Chimneys. 5.8** ★★ Notice the displaced block at the beginning that used to occupy the chimney. Start ten feet right of **On Golden Path**. Climb short face onto ledge. Continue up wide crack and chimney. then move left to vertical. right-facing dihedral that leads to top. Pro: Small to large nuts.
    Variation, 5.8 Instead of moving left after chimney. move right and follow vertical crack system to top Watch out for the bee hive. Pro: Medium to large nuts.

19. **No Mercy, 5.10d** ★ The leader had a classic line on the first ascent. "There's no place to hook!" The second gave an appropriate response; "I guess you'll have to stand and pound the bolt!"
    No mercy...Start 20 feet right and up from **Hidden Chimneys**. Climb face past small horizontal crack to bolt. Continue on thin face past two more bolts (5.10d) to small discontinuous cracks From here move right and up past large zenolith (5.10b) to horizontal crack. Continue on past bulge into a shallow gully and to top. Pro: Small to medium nuts, three bolts, Friends.

20. **Mad Man's Traverse, 5.7** (not shown on topo) Start at right end of wall. First Pitch: Scramble up easy chimney to thin crack diagonalling up and left. Climb crack to belay ledge on **Hidden Chimneys**. Second Pitch: Traverse left to **Hangover**, downclimb and continue left to **Layback**. Continue left to bolt. drop down to shelf. and traverse left past the Last Detail to the **Groin**. Finish to top via the **Groin**. Pro: Small to large nuts, three bolts.

21. **Down & Out In Phoenix, 5.9** ★ This challenging lead starts 40' right of **No Mercy** at thin face just left of thin seam. Climb face past three bolts to top. A third bolt was added after the first ascent (and by the first ascent party) to make the climb safer hurray! Pro: Three bolts, Friends

Satan's Slab

Located just below the Lower East Wall, Satan's Slab offers thin face climbs on predominantly sound granite As with the Lower East Wall. all the routes lend themselves to top-roping or leading. The access at this crag will most likely be tied into access to the Lower East Wall (see above).

22. **Satan's Slab, 5.8 (R)** Start just below middle of Lower East Wall at left side of prominent white slab. Climb detached flake. then continue on face left and up past one bolt to top Pro: One bolt.
    Variation, 5.8 (R) Climb face directly left of flake to bolt and regular route. Pro: None

23. **White Warlock, 5.10d** ★★ Originally rated 5.9. one wonders if the rating is still a "sandbag" Start just right of detached flake. Climb face past two bolts and small under cling to top. Be careful not to use the detached flake for climbing. Pro: Two bolts, small to medium nuts. Note: The arête between **White Warlock** and **Devil's Disciple** has been toproped at 5.10a.

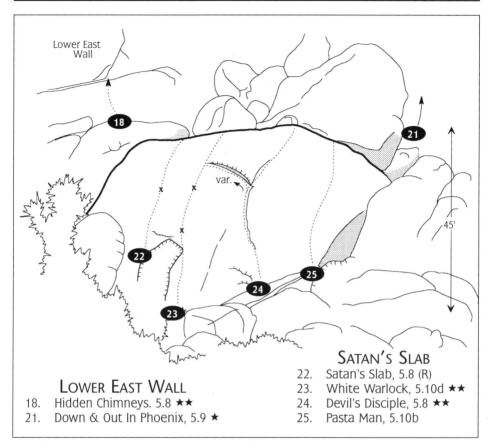

Lower East Wall

18. Hidden Chimneys. 5.8 ★★
21. Down & Out In Phoenix, 5.9 ★

Satan's Slab

22. Satan's Slab, 5.8 (R)
23. White Warlock, 5.10d ★★
24. Devil's Disciple, 5.8 ★★
25. Pasta Man, 5.10b

24. **Devil's Disciple, 5.8** ★★ Originally climbed as a free solo, this route has a variety of nice moves. Start at obvious crack just right of **White Warlock**. Make face moves to gain crack. then continue in crack up and right where a short face leads to the top. Pro: Small nuts, Friends

25. **Pasta Man, 5.10b** Pasta and hanging on hooks don't mix as grounders from "popped" hooks will testify! Ouch! Start just right and up from **Devil's Disciple**. Climb face up past one bolt (5.10b). then right and up past another bolt to top. Pro: Large nuts (lead belay), two bolts.

AMC Boulder

Three prominent right-arching cracks highlight the east face of this boulder pinnacle named for the Arizona Mountaineering Club. The aerial map below shows the location of routes within the AMC Boulder / Loafer's Choice Slab area. Standard Descent for AMC Boulder: Descend via short rappel off south or east side via large eyebolt on top.

26. **Reunion, 5.8 (R)** ★ Although originally done as a ground-up ascent, the bolts were stripped from this route by unknown parties. Until they are replaced, this route must be done as a toprope problem. Start at base of buttress that has three prominent, right-arching cracks (facing east). Climb face just left of left-most crack. Be careful to take the path of least resistance or this climb could be harder than 5.8 (hint: straight to the bolt is more like 5.9). Pro: Two bolts (removed by unknown party).

AMC BOULDER

26. Reunion, 5.8 (R) ★
27. Varicose, 5.6 ★
29. Mickey Mantle, 5.8 ★★
32. Mean Streak, 5.10a ★
33. Delayed Flight, 5.8 ★
35. Look Sharp, 5.10a

LOAFER'S CHOICE SLAB

36. Loafer's Choice, 5.10a (R) ★★
37. Dead Meat, 5.7 ★★

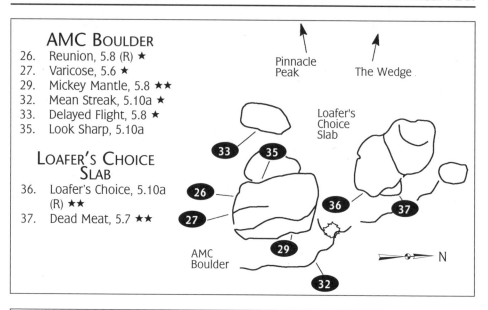

AMC BOULDER

26. Reunion, 5.8 (R) ★
27. Varicose, 5.6 ★
28. Rurpture, 5.10b ★

29. Mickey Mantle, 5.8 ★★

30. Diamond Back Crack, 5.6
31. Up In Smoke, 5.10b ★
32. Mean Streak, 5.10a ★
33. Delayed Flight, 5.8 ★

35. Look Sharp, 5.10a

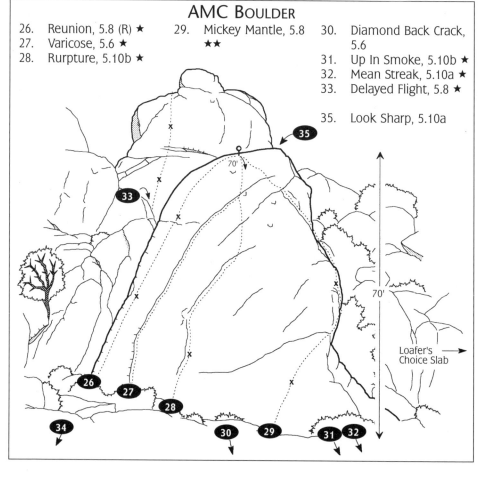

27. **Varicose, 5.6** ★ Start just right of **Reunion** at left-most crack on face. Climb left-most crack to top. Pro: Medium to large nuts, Friends.

28. **Rurpture, 5.10b** ★ This climb was named because the bolt was placed from a rurp in a seam. Originally rated 5.8. the rating was upgraded when a crucial foothold broke. Start just right of **Varicose**. Climb a short face past one bolt (5.10b) to gain a right-arching crack. Continue in crack until possible to climb directly up face past horizontal crack to top. Pro: One bolt, small to medium nuts, Friends.

29. **Mickey Mantle, 5.8** ★★ Start right of **Rurpture** under smooth face. Climb face past one bolt (5.8) to join crack just before corner. Continue over small over-hang past bolt to top (5.7). Pro: Two bolts, medium to large nuts.

30. **Diamond Back Crack, 5.6** This route is located on a rock wall (tan with a section of whi rock in the middle) 60 feet below the AMC Boulder. Start left of the white rock. Climb crack out roof and up to ledge, then climb right-arching crack in slot to top. Pro: Medium to large nuts.

31. **Up In Smoke, 5.10b** ★ Start approximately 100 feet northeast of AMC Boulder at northeast-facing wall. Climb face to horizontal crack and roof, then clear roof via thin crack and zenolith. Follow discontinuous seams past bolt to top. Pro: Friends, one bolt, small nuts.

32. **Mean Streak, 5.10a** ★ Start at northeast facing slab directly below **Mickey Mantle**. Climb face past two bolts to top. Pro: Two bolts

33. **Delayed Flight, 5.8** ★ Start approximately 100 feet west and above from the top of AMC Boulder at base of small face. Climb face past horizontal crack to top. Pro: Two bolts, Friends.

34. **Scar Wars, 5.12a** ★★ Start approximately 200' down (southeast) of AMC Boulder at east face of boulder pile with three prominent tiers. Climb flake to thin crack at second tier. Climb crack (5.12a), then move right at horizontal crack to another vertical crack. Climb crack to top. Pro: Small nuts, Friends.

Don Eydenburg nears the crux moves of **Mickey Mantle** (5.8) on the AMC Boulder.

35. **Look Sharp, 5.10a** Another ground-up route that has been stripped of it's bolts. Another lead turned toprope problem! Start on the back side (facing west) in a large boulder enclave. Approach from the north northeast (nne). Climb face just right of boulder (5.10a) to top. Pro: Two bolts (removed by unknown party)

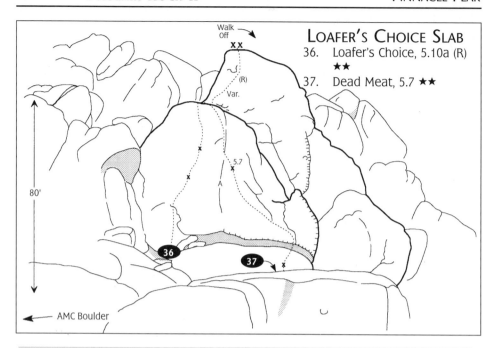

Walk Off

LOAFER'S CHOICE SLAB

36. Loafer's Choice, 5.10a (R) ★★

37. Dead Meat, 5.7 ★★

80'

← AMC Boulder

Loafer's Choice Slab

This slab, located just to the north of the AMC Boulder area, offers excellent face climbing and a unique belay position. It is also possible to finish out the last short (runout, but easy) section of the upper face to belay from bolts on top of the formation (see variation on topo).

36. **Loafer's Choice, 5.10a (R)** ★★ This climb is for those loafers who want a quick face climb. but don't want to go all the way to the Wedge. It's worth it! Start at base of smooth, east-facing slab. Climb small dihedral and face past two bolts to top. The belay involves wedging yourself behind the face and is surprisingly secure as long as your second doesn't outweigh you 2-to-1 - Har, Har! Pro: Two bolts.

37. **Dead Meat, 5.7** ★★ Start down and right of **Loafer's Choice.** Climb face past bolt to roof. Clear roof and continue on face using left-most crack until possible to move out left to arête. Continue to top via arête. One should take note that this is a very continuous 5.7 route. Pro: Two bolts, Friends.
     Variation, 5.9   After roof. continue in left-most crack and face (right of arête) to top. Pro: Small nuts.
     Variation, 5.3   After roof, climb right crack to top. Pro: Medium nuts.

The Wedge

This triangular-shaped pinnacle offers challenging face climbing with a classic summit. Notice the case-hardening on the west face (see geology section). Standard Descent for Wedge: Rappel (single line) from two-bolt anchor southeast or northwest.

38. **Hiliter, 5.7 (R)** ★ Start at middle of northeast face. Climb face past one bolt to top. Pro: One bolt, two belay bolts.
     Variation, 5.7   Instead of regular start, step off boulder on north side to gain northwest face and regular route. Pro: One bolt.

39. **Redemption, 5.9** ★★ Once again, another testimonial to Lance and Dane Daugherty's remarkably early free-climbing talents. Start at left side of southeast face. Climb face past two bolts to corner. then up corner to top. Pro: Two bolts, two belay bolts.

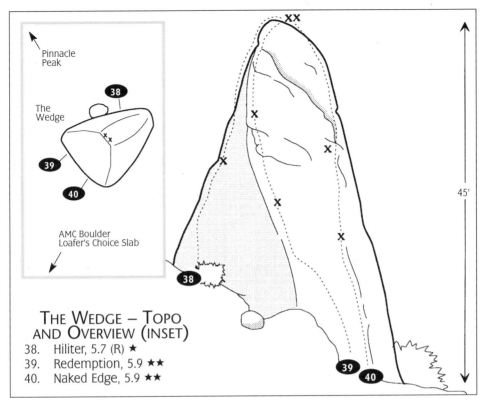

The Wedge – Topo and Overview (inset)

38. Hiliter, 5.7 (R) ★
39. Redemption, 5.9 ★★
40. Naked Edge, 5.9 ★★

40. **Naked Edge, 5.9** ★★ Beware of rope damage, if one falls around the corner (double ropes are recommended!). Start at right side of southeast face. Climb thin crack and face to corner, then up corner to top. Pro: Small nuts, two bolts, two belay bolts.

Y-Crack Boulder

This distinct boulder identified by the obvious off-width lies on top of a small knoll due north of Pinnacle Peak proper. Several routes have been done in this gathering of boulders and small towers. Standard Descent for Y-Crack Boulder: Rappel (single line) northeast.

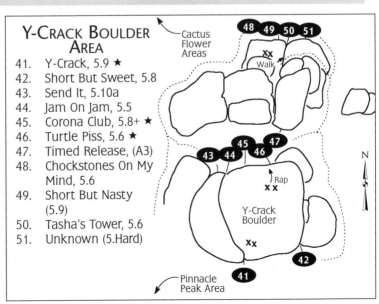

Y-Crack Boulder Area

41. Y-Crack, 5.9 ★
42. Short But Sweet, 5.8
43. Send It, 5.10a
44. Jam On Jam, 5.5
45. Corona Club, 5.8+ ★
46. Turtle Piss, 5.6 ★
47. Timed Release, (A3)
48. Chockstones On My Mind, 5.6
49. Short But Nasty (5.9)
50. Tasha's Tower, 5.6
51. Unknown (5.Hard)

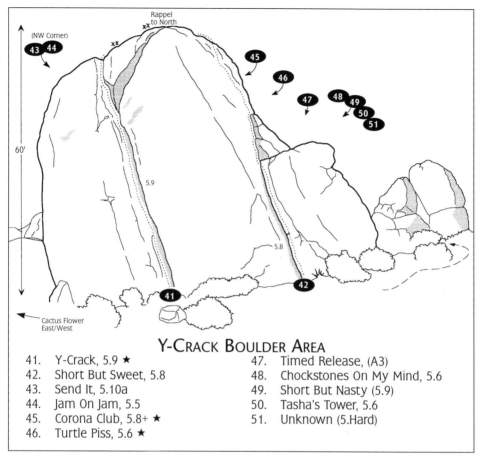

Y-CRACK BOULDER AREA

41. Y-Crack, 5.9 ★
42. Short But Sweet, 5.8
43. Send It, 5.10a
44. Jam On Jam, 5.5
45. Corona Club, 5.8+ ★
46. Turtle Piss, 5.6 ★

47. Timed Release, (A3)
48. Chockstones On My Mind, 5.6
49. Short But Nasty (5.9)
50. Tasha's Tower, 5.6
51. Unknown (5.Hard)

41. **Y-Crack, 5.9** ★ Start on south face. Climb obvious offwidth to "Y". Then continue up left crack to top. Pro: Medium to large, #4 or #5 Camelots, Big Dudes, Big Bros or tube chocks.

42. **Short But Sweet, 5.8** Maybe one of the more brutal 5.8's in the area. Start just right of Y-Crack at base of short. vertical crack. Climb crack to platform, then continue up east face to top. Pro: Medium to large nuts.

43. **Send It, 5.10a** Just to the right of **Jam On Jam** is a finger crack starting out of the same alcove. Ascend finger crack, avoiding a stem to the boulder behind. Break left when you absolutely have to and continue to top. Pro: Small to medium.

44. **Jam On Jam, 5.5** Start at northwest side of boulder. Climb jagged crack (loose rock) to top. Pro: Medium to large nuts.

45. **Corona Club, 5.8+** ★ Just right of **Turtle Piss**, climb face up thin seam past two bolts to top. Pro: Two bolts.

46. **Turtle Piss, 5.6** ★ Interesting name—on the first ascent Steve had to move a turtle away from the start. The turtle in its discontent decided to piss all over him, thus the name. Start at northeast side of boulder just right of northeast corner. Climb face past two bolts to top. Pro: Two bolts.

For the location of the remaining routes in the Y-Crack Boulder Area, see the overhead map.

47. **Timed Release, (A3)** Start on opposite wall from **Turtle Piss**. Aid left-leaning over-hanging seam until possible to free climb (be careful of loose rock at top). Pro: Pitons (Knifeblades to one-inch angle).

48. **Chockstones On My Mind, 5.6** This route is located on a large boulder massif just behind (northeast) from Y-Crack Boulder. From **Turtle Piss** walk east and north around corner until a large recess capped by two large chockstones is visible on left. Start in recess at south face under chockstone. Climb face to chockstone, then clear chockstone and proceed to top of **Tasha's Tower**. Pro: Medium to large nuts.

49. **Short But Nasty (5.9)** Located on the boulder just left of **Chockstones On My Mind**. Climb this fingertip crack to the alcove above. Essentially an extended boulder problem but an interesting seam. Pro: Small nuts and TCUs.

50. **Tasha's Tower, 5.6** Start north around corner from **Chockstones On My Mind** at northeast corner of boulder massif. Climb thin crack system just right of wide crack to gain left-leaning hand crack. Climb crack to top of tower. Pro: Small to medium nuts (large for belay).

51. **Unknown (5.Hard)** Start as for **Tasha's Tower**. Climb thin seam to bolt on right. Continue on face above (right of crack system) past another bolt to the top. Just in front of a boulder at the top, there are two 3/8-inch bolt studs with no hangers. Take medium to large pro for the belay. Walk off. Pro: Two bolts, medium-large pro (for belay).

Standard descent for **Tasha's Tower** Routes : Somewhat intricate downclimb via alcove just above **Chockstones On My Mind** and then around to east. Two bolts without hangers will be found at the top of **Tasha's Tower**.

CACTUS FLOWER AREA

52. Anarchist's Delight, 5.7+
53. Worm, 5.6
55. King Of Pain, 5.10a
59. Black Sunday, 5.10b (R)
60. Fabulous Fables, 5.10c
62. Palo Verde, 5.7
65. Pam's Jam, 5.7
66. Zenolith, 5.9 e
69. Mixed Feelings, 5.7
70. Cactus Flower, 5.10a ★
71. Crumbled Freak, 5.10a
72. You Can't Get There From Here, 5.11
73. I Just Wanna Be In The Guidebook, 5.7 ★

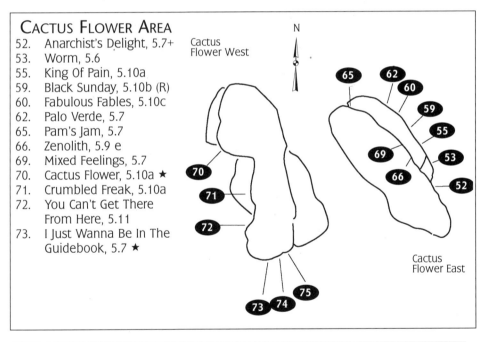

Cactus Flower West

N

Cactus Flower East

Cactus Flower East

This east-facing, wall has a good variety of crack and face climbing on it's two short levels.

52. **Anarchist's Delight, 5.7+** Climb 30-foot crack that is 30 feet to the left of **Zenolith**. Pro: Small to medium.

53. **Worm, 5.6** This route climbs the obvious hand crack 20 feet left of **King of Pain**. Pro: Small to medium nuts.

54. **Facist Pig, 5.9** Thin crack past bolt to ledge. Pro: Small to medium nuts, one bolt.

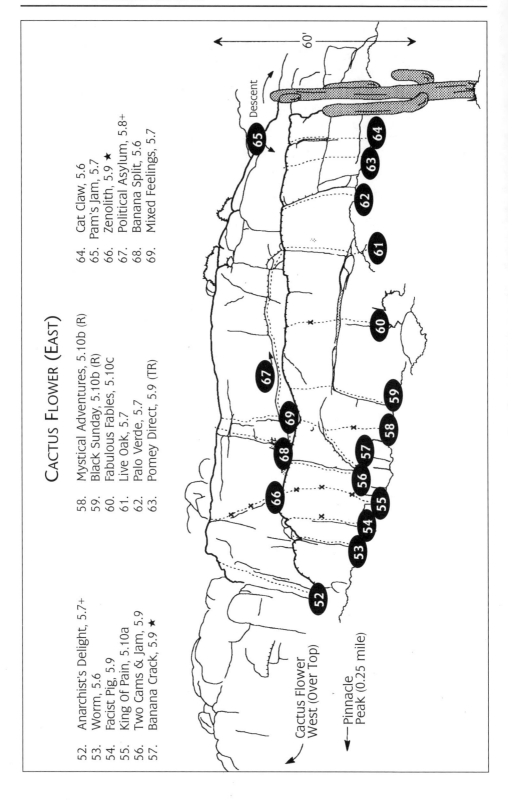

CACTUS FLOWER (EAST)

52. Anarchist's Delight, 5.7+
53. Worm, 5.6
54. Facist Pig, 5.9
55. King Of Pain, 5.10a
56. Two Cams & Jam, 5.9
57. Banana Crack, 5.9 ★

58. Mystical Adventures, 5.10b (R)
59. Black Sunday, 5.10b (R)
60. Fabulous Fables, 5.10c
61. Live Oak, 5.7
62. Palo Verde, 5.7
63. Pomey Direct, 5.9 (TR)

64. Cat Claw, 5.6
65. Pam's Jam, 5.7
66. Zenolith, 5.9 ★
67. Political Asylum, 5.8+
68. Banana Split, 5.6
69. Mixed Feelings, 5.7

55. **King Of Pain, 5.10a** Start at left side of lower wall. Climb face past three bolts to top. Pro: Three bolts (second bolt is bad.).

56. **Two Cams & Jam, 5.9** Start just right of **King of Pain**. Climb wide crack off ground. Move slightly left into thin crack. Climb this crack to top. Pro: Friends.

57. **Banana Crack, 5.9 ★** Start is same as **Two Cams & Jam**. Climb wide, right-arching crack until crack becomes horizontal. At this point climb straight up face (over zenolith) to top. Pro: Medium to large nuts, Friends.

58. **Mystical Adventures, 5.10b (R)** Start ten feet right of **Banana Crack**. Climb face past one bolt to horizontal crack. Finish is the same as **Banana Crack**. Pro: One bolt, Friends.

59. **Black Sunday, 5.10b (R)** Start six feet right from **Mystical Adventures**. Climb slightly right-leaning crack to horizontal crack. Continue past horizontal crack on face (5.10b (R)) to top. Pro: Medium nuts to large nuts, Friends.

60. **Fabulous Fables, 5.10c** Start 20 feet right of **Black Sunday** at thin seam. Climb thin seam to horizontal crack. Continue past horizontal crack on face (past bolt) to top. Pro: Small nuts, Friends, one bolt.

61. **Live Oak, 5.7** Start 30 feet right of **Fabulous Fables**. The route begins on the horizontal shelf to the right of the large block and follows the right slanting deteriorating hand crack. Pro: Small to medium nuts.

62. **Palo Verde, 5.7** Start 20 feet right of **Live Oak**. Climb hand crack to bulge. Turn bulge on left and continue up and past horizontal crack to top. Pro: medium nuts

63. **Pomey Direct, 5.9 (TR)** Climb loose face just right of **Palo Verde**. Pro: TR

64. **Cat Claw, 5.6** Start 10 feet right of **Palo Verde**. Climb face to short off-width. Somewhat loose. Pro: Medium to large nuts.

65. **Pam's Jam, 5.7** Around the corner on the northeast side in three-sided alcove. Climb 35 feet right-leaning hand crack. Pro: Medium to large.

66. **Zenolith, 5.9 ★** Start at wall directly above **King of Pain**. Climb face past two bolts and zenoliths to top. Pro: Two bolts.

67. **Political Asylum, 5.8+** This traverse starts just left of **Mixed Feelings** and goes out to the right, along horizontal crack system, exiting near the top of **Live Oak**. Pro: Medium to large.

68. **Banana Split, 5.6** Start five feet left of **Mixed Feelings**. Clear small roof and climb crack on right. Pro: Small to medium nuts.

69. **Mixed Feelings, 5.7** Start at wall directly above **Banana Crack**. Climb thin seam past horizontal crack (5.7). Continue in crack to top. Pro: Small nuts to medium nuts.

Cactus Flower West

This area, located up and over the hill to the west of Cactus Flower East has a variety of face and crack climbs. Watch out for the approach as it is possible to cross patches of incredibly rotten rock. See Cactus Flower East section for an aerial map of the Cactus Flower area.

70. **Cactus Flower, 5.10a ★** This climb was originally called **No Guts, No Glory** because the first ascent party felt they should have free climbed it. Its name was changed after the first free ascent. Start at southwest side. Scramble up short chimney, then up south-facing and right-arching crack (5.10a) to small stance. Continue up and left to top. Pro: Medium to large nuts.

71. **Crumbled Freak, 5.10a** It wouldn't be a good idea to disregard the name on this route. Just left of **You Can't Get There From Here**. Ledge past bolt to horizontal crack. Traverse right to bolt and continue past drilled pin to summit. Hard climbing on crusty rock! Pro: Two bolts, drilled piton, nuts, tri-cams.

72. **You Can't Get There From Here, 5.11** Start 25 feet up and right from **Cactus Flower**. Climb face up and right past three bolts (5.11d) to arête. Continue on face just right of arête to rappel anchor (or top if so desired). Pro: Five bolts. one drilled piton (used for belay and single line rappel).

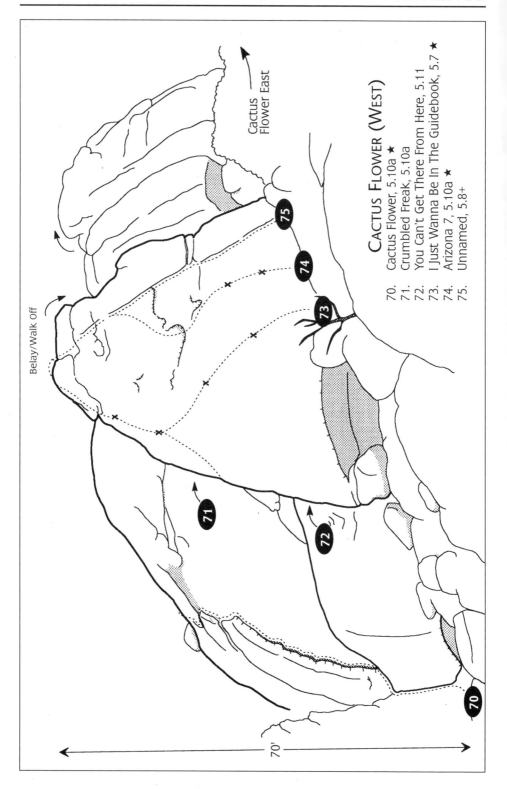

CACTUS FLOWER (WEST)

70. Cactus Flower, 5.10a ★
71. Crumbled Freak, 5.10a
72. You Can't Get There From Here, 5.11
73. I Just Wanna Be In The Guidebook, 5.7
74. Arizona 7, 5.10a ★
75. Unnamed, 5.8+

Cactus Flower East

Belay/Walk Off

70'

73. **I Just Wanna Be In The Guidebook, 5.7** ★ Start just right around corner from **You Can't Get There From Here**. Step off large boulder which lies right of large roof and climb low-angled face up and slightly left to arête. Continue on face right of arête to rappel anchor (or top if so desired). Follow same descent as **You Can't Get There From Here**. Pro: Three bolts, one drilled piton (used for belay and single line rappel).
74. **Arizona 7, 5.10a** ★ Start just right from **I Just Wanna Be In The Guidebook**. Climb face past two bolts (5.10a) to flake. Move left into prominent crack. then climb crack left of small roof until possible to move right above roof to fixed piton in another crack. Continue on face to top. Pro: Two bolts, one fixed piton, medium to large nuts.
75. **Unnamed, 5.8+** Climb the left leaning crack just right of the start of **Arizona 7** to join that route near it's top. This may look easy, but looks are deceiving in this case. Pro: Small to medium.

Pinnacle Peak East (Left)

This section of rock offers a variety of crack and face climbs that culminate at or near Sun Deck Boulder. The routes in this area can easily be combined with other routes on the Peak proper to make a longer day of climbing if so desired . Standard Descent for routes that top

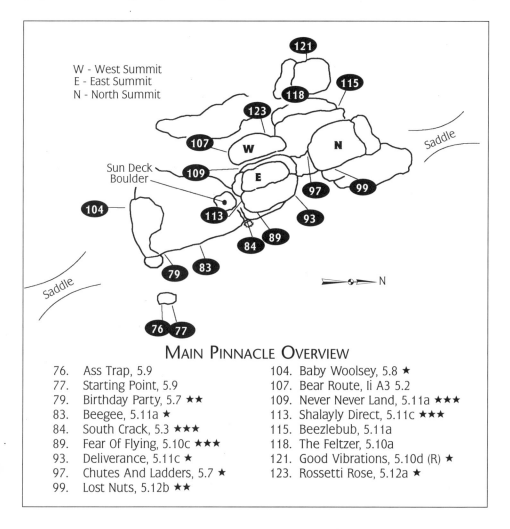

MAIN PINNACLE OVERVIEW

76. Ass Trap, 5.9	104. Baby Woolsey, 5.8 ★
77. Starting Point, 5.9	107. Bear Route, Ii A3 5.2
79. Birthday Party, 5.7 ★★	109. Never Never Land, 5.11a ★★★
83. Beegee, 5.11a ★	113. Shalayly Direct, 5.11c ★★★
84. South Crack, 5.3 ★★★	115. Beezlebub, 5.11a
89. Fear Of Flying, 5.10c ★★★	118. The Feltzer, 5.10a
93. Deliverance, 5.11c ★	121. Good Vibrations, 5.10d (R) ★
97. Chutes And Ladders, 5.7 ★	123. Rossetti Rose, 5.12a ★
99. Lost Nuts, 5.12b ★★	

East Summit: Rappel (single line) into The Notch. At this point, scramble down and right to a gully between the north and East Summits. Rappel east (single line) from bolts and chains past Chutes and Ladders.

Standard Descent for routes that top North Summit: Rappel single line (two bolt stance) off east face.

The following two routes are located on a short outcrop with two thin finger cracks, 200 feet below and left (southeast) of **Birthday Party** (#79).

76. **Ass Trap, 5.9** The left-hand finger crack. Watch out for the "trap"! Climb crack to top. Pro: Small to medium

77. **Starting Point, 5.9** The right-hand finger crack. Climb up to horizontal crack, then continue up face to top. Pro: Small to medium.

78. **Mr. Creamjeans, 5.10d** Start up and left from **Birthday Party** at slab. Climb face past one bolt to top. Pro: One bolt

79. **Birthday Party, 5.7 ★★** Move quickly or this climb will seem much harder than the rating! Also, whose birthday do you think this route is named after? Start about 50 feet

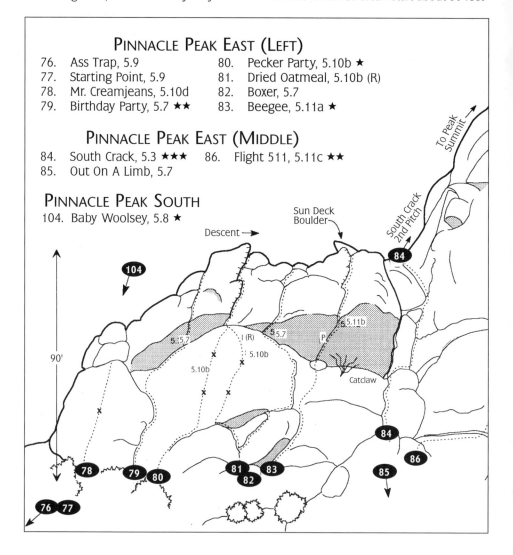

PINNACLE PEAK EAST (LEFT)

76. Ass Trap, 5.9	80. Pecker Party, 5.10b ★
77. Starting Point, 5.9	81. Dried Oatmeal, 5.10b (R)
78. Mr. Creamjeans, 5.10d	82. Boxer, 5.7
79. Birthday Party, 5.7 ★★	83. Beegee, 5.11a ★

PINNACLE PEAK EAST (MIDDLE)

84. South Crack, 5.3 ★★★   86. Flight 511, 5.11c ★★
85. Out On A Limb, 5.7

PINNACLE PEAK SOUTH

104. Baby Woolsey, 5.8 ★

Karen Schneider ready to start the overhang of **Birthday Party** (5.7), Upper East Wall at Pinnacle Peak. Photo by Tim Schneider.

left of **South Crack**. (**South Crack's** first pitch leads to Sun Deck Boulder.) Climb right-facing dihedral up and left to jumble of boulders. Traverse right under overhang to a vertical crack that splits the roof. Clear roof (5.7) and continue on easier climbing to Sun Deck Boulder area. Pro: Medium to large nuts.

80. **Pecker Party, 5.10b** ★ On the first ascent, both bolts were placed on stance. A credit to those "peckers". Start is same as **Birthday Party**. Follow ramp right until possible to climb face above past two bolts (5.10b) to roof. At this point traverse right and join **Dried Oatmeal** to top. Pro: Two bolts, Friends.

81. **Dried Oatmeal, 5.10b (R)** This climb was originally rated 5.9 because on the first ascent the leader moved right from the second bolt to somewhat easier terrain. Nowadays, most climbers climb straight above the second bolt creating a more sustained climb. Start 25 feet left of **South Crack**. Climb indistinct rib past two bolts (5.10b R) to crack. Continue up a crack to Sun Deck Boulder area. Pro: Small to large nuts, two bolts.

82. **Boxer, 5.7** Start 20 feet left of **South Crack**. Climb short, right-arching crack to small ledge. Continue up low-angled face, then traverse left to short vertical crack. Climb crack (5.7) to Sun Deck Boulder area. Pro: Medium to large nuts.

83. **Beegee, 5.11a** ★ Rumor has it that the leader taped a #7 hex to his chest so he could conveniently rip it off at the lip to place. Regardless, it took several falls to complete the first ascent. At that time it was thought to be 5.10, but the present consensus has it at 5.11a. This makes it Phoenix's oldest 5.11! Start 15 feet left of South Crack. Climb short. flared crack (5.10c) to reach small ledge. Continue up low-angled face to another short but drastically overhanging crack. Climb crack (5.11a) and trough (past beehive) to Sun Deck Boulder area. Pro: Medium nuts, one fixed piton.

Note: This route's namesake bees have moved down into the bottom of this crack! Inspect this route carefully before attempting it!

Pinnacle Peak East (Middle)

84. **South Crack, 5.3** ★★★ A classic beginning route to the top of Pinnacle Peak! Start at obvious gully-chimney system below Sun Deck Boulder. First Pitch: Climb gully-chimney system to Sun Deck Boulder (Cl. 4). Climbers should review the definition of 4th Class if this pitch seems underrated. Second Pitch: Scramble over broken boulders to gain crack system that arches slightly right. Continue up this crack system and chimney above to East Summit (5.3). Pro: Medium to large nuts,
    Variation, 5.6 Instead of starting in obvious gully-chimney system, move right a few feet and start in flared chimney. Climb chimney until possible to join regular route. Pro: Large nuts.
    Variation, 5.5 Climb open book just right of second pitch until possible to join regular route . Pro: Large nuts.
85. **Out On A Limb, 5.7** Start approximately 200 feet below **South Crack** at southeast facing pillar. Climb right-leaning arête past one bolt to horizontal crack, then move left to ledge. Continue to top via easy hand crack. Pro: One bolt, Friends
86. **Flight 511, 5.11c** ★★ Start just right of **South Crack**. Climb face right of squeeze chimney to horizontal crack, then move right to first bolt. Climb face past three bolts to ledge (5.11c). Pro: Three bolts.

Note: The following two routes, **Hades** and **Name It**, may be considered direct starts to **Fear of Flying**, **Powder Puff Direct**, **Lesson in Discipline** and **Sidewinder**.

87. **Hades, 5.10b** According to the first ascent leader, tube chocks were extremely hard to place and probably psychological at best. Start 25 feet right of South Crack. Scramble up wide chimney to prominent offwidth. Climb offwidth (5.10b) to belay ledge. Scramble left to Sun Deck Boulder Pro: Tube chocks (#5 & #6 Friends), medium to large nuts.
88. **Name It, 5.6** Start a few feet right of Hades. Climb right-arching crack and face to wide crack. Continue up cracks to belay ledge. Scramble left to Sun Deck Boulder Pro: Medium to large nuts.

Standard Descent for routes that top at Sun Deck Boulder: Either down-climb **South Crack's** first pitch (Cl. 4) or scramble down (south) and left (east) for several hundred feet.

Pinnacle Peak East (Right)

The routes presented in this section encompass the main east face on the Peak proper. the bowl-like area between the East/West Summits and the North Summit proper. Many of the finest routes in Phoenix are in this section. See Pinnacle Peak East (Left) section for an aerial map of the routes on and around the Peak.

89. **Fear Of Flying, 5.10c** ★★★ A Phoenix classic! Start under small overhang directly above **Name It**. Move out left under small overhang in left-leaning crack (5.10c) to southeast corner of face. Then continue up crack and face to horizontal crack and fixed piton (5.10b). At this point continue straight above on rib (5.10b) to East Summit. Note, the leader placed the bolts on the arête on stance. Pro: Small to medium nuts, Friends, one fixed piton, three bolts.

Note: The route **Requiem** has been omitted in order to straighten out the lines that exist on the main pinnacle, both east and south. There are ways to traverse back and forth between the routes, **Fear of Flying** and **Shalayly Direct**, if so desired.

90. **Powder Puff Direct, 5.11a** ★★★ Incredible exposure and strenuous climbing! Start is just right of **Fear of Flying**. Climb short dihedral until possible to move left onto face. Continue directly up face past five bolts to top of East Summit. Pro: Small to medium nuts, five bolts.

FA 1978 Stan Mish, Dave Black, Jim Waugh (Siege)/ 1978 John Steiger (Flash)

FA (Direct finish, straight above fifth bolt) 1979 Jim Waugh, Glenn Rink

91. **Lesson In Discipline, 5.11c ★★★** Perhaps. the finest face climb in Phoenix and certainly the most intimidating! On the first ascent, because of the extreme overhanging nature of the route, the first ascent party was compelled to place the bolts from rappel. Recognizing the difficulty they faced, the climbers trained hard for awhile before attempting the route. Although sieged when completed, it was a remarkable achievement in pushing the free climbing standards at that time. Start is same as **Powder Puff**

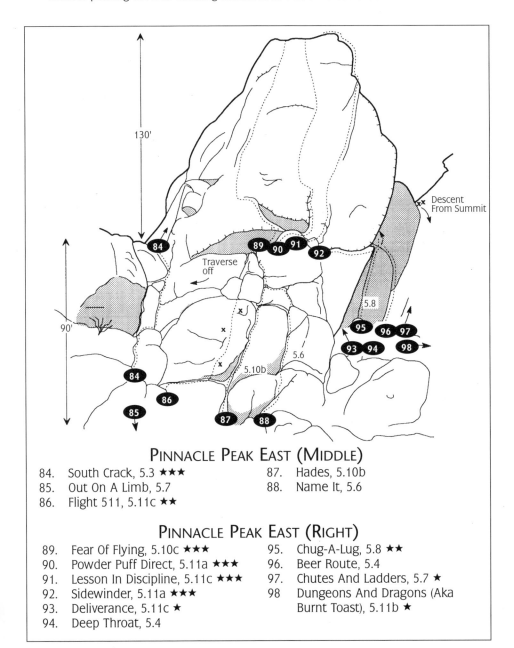

PINNACLE PEAK EAST (MIDDLE)

84. South Crack, 5.3 ★★★	87. Hades, 5.10b
85. Out On A Limb, 5.7	88. Name It, 5.6
86. Flight 511, 5.11c ★★	

PINNACLE PEAK EAST (RIGHT)

89. Fear Of Flying, 5.10c ★★★	95. Chug-A-Lug, 5.8 ★★
90. Powder Puff Direct, 5.11a ★★★	96. Beer Route, 5.4
91. Lesson In Discipline, 5.11c ★★★	97. Chutes And Ladders, 5.7 ★
92. Sidewinder, 5.11a ★★★	98 Dungeons And Dragons (Aka
93. Deliverance, 5.11c ★	Burnt Toast), 5.11b ★
94. Deep Throat, 5.4	

Direct. Climb short dihedral to near its end (for protection) . Then down- climb and step right to thin crack that leads to bolt (5.11a) . Continue up overhanging face (5.11c) past two bolts, then up less-angled face past another bolt to crack. Follow crack and face to top of East Summit. Pro: Small nuts, four bolts.

92. **Sidewinder, 5.11a ★★★** One of the first 5.11s in the area! Interestingly, the first recognized 5.11 in Phoenix is one of the few 5.11s that has been flashed on the first ascent. Start just right of **Lesson in Discipline**. Traverse horizontal crack right until crack becomes vertical around corner. Continue in crack (5.11a) until possible to move right into off-width (**Deliverance**). Climb off-width and crack to ledge. Continue to top of East Summit via **Feets Don't Fail Me Now** face (5.9). Pro: Small to large nuts, two bolts.

93. **Deliverance, 5.11c ★** The leader on the first ascent placed five bolts on rappel for protection not realizing that the top two bolts interfered with **Sidewinder**. The local purists promptly chopped the top two bolts. and later ascents proved that the two bolts were unnecessary for protection. Also, the climb was originally rated 5.12, but later ascents confirmed the present rating. Start 40' right and down around corner (west) at base of overhanging offwidth. Climb offwidth (5.11c) to belay ledge. Continue to top of East Summit via **Feets Don t Fail Me Now** face. Pro: 3 bolts, tube chocks. Large nuts.

94. **Deep Throat, 5.4** Start a few feet up and right of **Deliverance**. First Pitch: Climb shallow chimney and crack to belay at large boulder. Second Pitch: Continue to Notch via short wide chimney. Continue to top of summits via any Notch route (124-126). Pro: Medium to large nuts.

95. **Chug-A-Lug, 5.8 ★★** Many a climber has struggled with this crack! Start just right of **Deep Throat**. First Pitch: Climb crack to belay at large boulder (5.8). Second Pitch: Move up and right of large chimney (**Deep Throat**) to thin crack (5.7) which ends at Notch Continue to top of summits via any Notch route (124-126). Pro: Small to medium nuts.

96. **Beer Route, 5.4** Start 20' right of **Chug-A-Lug**. First Pitch: Climb gully until possible to traverse left over first pitches of **Chug-A-Lug** and **Deep Throat**. Continue traversing and up to cave-like chimney (cl. 4). Second Pitch: Continue up short chimney and dihedral to top of East Summit (5.4). Pro: Medium to large nuts.

97. **Chutes And Ladders, 5.7 ★** Start by scrambling up gully to base of thin crack in shallow dihedral (on right side of gully) that leads up over small overhang and right to top of North Summit. Pro: Small to medium nuts.

98. **Dungeons And Dragons (Aka Burnt Toast), 5.11b ★** Start just right of **Chutes and Ladders** at face. Climb face to bolt at roof. Clear roof (5.11b), then continue on face up and right to expanding flake. Surmount flake and continue to top via face and crack. Pro: 1 bolt. small nuts (sliders and a 3/4 Friend were used on the first ascent) .

99. **Lost Nuts, 5.12b ★★** Lacking a quality ascent, the rating is subject to controversy! On the first ascent and all known subsequent ascents the leaders have taken several falls while placing protection and executing moves. In addition the leaders completed their leads hanging off protection at some point on the route. Consequently, a bolt and fixed piton were added recently with the idea that it will now be possible for the lead to be done in good style. Start 30' up and right (north) of Dungeons and Dragons. Climb flared crack until crack pinches, then continue in crack to top of North Summit. Pro: Small to medium nuts, 1 bolt, "sliders", fixed piton (near top).

100. **Deathwatch, 5.10c ★** A back-breaking bolt (literally) was placed to make this route safe. The leader stood on a friend's back to make sure the bolt was high enough to keep the leader off the ground in the event of a fall. Start a few feet right of Lost Nuts. Climb right-arching cracks up (5.10c). then move back left to top of North Summit. Pro: 1 bolt. small to medium nuts, 1 fixed piton.

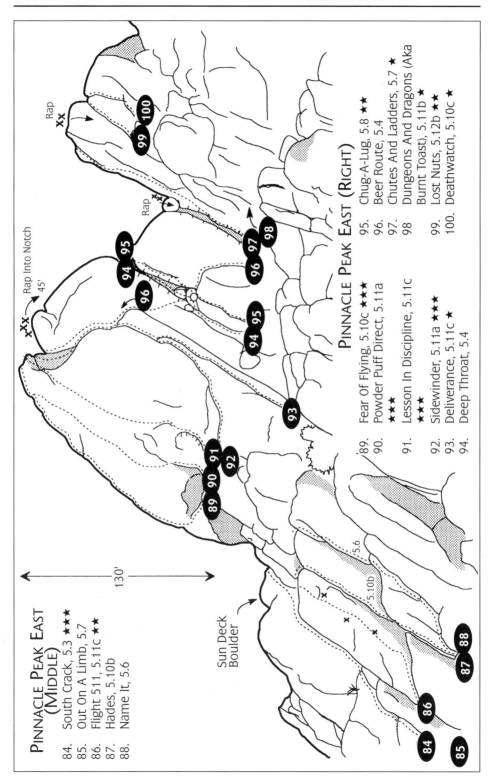

PINNACLE PEAK EAST (MIDDLE)

84. South Crack, 5.3 ★★★
85. Out On A Limb, 5.7
86. Flight 511, 5.11c ★★
87. Hades, 5.10b
88. Name It, 5.6

PINNACLE PEAK EAST (RIGHT)

89. Fear Of Flying, 5.10c ★★★
90. Powder Puff Direct, 5.11a ★★★
91. Lesson In Discipline, 5.11c ★★★
92. Sidewinder, 5.11a ★★★
93. Deliverance, 5.11c ★
94. Deep Throat, 5.4

95. Chug-A-Lug, 5.8 ★★
96. Beer Route, 5.4
97. Chutes And Ladders, 5.7 ★
98. Dungeons And Dragons (Aka Burnt Toast), 5.11b
99. Lost Nuts, 5.12b ★★
100. Deathwatch, 5.10c ★

Rap
xx

Rap
xx

Rap Into Notch
xx
45'

130'

Sun Deck
Boulder

5.6

5.10b

Pinnacle Peak South

This area yields some truly excellent face climbs. Most climbers approach by scrambling up South Crack's first pitch or by any of the routes listed in the Pinnacle Peak East (Left). See Pinnacle Peak East (Left) section for an aerial map of the routes on and around the Peak. Standard Descent for Pinnacle Peak South: See below.

101. **Happy Robots, 5.7 ★** To the west of Sun Deck Boulder (down and left of **Bear Route**), climb south-facing 80 foot buttress from the lower lefthand side angling up and right. The bottom of the route has a single bolt on it. Pro: 1 bolt, small to medium.

102. **On My Own Damn Couch, 5.6** Just left and behind the **Happy Robots** formation, climb short crack to top of pointed boulder. Pro: Small to large nuts.

103. **Vanishing Point, 5.9 ★** Start about 300' down (southwest) of Sun Deck Boulder. First Pitch: Climb short dihedral (5.9), then past brush onto low- angled slab with left-angling crack. Follow crack left and up to belay below obvious hand crack. Second Pitch: Climb crack above to top (5.9). Pro: Small to large nuts.

104. **Baby Woolsey, 5.8 ★** To the right of **Vanishing Point**, climb slab face up bolts and cracks. Pro: 5 bolts, nuts.

105. **Luna, 5.10b ★★** To the left of **Vanishing Point**, climb arête past 3 bolts to top. Pro: 3 bolts

106. **Sailin' Shoes, 5.9** Just left of **Luna**, climb short thin crack. Pro: Small

106a. **My Daddy's A Hard Man, 5.10b** Left of **Sailin' Shoes**, find a 15' offwidth crack. Climb the OW to a vertical crack which leads to a dished out face. Climb this to a horizontal crack and on to the top. Pro: Small to large.

107. **Bear Route, II A3 5.2** Start 20' left of South Gully or 50' left of Sun Deck Boulder. First Pitch: Aid bolt ladder out overhang to short, discontinuous crack. then up crack (A3) to hanging belay at horizontal crack (1 bolt). Second Pitch: Aid horizontal crack left around corner until it disappears (A3), then continue left past three bolts to thin, left-leaning crack that leads to large ledge (A1). Third Pitch: Continue aid up and right in crack to join **Spiral Staircase**. Continue on **Spiral Staircase** to top of West Summit (5.2). Pro: Small to medium nuts, pitons up to 1 1/4", Friends.

108. **South Of Heaven, 5.11c ★** Sport climbing comes to the Peak? This somewhat controversial route has lost some bolts since it's first ascent. It might be a good idea to look for missing bolts before starting up this one. Step off boulder left of South Crack to face past two bolts and horizontal crack. Then past 8 more bolts to top. Pro: 10 bolts (or maybe not)

109. **Never Never Land, 5.11a ★★★** This climb will give you the feeling of being all alone. On the first ascent the leader wanted to place the bolts on stance. He managed the first three but was forced to hook to place the fourth bolt. Start is same as South Gully. Climb South Gully until possible to traverse horizontal crack left to small ledge underneath bolt (5.7). Climb face past four bolts to top of West Summit. Pro: Small to medium nuts, 4 bolts.

110. **South Gully, 5.6** This route can be considered an approach to the Notch from Sun Deck Boulder. Start 30' left and up from Sun Deck Boulder. Climb wide crack up and right into Notch. Continue to top of Summits via any Notch route (124-126). Pro: Medium to large nuts.

111. **Twenty-Eighth Day, 5.9 (R) ★★** Guess what day of the month this route was completed? The second pitch involves classic face climbing on small knobs. Climb with care on this route. Tread carefully! The runout section of this climb has claimed a few broken ankles! Start from Sun Deck Boulder at **South Crack's** second pitch. First Pitch: Climb up **South Crack's** second pitch until possible to move left on large ledge about 10'. Continue up face to small right- facing flake, then up flake to another ledge. Traverse slightly left on ledge, then up face and corner (1 bolt) (5.7 R) to belay at hori-

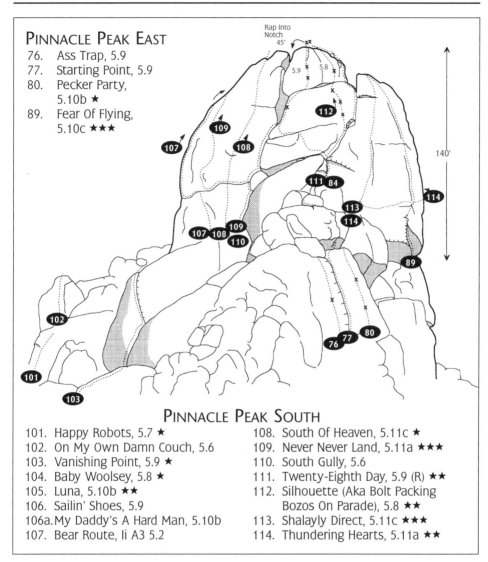

PINNACLE PEAK EAST

76. Ass Trap, 5.9
77. Starting Point, 5.9
80. Pecker Party,
    5.10b ★
89. Fear Of Flying,
    5.10c ★★★

Rap Into Notch 45'

5.9   5.8

112

140'

109

107   108

111 84

114

113

114

107 108 109

110

89

102

76 77 80

101

103

PINNACLE PEAK SOUTH

101. Happy Robots, 5.7 ★
102. On My Own Damn Couch, 5.6
103. Vanishing Point, 5.9 ★
104. Baby Woolsey, 5.8 ★
105. Luna, 5.10b ★★
106. Sailin' Shoes, 5.9
106a. My Daddy's A Hard Man, 5.10b
107. Bear Route, Ii A3 5.2

108. South Of Heaven, 5.11c ★
109. Never Never Land, 5.11a ★★★
110. South Gully, 5.6
111. Twenty-Eighth Day, 5.9 (R) ★★
112. Silhouette (Aka Bolt Packing
     Bozos On Parade), 5.8 ★★
113. Shalayly Direct, 5.11c ★★★
114. Thundering Hearts, 5.11a ★★

zontal crack. Second Pitch: Continue up face (2 bolts) and discontinuous crack to top of East Summit (5.9). Pro: Small to medium nuts, 3 bolts.

112. **Silhouette (Aka Bolt Packing Bozos On Parade), 5.8** ★★ Climb about 45' up the second pitch of **South Crack**, make a left and climb face on arête past three bolts to horizontal crack. Work to the right side to clip final bolt, then straight up (5.8) over bolt to top. Easier if you move right after clipping last bolt. Head straight up! Pro: Medium to large, four bolts.

113. **Shalayly Direct, 5.11c** ★★★ A truly demanding lead and one of Phoenix's best routes. As **Fear of Flying**, this route has evolved with much history. The first crux had been climbed years ago by Rick Fritz, but he retreated as he did not want to negotiate the climbing above without more bolts. Later, Dave Black repeated the first crux and finished the lead by traversing off left at the base of the **Requiem** crack. Most recently, the direct finish establishes a distinct route to the top of the East Summit. Start from Sun Deck Boulder 15' right of **South Crack's** second pitch. Climb face and indistinct rib past four bolts (5.11a) until possible to traverse right to crack in delicate

flake (5.9). Continue up crack (5.9) until it discontinues. Then continue up face above, past three bolts (5.11c) to top and East Summit. Pro: 7 bolts, small to medium nuts, Friends.

114. **Thundering Hearts, 5.11a** ★★ For those desiring a marvelous girdle. try this one! Start is the same as **Shalayly Direct**. First Pitch: Climb **Shalayly** until the third bolt (5.11a). At this point, downclimb slightly and traverse right passing a bolt to the first bolt on **Fear of Flying**. Belay at this point. (Be sure to

The author grasping at knobs on the second pitch of **Twenty-Eighth Day** (5.9). Photo by Tim Schneider.

carry a 3/8" cap- screw and hanger!) Second Pitch: Make a move up and clip into the second bolt on **Fear of Flying**. Step back down to the belay and traverse right to the second bolt on **Powder Puff Direct**, 5.10b. Continue up **Powder Puff** to its last bolt and traverse right to **Lesson in Discipline's** last bolt (5.10b) . Continue traversing right crossing **Sidewinder** just under the **Feets Don't Fail Me Now** face. Belay at this point. Third Pitch: Finish to top of East Summit via **Feets Don't Fail Me Now** face (5.9) or the last pitch of the **Beer Route** (5.4). Pro: Several bolts.

Pinnacle Peak West

For some reason this area has received little attention by climbers. Although the present climbs are not the Peak's best. the potential in this area for harder routes remains. See Pinnacle Peak East (Left) section for an aerial map of the routes on and around the Peak. Standard Descent for routes that top West Summit: Jump chasm between West and East Summits to reach East Summit. At this point continue on Standard Descent for routes that top East Summit.

115. **Beezlebub, 5.11a** Start on north side of North Summit below prominent off-width. Struggle up off-width and squeeze chimney (5.11a) to roof. then continue (5.7) to top and belay. Scramble south to North Summit for easiest descent. Pro: 2 bolts, tube chocks, small to large nuts.

116. **Voluptuous Ham, 5.5 (R)** Start 10' down (west) and right (south) of Beezlebub. Climb obvious chimney to small notch where moderate move south past bolt leads to top of North Summit. Pro: Large nuts, 1 bolt.
     Hamster Variation, 5.8 (R) After making entry moves into chimney. move out onto arête on left. Climb arête past two bolts to top. A moderate move south past bolt leads to top of North Summit. Pro: Friends, 2 bolts.

117. **Garbert's Chimney, 5.3** Start 50' slightly up and right of **Voluptuous Ham**. Climb chimney to Notch. Continue to top of summits via any Notch route (124-126). Pro: Medium to large nuts.

118. **The Feltzer, 5.10a** Start 45' right of **Voluptuous Ham**. Climb loose-looking section of rock split by crack until rock improves. Continue in thin crack just right of arête to

top. Continue to top of summits via any Notch route (124-126). Pro: Small to medium nuts, Friends.

119. **Brown Out (Originally The Chancre), A4** Start 60' right of **Voluptuous Ham** or up and just right of **The Feltzer**. Aid thin. bottoming crack to Notch. Continue to top of summits via any Notch route (124-126). Pro: Pitons (rurps to baby angles). small nuts, 1 fixed piton.

120. **Rastaman Vibration, 5.10c** ★ Start about 100' below (west) of **Brown Out** at left side of white slab. Climb face past three bolts to top. Pro: 3 bolts.

121. **Good Vibrations, 5.10d (R)** ★ On the first ascent, the leader saw a bolt part way up the route. Not realizing that the route was incomplete, he decided to rope solo as it looked like a nice line. He expected to find another bolt higher. Well, to his surprise and dismay, there was not another bolt nor any other protection. Fortunately, he did not fall. Later, he discovered that he had indeed done the first ascent. A remarkably lucky feat for its day. Incidently, the second ascent did not take place until 1983. Start 20' right of **Rastaman Vibration**. Climb discontinuous crack and face past one bolt to top of slab. Pro: 1 bolt, small nuts, Friends.

122. **Parallax View, 5.7** ★ Start six feet right of **Good Vibrations**. Climb chimney and crack to top . Pro: Tube chocks. large nuts

123. **Rossetti Rose, 5.12a** ★ This route was originally an aid line called **The Mystery** because no one knew who had done the first ascent. After the first free ascent the leader decided to rename the route as a dedication to a friend, Suzanne Rossetti, who had been tragically murdered. May her memory live on forever! Note, the pitons on this route were placed from rappel in case they are ever missing. Start 50' up and right from **Parallax View** or approximately 300' left (northwest) and up (north) from Sun Deck Boulder in southwest facing gully. Scramble up west gully until level with top of **Bear Route's** second pitch. Climb short dihedral (5.9), then move right past one bolt to base of slightly overhanging thin crack. Continue up thin crack past three fixed pitons (5.12a) to large ledge. then up face above to top of West Summit. Pro: Small to medium nuts. Friends, 1 bolt. 3 fixed pitons.

The Notch

This area has confused climbers in the past partially because the routes are somewhat contrived and partially because route descriptions were vague. Just remember that the routes presented never involve stemming or chimneying between the East and West Summits. Standard Descent for routes that top at the Notch: Same as descent for routes that top East Summit or West Summit.

124. **Spread-Em With Style Direct, 5.11a** ★★ Originally this route was climbed by stemming against the back wall. Subsequently, the route was climbed without assistance from the back wall and later ascents have shown this to be the more popular version. Start at west-facing wall at south end of chimney between East and West Summits. Climb right-arching crack. then up overhanging and slightly left-leaning crack (5.11a) to top of East Summit. Pro: Small to large nuts.

125. **Spiral Staircase, 5.6** Start at northeast corner of east-facing wall at north end of chimney between East and West Summits. Climb thin, winding crack (5.6) to ledge, then traverse south to other cracks that lead back to top of West Summit. Pro: Small to large nuts.
Variation, 5.6 (R) Avoid thin. winding crack by climbing face on right to reach ledge and regular route. Pro: None.

126. **Ezy Rider, 5.9** Start at east-facing wall 20' left of **Spiral Staircase** in chimney between East and West Summits. Climb crack to top of West Summit. (Be sure to not stem back against the west-facing wall behind you.) Pro: Small to large nuts.

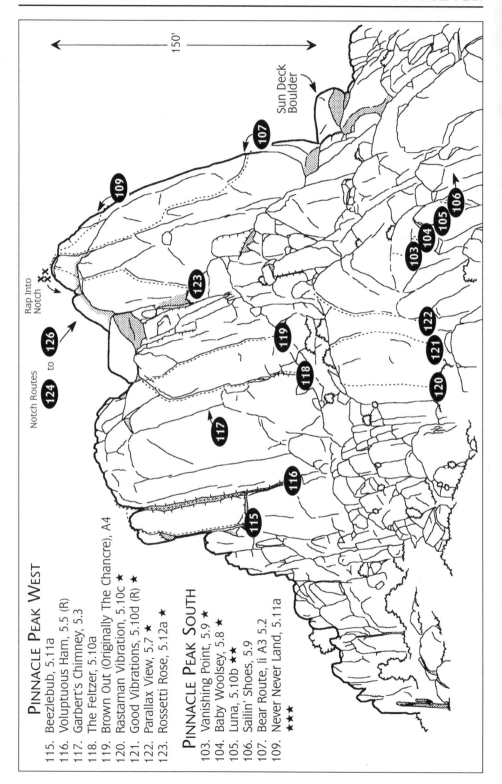

PINNACLE PEAK WEST

115. Beezlebub, 5.11a
116. Voluptuous Ham, 5.5 (R)
117. Garbert's Chimney, 5.3
118. The Feltzer, 5.10a
119. Brown Out (Originally The Chancre), A4
120. Rastaman Vibration, 5.10c ★
121. Good Vibrations, 5.10d (R) ★
122. Parallax View, 5.7 ★
123. Rossetti Rose, 5.12a ★

PINNACLE PEAK SOUTH

103. Vanishing Point, 5.9 ★
104. Baby Woolsey, 5.8 ★
105. Luna, 5.10b ★★
106. Sailin' Shoes, 5.9
107. Bear Route, ii A3 5.2
109. Never Never Land, 5.11a ★★★

Spectrum (5.7), Little Granite Mountain.

TROON MOUNTAIN DETAILED MAP

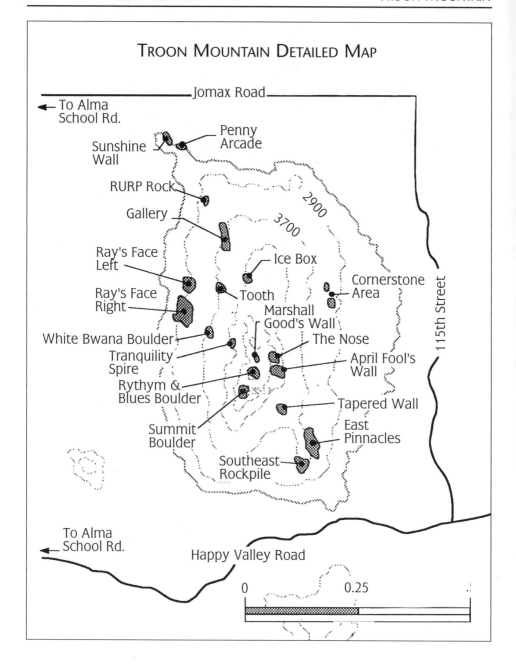

Jomax Road

To Alma School Rd.

Penny Arcade

Sunshine Wall

RURP Rock

Gallery

2900

3700

Ray's Face Left

Ice Box

Cornerstone Area

Ray's Face Right

Tooth

Marshall Good's Wall

White Bwana Boulder

The Nose

Tranquility Spire

April Fool's Wall

Rythym & Blues Boulder

Tapered Wall

Summit Boulder

East Pinnacles

Southeast Rockpile

115th Street

To Alma School Rd.

Happy Valley Road

0   0.25

Chapter 8

TROON MOUNTAIN

Troon Mountain, aka Windy Walks, is a 3500+-foot mountain located at the northwest end of the McDowell Mountains, northeast of Scottsdale proper. The routes on Troon are scattered along both sides of the mountain amid many large boulders, outcrops and rock piles. While some of the routes require a bit of a grunt to approach, the climbing here is widely varied and consistently interesting. One of the best crack climbs in central Arizona, Rhythm and Blues, is located near the summit.–certain proof that there are climbing jewels among the boulders of Troon. The side views of the mountain provided should help climbers to spot the various areas where routes are located. Plan your approach carefully. If you don't, some very strenuous and complicated hiking may be the result. Be advised that all trails are primitive (and hardly used) at best and the aerial topo only suggests the best possible directions to use.

The climbing on Troon is located on private property. Housing development around the perimeter of Troon is currently threatening access to this area in a big way. It is hoped that local climbers will be able to secure an access point to the mountain's climbing areas before it is lost forever. The chances of this are grim, however. Local climbing shops or the rock gym should be able to provide up to date information on efforts in this area, should any take place. In the

meantime, climbers should make every attempt to observe very low-impact climbing practices and remain respectful to landowners. At the time this book is published, the east side of Troon provides the only possible parking and access. Areas on the west side, although much harder to get to, also provide some very worthwhile climbing. As of this writing, most of them may still be reached via involved and arduous hiking to gain the west side of the mountain.

Along with the issue of respect, it is important that we maintain a presence on the mountain and it's climbing areas if we are to establish a desire for access. Let's make sure that people realize that climbers do use this area and would like to maintain access if possible.

Approach: Troon Mountain is across the street (and a bit south) from the east side of Pinnacle Peak (right behind all the houses). To get to Troon, use the driving instructions provided for Pinnacle Peak and then drive around on one of the roads (on the north or south of the mountain) to access parking on the east side. See map for details.

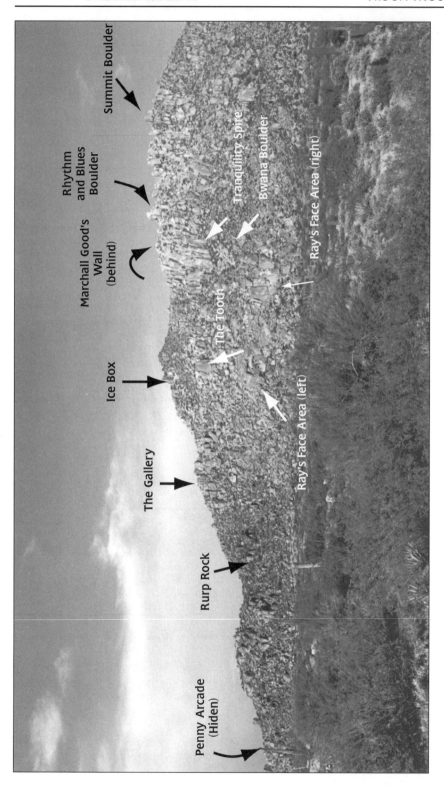

TROON MOUNTAIN COMPOSITE WEST

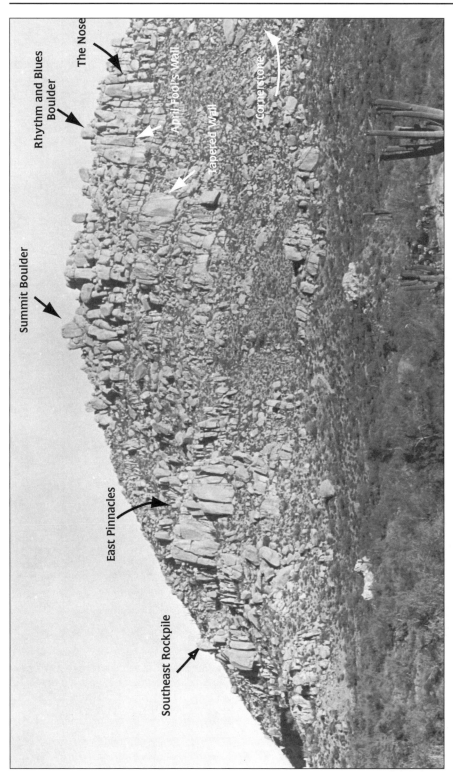

The Nose

Rhythm and Blues Boulder

April Fools' Wall

Cornerstone

Tapered Wall

Summit Boulder

East Pinnacles

Southeast Rockpile

TROON MOUNTAIN COMPOSITE EAST

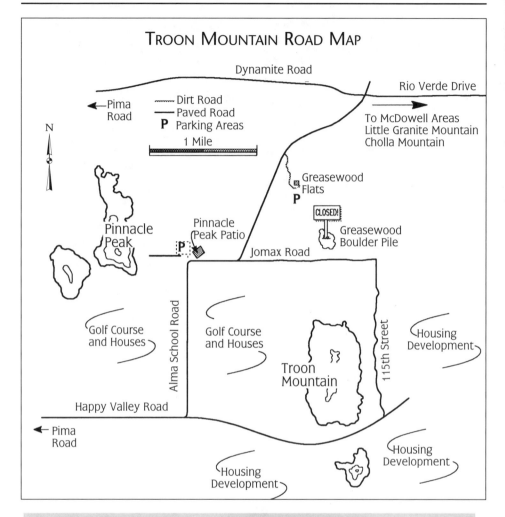

TROON MOUNTAIN ROAD MAP

Dynamite Road

Rio Verde Drive

←Pima Road

- - - Dirt Road
— Paved Road
P Parking Areas

1 Mile

To McDowell Areas
Little Granite Mountain
Cholla Mountain

N

Greasewood Flats
P

CLOSED!

Greasewood Boulder Pile

Pinnacle Peak

Pinnacle Peak Patio
P

Jomax Road

Golf Course and Houses

Alma School Road

Golf Course and Houses

Troon Mountain

115th Street

Housing Development

Happy Valley Road

← Pima Road

Housing Development

Housing Development

Housing Development

Greasewood Boulder Pile

This small climbing area is located on the north side of Jomax Road across from Troon Mountain's north end. Although this area has been popular in the past for climbing, the current owner and ongoing housing development has caused access to this area to be cut off. This is noted here so that trespassing will hopefully not occur. Please respect the owner's wishes!

Penny Arcade

This wall is located at the extreme northwest end of Troon Mountain and almost even with the valley floor. It faces north and is approximately 40 feet high. This area is one that will be lost to housing development (if it's not already by the time this is published), as you may one day be able to fall from this wall into someone's swimming pool. Please avoid conflict with landowners and climb elsewhere if trespassing is required. At such a time, the Penny Arcade should be calmly forgotten.

1. **Centipede, 5.9**   Start near left end of wall. Climb face past bolt and horizontal crack to top. Pro: One bolt, Friends.

PENNY ARCADE

1. Centipede, 5.9
2. Missile Command, 5.9
3. Pac Man (Comet), 5.5
4. Crazy Climber (Funnel), 5.8
5. Asteroids, 5.9
6. Battle Zone, 5.10d ★
7. Kong, 5.7

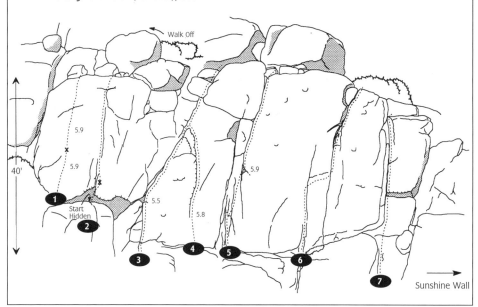

2. **Missile Command, 5.9**   Start ten feet right of **Centipede.** Climb overhang past bolt to top. Pro: One bolt, small to medium nuts.
3. **Pac Man (Comet), 5.5**   Start 15 feet down and right of **Missile Command.** Climb wide, right-arching crack to top. Pro: Medium to large nuts.
4. **Crazy Climber (Funnel), 5.8**   Start 20 feet right of **Pac Man.** Climb face to a crack passing a flake and on to top. Pro: Small to large nuts.
5. **Asteroids, 5.9**   Start 10 feet right of **Crazy Climber.** Climb short cracks to handcrack. Continue in crack passing roof to top. Pro: Small to large nuts.
6. **Battle Zone, 5.10d ★**   Originally rated 5.11 this climb has since had the right crack cleaned extensively thus lowering its rating. Nevertheless, the route still guarantees a "pump." Start 25 feet right of **Asteroids.** Climb double cracks to top. Pro: Small to large nuts.
7. **Kong, 5.7**   Start 20 feet right of **Battle Zone** or at right end of wall. Climb obvious overhang to top. Pro: Medium to large nuts.

Sunshine Wall

This small wall is located due west-northwest (wnw) from Penny Arcade. No topo is shown for the climbs.

8. **Sunshine, 5.7**   Start down and left at thin crack. Climb crack to bulge. Surmount bulge to top. Pro: Small to medium nuts.
9. **Two Easy, 5.2**   Start up and right from **Sunshine.** Climb wide, left-arching crack to top. Pro: Medium to large nuts.

RURP Rock

Located just below the ridgecrest and north-northwest (nnw) from The Gallery, this small south-facing wall displays a unique formation that gives the appearance of a gigantic RURP stuck in an appropriate crack.

10. **Fist Fight, 5.9**   Above RURP Rock, a prominent, southwest-facing crack can be seen splitting a boulder. Climb crack to top. Pro: Small to medium nuts.
11. **Tea Cups, 5.8**   Start 100 feet down and left of RURP Rock at south-facing boulder. Climb left-angling four-foot crack. Pro: Large nuts, Friends.
12. **Jelly Roll, 5.9**   Start at prominent "Y" crack at center of RURP Rock. Climb crack exiting right at "Y" to top. Pro: Medium nuts, Friends.
13. **Tender Vittles, 5.8**   Start at base of chimney at right side of RURP Rock under the "RURP." Climb chimney to four-foot crack. Continue in crack to roof (the "RURP"). Exit roof left to top. Pro: Medium to large nuts, Friends.

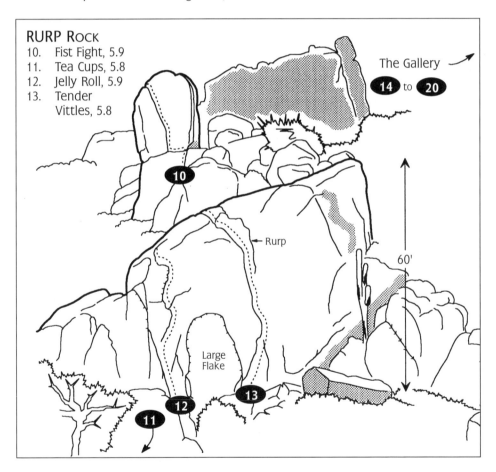

RURP ROCK
10. Fist Fight, 5.9
11. Tea Cups, 5.8
12. Jelly Roll, 5.9
13. Tender
    Vittles, 5.8

The Gallery

14 to 20

Rurp

60'

Large
Flake

The Gallery

Located on the west side, just below the ridgecrest and far to the north, this wall yields a wide range of difficulty in its climbs.

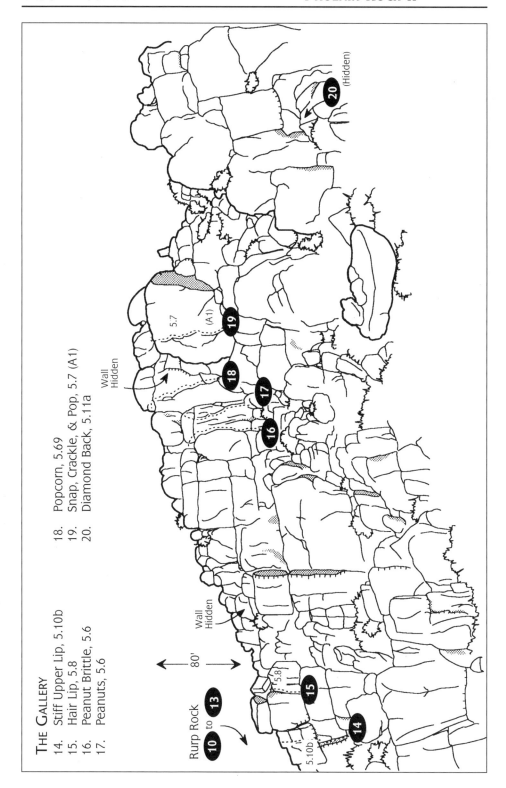

THE GALLERY

14. Stiff Upper Lip, 5.10b
15. Hair Lip, 5.8
16. Peanut Brittle, 5.6
17. Peanuts, 5.6

18. Popcorn, 5.69
19. Snap, Crackle, & Pop, 5.7 (A1)
20. Diamond Back, 5.11a

Rurp Rock

10 to 13

← 80' →

Wall Hidden

5.8

5.10b

5.7

(A1)

Wall Hidden

(Hidden)

10 13 14 15 16 17 18 19 20

14. **Stiff Upper Lip, 5.10b**   Start at upper northwest end of The Gallery wall. Climb broken cracks to obvious roof. Climb over roof to top. Pro: Small to medium nuts.

15. **Hair Lip, 5.8**   Start 15 feet right from **Stiff Upper Lip**. Climb chimney to hand-and-fist crack. Continue in crack to top. Pro: Medium to large nuts.

16. **Peanut Brittle, 5.6**   Start 20 feet left of **Peanuts**. Climb vertical hand-and-fist crack to top. Pro: Medium to large nuts, Friends.

17. **Peanuts, 5.6**   Start approximately at the middle of The Gallery wall at south-facing wall. Climb left-angling "z" crack to top. Pro: Medium nuts, Friends.

18. **Popcorn, 5.6**   Start 2 feet right of **Peanuts**. Climb hand-and-fist crack to top. Pro: Medium to large nuts, Friends.

19. **Snap, Crackle, & Pop, 5.7 (A1)**   Start on small wall below The Gallery approximately 125 feet right of **Peanuts** and **Popcorn** or 75 feet left of **Diamond Back**. First Pitch: Climb left-angling crack (A1) to horizontal crack. Climb back right to thin crack and belay. Second Pitch: Climb thin crack to top (5.7). Pro: Short thick lost arrows, small nuts, Friends.

20. **Diamond Back, 5.11a**   Start at small boulder pile approximately 75 feet below and right from **Snap, Crackle, & Pop**. Climb face to overhanging 1½-inch crack. Continue in crack to top. Pro: Medium nuts, Friends.

The Tooth

Located on the west side almost directly above Ray's Face Area Left and due south of The

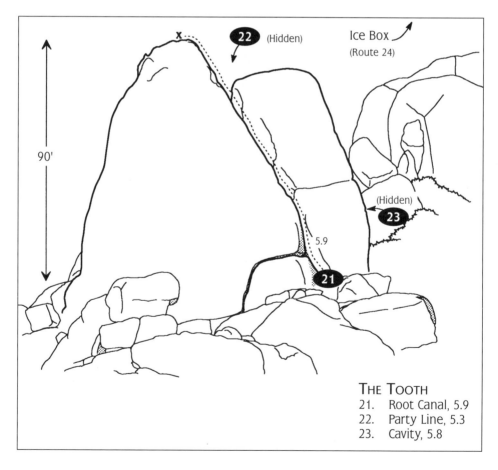

THE TOOTH
21. Root Canal, 5.9
22. Party Line, 5.3
23. Cavity, 5.8

Gallery, an obvious tooth-like triangular formation can be found. No routes exist up the blank exposed west face, but other routes may be located around the other sides of this pinnacle. Standard Descent: Rappel (single line) from runner and nut or downclimb **Party Line** (5.3) into notch.

21. **Root Canal, 5.9**   Start on south side. Surmount boulder to triangular alcove. Climb left-angling crack past horizontal crack to chimney. Continue on **Party Line** to top. Pro: Small to medium nuts, one bolt.

22. **Party Line, 5.3**   Start in notch on top. Approach from southeast side of The Tooth. Climb face past bolt to summit. Pro: One bolt.

23. **Cavity, 5.8**   Start 25 feet right of **Root Canal**, around corner. Climb chimney and traverse right on horizontal crack to a seam/crack. Climb crack and face past two pitons to top. Descend via single line rappel north into notch. Pro: Small to large nuts, two pitons, one bolt (for rappel).

Ice Box

Located almost directly above The Tooth and on the ridgecrest, this area, which encompasses several large boulders, will be a challenge just to find. Your only clue is that the start of the individual route in this area is hidden in a boulder enclave; thus the "Ice Box." No topo is shown.

24. **Thin Ice, 5.10b**   Start on northeast side in top of chimney. Climb horizontal finger crack past two pitons to corner. Continue in corner to top. Pro: Two pitons, Friends.

Ray's Face Area Left

This area is best identified by the large roof-like system on its right flank. It hosts both face and crack climbs. See topo, page 186.

25. **Cleavage, 5.7** ★   Start at base of slab at left end of Ray's Face Area Left. Climb face via water trough past one bolt to top. Pro: One bolt.

26. **Extra-Strength Tylenol, 5.9 (R)** ★   After this lead you will want some Extra-Strength Tylenol™ or feel like you got a tampered batch of the pain killer. Start 30 feet right of **Cleavage**. Step off boulder left to gain face, then climb face past two bolts and horizontal crack to top. Pro: Two bolts, medium nuts.

27. **Dual Identity, 5.9**   Start at left (north) end of large prominent roof. Climb wide, flared crack to top. Pro: Medium to large nuts, tube chocks.

28. **Basket Case, 5.9**   Start 30 feet right of **Dual Identity**. Climb obvious dihedral to top. Pro: Medium to large nuts.

29. **Creep From The Deep, 5.10b**   Start 150 feet right of **Dual Identity** or 120 feet right of **Basket Case**. Climb obvious wide crack to top. Pro: Tube chocks, large Friends.

Ray's Face Area Right

This area has the greatest concentration of routes on Troon Mountain. Excellent cracks and superb faces abound on this almost 200-foot-high crag. It is speculated that this area was named after either Ray Garner (see history section) or Ray Stauffer who participated in the first known route in this area, **Picture Window Route**. Topo, page 187.

30. **#1, 5.6**   Start 200 feet left of **Picture Window Route** or near left (north) end of face. Climb crack in dihedral to top. Pro: Medium to large nuts.

31. **Only The Strong Survive, 5.11a** ★★★   Indeed, a Phoenix face-climbing classic! Start is the same as **Picture Window Route**. Climb the first pitch of **Picture Window Route** to bolt on left on face. Continue on face up and slightly right past three more bolts to top. Pro: Four bolts, small to medium nuts.

32. **Picture Window Route, 5.3**   Start near left end of Ray's Face at base of wide crack (hidden behind boulder) that splits the whole face. First Pitch: Climb crack to over-

RAY'S FACE AREA LEFT

25. Cleavage, 5.7 e
26. Extra-Strength Tylenol, 5.9 (R) ★

27. Dual Identity, 5.9
28. Basket Case, 5.9

29. Creep From The Deep, 5.10b

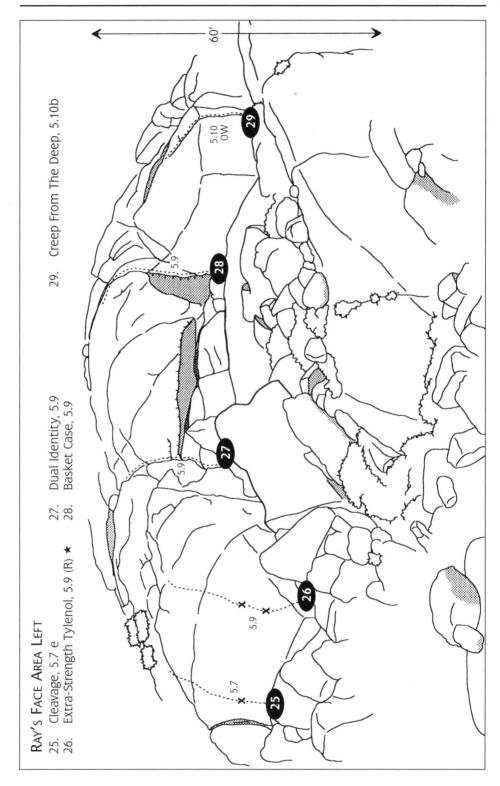

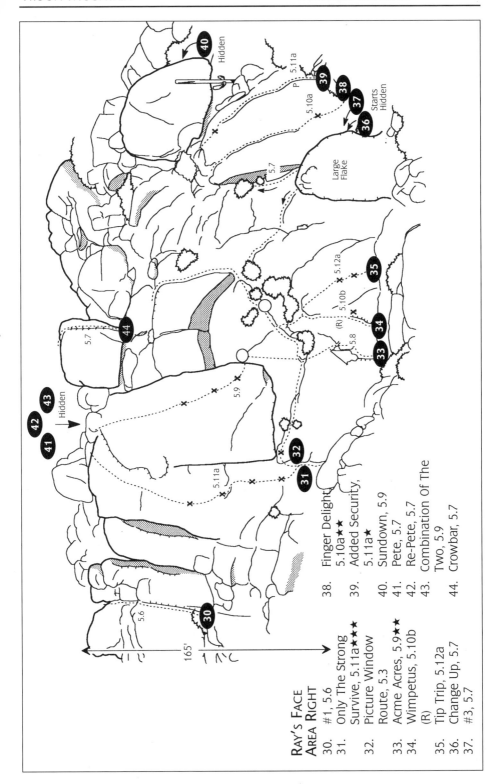

RAY'S FACE
AREA RIGHT

30. #1, 5.6
31. Only The Strong
     Survive, 5.11a★★★
32. Picture Window
     Route, 5.3
33. Acme Acres, 5.9★★
34. Wimpetus, 5.10b
     (R)
35. Tip Trip, 5.12a
36. Change Up, 5.7
37. #3, 5.7
38. Finger Delight
     5.10a★★
39. Added Security,
     5.11a★
40. Sundown, 5.9
41. Pete, 5.7
42. Re-Pete, 5.7
43. Combination Of The
     Two, 5.9
44. Crowbar, 5.7

hang (5.3). Second Pitch: Drop down and traverse right across ledge to its end, then scramble up and over to palo verde tree. Third Pitch: Finish by climbing left, then up large crack to top. Pro: One bolt, medium to large nuts.

33. **Acme Acres, 5.9 ★★**   Start approximately 25 feet right of **Picture Window Route**. First Pitch: Climb right-facing corner and short face to obvious belay right and above large roof but below large crack and left of another large roof. Second Pitch: Climb face left and up from belay past three bolts to top (5.9). Pro: Small to large nuts, three bolts.

34. **Wimpetus, 5.10b (R)**   Start 10 feet right from **Acme Acres**. First Pitch: Climb indistinct left-facing corner past one bolt to small ledge on right (5.10b). Continue on face to vegetated ledge. Second Pitch: Join **Acme Acres** or **Picture Window Route** to top. Pro: One bolt, medium to large nuts.

35. **Tip Trip, 5.12a**   Start just right (south) from **Wimpetus** below obvious white face. Climb face past two bolts and slightly left to ledge. Continue up and right on ledge to palo verde tree for belay. At this point either continue on **Acme Acres** or **Picture Window Route** to top. Note: This face has had many holds broken since the first ascent. The rating is reflective of the present difficulty. Pro: Two bolts, medium to large nuts.

36. **Change Up, 5.7**   Start right from **Tip Trip** behind right edge of large block. Climb thin crack to boulder and continue up and left to palo verde tree. Palo verde tree is same as top of **Tip Trip**. At this point continue on **Picture Window Route** to top. Pro: Small nuts, one piton.

37. **#3, 5.7**   Start just right from **Change Up** and the large block. Climb obvious hand-and-fist crack to top. Pro: Medium to large nuts.

38. **Finger Delight, 5.10a ★★**   An excellent climb that was originally done without the first bolt. Most will be glad it is there now. Start 50 feet right from **#3**. Climb face past bolt into finger crack. Continue in crack to top. Pro: One bolt, small to medium nuts, Friends.

39. **Added Security, 5.11a ★**   Start 20 feet right of **Finger Delight**. Climb thin crack until possible to move left onto face. Continue on face past bolt to top. Pro: Small nuts, one piton, one bolt.

40. **Sundown, 5.9**   Start up and right from **Added Security** around corner of large boulder. Climb obvious open book to top. Pro: Medium to large nuts.

41. **Pete, 5.7**   Start at north side of large boulder on top of Ray's Face and directly above **Picture Window Route**. Climb right crack to horizontal crack, then continue to top. Pro: Small to medium nuts.

42. **Re-Pete, 5.7**   Start just left of **Pete**. Climb crack to horizontal crack, then continue in crack to top. Pro: Small to medium nuts.

43. **Combination Of The Two, 5.9**   Start left of **Re-Pete** at northeast corner. Climb face past bolt to horizontal crack, then continue directly above to top. Pro: One bolt, medium nuts.

44. **Crowbar, 5.7**   I understand that a crowbar was used to do a little gardening. Start at south side of large boulder on top of Ray's Face and directly above. Climb overhanging crack in dihedral to top. Pro: Medium to large nuts.

White Bwana Boulder

This large boulder is located half way between Ray's Face Area Right and Tranquility Spire. Look for an overhanging west face as an identifying characteristic. Two face routes exist on the north face. No topo is shown.

45. **A Bone For Bwana, 5.7**   Start at the right side of the north face. Climb well-protected face past two bolts to top. Pro: Two bolts, one belay bolt.

46. **Call Me Bwana, 5.10a**   Start at left side of north face. Climb face past two bolts to top. Pro: Two bolts, one belay bolt.

Tranquility Spire

This approximately 100 foot high spire gives one the feeling of what it must be like to climb in the Needles of South Dakota. It is located almost directly above Ray's Face Area Right and is hard to see because the pinnacle blends into the rock behind it. Standard Descent: Rappel single line east from summit to notch. Note: Climbers might carry a large runner in case runners around the summit are old or missing.

47. **Shaboomy, 5.10b** ★   Start at the northwest side of the spire just right and up from loose chimney. Step off boulder and traverse face and crack to same crack as loose chimney (one should be above chimney and loose section). Climb narrowing crack to its end, then continue on arête above past three bolts to top. Pro: Small to medium nuts, three bolts.

48. **Sanity Route, 5.9**   Start on east side of spire. Climb thin crack and face past two bolts to top. Pro: Small to medium nuts, Friends, two bolts.
FA: 1971 Lyle Huff, Jon Biemer.
Insanity Variation, 5.6 (R)   Instead of regular start, start down and left (south). Hand traverse flake to reach south face, then climb unprotected face to join regular route 40 feet up. Pro: None.

49. **Death Of Ethos, 5.10a** ★★★   On the north side of Tranquility Spire, climb face past five bolts to summit. Pro: Bolts.

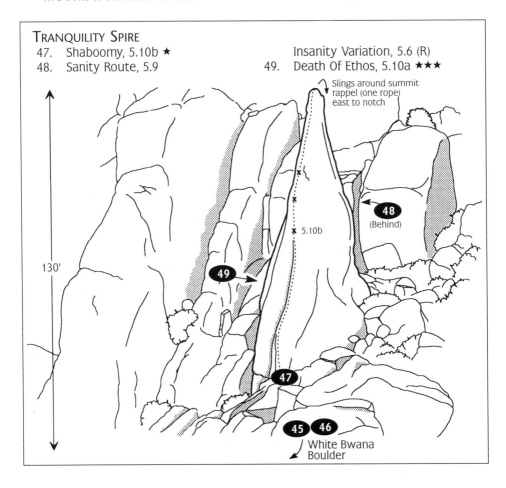

TRANQUILITY SPIRE
47.   Shaboomy, 5.10b ★
48.   Sanity Route, 5.9

Insanity Variation, 5.6 (R)
49.   Death Of Ethos, 5.10a ★★★

Slings around summit rappel (one rope) east to notch

48 (Behind)

5.10b

49

130'

47

45   46
White Bwana Boulder

Marshall Good's Wall

Located high on the summit crest, this north-facing wall is best found by first locating Rhythm and Blues Boulder. From Rhythm and Blues Boulder move approximately 125 yards north-northwest (nnw) through large boulders and down to base of wall. It will be recognized by its distinctive vertical cracks that cut through two small roofs and its horizontal cracks that cut the face in two. This wall gives one a small taste of what it is like to climb in the Schwangunks.

50. **Pasta Man's Ride, 5.10b**   Start below two north-facing cracks that split double overhang. Climb left crack system to top. Pro: Small to large nuts, Friends.
51. **Marshall Good's Ride, 5.10d ★**   This climb works its way out two roof systems and gives quite the ride before its over. Start is the same as **Pasta Man's Ride**. Climb right crack system to top. Pro: Small to medium nuts, Friends.
52. **Lateralito Bandito, 5.9 ★**   It seems that there is always a bandito trying to cross the path of Marshall Good. Start at right end of wall on top of broken boulders. Traverse horizontal crack system left crossing both **Marshall Good's Ride** and **Pasta Man's Ride** under the second roof system all the way to the left end of the wall. Pro: Medium to large nuts, Friends.
53. **Mistaken Identity, 5.8 ★**   This climb was so named because it is often confused with **Rhythm and Blues**. Although much shorter, it still yields aesthetic climbing. Start approximately 125 yards north from Rhythm and Blues Boulder and due east of

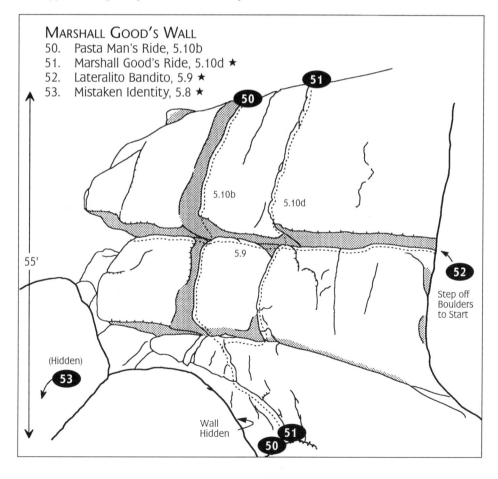

MARSHALL GOOD'S WALL
50. Pasta Man's Ride, 5.10b
51. Marshall Good's Ride, 5.10d ★
52. Lateralito Bandito, 5.9 ★
53. Mistaken Identity, 5.8 ★

Marshall Good's Wall. Approach crack (between green lichen) 40 feet off the ground from right (5.7). Climb crack to top (5.8). Descend via scramble off south side. Pro: Medium to large nuts.

Rhythm And Blues Boulder Area

This massive boulder is one of the highest points on Troon Mountain. Although from many angles it appears to be the summit, it is not. Two great crack climbs are located on its north face and other climbs exist in the immediate area. Standard Descent: Rappel (single line) or scramble Cl. 5 down southeast side (one crappy bolt, angled hanger with ring, no slings).

54. **Heavy Metal, 5.9 ★**   Start at northeast corner of Rhythm and Blues Boulder under large detached flake. Climb wide right-arching crack to top. Pro: Medium to large nuts, tube chocks.
55. **Rhythm And Blues, 5.10b ★★★**   A classic overhanging handcrack with a spectacular view of Pinnacle Peak. This is one of the best crack climbs in central Arizona!!! Start below north face of Rhythm and Blues Boulder. Climb slightly overhanging crack to top. Pro: Medium to large nuts, Friends.
56. **Everybody And His Brother, 5.11a**   Start underneath boulder-roof just west of Rhythm and Blues Boulder. Climb short vertical crack, then traverse right under roof to overhanging crack that splits roof. Climb crack out roof and into chimney. Climb chimney to top. Pro: Medium to large nuts, Friends.

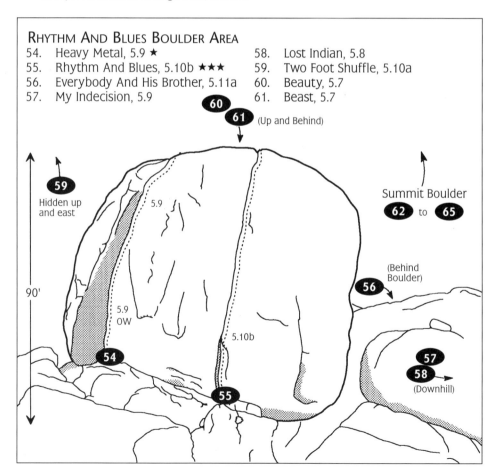

RHYTHM AND BLUES BOULDER AREA
54. Heavy Metal, 5.9 ★
55. Rhythm And Blues, 5.10b ★★★
56. Everybody And His Brother, 5.11a
57. My Indecision, 5.9
58. Lost Indian, 5.8
59. Two Foot Shuffle, 5.10a
60. Beauty, 5.7
61. Beast, 5.7

60
61 (Up and Behind)

59
Hidden up and east

5.9

Summit Boulder
62 to 65

(Behind Boulder)
56

90'

5.9 OW

54

5.10b

55

57
58
(Downhill)

57. **My Indecision, 5.9**   Start approximately 50 yards directly west of Rhythm and Blues Boulder below north-facing wall. Climb short face between large horizontal cracks to thin vertical crack. Continue up vertical crack to top. Pro: Medium to large nuts.
58. **Lost Indian, 5.8**   Start about 70 yards southwest of Rhythm and Blues Boulder and 25 yards south and around corner from **My Indecision** at north-facing slab. Step north off large block onto corner of face to gain crack. Climb crack to top. Descend via easy chimney off east side. Pro: Small to large nuts, Friends.
59. **Two Foot Shuffle, 5.10a**   Start about 90 yards southeast of Rhythm and Blues Boulder at southeast corner of large boulder-pinnacle. Climb slightly overhanging crack in dihedral to top. Descend via tandem rappel. Pro: Medium to large nuts, tube chocks.
60. **Beauty, 5.7**   Start about 80 yards south of Rhythm and Blues Boulder at base of north-facing slab split by two cracks. Climb left crack to top. Pro: Medium to large nuts.
61. **Beast, 5.7**   Start just right of **Beauty**. Climb crack to top. Pro: Medium to large nuts.

Summit Boulder Area

From Alma School Road it appears that to reach the summit of Troon Mountain all one has to do is hike. This is not the case as it requires Cl.5 climbing to reach the top of Summit Boulder. Two new technical routes have been done here since 1987, both recommended.

62. **North Crack, 5.8**   Start on north side of Summit Boulder in boulder enclave. Climb crack system up to wide ledge, then continue up and right in thin crack to top. Descend via rappelling (single line) route. Pro: Small to medium nuts, two belay bolts.
63. **Happy Hooker, 5.10b** ★★   Climb the right side of the north face past four bolts to top. Pro: Four bolts
64. **By Hook Or By Crook, 5.10c** ★★   Climb the west face past three bolts to ledge, then continue up arête past another bolt to top. Pro: Four bolts
65. **Diaphragm Slip, 5.10a**   Start about 30 yards northwest of Summit Boulder below northwest facing crack on indistinct pinnacle. Climb face (5.10a) to gain crack, then up widening crack to top. Pro: Small to large nuts, tube chocks.

Southeast Rockpile

This area along with Ray's Face Area and the East Pinnacles was one of the first areas to receive attention on Troon Mountain. This can be attributed to the relatively short approach. Most of the routes are short and hard to locate, as many of the starts are hidden. One of the best routes on the mountain, **Pussyfoot,** is found in this area. Standard Descent: Scramble Cl. 3 off northeast side.

66. **Warm And Windy, 5.9**   Start at base of large indistinct pinnacle capped by over-hanging boulder approximately 400 yards due west of the Southeast Rockpile. Climb chimney and overhanging crack to low-angled slab (5.9), then continue right underneath overhanging boulder and up to top. Pro: Medium to large nuts.
67. **Breakfast Of Champions, 5.7**   Start on north side in boulder enclave at obvious crack system. Climb left crack to small platform (5.7). Continue in crack to top. Pro: Medium to large nuts.
   Variation, 5.4   Instead of climbing left crack, climb right crack to join regular route. Pro: Medium to large nuts.
68. **Hangin Out, 5.10c** ★   On the first free ascent, the leader wasn't sure whether to rate the climb 5.10. What the leader failed to take into account was that he is well over 6' tall. The rating on this route might vary with an individual's height. Also, this route has not received a second ascent to the author's knowledge. Start on west side at prominent boulder-pinnacle that begins with overhang. Climb overhang past bolt, then continue on face past four bolts to top. Pro: Five bolts, medium nuts.

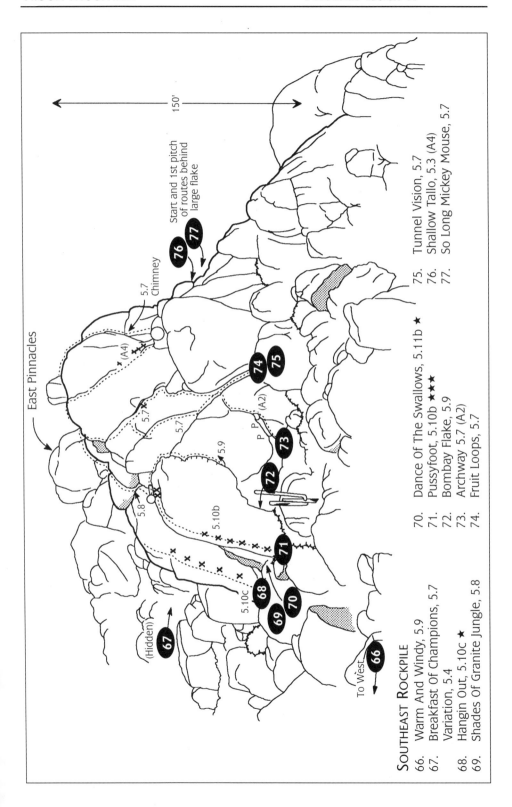

East Pinnacles

150'

Start and 1st pitch
of routes behind
large flake

5.7
Chimney

(A4)

5.7

5.7

5.9

P.P. (A2)

5.8

5.10b

5.10c

(Hidden)

To West

SOUTHEAST ROCKPILE

66. Warm And Windy, 5.9
67. Breakfast Of Champions, 5.7
    Variation, 5.4
68. Hangin Out, 5.10c ★
69. Shades Of Granite Jungle, 5.8
70. Dance Of The Swallows, 5.11b ★
71. Pussyfoot, 5.10b ★★★
72. Bombay Flake, 5.9
73. Archway 5.7 (A2)
74. Fruit Loops, 5.7
75. Tunnel Vision, 5.7
76. Shallow Tallo, 5.3 (A4)
77. So Long Mickey Mouse, 5.7

69. **Shades Of Granite Jungle, 5.8**   Start underneath prominent large-leaning flake on west side and 20 feet right of **Hangin Out**. Climb left side (wide crack) through huge boulder chockstones to top. Pro: Medium to large nuts.

70. **Dance Of The Swallows, 5.11b ★**   This route starts around the corner to the left of the start of **Pussyfoot**. The route ascends to the same belay as **Pussyfoot** past six bolts. Rap off slings in gully east of route. Pro: Six bolts.

71. **Pussyfoot, 5.10b ★★★**   Start at left edge (northwest) corner of prominent large-leaning flake on west side and 20 feet right of **Hangin Out**. First Pitch: Climb arête past six bolts to top (5.10b). Second Pitch: Scramble off flake (northeast) to short off-width (**Shades of Granite Jungle**). Climb off-width (5.8) to top. Pro: Six bolts.

72. **Bombay Flake, 5.9**   Start underneath prominent large-leaning flake on west side. First Pitch: Climb block-crack system to roof (where flake rests against wall). Then traverse right, out and over roof, to top of flake (5.9). Second Pitch: Scramble north to short off-width (**Shades of Granite Jungle**). Climb off-width (5.8) to top. Pro: Small to large nuts.

73. **Archway 5.7 (A2)**   Start 20 feet right of **Bombay Flake**. Turn overhang to get on main wall. Climb horizontal crack to vertical crack. Continue up and right to join **Fruit Loops** (5.7) or **Tunnel Vision** (5.7). Pro: Two fixed pitons, small nuts.
   FA: 1982 Jason Sands, Mike Long

74. **Fruit Loops, 5.7**   Start at large-sloping platform beneath large-leaning flake on south side. Climb ramp left past broken-block crack system (**Tunnel Vision**) to flared crack. Climb crack until possible to traverse right to join **Tunnel Vision** (5.7). Continue to top via **Tunnel Vision**. Pro: Small to large nuts.

75. **Tunnel Vision, 5.7**   A crawling chimney–off-width will give you "tunnel vision" for sure. Start is same as **Fruit Loops**. Climb ramp left to broken-block system that leads up and right. Climb crack system on left to wide crawl space (5.7). Follow wide crawl space up and left until possible to move left out of crawl space past bolt (5.7). Continue to top via crack above (5.7). Pro: Small to medium nuts, one bolt.

76. **Shallow Tallo, 5.3 (A4)**   Start just right of **Tunnel Vision**. First Pitch: Climb chimney to large platform (5.3). Second Pitch: Aid bolt ladder (three bolts) to insipid crack, then follow crack diagonally up and left past bolt to top (A4). Pro: Small to medium nuts, Friends, four bolts, pitons (RURPs to two inches).

77. **So Long Mickey Mouse, 5.7**   Named after a Stanley Clarke song, this route is "Mickey Mouse" at its best. Start just right of **Shallow Tallo**. First Pitch: Climb face on indistinct prow past bolt (5.7), then step left and up broken cracks to large platform. Second Pitch: Move east to base of wide, flared chimney. Climb chimney past bolt (5.7) to top. Pro: Small to medium nuts, two bolts.

East Pinnacles

This impressive area yields several pinnacles and/or buttresses of rock that are all east-facing. Some very good climbing can be found here. Great care has been taken by the locals not to crowd the individual pinnacles with routes exercising the belief that too much of a good thing loses its appeal.

78. **Desolate Sojourner, 5.10b ★★**   Start approximately 100 yards down and left from **Graham Cracker** or left (south) end of East Pinnacles at small dihedral beneath obvious roof. The wall and roof are east-facing; the dihedral is at the left side of the roof. First Pitch: Climb corner past bolt to horizontal finger crack. Traverse finger crack right until possible to swing out on horn above roof (5.9). Mount horn and belay at two bolts. Second Pitch: Climb face straight up past two bolts to top (5.10b). Pro: Small nuts, three bolts, two belay bolts.

79. **Graham Cracker, 5.10c ★★**   Start on south facing wall split by horizontal cracks at left end of East Pinnacles around corner from **Ginger Bread**. Climb face (5.10c) and crack in corner until last full horizontal crack is reached. Traverse left to fixed piton below vertical crack. Climb over pin (5.9) to crack and on to top. Pro: Friends, one fixed piton.

EAST PINNACLES

78. Desolate Sojourner, 5.10b ★★
79. Graham Cracker, 5.10c ★★
80. Ginger Bread, 5.9 ★

81. Face Sandwich, 5.9 ★
82. Lookin' For Trouble, 5.10b(R)
83. Pit Or Pendulum, 5.5
84. Thunder Roe, 5.7

85. Short And Sassy, 5.5
86. Melena, 5.10b ★
87. What A Drag, 5.7

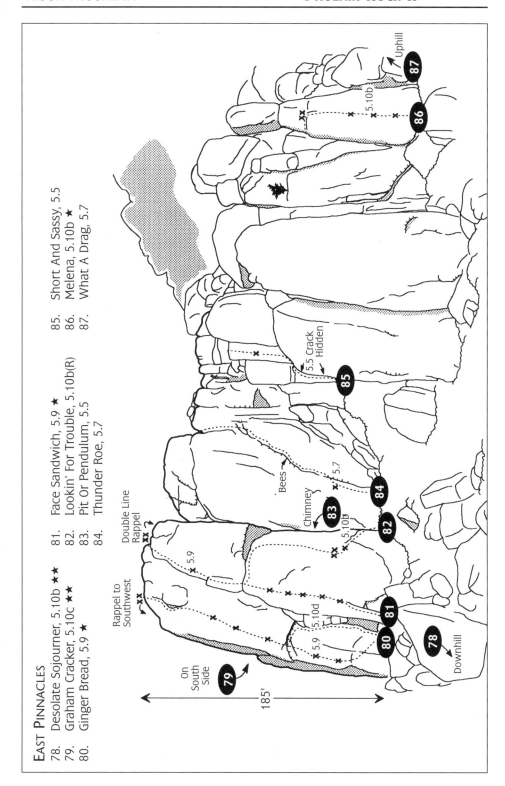

80. **Ginger Bread, 5.9** ★   Start at left pinnacle below east face. Climb past vertical crack (right to left) to reach bolt, then continue on face past another bolt and small horizontal crack to ledge (5.9). Descend via single line rappel off southwest side (two bolts). Pro: Small nuts, Friends, five bolts, two belay bolts.
    Ginger Snap Variation, 5.10d   Instead of regular start, move up to just below overhanging block. Climb crack on left side of block up and left to join regular route. Pro: Medium to large nuts, Friends.

81. **Face Sandwich, 5.9** ★   This climb will give the leader quite an adrenaline rush as they move over its flakes. Start at pinnacle right of **Ginger Bread** below east face. Climb past arched overhang (5.9), then continue on face near small crack to bolt. Continue past four bolts to horizontal crack, then up face and crack to mount block. Continue on corner past bolt to top (5.9). Descend via rappelling route (double line–two bolts) or join **Pit and Pendulum**'s second pitch to top of pinnacle due south. Rappel (single line) off southwest side (two bolts). Pro: Small to large nuts, Friends, six bolts, two belay bolts.

82. **Lookin' For Trouble, 5.10b (R)**   Information was scant on this route at time of publication so exercise great caution. Start right and around corner from **Face Sandwich** at left-arching crack. First Pitch: Climb thin crack around corner to east face and two-bolt belay (5.10). Second Pitch: Climb face above to horizontal crack (5.9 (R)), then traverse right in crack to join **Face**

Unknown climber top-ropes **Face Sandwich** (5.9).

Sandwich. Continue to top via **Face Sandwich** (5.9). Descend via rappelling **Face Sandwich** (double line) or join **Pit and Pendulum**'s second pitch to top of pinnacle south. Rappel (single line) off southwest side (two bolts). Pro: Small to large nuts, Friends, two belay bolts. one bolt.

83. **Pit Or Pendulum, 5.5**   Start at pinnacle right of Ginger Bread in chimney at northwest corner. First Pitch: Climb chimney past chockstone to platform (5.5). Second Pitch: Scramble south and east into abode onto large flake. Climb flared chimney past bolt to large ledge (5.5), then step south onto next pinnacle and scramble to top. Descend via single line rappel off southwest side (two bolts). Pro: Small to medium nuts, tube chocks, one bolt, two belay bolts.
    Variation, 5.7   Instead of climbing chimney, ascend crack on right (west) wall to join

regular route. Pro: Small to medium nuts.

84. **Thunder Roe, 5.7**   Start 30 feet right of **Pit or Pendulum**. Climb dihedral past bolt (5.7), then continue in crack and on ramp to bulge on left. Clear bulge and move left to top. WATCH CAREFULLY FOR BEES ON THIS ROUTE!! THERE IS TRADITIONALLY A LARGE HIVE IN THE SLOT TO THE LEFT OF THE RAMP ABOVE THE FIRST BOLT! Pro: One bolt, small to large nuts.

85. **Short And Sassy, 5.5**   Start 45 feet right of **Thunder Roe**. Climb short, obvious handcrack until angle breaks (5.5). Avoid temptation of scrambling up vegetated crack. Instead move right and climb low-angled slab past bolt to top (5.5). Pro: Medium to large nuts, one bolt.

86. **Melena, 5.10b** ★   Start approximately 100 yards north (or three pinnacles north) of **Face Sandwich** pinnacle below east face. Climb face past three bolts to two bolt hanging belay. Either rappel route (single line) or scramble left around corner and off. Pro: Three bolts, two belay bolts.

87. **What A Drag, 5.7**   Start approximately 100 feet right and up from **Melena**. Climb short crack to ramp . Continue on arête to crack in corner. Climb corner to roof, then exit roof on right and continue in crack to top. Pro: Small to large nuts.

Tapered Wall Area

This area hosts climbs that are scattered all over and can easily occupy a full day's worth of climbing. The routes on the Tapered Wall are the easiest to locate as they are the longest and most distinct. The other routes will be found in proximity to these climbs. Topo, p. 198.

88. **Hand Job, 5.10b**   Start 50 feet below and left of **Bar None** or 200 feet left of Tapered Wall. Climb short thin crack to definite overhanging handcrack. Continue in crack to top. Pro: Small to medium nuts, Friends.

89. **Joke Book, 5.7**   Start approximately 150 feet up and left of Tapered Wall. Climb obvious open book to roof. Turn roof by traversing left to ledge and belay. Pro: Medium to large nuts.

90. **It Don't Get No Traddern' That, 5.8**   Just down and right of **Joke Book**, climb up dark, flaring chimney crack to small ledge on the left side. This one is quite burly. Pro: Medium to large nuts.

91. **Bar None, 5.7**   Start 50 feet left of **Bee Direct** or just left of Tapered Wall at dihedral system. Climb short dihedral to top. Pro: Large nuts, Friends.

92. **Bee Direct, 5.7**   Start at left end of Tapered Wall just left of overhang and below obvious off-width. Climb crack and off-width to ledge and tree. Note: The "BEE" in the route name (as in Beeware!) Pro: Medium to large nuts.
   Variation, 5.9   Climb regular route until you can traverse 8 feet right to vertical thin crack. Continue up thin crack to top. Pro: Small to large nuts.

93. **The Perch, 5.9** ★   Start approximately 50 feet right of **Bee Direct**. Climb brown-stained crack past bolt to top. Exit on right side of large chockstone. Pro: Small to large nuts, one bolt.

94. **Transformation, 5.8** ★   Start 10 feet right of **The Perch**. Climb crack where flake meets wall to ledge. Continue up obvious left-arching crack past off-width to thin crack on left. Continue in thin crack to top. Pro: Small to large nuts.

95. **Step In Line, 5.6**   Start on wall below Tapered Wall and 50 feet to the left of obvious large overhang. Climb open book to top. Pro: Medium to large nuts.

96. **Skid Marks, 5.8**   Start is the same as **Step In Line**. Scramble boulder-filled gully until obvious short right-arching handcrack is visible on right. Climb this crack right and up to top. Pro: Medium to large nuts, Friends.

97. **Goob's R'out, 5.7**   Start just left of the start for **Step In Line** and **Skid Marks**. Climb up handcrack up small overhang to discontinuous cracks above. Finish up crack to top. Pro: Small to medium-large nuts.

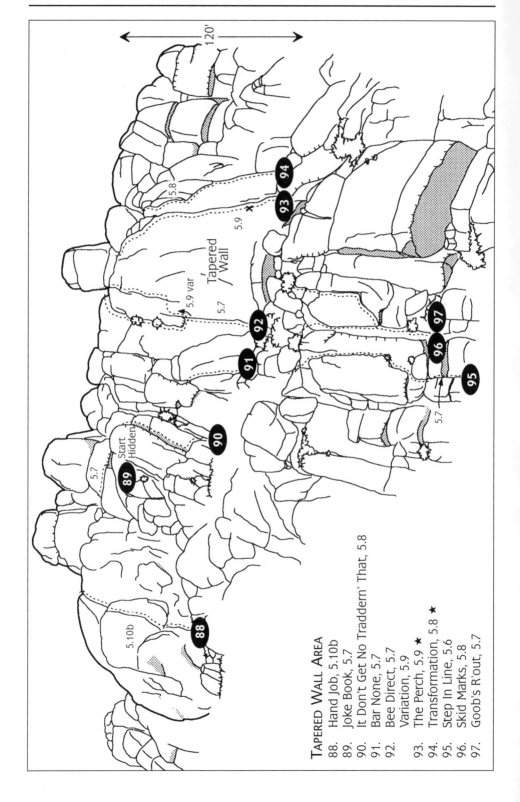

TAPERED WALL AREA

88. Hand Job, 5.10b
89. Joke Book, 5.7
90. It Don't Get No Traddern' That, 5.8
91. Bar None, 5.7
92. Bee Direct, 5.7
    Variation, 5.9
93. The Perch, 5.9 ★
94. Transformation, 5.8 ★
95. Step In Line, 5.6
96. Skid Marks, 5.8
97. Goob's R'out, 5.7

April Fool's Wall

Named because the first route established was done on April 1st, this wall is the largest on the east side of Troon Mountain. Only two routes exist at this time, but the author feels that there are more routes possible for those first ascent seekers.

98. **April Fool, 5.9 (R)** ★ This 200 foot climb is one of the longer routes at Troon Mountain. Start at center of wall in large boulder enclave. First Pitch: Climb vertical crack to large ledge (5.9). Second Pitch: Climb right side of detached flake (5.7), then continue up crack and indistinct prow directly above to top. (5.7 (R)). Pro: Small to large nuts, Friends.

99. **May Day, 5.9 (R)** ★ Except for some loose rock at the roof, this climb offers excellent rock and aesthetic climbing. Start up and right from **April Fool**. Approach from right side of wall on ledge system veering left, which places you underneath large overhang. Three crack systems split overhang. Climb to the middle crack system by easiest means. Clear overhang via this system and continue up discontinuous cracks and face clearing small roof on left to top. Pro: Small to large nuts, Friends.

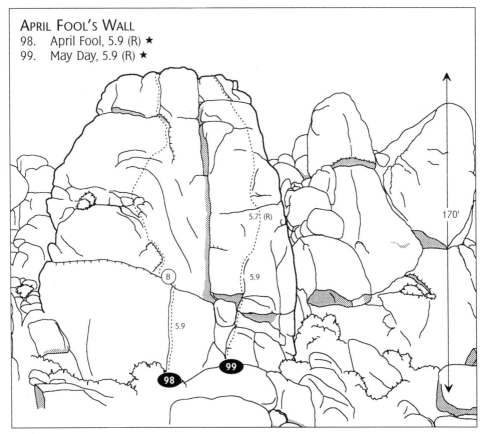

APRIL FOOL'S WALL
98. April Fool, 5.9 (R) ★
99. May Day, 5.9 (R) ★

The Nose

Many climbers looked and attempted to establish a route up this formation before any success was finally achieved. The routes that now exist are serious leads and should be heavily considered before any attempt at leading. The wall was named for the prominent triangular roof that resembles a nose.

THE NOSE
100. Risky Business, 5.10a (R)
101. The Nose, 5.11a (R)

100. **Risky Business, 5.10a (R)**   Lead-outs on risky protection make this a serious lead. Start at ledge system located slightly up on left side of wall. Climb indistinct rib on face to overhang split by crack. Clear overhang via crack and continue in crack (R) passing bolt (5.10a) until a short enjoyable face leads to top. Pro: Small to large nuts, Friends.

101. **The Nose, 5.11a (R)**   The leader on this route may potentially hit his belayer if he falls after clearing the roof. Start at right side of wall. First Pitch: Climb face to bolt belay slightly below overhang (5.7). Second Pitch: Climb up to overhang and use horizontal crack to clear overhang (5.11a). Traverse left (R) to crack and continue in crack past bolt until a short enjoyable face leads to top. Pro: Bolts, small to medium nuts, Friends.
   Note: The first pitch of this route is a fine 5.7 lead for moderate climbers! Rappel off.

Corner Stone Area

This area is located on the east side far to the north. It is best identified by the large prominent dihedral (**Corner Stone**). The approach is fairly short and painless by Troon standards. Descent: Scramble off the backside of the formation, down and to the north, then back around to the base of the rock.

102. **Lead It, Or Leave It, 5.10b (R)** ★   Be prepared for this lead as there are only three bolts for approximately 90 feet of face climbing. Start 20 feet left and around corner from **Corner Stone**. Climb face past three bolts to top. Pro: Three bolts (2nd bolt suspect).

103. **Corner Stone, 5.9** ★   Start at the obvious dihedral. Climb chimney to ledge. Continue on face past two bolts to handcrack. Finish in crack to top. Pro: Two bolts, medium to large nuts, Friends.

104. **Truth Or Consequences, 5.9**   Start at next major wall, up and right from **Corner Stone** off small platform on left side of wall. Climb face along seam until it widens, then continue up crack to easy face and top. Pro: Small to medium nuts, Friends, ?– fixed piton.

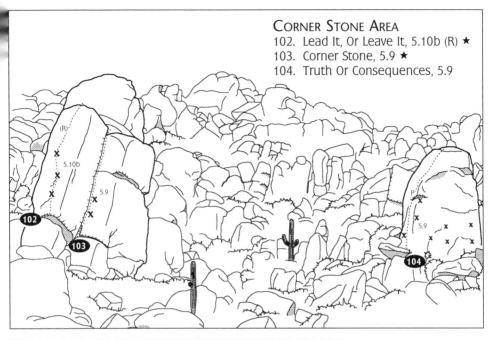

Corner Stone Area
102. Lead It, Or Leave It, 5.10b (R) ★
103. Corner Stone, 5.9 ★
104. Truth Or Consequences, 5.9

Left:
Scott Aldinger leads
the **Corner Stone** (5.9).

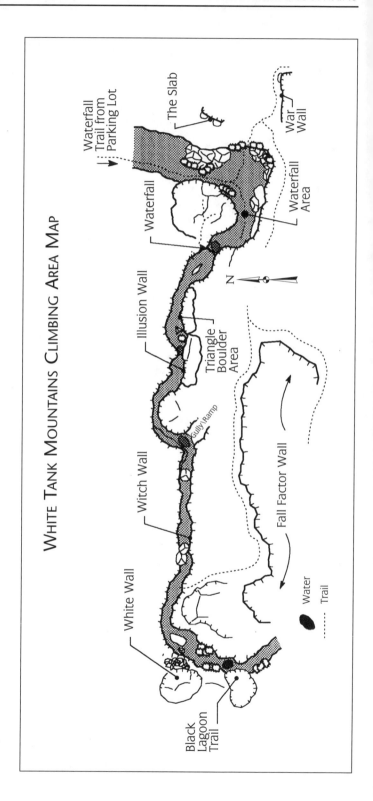

WHITE TANK MOUNTAINS CLIMBING AREA MAP

Waterfall Trail from Parking Lot

The Slab

War Wall

Waterfall

Waterfall Area

N

Illusion Wall

Triangle Boulder Area

Gully Ramp

Witch Wall

Fall Factor Wall

White Wall

Water

Trail

Black Lagoon Trail

Chapter 9

WHITE TANK MOUNTAINS

The White Tank Mountains are a rugged desert mountain range that runs in a roughly north-south alignment off to the west of the Phoenix metro area. The peaks of the White Tanks can be seen from central Phoenix on low-pollution days when the smog and haze don't obstruct the view. In general, the White Tanks can provide an interesting climbing experience, away from the more populated crags closer to town. Be advised that the rock in the White Tank is extensively fractured and can be quite loose in a lot of places. The numerous crack systems and rather vague descriptions can also make route finding part of the crux of the climbs. The longest routes (and some of the loosest!) in the area will be found on Fall Factor Wall, the obvious 350-foot formation up and behind the Waterfall Area. The other formations with established climbs are distributed along the wash starting at the top of the Waterfall Area (see map). Note: It is a very good idea to be extra careful when climbing on suspect rock. Wearing a helmet while climbing is also recommended highly.

Development of the climbing in the White Tanks has been mostly due to the efforts of local climber, Bob Blair, who's been dodging White Tanks rockfall for nearly twenty years. Recently, it has been reported that an unknown party (or parties) had been stripping bolts from some of the routes in this area. As of November of 1995, the bolts on routes in Waterfall Area and along the wash above the waterfall seemed to still be in place (All bolts not verified). This inspection did not include routes on Fall Factor Wall. Be forewarned, bolts may be missing from some of the routes described in this chapter. It is nearly impossible for a guidebook to reflect the current situation as it relates to fixed protection in this (or any) area. If you choose to climb any of these routes, you may find that the bolts mentioned in the route descriptions (and/or shown on the route topos) no longer exist. Climb carefully and with a healthy amount of cynicism.

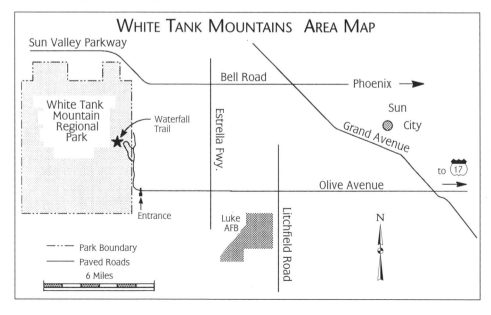

A Word About Petroglyphs: When climbing in the areas outlined in this chapter, it will be very hard for you to miss seeing all the native American artwork which adorns this section of the park. Many examples of prehistoric petroglyphs can be viewed on the main Waterfall Trail, as well as on a few of the rock walls lining the wash above the waterfall, roughly from the Triangle Boulder all the way to the Black Lagoon. Please be respectful and avoid climbing ON any of these historical renderings. Climbing shoes can damage or erase the petroglyphs. A little care goes a long ways!

How To Get There: Drive west out of Phoenix on Olive Avenue (see map), which may be reached from I-17 or via 99th Avenue/Loop 101 from I-10. Heading west on Olive will take past a lot of farmland right on into the White Tanks Regional Park. A $2 fee per vehicle will be collected at the entrance to the park. Continue into the park on the main road. Keep an eye out for the sign to the Waterfall Trailhead (just past the Horse Staging Area). Park at the trailhead. The hike is an easy one mile jaunt on relatively flat ground into the waterfall canyon. The first half of the trail looks like an overtended golf cart path. The drive from central Phoenix takes about 45 minutes. The Waterfall Trail takes you to all of the areas described in this chapter starting, obviously, with the Waterfall Area climbs. The drive to the Waterfall Trailhead is entirely on paved roads.

Access: The climbing areas in this chapter fall within the boundaries of the White Tanks Mountain Regional Park. Hopefully this will preserve it for future Phoenix climbers. Please be nice to the tourists and hikers! There have been some conflicts in the past with the park rangers due to climbers placing bolts next to and above the hiking trail. This practice is not recommended and bolts will be removed. Rumor has it that, due to budget cutbacks, the park may only be open on the weekends now. It might be worth a phone call to the Maricopa County Recreation Department (506-2930) if you're thinking about going to the White Tanks during the week.

Waterfall Canyon Area

This area is rather complex. First, the rock can be very water polished in one section and very coarse and loose in another. Second, over the years this area has become popular for "sport rappelers", "trundlers", and careless hikers (the trail winds around and directly above). Climb and enjoy, but be careful!

Waterfall Area Left

1. **Rusty Piton, 5.4**   The ascent party suspects this route may have had a previous attempt as they found a rusted angle piton with a retreat sling on it part of the way up the route. Either way, look out for loose rock on this route! The start is located about 50 feet to the left of the Banana Peel Slab. First Pitch: Climb a low-angle slab that arches right over the Banana Peel Slab. Continue in a low-angle crack up and right past the "Rusty Piton" on sound rock to a ledge. Second Pitch: Join the third pitch of Easy Ledges. Climb loose rock left and then right to the top of the wall. Pro: Small to large.
2. **Easy Ledges, 5.2**   Start at left side of Banana Peel Slab. First Pitch: Climb ramp and vegetated crack to large ledge (Cl. 4). Second Pitch: Wander up crack systems until possible to move back right to ledge (5.2). Third Pitch: Wander up crack systems left, then back right, and finally straight up to top (5.2). Pro: Small to large nuts.
   Banana Peel Variation, 5.8 (R)   Instead of regular first pitch start 20 feet right at left edge of indistinct 5-foot high by 2-foot wide dihedral. Climb smooth, low-angled face to large ledge. At this point join the regular route. Pro: Small nuts.
3. **Z Crack, 5.11 TR ★★**   This obvious crack system is located on the Banana Peel Slab. A belay can be set up by climbing the first pitch of **Easy Ledges** or **Wombat Indirect**. Expect good rock and tough climbing. It is unknown if this route has seen a lead at this time. (50 feet.) Pro: Toprope.
4. **Wombat Indirect, 5.9 ★★**   This route starts on the south side of the Waterfall Area, about 10 feet to the left of **Staircase**. First Pitch: Climb vertical slippery rock (5.8)

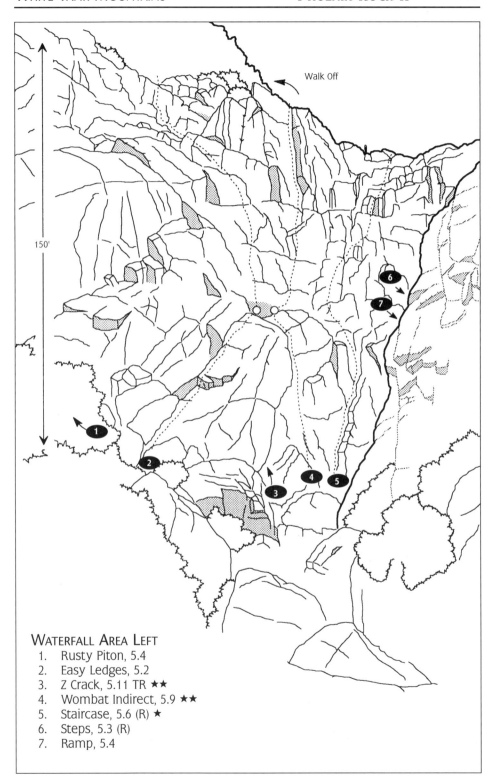

Walk Off

150'

Waterfall Area Left
1. Rusty Piton, 5.4
2. Easy Ledges, 5.2
3. Z Crack, 5.11 TR ★★
4. Wombat Indirect, 5.9 ★★
5. Staircase, 5.6 (R) ★
6. Steps, 5.3 (R)
7. Ramp, 5.4

WATERFALL AREA RIGHT
8. Electrophilic Aromatic Substitution, 5.5
9. Crunchy Frog, 5.8 ★
10. Sweet Dream, 5.9- ★★
11. Leaping Lizards, 5.4 ★
12. Bob And Eric's Excellent Adventure, 5.9 ★★
13. Warmup, 5.4 ★

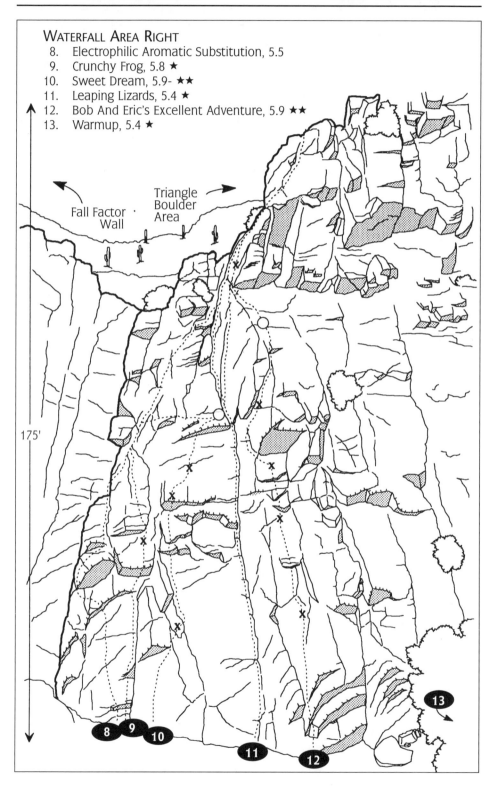

to a bolt. Veer up and slightly right to another bolt. Continue up and left to a ramp, which is followed to the top of the Banana Peel Slab. Second Pitch: Move 15 feet right on the ledge and climb up (mantle) to a small ledge above, using a bolt for protection. A few small ledges lead to the base of an overhung dihedral with a crack. Jam your way up an overhang to the dihedral (5.9) and climb it to the top of the wall. Pro: Small to large, three bolts.

5. **Staircase, 5.6 (R)** ★   Start a few feet right of **Wombat** and opposite ringbolt on opposite wall. First Pitch: Climb wide staircase right and up to small hole (toilet-seat–bucket) (5.6). Second Pitch: Continue directly up and right on face and crack systems to top (5.6). Pro: Small to large nuts, Friends.

6. **Steps, 5.3 (R)**   Start at back of arroyo above and left of first pool of water. Climb face directly to top. Pro: Small to large nuts, Friends.

7. **Ramp, 5.4**   Start on right side of arroyo above band of rock between first and second pool of water. First Pitch: Climb right-facing dihedral and ramp up to broken dihedral system. Continue up broken dihedral system to ledge (5.4). Second Pitch: Continue (short distance) up to top (Cl. 4). Pro: Small to medium nuts.

   Romp Variation, 5.4. Instead of climbing right-facing dihedral and ramp up to broken dihedral system, climb crack on right side of low-angled ramp up to broken dihedral system to join regular route. Pro: Small nuts.

Waterfall Area Right

8. **Electrophilic Aromatic Substitution, 5.5**   Start at low-angled slab 20 feet right of ringbolt. First Pitch: Climb up slab to hidden dihedral system (same as Ramp) that leads to ledge (5.5). Second Pitch: Continue (short distance) up to top (Cl. 4). Pro: Small to medium nuts.

9. **Crunchy Frog, 5.8** ★   Ribbbbit crrrunnnnnch! The start of this climb is located about 30 feet left of **Leaping Lizards** at a low-angle dihedral. First Pitch: Climb up the easy low-angle dihedral for about 30 feet to a big overhang. Clip a bolt and climb the overhang. Move up and left following a crack to the spacious belay alcove (50 feet to 60 feet). Second Pitch: Two possible finishes to the route: a) Climb the second pitch of **Sweet Dream**, or b) Climb straight up to the ledge of **Leaping Lizards,** then continue on Cl. 4 to the top. Pro: One bolt, Small to large.

10. **Sweet Dream, 5.9-** ★★   Probably the best lead in the waterfall area, according to the first ascent team! The start of the climb is located about 15 feet to the left of **Leaping Lizards** below an overhanging arete. First Pitch: Climb up a smooth ramp to a bolt. Move right (5.9-) and climb vertical jugs to the base of the arete and another bolt. Climbing up and right leads to a third bolt and easier rock to a spacious belay alcove. Second Pitch: Climb thin jagged crack on the right-hand wall of the belay alcove. After 20 feet, the crack ends and the alcove of **Bob and Eric's Excellent Adventure** is reached. Continue left around the corner of the alcove to bolt on a slab. Climb straight up the slab to the top of the wall. Pro: Four bolts, Lowe Balls, TCUs, small to large.

11. **Leaping Lizards, 5.4** ★   Start 45 feet right of ringbolt. First Pitch: Climb obvious classic dihedral to ledge (5.4). Second Pitch: Continue up (short distance) to top (Cl. 4). Pro: Small to large nuts.

12. **Bob And Eric's Excellent Adventure, 5.9** ★★   This route starts about 15 feet to the right of **Leaping Lizards** and weaves through some spectacular overhangs. First Pitch: Climb sound rock past a bolt to gain a low-angle dihedral. Continue up to a large white overhang and another bolt. Traverse left around a corner and move up a few feet to bolt number three. Climb up and right under a small overhang (5.9) to gain a small crack–dihedral system which is ascended to a horizontal crack (belay). (50 feet.) Second Pitch: Climb up and left on a low-angle unprotected ramp for about 40 feet (easy) to an alcove. Continue left around the corner of the alcove to bolt on a slab. Climb straight up

the slab to the top of the wall (70 feet). Pro: Four bolts, Lowe Balls, medium to large cams.

13. **Warmup, 5.4** ★   Start 40 feet right of **Leaping Lizards**, where a trail goes up against the wall behind bushes. Climb large broken dihedral system to top. Pro: Small to large nuts.

War Wall

The War Wall is a 50-foot formation that sits above and left (southeast) of the Waterfall Area. The wall is not obvious from the Waterfall Area, but glimpses of it can be seen from the trail just before reaching the mouth of the Waterfall Area. Across the small canyon from **Sweet Dreams**, a trail leads up and left until it passes below the War Wall. Some minor scrambling may be required. Watch out for loose rocks! Routes are described from left to right. Topo, page 208.

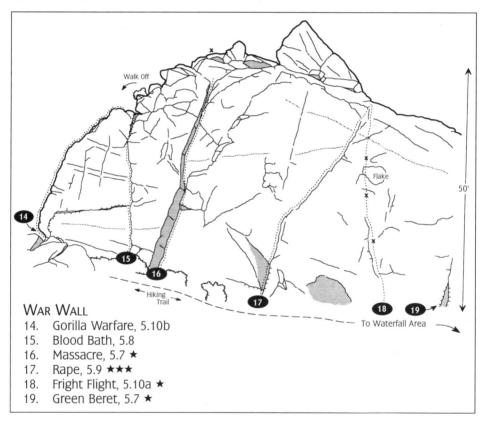

WAR WALL
14. Gorilla Warfare, 5.10b
15. Blood Bath, 5.8
16. Massacre, 5.7 ★
17. Rape, 5.9 ★★★
18. Fright Flight, 5.10a ★
19. Green Beret, 5.7 ★

14. **Gorilla Warfare, 5.10b**   This route is located on the left edge of War Wall to the left of **Blood Bath** and **Massacre**. Climb a gymnastic overhang (heel hook) to easier ground above. A spotter is a good idea on the overhang moves. Pro: Lowe Balls.

15. **Blood Bath, 5.8**   Start at far left corner of wall. Climb handcrack to top. Pro: Medium to large nuts.

16. **Massacre, 5.7** ★   Start just right of **Blood Bath**. Climb obvious dihedral to top. Pro: Small to medium nuts.

17. **Rape, 5.9 ★★★**   This route was listed as a (TR) in the first and second Phoenix guidebooks. In February of '91, Bob led it using rappel placed TCUs. Climbs the dihedral to the right of **Massacre** by "ape hanging" on it's right margin (35 feet and overhung).

18. **Fright Flight, 5.10a ★**   Directly below the top of **Rape**, climb overhanging face on big holds to top. The route was originally established as a toprope. Later, another climber led the route using rappel-placed natural protection. Since that time, an unknown party has "equipped" the route with three bolts. Make sure the bolts are still there if you're planning to lead this one. Pro: Three bolts.

19. **Green Beret, 5.7 ★**   This climb starts approximately 25 feet to the right of **Rape**. Climb a "greenish epidate" dihedral system (35 feet). The ascent party suspects that this route may have seen an earlier ascent.

The Slab

This formation is on the south side of the streambed down the hill from War Wall, facing to the north. It is about 150 feet to the southeast of the Waterfall Area. No topo shown.

20. **You Name The Route, 5.4**   This route ascends the left-leaning discontinuous crack on the right side of The Slab. Start down between the two large boulders at the base. Climb the crack and face, exiting right of the capstone boulder (60 feet). Pro: Small to medium.

21. **Therapy, 5.7 R**   About 15 feet to the left of **You Name the Route**, climb 25 feet of unprotected easy face to a horizontal crack. Step right and climb a thin left-leaning crack to the left edge of The Slab. Climb straight up the face and over the summit boulder to the top (60 feet). Pro: Small to large.

Triangle Boulder Area

After crossing over the Waterfall area, drop back down into the wash. In a short distance there is an area with petroglyphs on both sides of the wash. In the middle of the wash, one should notice the Triangle Boulder. The climbing rests on a 45-foot wall to the left.

22. **Exit Stage Left, 5.9 ★**   Start near left end of wall. Climb face to horizontal crack, then continue up face just right of thin crack until exit left is possible. Pro: Small to medium nuts, Friends.

23. **Layback, 5.5**   Start 12 feet right of **Exit Stage Left.** Climb obvious right-facing dihedral to ledge, then move right climbing blocks and face to top. Pro: Small to large nuts.

24. **Arpeggio, 5.7**   Start 15 feet right of **Layback.** Climb thin left-leaning crack to ledge, then join **Layback** to top. Pro: Small to large nuts.

Illusion Wall Area

This modest area is located approximately 100 feet to the west (upsteam) of the Triangle Boulder Area. It faces north and has three established routes, described left to right. This is maybe the best area along the wash for viewing ancient petroglyphs. Many examples can be seen on the short wall that faces Illusion Wall, as well as the "chain" petroglyphs that can be seen atop the **Joe Schmidt Route**. Standard descent for Illusion Wall: Walk off and down Third-class terrain to the right of the wall or single line rappel from bolts above **Illusion**.

25. **Joe Schmidt Route, 5.6**   This route is best identified by the obvious petroglyph "chains" on a square buttress directly above this route. The basic line follows a crack/gully system over big ledges to a belay on top of the "petrocliff." Climb an easy crack gully for 20 feet to a large ledge. Climb up broken crack to a shallow groove. A layback on the edge of the groove and more climbing take you past a bush on the left. Climb up to and surmount the summit block to belay on top (100'). Pro: Small to large.

26. **Memory Lane, 5.8 ★**   This climb is located on a 50' block-shaped wall (the Illusion Wall) about 25 feet right of the **Joe Schmidt Route**. This is the left-hand route of two

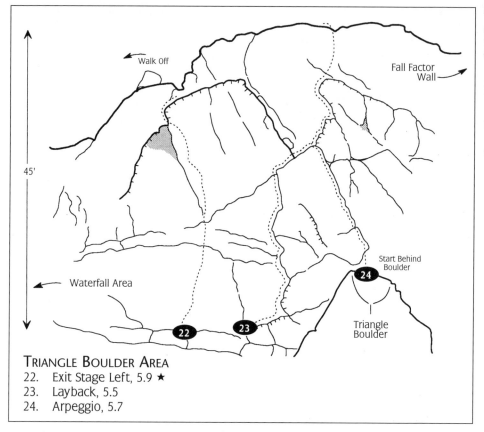

45'

Walk Off

Fall Factor Wall

Start Behind Boulder

Waterfall Area

Triangle Boulder

TRIANGLE BOULDER AREA
22.　Exit Stage Left, 5.9 ★
23.　Layback, 5.5
24.　Arpeggio, 5.7

existing lines on the wall. Climb slick rock to a bulge. A couple of committing moves over the bulge lead to a ¼" crack. Continue up the face (horizontal pro placements) to varnished knobs and jugs leading to a two-bolt belay on top. Pro: Small to medium-large, two belay bolts.

27.　**Illusion, 5.7 ★★**　This nice route is on the right side of the Illusion Wall, just to the right of **Memory Lane**. Climb slippery rock up to a bulge. Climb past bulge to a bolt. Continue up to a varnished crack with lots of knobs and jugs and follow this to the 2-bolt belay on top. Pro: One bolt, small to large, two belay bolts.

Witch Wall

This area is found if you continue up the wash from the Illusion Wall area, to the west (a few hundred feet west of the Triangle Boulder area). You will make a left turn, pass a gully on the left and then contine up the wash past a boulder (in the wash) to a spot where the wash is about 15 feet wide with a sandy bottom. The wall faces to the north and is about 30 feet high. Although short, the climbing and the rock is of reasonably good quality (although slicker'n-snot-on-a-glass-doorknob). Routes are described from left to right. Standard descent for the Witch Wall: Walk off and down sloping ground to the right of the wall.

28.　**Poison Apple, 5.8 ★**　On the left side of Witch Wall, climb slippery rock to a horizontal space. Climb over an overhang on big slippery jugs and continue to top on easy ground. Pro: Lowe Balls and TCUs.

29.　**Mirror, Mirror, 5.9 ★**　Mirror, mirror on the wall, which is the slipperiest route on the wall? Put on your skates 10 feet to the right of **Poison Apple**, climb slippery rock to a horizontal space. Thrutch through the overhang using a weird movable knob hand-hold. Continue straight up to the top. Pro: Lowe Balls, small nuts.

30. **Sleeping Beauty, 5.9** ★   This route is located on the right hand side of Witch Wall, about ten feet to the right of **Mirror, Mirror**. A large boulder will be above you and to the right. Climb slippery rock...hey, it's the same! Climb slippery rock to a horizontal crack. Burly jams get you by the overhang where you can jam your way to the top. Pro: Small to medium large.

The White Wall

This wall is located up the streambed from Witch Wall, just past the Tiger Tooth Boulder (a 20-foot boulder in the streambed). The wall is formed of a light-colored rock and is easily identified by the horizontal overhang running across the face. This is approximately 0.25 mile west of the Waterfall area and about 200 yards upstream from the Witch Wall area around a bend in the wash. The rock is somewhat loose but faces south and is decently sheltered, making it good for cold winter days. Routes are described from left to right. Standard Descent for the White Wall: Walk off the back and down to the right.

31. **Red Dog, 5.8**   On the left side of the White Wall, climb up face past a bolt to a right-leaning dihedral (large cam). Continue up and left around the corner of the dihedral to clip a bolt. Climb straight above to a third bolt and small cam placement to the top of the wall. Pro: Three bolts, TCUs, Lowe Balls, and medium to large cams.

32. **Scorpion's Last Dance, 5.8** ★   Start ten to15 feet right of **Red Dog**, near the center of the wall. Climb straight up past two bolts to an overhang. Surmount the overhang directly to another bolt. Continue to the top of the wall. Pro: Three bolts, small to medium cams.

The White Wall
31. Red Dog, 5.8	33. Timmie's 5.12 Route, 5.7 (R)
32. Scorpion's Last Dance, 5.8 ★	34. Serrated Edge, 5.7 ★

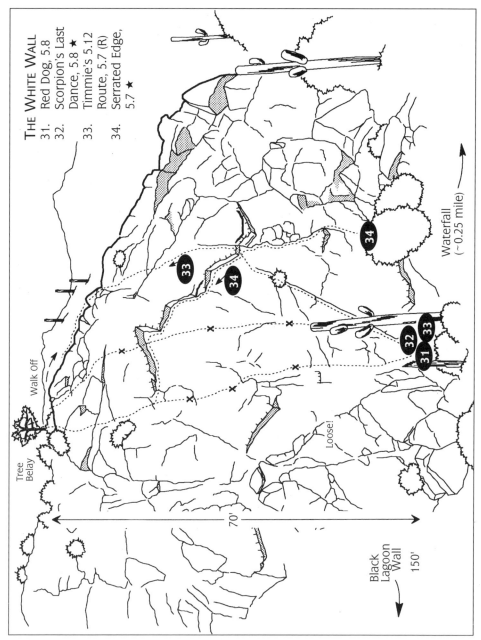

THE WHITE WALL
31. Red Dog, 5.8
32. Scorpion's Last Dance, 5.8 ★
33. Timmie's 5.12 Route, 5.7 (R)
34. Serrated Edge, 5.7 ★

Waterfall (~0.25 mile)

Walk Off

Tree Belay

Loose!

70'

Black Lagoon Wall 150'

33. **Timmie's 5.12 Route, 5.7 (R)**   This shares the same starting spot as for
Scorpion's Last Dance. Near the center of the wall, climb up a right-leaning, narrow
ramp for 25 feet. Continue up a vertical dihedral until possible to traverse right around a
corner. Climb runout face to the top of the wall. Pro: Small to medium large.

34. **Serrated Edge, 5.7 ★**   Along the right side of the White Wall, climb an obvious vertical dihedral that arches left after about 35 feet and turns into an overhang. Climb past
loose rock to gain the dihedral. Layback up the dihedral until you reach the overhang.
Undercling out to the left past the overhang and then continue up the face above to the
top of the wall. Pro: Small to medium-large, Lowe Balls.

The Black Lagoon Wall

This wall is the obvious dark buttress of rock located just up the streambed from the White Wall above a dark pool that resembles an Exxon oil pond. It is on the north side, facing south, and is about 75 feet high. Watch out for loose rock! Petroglyphs may be seen along the lower righthand side of the Black Logoon Wall. Some latter-day moron has also added examples of modern rock grafitti as well, just left of the petroglyphs. Standard Descent for the Black Lagoon Wall: Walk off the back and to the right down the saddle and gully between the White Wall and the Black Lagoon Wall.

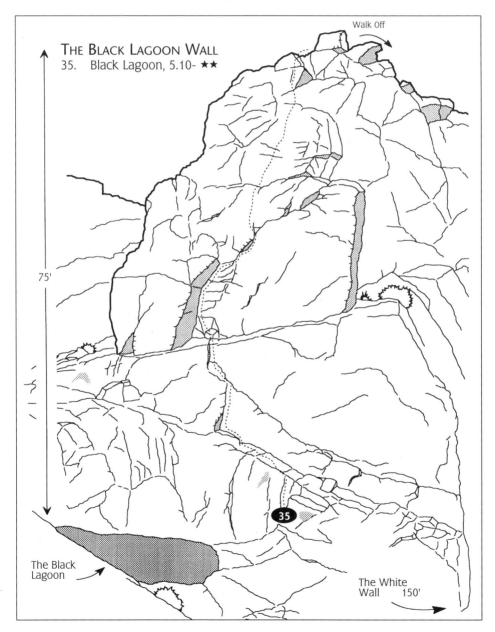

THE BLACK LAGOON WALL
35.　Black Lagoon, 5.10- ★★

Walk Off

75'

The Black Lagoon

The White Wall　150'

35

35. **Black Lagoon, 5.10- ★★**   Start at right side of pool. Climb up good rock past a short dihedral to a ledge. Continue up steep cracks in a corner to an overhang. Handrail right and jam a crack to turn the overhang and gain the face above. Climb to the top past two bolts. Pro: Two bolts, Lowe Balls, small to medium cams.

Fall Factor Wall

Although this is the largest wall in the area by far, it doesn't necessarily yield the best climbing and definitely not the best rock. Please keep in mind that because the wall is extremely fractured, loose rock is almost certain, and route descriptions are unavoidably vague. Bob Blair writes:

> *"It would probably be a good idea to wear a catcher's mask, crash helmet, and body armor if you intend to belay off the chains while your partner leads the hanging buttress pitch of Atilla the Hun. You will be in harm's way if he trundles a wobbly."*

I suggest that you take this as a potential warning for the entire wall! Climb carefully and definitely wear a helmet for this one!!!! Topo, page 216.

36. **Hangbelly Crack, 5.7**   Start at far left side of wall. There are two vertical cracks; **Hangbelly** starts at the right one. First Pitch: Climb crack and dihedral, then face to ledge (5.7). Second Pitch: Continue to top via easiest means (5.2). Pro: Small to medium nuts.

37. **Potent Pudding, II 5.6**   Start where **Cactus Candy** ledge meets base of wall. First Pitch: Climb crack up and left on low-angled slab to bushy ledge (5.3). Second Pitch: Climb up and right (5.4) towards **Crotch Notch** (recognized by ocotillo on top of wall). Belay on ledge below and right of **Crotch Notch** dihedral-chimney. Third Pitch: Climb up and through notch to top (5.6). Pro: Small to large nuts.

38. **Milkrun, II 5.6**   Start is just right of **Potent Pudding**. First Pitch: Climb straight up crack to ledge (5.5). Second Pitch: Continue up and left toward a big loose-looking flake, then past flake to ledge with saguaro (5.4). Third Pitch: Climb up to overhang, then over, and on to top (5.6). Pro: Small to large nuts.

39. **Cactus Candy, II 5.5**   Start 40 feet right of **Milkrun**. First Pitch: Climb up crack to black band and **Cactus Candy** ledge. (5.3). Second Pitch: Continue up crack system to steep section, then left and up right to standing belay (5.5). Third Pitch: Continue on easy climbing to top (5.3). Pro: Small to large nuts.

40. **Snorfy Elaticor, II 5.7**   Start at base of large right-facing dihedral under the great roof. First Pitch: Climb dihedral on right side to roof. Climb over "frisbee" turning overhang on left, then up to **Cactus Candy** ledge (5.6). Second Pitch: Climb up to hanging thin flake, then past flake to ledge. Continue on to another ledge and belay (5.7). Third Pitch: Easy climbing leads to top (5.3). Pro: Small to large nuts.
    Turkey Traverse Variation, 5.3   Instead of climbing over "frisbee" and turning roof, traverse left onto left face of the dihedral and up to rejoin route. Pro: Small to large nuts.
    FA: 1975 Bob Blair, Joe Schmidt

41. **The Jaws Of Rockomatic, II 5.7**   Start 25 feet right of **Snorfy Elaticor**. First Pitch: Climb face and flakes under great roof to bolt. Diagonal left to small crack, then up and right to roof and left-leaning horizontal space. Launch into space and crawl out to edge of overhang. Clear overhang and move left to belay (5.7). Second Pitch: Climb up to **Cactus Candy** ledge (5.2). Third Pitch: Move up and right on **Cactus Candy** ledge, then climb left side of hanging buttress above to top (5.7). Fourth Pitch: Easy climbing leads to top (5.1). Pro: Small to large nuts, Friends. Note: Bob has added bolts to the first three pitches of **Atilla**. There are four new bolts on the first pitch, and two belay bolts. The second pitch now has four bolts and two belay bolts. The third pitch has one bolt. Please see the warning about stripped bolts in the introduction to this chapter!

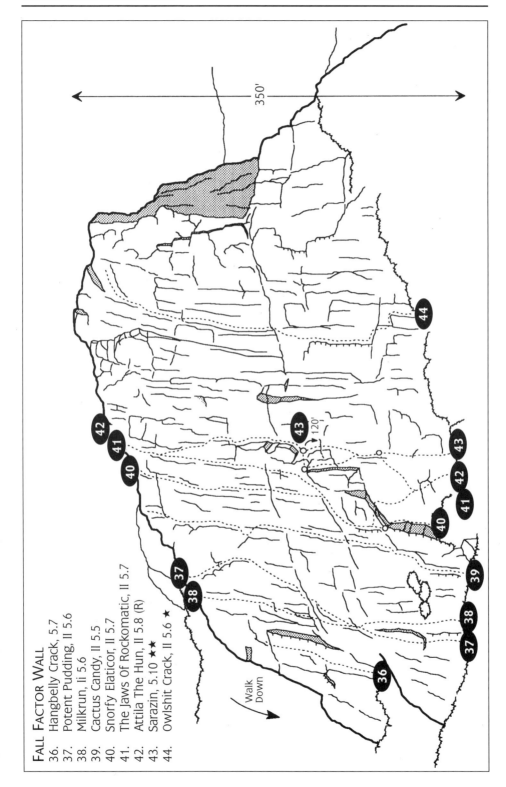

Fall Factor Wall
36. Hangbelly Crack, 5.7
37. Potent Pudding, II 5.6
38. Milkrun, II 5.6
39. Cactus Candy, II 5.5
40. Snorfy Elaticor, II 5.7
41. The Jaws Of Rockomatic, II 5.7
42. Attila The Hun, II 5.8 (R)
43. Sarazin, 5.10 ★★
44. Owlshit Crack, II 5.6 ★

350'

120'

Walk
Down

42. **Attila The Hun, II 5.8 (R)**   Start is same as **The Jaws of Rockomatic**. First Pitch: Climb face and flakes under great roof to bolt. Traverse right and up passing two bolts to sling belay (two bolts, 5.6). Second Pitch: Climb up into small right-facing dihedral (bolt), then up until possible to move left onto **Cactus Candy** ledge (5.6). Third Pitch: Move back right off of **Cactus Candy** ledge and traverse face up and right to right side of hanging buttress.Climb right side of buttress to its top (5.8). Fourth Pitch: Easy climbing leads to top (5.1). Pro: Four bolts, two belay bolts, small to large nuts, Friends.

43. **Sarazin, 5.10 ★★**   This well-bolted climb starts 15 feet to the right of **Atilla the Hun**. Climb steep rock past five bolts straight to the standing belay on **Atilla**. Don't belay. Continue up the wall, passing three more bolts. Move right and climb up past more bolts to a bulge protected by a #3 Friend. Climb bulge to a bolt and then move up to a two bolt belay. To descend, rappel (two ropes!) from belay chains (120 feet) back to the ground. Pro: 12 bolts, #3 Friend!!

44. **Owlshit Crack, II 5.6 ★**   Start 100 feet right of **Attila the Hun**. First Pitch: Climb short right-facing dihedral until possible to move left to another dihedral and up to large ledge (5.6). Second Pitch: Climb a dihedral to an overhang, then over overhang to crack that widens into dark chimney. Continue up chimney until possible to exit right on large ledge (5.6). Third Pitch: Easy climbing leads to top (Cl. 4). Pro: Small to large nuts. **Fritz Fell Here Variation, 5.8**   After climbing short right-facing dihedral, move left past the regular dihedral to a short face that leads to another large dihedral with wide crack. Climb crack until possible to exit right and rejoin regular route. Pro: Small to large nuts.

Chapter 10

ODDS 'N ENDS

In the old days of the Climber's Guide to Central Arizona, this chapter went under the title of "Outback." Although I had hoped to retain this name, some of the areas I wanted to include weren't all that outback in nature and weren't really deserving of a chapter of their own, "Odds-'n Ends" seemed a more and more applicable designation for the chapter. The name seems to fit, since I had lots of weird little formations and crags dispersed throughout the general area to throw into the bin, this seemed the logical place to do it.

In general, this chapter contains information on several smaller climbing and less-developed areas scattered throughout this part of the state. Most of them are interesting and rather obscure crags that are worth a visit or two if for no other reason than they offer something different than the standard climbing day at the local spots. Details may be a bit sparse for some of the areas, but I'll invoke the traditional guidebook author's bailout response and say that any lack of information should be seen as an opportunity to have a good adventure in the unknown.

Regarding the greater portion of the climbs in this chapter: As you might expect with more or less "backcountry" climbs, you're gonna have to work a bit to do some of these. In most cases, this probably boils down to a long, involved, uphill approach, but may involve other challenges as well (bushwhacking, descents, loose rock, etc.). Although the popularity of sport climbing has led a lot of climbers to appreciate crags where it's nearly possible to belay off the bumper, I can highly recommend a day of climbing where you can enjoy the desert and the rock in a remote location, far from the crowds. That's what most of the climbs in this chapter offer. Routes described are found in the Bradshaw Mountains to the north (Crown King/Bloody Basin area), the Mazatzal Mountains to the northeast (Four Peaks), and the Eagletail Mountains to the southeast (Courthouse Rock and the Eagle Feathers).

Information on the rather "after work" climbing locations at Lookout Mountain and the Ice Castle areas has also been included here, although neither is really an "outback" location. Those are the breaks. They had to go somewhere.

Lookout Mountain

Lookout Mountain is located in northern Phoenix and is part of the Phoenix Mountain Preserve system. Until a couple of years ago, the area had not seen any real attempts at route development other than a foray by Paul Paonessa and Chuck Johnson in 1986 to check out the climbing potential. After climbing a couple of routes on Dead Dobie Wall (the only wall in the area that resembles something climbable), they decided there was much better rock around to put up first ascents and moved on to the much-better granite formations of the McDowell Mountains areas. The main reason for this seems to have been somewhat associated with the somewhat unstable rock they found at Lookout Mountain. Zoom forward to 1993. Marty Karabin and Chris Bastek break out the drill and install several bolted lines on Dead Dobie Wall, dragging it into the sport climbing decade. I suspect the hardest part of this bolting effort was finding something solid to drill an anchor into.

Although it's one of the closest "climbing" areas in the metro Phoenix area, and one of the few that you can hit as an "after work" climbing fix, if you head out to climb at Lookout Mountain, expect to find some crumbly rock and climb appropriately. Recent traffic on the wall has probably cleaned off some of the loosest obvious holds, but it might be a good

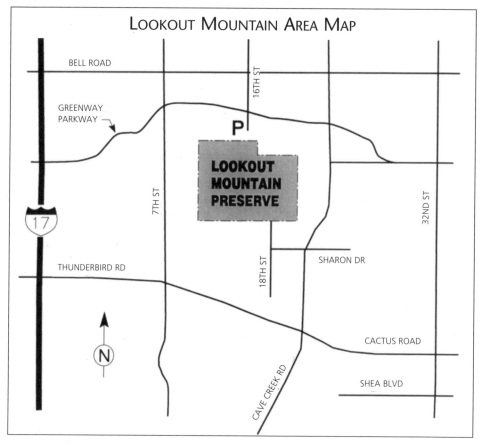

idea to bring helmets and belay to the side of a direct path below your climber to avoid potential handhold and foothold fallout. Also keep an eye on those climbing next to you, as they might send some surprises down the wall as well.

The established routes described in this chapter are all on Dead Dobie Wall. This 75 foot (at its highest point) volcanic wall in the middle of the Lookout Mountain Preserve can easily be seen from the 16th Street parking area, although it doesn't look like much. The wall faces west, so expect no shade after noon. As expected under a wall this loose, the footing on the steep, loose hill-side can be tricky. Move carefully in this area!

Approach: As mentioned above, the Lookout Mountain Preserve is located smack within the Phoenix Metro area. A short, and relatively easy 15-minute approach hike can be done from the trailhead

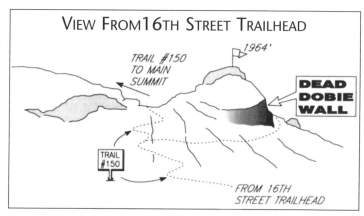

parking lot on the north side of the preserve, where 16th Street dead ends at the trailhead after going south from Greenway Parkway. This is easily accessed by taking the Greenway exit from I-17 or by accessing the parkway from Cave Creek Road and heading west to 16th Street.

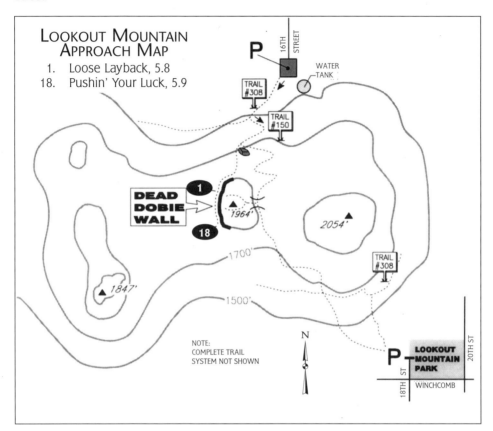

From the parking area, hike out on trail #308, heading west. Trail #308 travels the perimeter of the park. Approximately one hundred yards out of the parking lot, a trail marker shows the intersection of that trail with trail #150 (the summit trail). Turn onto trail #150 and hike up through some switchbacks. There is a turnoff where a large boulder sits in the wash coming down from the saddle above. Take this side trail to the west to go around to the bottom of Dead Dobie Wall. There are a few braided trails going in the correct general directions, so follow your nose on the best looking option to gain the bottom of the wall.

Routes are described from left to right (north to south).

Dead Dobie Wall

1. **Loose Layback, 5.8**   This is the leftmost route on the wall (left of **I Love Loosie** and **Junkyard Dog**). A low section of Class 4 crumbly rock leads to a short two-bolt face. Climb this to bolted anchor. Not shown on topo. Pro: Two bolts, two-bolt anchor.
2. **The Gnome, 5.10–**   Just right of **Loose Layback**, another two bolts lead to anchor. Not shown on topo. Pro: Two bolts, two-bolt anchor.
3. **I Love Loosie, 5.9 R**   This starts at a crack system below a small open book right at the top of the wall. Climb runout crack to a two-bolt face above (bolts may be hard to spot from the ground). Rap from anchor. Pro: Two bolts, two-bolt anchor.

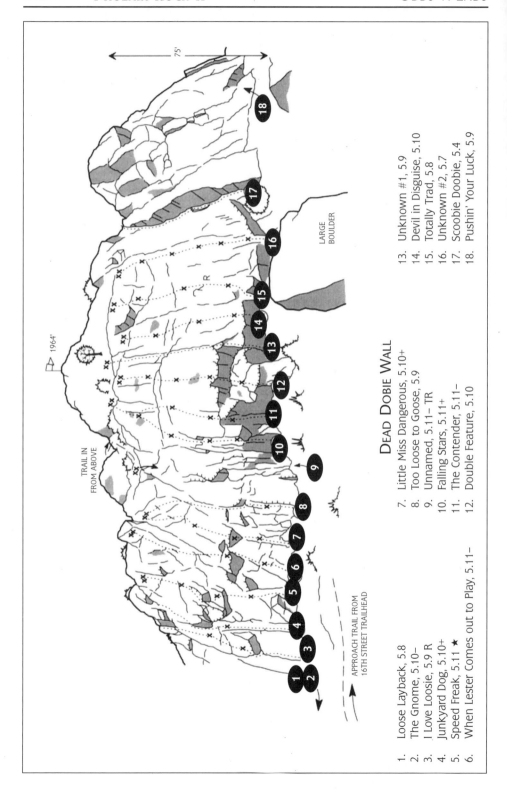

75'

18

17

16

15

14

13

12

11

10

9

8

7

6

5

4

3

2

1

1964'

R

TRAIL IN
FROM ABOVE

LARGE
BOULDER

APPROACH TRAIL FROM
16TH STREET TRAILHEAD

DEAD DOBIE WALL

1. Loose Layback, 5.8
2. The Gnome, 5.10–
3. I Love Loosie, 5.9 R
4. Junkyard Dog, 5.10+
5. Speed Freak, 5.11 ★
6. When Lester Comes out to Play, 5.11–

7. Little Miss Dangerous, 5.10+
8. Too Loose to Goose, 5.9
9. Unnamed, 5.11– TR
10. Falling Stars, 5.11+
11. The Contender, 5.11–
12. Double Feature, 5.10

13. Unknown #1, 5.9
14. Devil in Disguise, 5.10
15. Totally Trad, 5.8
16. Unknown #2, 5.7
17. Scoobie Doobie, 5.4
18. Pushin' Your Luck, 5.9

4. **Junkyard Dog, 5.10+**   Just right of **I Love Loosie,** climb overhanging fingercrack to a bolt, then continue on two-bolt face past left facing corner above to anchor. Pro: Small pro, two bolts, two-bolt anchor.

5. **Speed Freak, 5.11** ★   In the left central part of the wall, there are four routes with bolts near the ground. This is the leftmost line. Climb up corner of buttress to a bolt. Head slightly left to second bolt just above a small roof, then past two more bolts to anchor. Pro: four bolts, two-bolt anchor.

6. **When Lester Comes out to Play, 5.11–**   Just right of **Speed Freak**, climb up overhang leading to crack. More face and crack moves lead past four bolts to anchor. Pro: four bolts, two-bolt anchor.

7. **Little Miss Dangerous, 5.10+**   This route starts just below a triangular roof just right of **When Lester Comes out to Play**. Climb up small corner past a bolt to the triangular roof, clip second bolt and turn roof, then continue up face to last bolt. Go right and up at the third bolt to find the anchor. Pro: three bolts, two-bolt anchor.

8. **Too Loose to Goose, 5.9**   This is the jagged crack that doesn't quite reach the ground just right of **Little Miss Dangerous**. Climb face past one bolt in skinny right-facing corner to gain crack. Continue in crack (turns into r-facing overlap) and veer left to anchor (shares anchor with **Little Miss Dangerous**). Pro: One bolt, small to medium pro, two-bolt anchor.

9. **Unnamed, 5.11– TR**   The grungy section of the wall just right of **Too Loose to Goose** has been climbed on toprope. This is below the rap anchor on the trail at the top of the wall. Pro: Toprope! Two-bolt anchor.

10. **Falling Stars, 5.11+**   Right of the crumbly middle of the wall. Start at a cracked-up, left-facing buttress corner. Climb the steep, loose face over bulge and corner. Continue to anchor, staying right of the crack past three more bolts. Watch for loose rock at the start! Pro: four bolts, two-bolt anchor.

11. **The Contender, 5.11–**   Just right of **Falling Stars**, climb up into a grey alcove below roof with a bolt. Continue to roof (second bolt) and then over to face above. Two more bolts lead to the anchor (shares last bolt and anchor with Falling Stars). Pro: four bolts, two-bolt anchor.

12. **Double Feature, 5.10**   Right of **The Contender**, this route starts at a bulge right at the bottom of the wall with a bolt you can nearly clip from the ground. Continue above over another bulge/roof and then past two horizontal railings and steep last section to anchor. Pro: four bolts, two-bolt anchor.

13. **Unknown #1, 5.9**   Ten feet to the right of **Double Feature** is a black flaring crack system with two old self-drive bolts (no hangers). Climb crack to anchor at top. Watch pro placements in this sucker! Pro: Small to medium, two-bolt anchor.

14. **Devil in Disguise, 5.10**   Six feet right of the unnamed crack route, climb overhang to face above, passing three bolts to anchor. Pro: three bolts, two-bolt anchor.

15. **Totally Trad, 5.8**   The name is somewhat ironic here although the runout nature might be the source. Six feet right of **Devil in Disguise**, climb out of short right-facing corner, through overhang, and onto the face above. Watch the crater possibilities when moving to the second bolt! Somewhat runout! Pro: three bolts, two-bolt anchor.

16. **Unknown #2, 5.7**   This route scales the highest part of Dead Dobie Wall (~75 feet). Ten feet right of **Totally Trad**, climb face just left of discontinuous thin cracks past five bolts to anchor. Pro: five bolts, two-bolt anchor

17. **Scoobie Doobie, 5.4**   This route climbs the obvious chimney up the left side of a "pillar" formation on the right side of the wall. Pro: Mostly large. Bring sling for chockstone thing.

18. **Pushin' Your Luck, 5.9**   About 30 feet to the right of the **Scoobie Doobie** pillar, climb a face just right of a right-facing corner past three bolts to anchor. Watch for loose rock! Pro: three bolts, two-bolt anchor

Ice Castles

This area lies in the far northwestern sector of the Phoenix metro area, just south of the Carefree Highway between 99th Avenue and 51st Avenue (see map). Some of the original development of this extended bouldering area was done by Ted Olsen and Phil Falcone in 1987-1988. They snagged most of the longest possible lines. Marty Karabin, filled in the existing lines with a few additional routes in '93-'94, most of which were one- and two-bolt face climbs.

The nature of the climbing here is generally decomposing desert granite. Many routes will have loose rock, so be prepared to deal with the possible consequences of those temporary handholds! (spotters, toprope, other protection...). Broken ankles aren't much fun. The climbs here are also short, with the longest topping out at 65 feet. A few nuts/cams and a few Quickdraws should be enough to adequately protect most routes.

NOTE: As you will see while collecting spent shells for your collection, this area is a popular spot for rednecks to bring out their guns and beer and spend an afternoon plunking away at anything that ain't tied down. Your best bet is to keep an eye out for these types and stay clear of the firing line!

Only approach information will be included in this guide. For more information, Marty Karabin has authored a detailed 11"x17" guide which is available at the local climbing shops for $2.00.

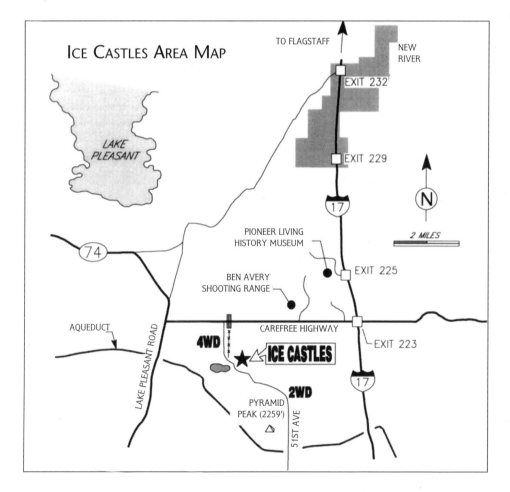

Approach: There are two ways to get to the Ice Castles area (also see map):

1) 2WD: This means fairly high-clearance vehicles! Head north on Black Canyon Highway (I-17), take the Happy Valley Exit and drive west to 51st Avenue (dirt). Drive north on the rutted dirt road (rough) around the north side of Pyramid Peak and park where convenient. This will put you (depending on where you park) on the eastern side of the climbing area. Warning! This road may be fairly impassible following heavy rain.

2) 4WD: Drive north on Black Canyon Highway (I-17) to the Carefree Highway exit (also for Ben Avery Shooting Range). Head west on the Carefree Highway for four miles. Just past a cattle guard, head south on a straight-forward (easy) 4WD dirt track, following the fenceline for approximately 2.0 miles. This will lead to the northwest corner of the Ice Castles Area.

Crown King Area

Although climbing development has been ongoing at the many granite formations lining the canyons near Crown King since at least the early 1970s, documentation on routes is pretty much non-existent. Rumor has it that Jim Guan and Rand Black climbed a few routes on the Bloody Basin granite, but again, information is sparse to non-existent. If you chance to climb in this area, you may be re-ascending routes that have previously been climbed by this duo. No matter. If you're into a little adventure and don't mind a little dirty work (scrambling to the formations through somewhat scrubby brush and loose slopes), there are some route development possibilities in this area.

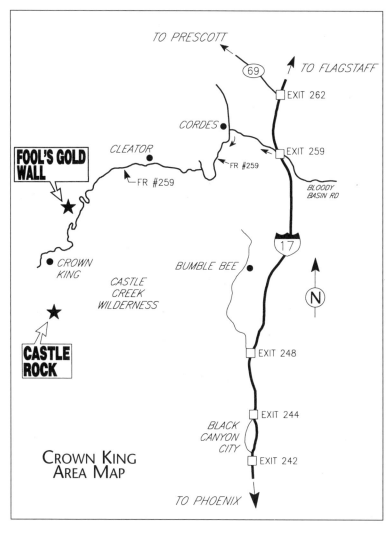

CROWN KING
AREA MAP

Fool's Gold Wall

Fool's Gold Wall is located just off the road from Cleator to Crown King. Although this is one of the largest and most obvious formations in the area, and may have had climbers on it in the past, the routes below represent efforts made by local climbers who saw the wall on the side of a hill on the way from Cleator to Crown King. When Flakey Bats was done, there was absolutely no evidence of climbing or anchor slings at the top of the wall, so it is not known if the wall had been climbed before.

The wall is approximately 230 feet high and can be roughly compared to Gardener's Wall in the McDowell Mountains in general size. The rock seems to be of the Granite Mountain (Prescott) type of pink granite that is extremely hard. It has a fine texture and doesn't lend itself readily to face routes either for putting in bolts, or for facial features. The cracks present some interesting climbing possibilities.

Approach: From the Phoenix area, drive north on I-17 to the Bloody Basin Road exit (#259). This is approximately 42 miles from Deer Valley Road. Take the Bloody Basin Road exit and head west on the dirt road. This road is generally good and should present no problem for most vehicles. It is a little bouncy and "washboard" in places. Follow the dirt road for three or four miles to a stop sign. Take a left at the stop sign onto Forest Service road #259 headed for Cleator. Continuing on, you will come to a split in the road. Take the left fork. This leads to another stop sign where you turn left and drive on through Cleator, Arizona; "Gateway to the Bradshaws." Don't blink or you'll miss downtown. Approximately 8.5 miles past Cleator you will see the wall up on the right side on the hill. Drive up through two 180-degree switchbacks and park in a pullout below the wall. Almost directly below the wall, there is a gully where a large corrugated pipe runs under the road. This is a good place to start up to the wall. It's a short and steep approach through prickly pear cactus, dirt slopes and loose rock, but can be traversed pretty easily.

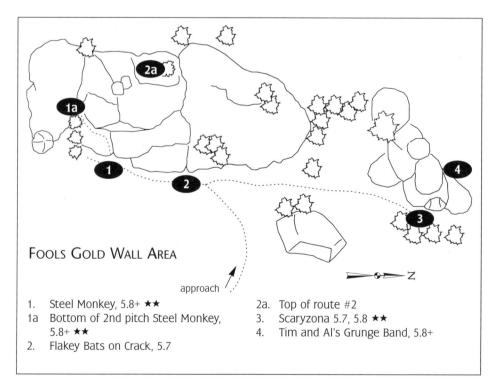

FOOLS GOLD WALL AREA

approach

1.   Steel Monkey, 5.8+ ★★
1a Bottom of 2nd pitch Steel Monkey, 5.8+ ★★
2.   Flakey Bats on Crack, 5.7

2a. Top of route #2
3.   Scaryzona 5.7, 5.8 ★★
4.   Tim and Al's Grunge Band, 5.8+

Route Descriptions
The routes are described from left to right (see map).

1. **Steel Monkey, 5.8+ ★★**
Although the first pitch of this route (at least the start done so far...) ain't much to write home about, the upper pitch (stars for the second pitch only) makes up for any discomfort incurred on the starting pitch. The route begins in a rather wide slot to the left side of the wall. First Pitch: Climb up wide slot to gain a ledge above. Second Pitch: Move the belay along the

FOOL'S GOLD WALL
1. Steel Monkey, 5.8+ ★★★

ledge to the left side of the wall and around the corner to a point below a nice looking crack running up the vertical wall above. The second pitch ascends this crack to the

FOOL'S GOLD WALL
1. Steel Monkey, 5.8+ ★★★   3. Scaryzona 5.7, 5.8 ★★   4. Tim and Al's Grunge Band,
2. Flakey Bats on Crack, 5.7   5.8+

summit. See **Flakey Bats on Crack** for the descent (take two ropes). Pro: Small to large (TCUs for Pitch 2 helpful).

Note: The second pitch of **Steel Monkey** can be toproped after climbing **Flakey Bats on Crack** and setting an anchor (TCUs and slings).

2. **Flakey Bats on Crack, 5.7**   Start in the obvious weakness nearly in the center of the large formation. First Pitch: Climb the center fracture past some grassy tussocks in the crack (5.7) to gain a ledge with a good-sized tree on it. From the large tree, move up and left, to a narrower ledge. Belay here from a small tree. Second Pitch: Exit to the right end of this ledge, (east) then follow a ramp/ledge system over a hollow flake to the top. Belay at a good tree on top of the wall. Descent: Rap from the tree at the summit (two ropes!), down to the large tree on the first pitch, then rappel from there to the base of the wall. Pro: Small to medium large.

3. **Scaryzona 5.7, 5.8 ★★**   Start at the base of the formation with a huge slightly detached flake. Climb up, past/through a tree at the base over slightly loose rock to gain the left side of the flake. Ascend the flake, until it thins out and you can mantle onto it. From here, clip a bolt on the face, then work your way up the face past several more bolts, until you can exit left to a ramp/wide crack system to the top and two-bolt anchor. Descend by either rapping (two ropes) from the summit anchors or downclimb off the back and scramble down the obvious gully to the base. Pro: Medium to large pro, bolts.

Variation 1   Climb straight up the face, then turn the small roof by climbing up onto the summit block/boulder directly. The first ascent party has plans to protect this option with a bolt, although none exists at the current time.

FOOL'S GOLD WALL
3.   Scaryzona 5.7, 5.8 ★★

Variation 2   Climb the right side of the flake at the bottom, then continue on the regular route to the anchors.

4. **Tim and Al's Grunge Band, 5.8+** Start around the right from **Scaryzona** in a recess, climb up and right to gain a lieback (fingertip) crack which follows a ramp. Overcome this, then continue up a wider (lichen covered) slot to the top. Pro: Small to medium-large.

Castle Rock

Castle Rock is a small quartzite crag south of Crown King that probably doesn't see a whole lot of climbing traffic since the days when the *Climber's Guide to Central Arizona* went out-of-print. Its remote location and mostly moderate climbing may keep it from becoming a climbing hot spot even now, but in the interests of historical documentation, I wanted to include the available route information. The established routes have been done on fairly solid rock and

mostly face climbing on incut holds at an angle of 80-degrees or more. All the routes protect nicely with conventional protection.

Approach: Follow the directions given for Fool's Gold Wall (above). Continue on the road past that formation and on into Crown King. Continue south of Crown King 1 mile then turn right (west) on the Senator Road. After 1 more mile, turn left on the Fort Misery Road (sign). Follow this interesting road generally south about 5 miles, where the road passes to the right of Castle Rock, an obvious light-colored crag a few feet from the road. Castle Rock is at about 4800 feet elevation in a deep canyon, so weather is best in the spring and fall.

Routes are described from left to right, when looking at the west face from the road. No topo is shown.

Whillan's Bloodbath, 5.6 Start at the second crack from the left of several cracks that split the west face of northernmost buttress. Approach start by hiking up tree-covered talus at left. Climb crack to top. Pro: Medium nuts.

Last Will & Testament, 5.6 Start on buttress left on center of main west face. First Pitch: Climb steep face (5.6) which leads to easier climbing and belay ledge at top of buttress. Second Pitch: Above, climb several large detached flakes to large belay ledge. Third class climbing leads to summit. Descend via Class 2 scramble down east side. Pro: Small to large nuts.

Twenty Tiny Fingers, 5.4 Start at buttress further back from road and right of **Last Will and Testament**. Avoid smooth west face by scrambling up right side to corner formed by west and south faces. First Pitch: Climb corner avoiding roof by traversing onto west face. Continue climbing steep face (5.4) to belay ledge atop buttress. Second Pitch: Continue up broken rock (Cl. 3-4) to summit. Pro: Small to large nuts.

The Dreaded South Stack, 5.1   Start at west face of the buttress closest to road at right end of crag. Climb west face to top. Descend left via Cl. 3. Pro: Small nuts.

Eagletail Mountains Area

The Eagletails are a low desert mountain range located at the western edge of the Harquahala Plain, about 60 miles west of Phoenix. The range is characterized by steep eastern slopes and gentle western slopes. This is the craggy looking range and impressive rock formation (Courthouse Rock) visible to the south of the highway when driving west to Joshua Tree.

The rock here tends to be of an "adventurous" nature, although quite a few ascents of the Courthouse Rock route have been done over recent years by Arizona Mountaineering Club members. One only has to keep an eye out for unexpected surprises in order to have an enjoyable day of climbing there. The Eagletail climbs have most likely not received many ascents (if any!) in the last ten years or so. This is mainly due to a long approach and nebulous route information. As this section won't do much to improve on the previously existing route information, it is more of a historical record than a source of beta for detail hungry climbers. The adventure lives!

Approach:
From Phoenix drive west on Interstate 10 for about 60 miles to the Salome exit (exit 81). Go south under the freeway, then take the first right past the eastbound freeway exit ramp onto Harquahala Valley Road.

For Courthouse Rock: After turning onto Harquahala Valley Road, continue

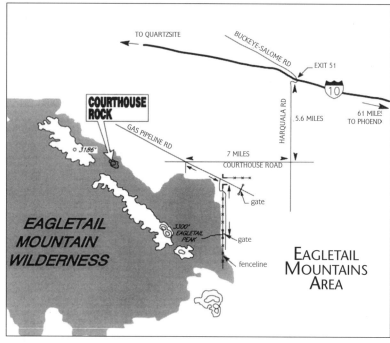

south until possible to turn right (west) on Centenial Rd. Continue west for approximately 7 miles, then turn northwest onto a pipeline road. After 4.1 miles, turn left (southwest) onto a narrow dirt road which leads past the base of the rock. (Courthouse Rock is visible at the foot of the Eagletails while approaching).

For Eagletail Peak routes: After turning onto Harquahala Valley Road, continue south passing Centenial Rd. and Courthouse Road for 2 miles until possible to turn west on Buckeye Rd. Continue 4 miles, at which point the road passes a house and becomes rougher. After another 4.3 miles, the road degenerates still further into a jeep trail. Eagletail Peak is southwest less than 2 miles.

Courthouse Rock

1. **Standard Route (5.5)** The standard climbing route ascends the deep gully on the far left side of the east face of the rock. The approach to the route is on the left side of an obvious talus slope directly below the huge gully.

   First Pitch: Climb up right side of gully for 50', then right 10' to arête. Follow arete for 75' to two-bolt belay on left wall of a small alcove.

   Second Pitch: Continue up short steep wall past two bolts on right and proceed directly up right side of gully for 160'. The belay bolts are on a high ledge on the far right side of gully.

   Third Pitch: This pitch climbs straight up the center of the gully for 160' to an obvious large ledge and belay at bottom of left side of steep wall.

   Fourth Pitch: Climb directly above two-bolt belay to a higher ramp and two bolts. Ascend steep crack system (5.5) past another bolt, then traverse right around arete and up to belay bolts on small ledge 160' above bottom of pitch.

   Fifth Pitch: Proceed up short dihedral then straight up a large, loose face to two-bolt belay just below top of main gully.

   Sixth Pitch: Traverse Class 3 terrain 0.25 mile north, then northwest into large hard rock gully below main peak. Ascend Class 4 ledge systems on north wall of gully past huge saguaro cactus to belay about 30' below top of wall. There are two hidden pitons stuck in cracks facing the wall.

   Seventh Pitch: Climb up and left to small dihedral, then make tricky step to the right over bulge. Scramble up and left to four-bolt anchor in alcove just below and west of main summit saddle.

   Eighth Pitch: Walk east across saddle, then up and left over Class 4 rock. Pass false summit to the left, pass chimney top, then scramble up to summit.

Descend the climbing route (except from the four-bolt belay at the top of Pitch 7–here climbers should descend via two ropes all the way to hard rock gully), being careful not to

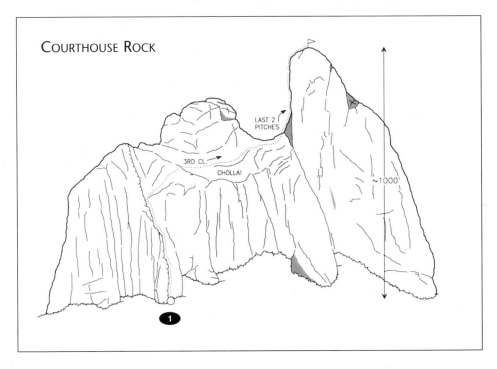

COURTHOUSE ROCK

LAST 2 PITCHES

3RD CL.

CHOLLA!

~1000'

1

rappel past belay bolts. The loose rock hazard is omnipresent, especially on Pitches 4 and 5. Pro: Large camming devices, Quickdraws. Take a few slings to leave at rappels.

The Eagletail Mountains 15-minute topographic map (USGS) may be useful..

Eagletail Peak

Eagletail Peak (aka North Feather), 5.6   Start by hiking southwest from road to below prominent saddle northwest of summit. Climb Class 4 rock to saddle. Scramble southeast up large gully to base of summit pinnacle. Climb enjoyable cracks on north corner to summit. Descend via 90' rappel (two bolts) just southeast of route. Pro: Several bolts, small to medium nuts.

Middle Feather, 5.5   Start at north corner of Eagletail summit pinnacle. Scramble southeast down gully to notch. Climb up Class 3 rock to base of Middle Feather's east face. Climb face and cracks On northeast face to summit stance and single bolt belay. From here, one can touch the very pointed summit with hand. Descend via 50' rappel (one bolt) down route. Pro: Small to medium nuts, one belay bolt.

South Feather, 5.0   Start by scrambling southeast from **Middle Feather** to base of South Feather's northeast face. Climb prominent chimney to summit. Descend via 60' rappel (one bolt) down route. Pro: Small to medium nuts, one belay bolt.

Justice of the Peace, 5.8   Start at large cone-shaped pinnacle well below and northeast of Eagletail Peak on north face. Climb wide chimney until one can exit left onto large ledge (5.5). From left end of ledge, climb bulge (5.8) past bolt to easier climbing. Climb up obvious ridge to summit. Descend via 130' rappel down south face (two bolts). Pro: Two bolts, medium nuts.

Four Peaks

Four Peaks is a group of 7,000-foot peaks at the southern end of the Mazatzal Mountains, 40 miles northeast of Phoenix. Although once a densely wooded and beautiful area, in May of 1996 the "Lone" fire broke out on the east side of the mountain ridge, gutting over 60,000 acres of forest while passing directly over the top of Four Peaks. An unusually dry winter left the area dry as a bone and ripe for fires. Once started, the raging fire swept through the area in only a couple of days, decimating this beautiful mountain area despite the best efforts of firefighters to stop the blaze. Biologists estimate that it will be over 100 years before this area returns to it former condition. I can't express what a tragic loss of beautiful forest acreage this fire has caused to what was a very beautiful and peaceful place to climb. Best wishes for a speedy recovery!

The climbing area detailed here, is located near the 7,657-foot summit of Brown's Peak, the northern-most and highest of the four peaks. A well-traveled hiking trail leads to the climbing on a north-facing buttress just off the trail. The rock in this area is known as Mazatzal Quartzite, a fine-grained rock similar to sandstone except much harder. The fractured nature of this rock can yeld some great holds, but with all those cracks, there's a bit of loose rock to go with all those handholds. You will also find that (in general) the rock gets more fractured and looser the closer you get to the top of the climbs. Additional care must be exercised when descending from these routes! Also, this area is no place to be if a storm is coming in. Lightning strikes can and do occur here!

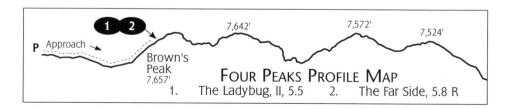

FOUR PEAKS PROFILE MAP
1.   The Ladybug, II, 5.5   2.   The Far Side, 5.8 R

Approach: From Phoenix drive northeast on AZ 87 (Beeline Highway) until you can turn right onto Cline Cabin Road (US Forest Rd. 143). This is approximately 13.5 miles past Shea Road. Drive on this relatively good dirt road for another 16 miles until you can make a right onto the road leading south (US Forest Rd. 648). Go south approximately 2.5 miles to the Lone Pine Saddle trailhead.

From the parking lot, take the well-traveled trail up the railroad ties (stairs) to the south. The weaving trail will take you all the way to the base of the "hiker's" gully leading to the top of Brown's Peak. The trail is between 2 and 2.5 miles long. Gentle inclines and great scenery (at least before the fire) make this worth doing just for the hike. Spectacular views of Roosevelt Lake can be seen from this ridge, to the east. Just below the summit run, you come out on a saddle. Exposed rock buttresses on the peak will be in plain view to the south. The Ladybug Route goes up the buttress just right of the obvious large gully that leads to the summit of Brown's Peak. Continue up the last steeper section on the ridge, passing over a small notch at the top. This drops you down into the bottom of the gully. The route starts just to the right of the bottom of the gully.

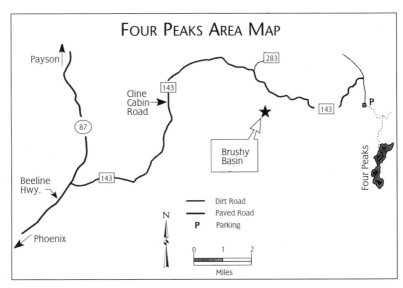

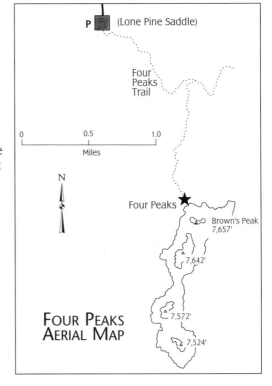

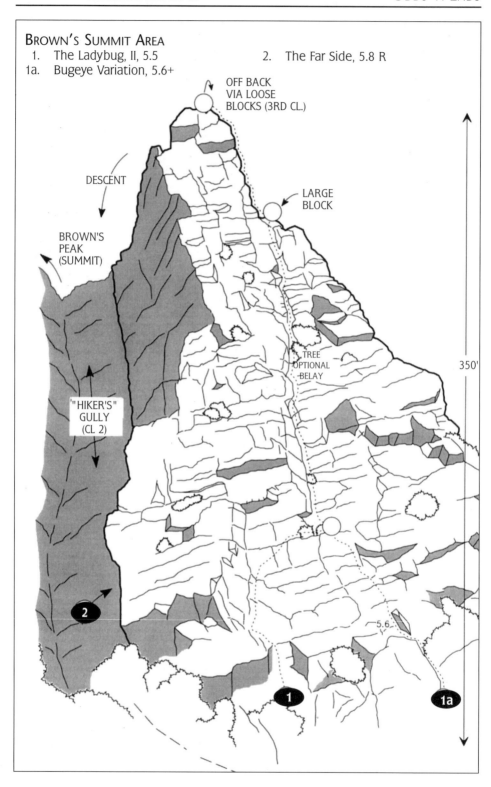

BROWN'S SUMMIT AREA
1. The Ladybug, II, 5.5   2. The Far Side, 5.8 R
1a. Bugeye Variation, 5.6+

OFF BACK
VIA LOOSE
BLOCKS (3RD CL.)

DESCENT

LARGE
BLOCK

BROWN'S
PEAK
(SUMMIT)

TREE
OPTIONAL
BELAY

"HIKER'S"
GULLY
(CL 2)

350'

5.6

1. **The Ladybug, II, 5.5**   Start from upper saddle at north face of closest peak (Brown's Peak, 7,657 feet). Right side of face is split by a deep gully. **The Ladybug** ascends north face of buttress to right of gully. Walk up ridge following rough trail to base of rock, then scramble over notch and into gully. The hiker's route continues up gully. The Ladybug starts at foot of buttress, right and slightly lower. First Pitch: Using tree for belay, climb easy rock, avoiding overhang on left, to reach smooth face above. Climb left side of face to reach small belay ledge with crack for anchor. Second Pitch: Climb up corner system and through overhangs on good holds. Continue another 30 feet to a large sloping ledge with a large tree. You may belay here if you wish to split this pitch. Otherwise, climb through the tree to gain the corner system once again and follow it through another overhang to gain easier rock above. Continue up to a large ledge with a humongous fallen block and belay (150', 5.5). Third Pitch: A short dihedral can be seen up and right of the belay block

The northern end of Brown's Peak (Ladybug Route) on Four Peaks.

past some ledged face climbing. Work your way up and right across good holds to gain the dihedral. A short bit of jamming (5.5) will get you past the dihedral and onto loose ledges above. Watch that you don't dump rocks (or yourself!) by grabbing the wrong thing. Belay above on the broken ledge. Fourth 4: Work your way around the left side (east) of the summit ridge, climbing up and over loose blocks to gain the top. Pro: Medium to large.

1a. **Bugeye Variation, 5.6+**   This variation is an interesting alternative starting pitch for **The Ladybug** and may have been done before by other climbers as lost as we were. From the bottom of the buttress, scramble (staying right against the bottom of the wall) through the bushes and trees to a small cleared-out spot next to a strange tree which sticks out horizontally from the ground. An obvious crack system leads directly up the wall. Climb crack (5.6+) which goes through slightly overhanging rock. The crack goes to a small ledge below a rather large flake leading up and to the left. Layback the edge of the flake (5.6) to gain a good stance above. From there, move up and slightly left to climb up the right side of polished face past discontinuous cracks. Work to the left at the top and belay on a small ledge by two bushes at the bottom of a right-facing dihedral that leads to more overhangs. This joins **The Ladybug** at this point (110, 5.6+). See route topo. Pro: Medium to large.

2. **The Far Side, 5.8 R**   This two-pitch route starts inside the lefthand wall of the same buttress where **The Ladybug** route is located (about 70 feet up the right side of the hiker's gully). Expect loose rock and possible tricky pro placements. First Pitch: Scramble to the base of a 10- to 15-foot dihedral. Climb the dihedral to a series of overhangs. Turn the overhangs to a stem section. Climb this to a layback ending at a belay

stance. Second Pitch: Climb the slightly overhanging wall above. Look for a #2 (fixed) wired Camlock. Turn one last roof; move right onto the arête and up, finishing on the third pitch of Ladybug. Pro: Small to very large. Descent: Scramble over loose blocks and top of peak into a notch on the south side. Take care here and watch for loose holds. Some may want to remained tied in for this scramble. Continue across slopes the easiest way from here into the hiker's gully. From there, you can either scramble your way to the top of the peak, or work your back down the hiker's gully to your packs.

Brushy Basin Area

The routes listed here have been done on a group of granite formations that are seen across Brushy Basin to the right of the road on the drive into Four Peaks (approximately 13 miles in from the turn onto Forest Road 143 from the Beeline Highway). A fairly decent looking slab formation (Valentine Wall) is the

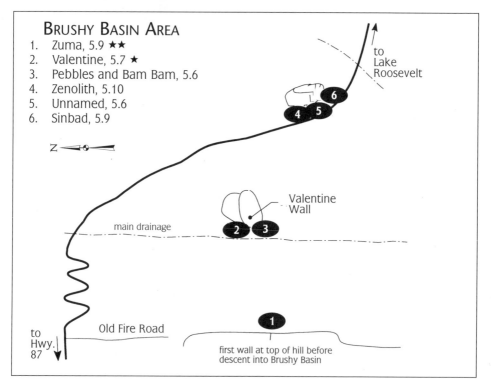

BRUSHY BASIN AREA
1. Zuma, 5.9 ★★
2. Valentine, 5.7 ★
3. Pebbles and Bam Bam, 5.6
4. Zenolith, 5.10
5. Unnamed, 5.6
6. Sinbad, 5.9

to Lake Roosevelt

Valentine Wall

main drainage

to Hwy. 87

Old Fire Road

first wall at top of hill before descent into Brushy Basin

most obvious indication of the proper area from the road. In all likelihood, this area was also burned over by the fire described above. Route information was fairly sketchy and incomplete, but hopefully the information that I was able to piece together from the clues I had will get more adventurous climbers to the right spot. Advance apologies if misleading info is contained here.

THE
VALENTINE
WALL

Valentine Wall

1. **Zuma, 5.9 ★★**
   This route is located up on the hillside crag behind Valentine Wall (see map). On the first ascent of this route, Chris Dunn took a 25-foot screamer in the company of a 300-pound block of rock that decided to head for the bottom of the route. Lucky for him, the block bounced clear of his belayer! Pro: Assorted nuts and cams.

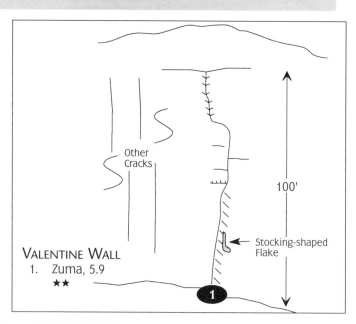

Other
Cracks

100'

Stocking-shaped
Flake

VALENTINE WALL
1. Zuma, 5.9
    ★★

1

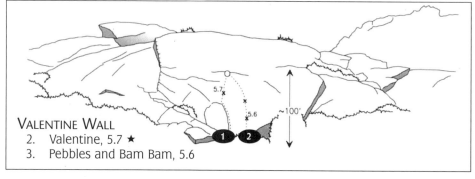

VALENTINE WALL
2. Valentine, 5.7 ★
3. Pebbles and Bam Bam, 5.6

5.7

5.6

~100'

1 2

2. **Valentine, 5.7** ★ This route follows a left-leaning crack, finishing with a featured face to a belay. An easy slab can be climbed to the top. Pro: Small to medium, one bolt.

3. **Pebbles and Bam Bam, 5.6** This route is located to the right of the start of Valentine. Slab climbing leads to that route's belay. From the belay, easy slabs lead to the top of the wall. Pro: Two bolts.

Dave Houchin on the first ascent of **Valentine**.

The following three routes are located up the road (on the other side) from the other formations. Not much is known about identifying this crag, but look for something nearby and off of the left side of the road around mile 13 on Forest Road 143 on the way into the Four Peaks area.

4. **Zenolith, 5.10** Climb up zenoliths on face left of crack. Area has been burned over. Pro: Bolts.

5. **Unnamed, 5.6** Short crack located in between **Zenolith** and **Sinbad**. Pro: Small to medium-large.

6. **Sinbad, 5.9** Short, finger crack located up and right of **Zenolith**. Pro: Small to medium.

Picket Post Mountain

The subject of Picket Post Mountain comes up now and then, as it is impossible for climbers to miss this impressive-looking spire off the south side of the road when driving to and from the eastern Superstition Mountains or Queen Creek climbing areas. As is the case with many of the more impressive and eye-catching formations that sprout in the local area, legendary Arizona climber Bill Forrest and partner Gary Garbert were responsible for the first ascent of

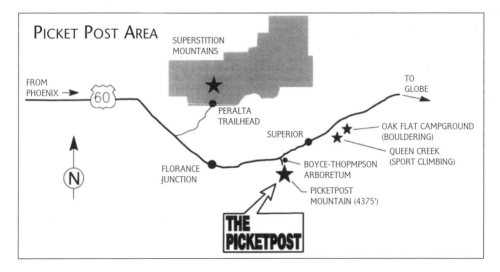

the Picket Post in 1965. The route material below is included mainly for information purposes and to somewhat provide a record of efforts that have taken place on the spire. The rock on this formation tends to be loose and the route ratings (due mainly to a lack of protection) lean into the "X" zone (death falls possible!), so in no way is this a recommendation to climb on the Picket Post. But, as an old partner of mine used to say, "It's your party...fly if you want to."

Although Picket Post Mountain might be considered an outlier of the Superstition Mountains, I have included it here as one of the "Outback" formations because of it's "odds 'n ends" nature. The Picket Post is accessed through the Boyce Thompson Southwestern Arboretum. This park is located a few miles west of Superior, Arizona; gateway to the Queen Creek climbing areas. The arboretum itself is approximately 40 miles east of Phoenix, give or take a few miles. Although the mesa-like main peak of Picket Post Mountain is surrounded by steep walls, the only activity has been an ascent of the "Picket Post," a large pinnacle on the north side. Questionable rock and some nasty rock can be listed as reasons for this.

Approach: Drive east from Phoenix towards Superior on US 60-70. When approximately a few miles from Superior, one will notice Picket Post Mountain on the right (south). Park at the Southwest Arboretum which is just off the highway on the right (south). Walk up the talus on the right (west) side of the pinnacle to reach the routes.

1. **The Picket Post, 5.7 X**   Start at saddle between pinnacle and Picket Post Mountain. Climb up 25 feet past a bolt, then traverse right to obvious crack. Climb crack and face to overhang, then scramble right to summit. Descend via 150-foot rappel (one bolt). Pro: two bolts, large nuts.
2. **Hudson Route, 5.9 R/X**   Drop down the west side from the start of the **Picket Post** route. Starts on the west-northwest side. Reports say the route climbs to a ledge with a tree, then on to the top. Pro: Unknown

Yarnell Wall

Yarnell Wall is a large (and relatively unknown) granite wall located between Yarnell and Congress, northwest of Phoenix. The routes done here were mainly pioneered by the Los Banditos, a rather unorthodox clan of local climbers consisting of Dan Langmade, Stan Mish, Glen Rink and others. Although there aren't that many climbs here, the fine-grained granite here is sound and offers good protection. Occasional bolts will be found, but for the most part Yarnell Wall has been purposely left clean of fixed protection.

Approach: From Phoenix, drive to Wickenburg on highway 60. Upon entering the main area of town, you will see the turnoff for highway 93 to Las Vegas. Make a right turn onto highway 93 and drive northwest to its junction with highway 89 (approx. 6.2 miles). Make a right onto 89 and drive north through Congress, approximately 13.5 miles

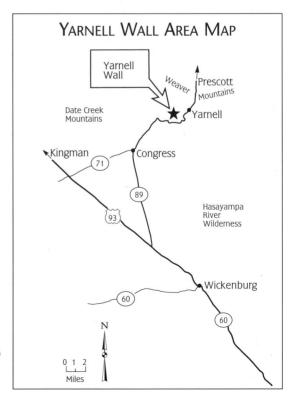

YARNELL WALL AREA MAP

from the 93/89 junction, to a large pullout on the right side of the road just before the highway splits. Park here. The wall may be seen uphill and to the left (west).

The hike to Yarnell Wall from the road below has got to qualify for the worst approach in this book. Long, uphill, and involved, there's no easy way to get there. You have my admiration if you undertake this hike to sample the climbing at Yarnell Wall. The lack of quality ratings for the routes below only indicates a lack of information and in no way reflects the worthwhile nature of the routes themselves. Go and find out!

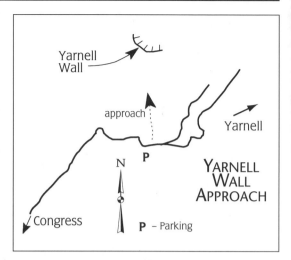

YARNELL WALL

1. Wide Glide, 5.9
2. Languish 5.9
3. L.B.'s Panhead, 5.5
4. Mish Mash, 5.8
5. The Sultan, 5.10
6. The Knucklehead, 5.8

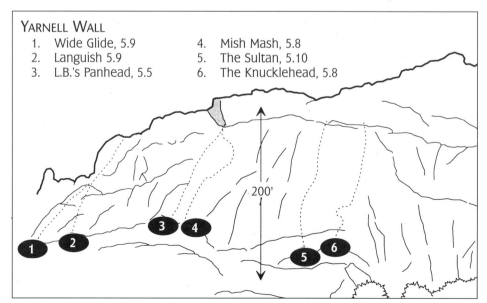

1. **Wide Glide, 5.9**   Start 15 feet right (southwest) of large flake at extreme left (northwest) end of wall. Climb seam and face to top. Pro: Small to medium nuts.
2. **Languish 5.9**   Start in right-facing corner 30 feet right of low-angled ramp right (southeast) of Wide Glide. First Pitch: Climb dihedral to ramp (5.8). Second Pitch: Climb crack through roof to convenient belay (5.9). Third Pitch: Scramble to top (5.2). Pro: Small to large nuts.
3. **L.B.'s Panhead, 5.5**   Start right of Languish and directly below left (northwest) end of left-most roof (at top of wall). Climb cracks leading to and through left-most roof. Pro: Small to large nuts.
4. **Mish Mash, 5.8**   Start 15 feet right (southeast) of L.B.'s Panhead. First Pitch: Climb thin flake until possible to move right to right-arching thin flake. Climb flake (5.8) and then face to ledge. Second Pitch: Scramble left to join L.B.'s Panhead at left end of left-most roof. Pro: Small to medium nuts.
   Variation, 5.10   Instead of regular second pitch, climb dihedral on right side of left-most roof to top. Pro: Medium nuts.
5. **The Sultan, 5.10**   Start at left-leaning, left-facing dihedral far right (southeast) of Mish Mash. Climb left-leaning dihedral and crack above through bulge (5.10), then move left and follow crack to top (5.8). Pro: Small to large nuts.
6. **The Knucklehead, 5.8**   Start right (southeast) of The Sultan below small roof. Climb face past bolt to roof, then over roof and past two more bolts to top. Pro: Three bolts, medium nuts.

Vulture Peak

I debated a long time before including the two climbs on Vulture Peak in this guide. Include the choss pile, don't include the choss pile.... In the end, the climbing here isn't really the type that most climber's are looking for, and the quality of the rock certainly isn't a reason to go running there to put up additional routes. However, the east face of the peak was the scene of some significant routes in Arizona climbing history, so in the interests of maintaining the historical record, I finally chose to include these two routes. Only rudimentary data will be given below in an effort to keep accidents near the zero mark. If you go to climb here, be forewarned that it is quite serious and you need to be responsible for your own safety and self-rescue!

The Bottom Line

Before anyone goes charging off to Vulture Peak, let me say here for the record that the rock on this formation is some of the most rotten you may ever encounter! This is not a point of debate and is not really a subjective opinion on what you will find here. The stuff is loose, boggy, flaccid, lax, slack, insecure, unattached, and unfastened. Get the point? There is enough loose rock here to build a stone wall from downtown Phoenix to the base of the Peak. There! Is that clear? Does that leave room for questions? So...if you go out here with a glow in your eyes to repeat the climbs described below, you are on your own! Don't blame me if something breaks off and sends you plunging to the ground! Climb responsibly! On to the info....

The rounded summit of Vulture Peak sprouts rather blatantly out of the desert 10 miles south of Wickenburg to an elevation of 3658 feet. The east face of the peak is the location of two of the states earliest forays into the realm of hard aid climbing by local climbers Bill Sewrey and Larry Treiber in 1967 and 1968. Two routes have been climbed on the 600-foot east face of the peak. About 450 feet of this is vertical to overhanging, with the last 150 feet or so rolling off to scrambling (and more loose rock).

Location: The peak resides off the east side of Vulture Mine Road, which travels south out of Wickenburg. Drive northwest from Phoenix on highway 60 to Wickenburg. Take the left turn to stay on highway 60 (at its intersection with Highway 93) and continue west for approximately 2.5 miles to a stoplight at Vulture Mine Road. Turn left and drive south on Vulture Mine Road. The peak can be seen to the southeast along this road. After about 6.5 miles, you'll be just about straight west of the peak's back side. Bear in mind that the climbing is on the east face. According to those in the know, there are several possible 4WD roads that lead to spots close to, and below the wall. I leave it up to you to find the proper way to this spot, as it

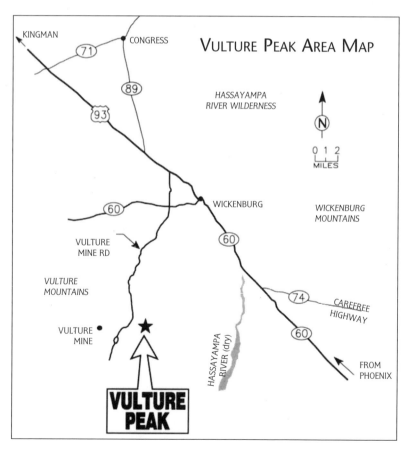

would nearly be impossible to describe accurately. Please be low-impact if you undertake this drive and don't braid new roads through undisturbed desert areas in the interests of making things easier.

The Climbs

The Vulture, 5.5 A4   This is the original route up the peak. The first ascent of **The Vulture** was done in October of 1967. A brief description of the two-day climb appeared in the 1969 American Alpine Journal (pg. 398), in which it was given the rating of NCCS IV, F5, A4. The climb was repeated by another team of Phoenix climbers, Lance and Dane Dougherty (see History section). According to Bill, the Dougherty brothers found the route to be "interesting" and eliminated a bit of aid on the second pitch, by free-climbing a traversing section to the ledge which Bill had led on skyhooks, rurps and slings "just for the fun of it." As far as Bill knows, this is the only time the route has received a repeat ascent.

Bill Sewrey says he just "wanted to engineer a route up the wall." I got the idea he just did it to see if it could be done. His partner in the final ascent push was another well-known Phoenix climbing pioneer, Larry Treiber, although Don Weaver was involved in the early going. Evidently, a night spent trying to sleep sitting up on a ten-inch ledge was enough for Don and he bailed from the effort.

After a few trips up to clean and do the lower pitches, they went for the top, spending one night in belay seats on the route. Tom Taber was involved in the project early as well, but wasn't in on the final complete ascent. The A4 nature of the climbing was largely due to the decomposing rock, commonly referred to as "desert junkoid." The route weaves up the face, bypassing ledges and overhangs to a phallic formation at the top, which Bill referred to as the "dork." They liked to use that term in those days (that was the original name of Tom's Thumb).

The route consists of five pitches of climbing, going up the left side of the face. Pitch One ascends a vertical weakness. Pitch Two traverses left along a ledge system. Pitch Three goes vertical again, leading to 1/4"-bolt ladder on the fourth pitch. The bolt ladder takes you to the to the fifth pitch crux traverse below an overhang leading to the "dork" above. Scrambling leads to the top. All belays have 3/8" stud anchors, albeit 30-year-old ones.

The Talon Traverse, 5.8 A2   This route was done sometime after **The Vulture,** although Bill couldn't shed much light on an exact date of the final first ascent. It was much easier in terms of aid, but the first ascent took a period of two years to complete! The original effort consisted of Bill Sewrey, Bob Box and Larry Treiber. Box left the effort before completion of the route. Two years (yes, you heard right) later, Sewrey and Treiber returned to the wall to finish the route. The lead from the ledge went up and right, leading to much easier climbing above, and the top of the wall. Bill couldn't remember what they rated it at the time, but the subsequent second ascent (see below) gave it a rating of 5.8 A2 for the four pitches.

The second ascent of the route wasn't made until October of '88 by Paul Paonessa and John "Chew" McHugh, who repeated the route in a single day. Paul reports that they actually started up The Vulture, hoping to climb "anything." After the first pitch, they traversed right across the "vulture ledge" in the center of the wall and joined **The Talon Traverse** for its last three pitches to the top.

This route ascends the wall in four pitches, starting to the right of the start of The Vulture. The first three pitches each end on ledges and consist of mixed aid and free climbing. Pitch Three has a few bolts interspersed with pro placements. The last pitch is 5.8 face climbing with natural protection available. Other details are sparse about the route, but basically goes up and to the right side of the face before ending on top.

Descent (for either route): Once you get to the top of the wall, you can walk off the south end and work your way back down (possible downclimbing and scrambling) and around to the east side. There's supposed to be a register on top to sign in as well.

Chris Dunn on the first
ascent of **Zuma** (5.9)
on the Valentine Wall,
Brushy Basin Area,
Odds 'n Ends chapter.
The route description
is on page 233.

Chapter 11

First Ascent List

Beardsley Boulders

Fear Rock Area

Black and Decker Pecker Wrecker   Bob Blair and Jay Abbas, 11/86
Naked Bimbos From Mars   Bob Blair and Andy Linkner, 3/85
Brown Sugar   Jim Guadnola and Bob Blair, 12/90
Grandma Got Run Over By A Reindeer   Bob Blair and Paul Paonessa, 12/87
The Fear Of Having Sex With Dead People   Bob Blair and Andy Linkner, 3/85
The Flake   FA Unknown
Teenage Enema Nurses In Bondage   Jay Abbas and Bob Blair, 11/85
Wait Until Dark   Ted Olsen and Phil Falcone, 12/88

Tombstone Area

Sad But Sweet   Greg Elbert, Gary Elbert, and Bob Blair, 3/91
A Little Loose In The Attic   Marty Karabin, 11/94
Deception   Marty Karabin, 11/94
Black Bart   Jim Guadnola and Bob Blair, 12/90
Less More   Bob Blair and Jeff Hill, 12/88
Slap Leather   Bob Blair and Jeff Hill, 12/88
Rode Hard, Put Away Wet   Bob Blair and Jeff Hill, 12/88

Lower Main Area

Spank Your Monkey   Bob Blair and Jay Abbas, 11/84
The Gripper   (Solo) Jim Waugh - (Bolted) Bob Blair and Jay Abbas, 3/85
Anarchy Crack   Unknown
Slewgundymegahawk   Andy Linkner and Bob Blair, 1/84
Classic Orange   Unknown
Entrails   G. Opland, Solo, 7/95
Hot Sweaty Buns   (Gear) Unknown - (Bolted) Andy Marquardt, Rich Shoup and Bob Blair, 4/87

Camelback Mountain

Neck Routes

Line Of Fire   Dana Hollister, Dave Youkey, 1983
Neck Route   Ben Pedrick, Lee Pedrick, Bill Mcmorris and Ralph Pateman, Jan. 1949

South Camel's Head

South Route   Kachina Members, 1946
Open Book   Bill Forrest and Ted Roy, 1966 FFA Chuck Parker and Vic Thomason, 1972
Anguish   Chuck Parker and Vic Thomason, 1972
June Bug Crack   Chuck Parker, 1972
Sewery's Roof   Bill Sewery, Larry Treiber, and Gary Garbert, ?

Headwall

Class Three Gully Unknown
The Walk Up Unknown
Rappel Gully Unknown
Headwall Route Ray Garner, 1946 Var. Ray Garner, 1946
George Route Ed George, Ben Pedrick, 1947

Praying Monk

Unnamed Unknown
Southeast Corner Bill Forrest, ?
East Face Gary Driggs, Dec. 1951
Excess (XS) Jason Sandidge, John Ficker, Chuck Hill, 1985
Roof Aid Route Unknown
Exorcist Dana Hollister (Solo), 1980 FFA, Stan Mish, Dan Langmade, 1980
Next Time Var Jim Finn, Dana Hollister, 1980
Monk's Ass Bill Forrest and Gary Garbert, 1965

Gargoyle Wall

Pockets Phil Falcone and Ted Olsen, 5/87
Pedrick's Chimney Ben Pedrick, 1946-47
Misgivings Larry Treiber, Pete Noebels, Bruce Grubbs, 1978 FFA, Larry Treiber, Dennis Abbink, Bruce Grubbs, 1978
Hart Route Dick Hart, 1946
N. Central Var Kachina Members, 1946
Cholla Traverse Jim Dean, Chris Struckmeyer, 1970
Fresh Air Traverse Key Punches, Art Murphy, 1965
August Traverse Unknown
Hard Times Larry Treiber, Doug Frericks, 1978
Beehive Jack Turnage, Bill Forrest, 1965
Rotten Chimney Doug Black, ? FFA, Lance and Dane Daugherty, ?

August Canyon

Doug's Dandy Doug Black, Bill Forrest, ?
Fixed Line Traverse Arizona Mountaineering Club Members, ?

Western Headwall

Suicide (Pitch One) Herb and Jan Conn, May 15, 1949
            (Entire Route) Bill Forrest, Doug Black, ?
            Var: Rex Lambert, Pat Copeland, Joe Theobald, ?
Suicide Direct Ralph Pateman, Bob Owens, 1949 FFA, Lance and Dane Daugherty ?
Black Direct Manny Rangle, Et Al. 1993

Boulder Canyon

Ridge Route Ben Pedrick, John Goodson, Jack Allen, Ralph Pateman, Jan and Herb Conn, May 1949
Tarantula Var Jack Turnage, Bill Sewrey, 1966
Bloody Toes Larry Treiber, Bill Ellis, 1968
The Yellow Wall Unknown

Camel's Foot

Otherwise Dana Hollister, Herb North Jr., 1978
Camel's Foot Tom Kreuser, Ron Treiber, Larry Treiber, R. Stepphun, ?

Bobbie's Rock

Pedrick's Split Ben Pedrick, 1947-1948
Pateman's Cave Ralph Pateman, Stan Lerch, Gene Lefebvre, 1950 Var Bill Forrest, Key Punches, 1965
Fry Babies Bill Sewrey, Gary Garbert, 1964 FFA, Jim Waugh, Chris Raypole, 1985
The Flute Unknown

Camel's Ear

Chase The Dragon Dana Hollister, Jim Finn, 1980
Dragon Var. Dana Hollister, Brad Smith, 1979

The Hump

Humpty Pumpty Cory Hove, 1992

Cholla Mountain

Saguaro Hotel Area

Saguaro Hotel Andy Cary and Paul Paonessa, 2/90
Cholla, Cholla, Cholla Paul Paonessa and Andy Cary, 2/90
Room Service (Doubtful): Greg Opland, Scott Aldinger, and Mike Kaczocha, Fall '94
Mish Mash Stan Mish, Et Al, ?
The Panty Route Greg Opland, Lisa Schmitz, Rick Forbes, 12/94
Thrash Compactor Greg Opland, Scott Aldinger, Mike Kaczocha, 12/94
Dado Jan Holdeman, Rick Forbes, Steve Holmquist, 2/91
Cherry Jam Jason Sandidge and Sherry Duncan, 1987
Cup-A-Jam Mike Cook and Jason Sandidge, 1987
Famous Last Moves Glen Dickenson and Sherry Duncan, 1987
Slab Shit Dave Insley (Solo), 1987
Sherry's First Sherry Duncan and Jason Sandidge, 1987
Route Cellar Jan Holdeman, Don Thomas, Eric Ramsey and Peggy Bonanati, 3/92

Chorus Line Area

The Potato Greg Opland, Lisa Schmitz, Rick Forbes, 12/94
Chorus Line Tom Brecke, Andy Cary, and Paul Paonessa, 3/91
Room Service (probably not) Greg Opland, Scott Aldinger, and Lisa Schmitz, 12/94

Econoline Area

Econoline Paul Paonessa, Jan Holdeman, Andy Cary and Tom Brecke, 3/91
Mainline Undone
Bloodline (Aka Deadline) Jan Holdeman and Ron Futrell, 1991

Stiletto Area

Meander Jan Holdeman and Matt Lynch, 2/88
Blockwatch Jan Holdeman, Et Al., 1991 Or So...
Stiletto Jan Holdeman Et Al, 1991 Or So...
Contrivance Jan Holdeman and Don Thomas, 1991
Bandito's Route Los Banditos, ?

The Whale

Save Your Desert Jan Holdeman and John Mchugh, 3/88
Watch Your Wait Jan Holdeman and John Mchugh, 3/88

Twat Me One Time John Mchugh and Jan Holdeman, 3/88
Unknown FA: ?
Unknown FA: ?
Sump Pump Jan Holdeman and Matt Lynch, 2/88

Jaid Boulder Area

J-aid John Mchugh and Jan Holdeman, 2/88
Carborundum Undone...

The Scimitar

Trial Separation John Mchugh and Jan Holdeman, 1991
Chips Ahoy Jan Holdeman and John Mchugh, 1991
Border Crossing Jan Holdeman and Don Thomas, 3/92

Defacement Area

Defoliation Tim Bombaci, Rick Forbes, and Jan Holdeman, 2/91
Defacement Tim Bombaci, Rick Forbes, and Jan Holdeman, 2/91
Bombaci Route Tim Bombaci, Rick Forbes, and Jan Holdeman, 2/91
Birdland Jan Holdeman and Paul Paonessa, 2/92
Gullet Paul Paonessa and Jan Holdeman, 2/92

The Far Side

VW Roof Jan Holdeman and John Mchugh, 1/88
Geronimo's Cadillac Jan Holdeman and John Mchugh, 1/88
Close Quarters Jan Holdeman and John Mchugh, 1/88
Crazy Man Driver Jan Holdeman, Paul Paonessa and John Mchugh, 2/88
Wotme Two Step Jan Holdeman and John Mchugh, 1/88
Grotto Jan Holdeman, Rick Forbes, and Tim Bombaci 2/91

Jacob's Wall

38 Weeks Terry Reisner, Paul Bennett, 2/88
Wipe Your Feet Jan Holdeman, Terry Reisner, John Mchugh 2/88
Transition Jan Holdeman and Ron Futrell, 1/91

Indian Rocks

Inside Moves Jan Holdeman and Paul Paonessa, 2/92
Hallowed Ground Jan Holdeman and Paul Paonessa, 2/92

Jacuzzi Spires

First Jacuzzi Spire

Four Flakes John Ficker, Jason Sandidge Et Al., ?
Jason's Route Jason Sandidge Et. Al, ?
Don't Bug Me Paul Diefenderfer, Bob Blair, and Andy Linkner, 3/84
Up Tempo and Dynamic Bob Blair and Andy Linkner, 12/84
Bugati Cafe John Ficker and Dave Gunn, ?
Harcourt Fenton Mudd Bob Blair and Andy Linkner, 4/84
Alice's Restaurant Andy Marquardt, ?
Red Tail Diner Paul Dief, Et Al...
Four Star Daydream Andy Marquardt, ?
5.12 Face Andy Marquardt, ?
Second Pitch Of Something John Ficker, Bob Blair, Larry Braten, and Andy Marquardt, 11/86
Play Dough Bugs John Ficker, Jim Zahn, George Theilman, and Andy Linkner, 4/84

Second Jacuzzi Spire

Ficker-Braten John Ficker and Larry Braten, ?
Braten-Ficker Larry Braten and John Ficker, ?

Third Jacuzzi Spire

John Ficker's Radically Overhung Crack John Ficker and Russ Theilman, 12/84
Penetration John Ficker, George Thielman, and Bob Blair, 4/84
Top Out Larry Braten and John Ficker, ?
Maybe Whitey Bob Blair and Larry Braten, 11/86
Easy You Fucking Wino Tom Martin, Bob Blair and Jim Guadnola, 1/91
Where's My Whitey Larry Braten and Bob Blair, 11/86
Bug Shit Andy Marquardt, His Girlfriend, and Bob Blair, ?
Tom's Wonderful Thing Bob Blair, Tom Martin, and Jim Guadnola, ?
Okay Whitey Larry Braten and Bob Blair, 11/86

Little Granite Mountain

Pasta Pinnacle

Pasta Man Unchained Frank Valendo, Jim Waugh, 1982
Freducini Al-Fred-O Greg Opland and Fred AmRhein, 1/93

The Cone

Unknown TR Unknown
Kate's Fault Kate Nisselson, Doug Fletcher and Jan Holdeman, ?
Sideshow Jaime Moore and Jan Holdeman, 11/91
Three Dopes On A Rope John Mchugh, Doug Fletcher, Jan Holdeman, 2/88

Riven Wall

Off Your Rocker Jan Holdeman, Noel Aronov, Amy Barrington, 1986
Codgers Jan Holdeman, John Mchugh and Noel Aronov, 1986

Lost Bandana Wall

Dueling Hammers Peter Hogan, John Mchugh 1986
Slot Glen Dickinson, John Ficker, 1981
Climb At First Sting (Known) Richard Horst, '94
Limbo Glen Dickinson, Cindy Zarlengo, Jim Zahn, John Ficker, 1981
Spectrum John Ficker, Glen Dickinson, Jim Zahn, Cindy Zarlengo, 1981
Lawless and Free Dan Loden, Glen Dickinson, 1987
Loosy Loose Richard Horst, 10/94
Seemingly Useless Jim Zahn, Glen Dickinson, John Ficker, 1981
Owl Out Glen Dickinson, Cindy Zarlengo, 1981
Footloose Glen Dickenson and J. Schmit, 1987
Family Affair Steve Smelser, Sherry Duncan, and Jason Sandidge, 1987
Group W Bench Jan Holdeman, Noel Aronov, and Amy Barrington, 1986
Deathics Jason Sandidge, Sherry Duncan, and Andy Marquardt, 1987

The J-Wall

J-Indirect Jaimie Moore and Jan Holdeman, Et. Al. 4/91
J-For Play Jaime Moore, Candace Luther, and Tom Matthews, 4/91
Bee Careful Doug Fletcher, Dan Stough, and Caryl Parker, 1987
Cricket Patrol Doug Fletcher, Dan Stough, and Caryl Parker, 1987

Good, Bad And Ugly Pinnacle

Shades Of Vertical Eric Putnam, Mike Covington, 3/88
Grim Ripper Mike Covington, 3/88

Morning Glory Boulder Area

Flim Flam Mike Covington, Eric Putnam, 3/88
On A Nice Windy Day Mike Covington (Free Solo), 3/88
Seem Dream Eric Putnam (Free Solo), 3/88
Groove Tube Mike Covington, Eric Putnam, 5/88
Kadywompus Eric Putnam, Mike Covington, 5/88
Overhung Thing Mike Covington, Eric Putnam, 5/88
Hallucination (TR) P. Putnam, M. Covington, B. Mattingly, J. Mcqueen, 11/87
            (Lead) Putnam, Covington, Mattingly, 12/87

Bobcat Boulder

Impossible Larry Sallee, Ed Cordium, and Mike Kelley, 2/88
Next To Impossible Ed Cordium, Larry Sallee, Mike Kelley and Walt Wright, 2/88
Loosinda Linda Savage, Doug Fletcher, 1986
Grin & Bear It Doug Fletcher, John Mchugh, 1986
Crystalline Grin Glen Dickenson?
Snakes Are Poodles Too Jan Holdeman, Doug Fletcher, 1986
Missing Lynx Todd Swain (Rope Solo), 3/88

The Loaf

Shake 'n Bake Glen Dickinson, John Ficker, Cindy Zarlengo, 1981
Shake 'n Flake John Ficker, Glen Dickinson, 1981
Wimpy John Ficker, Glen Dickinson, 1981
Young Monkeys (Free Solo) Chuck Hill, 1986
            (Bolted Ascent) Doug Fletcher, John Mchugh, 1986
Blow Fly's Last Ride Chuck Hill, Tom Mcmillan, Dave Insley, Dave Gunn, 1986
"A" Crack Tom Mcmillan, Chuck Hill, Dave Insley, 1986
Dike Walk Dave Insley, Chuck Hill, Tom Mcmillan, 1986
Sweet Surprise Jim Zahn, Glen Dickinson, John Ficker, 1981
Lose Yer Stance, Shitcher Pants Greg Opland, Scott Aldinger and Tim Schneider, 1995
Gender Blender Chuck Hill, Dave Insley, Gary Perkins, 1984
Arm and Hammer Steve Smelser, Glen Broughton and Tony Mazzei, 11/87
Old & Slow Noel Aronov and Mike Taylor, 1/87

Torrid Wall

Blue Highways Bill Hatcher, Jim Waugh, Frank Valendo, 1986
Desert Solitaire (Free Solo) Jim Waugh, Frank Valendo, Bill Hatcher, 1986

Trundling Pinnacle

Some Like It Hot Jim Waugh, Frank Valendo, Bill Hatcher, 1986
Fear The Reaper Steve Smelser, Tony Mazzei, J. Duval, Glen Broughton, T. Standing, Larry Braten, 2/88
Auger Refusal Steve Smelser and Tony Mazzei, 11/87

Roofer Madness Wall

Roofer Madness John Ficker, Jim Zahn, Mike Long, 1981

Fair Weather Wall

Flare Thee Well   Frank Valendo, Jim Waugh, Bill Hatcher, 1986
Fair Thee Well   Jim Waugh, Bill Hatcher, Frank Valendo, 1986
Fire and Ice   Steve Smelser, Larry Braten, 12/88

Harp Wall

Walkaway   Jim Zahn, Mike Long, John Ficker, 1981
Runner-Up   Cindy Zarlengo, Glen Dickinson, John Ficker, 1981
Angle Of The Dangle   John Ficker, Glen Dickinson, Cindy Zarlengo, 1981
The Beginning and The End   Glen Dickinson, John Ficker, 1981
Endure The Elements   Mike Covington and Eric Putnam, 4/88

Sleeping Cactus Wall

Left Face   (Bolted) Tim Schneider, Greg Opland, and Scott Aldinger, 1/92
Dublin – High Road   Doug Fletcher and Ron Futrell, 1987
Dublin – Low Road   Jan Holdeman and John Mchugh, 1987
The Bickerson's Dirty Habits   Doug Fletcher and Jan Holdeman, 1987
Tupelo Honey   John Mchugh and Bart Garlotte FFA, Jan Holdeman and John Mchugh, 1987
Jibbering Seconds   Glen Dickenson, 1981 Named: Jan Holdeman and Noel Aronov, 1987
Chasm View   Jan Holdeman and John Mchugh, 1987
Fake Out Flake   Fernando Schrader Et Al, ?
Greg and Al's Excellent Adventure   (TR) Doug Fletcher and Jan Holdeman, Late 80's
     (Bolted) Greg Opland and Al Muto, 1/92
Martin Luther King   Jan Holdeman and Doug Fletcher, 1987

The Roost

Indecent Exposure   Steve Smelser and Larry Braten, 12/87
Riff Roof   Steve Smelser and Larry Braten, 12/87
Blind Faith   Steve Smelser and Larry Braten, 12/87
Crater Maker   Dave Insley and Kevin Tank, 9/86
Deviant Behavior   Steve Smelser and Larry Braten, 12/87
Grand Illusion   Bill Golightly and Glen Broughton, 12/87
Peter's Out   Jan Holdeman, Peter Hogan, 1987
Bumps   Al Muto, Greg Opland, Tim Schneider, 12/91
Matterhorn   Bill Golightly and Glen Broughton, 12/87
Wetterhorn   Bill Golightly and Glen Broughton, 12/87
Cap'n Crunch   Bill Golightly and Glen Broughton, 12/87

Mogul Wall (a.k.a. Teenage Face)

Incognito   Andy Cary and Paul Paonessa, 1990
Duckin' For Jesus   J. Ficker, B. Ficker, John Mchugh, 2/87
Writer's Block   Avtar Singh Khatsa, 4/87
Buckets Of Quicksand   Avtar Singh Khatsa, 4/87
Made In The Shade   Steve Smelser and Tony Mazzei, 11/87
Where The Fughowi   John Mchugh, Becky Ficker and John Ficker, 2/87
Bitches' Itch   Larry Braten and Rich Shoup, 11/87
Moguls   Larry Braten, Glen Dickenson, John Ficker, 3/87
Rampit   John Ficker and Glen Dickenson, 1987
Tolkien Roof   Steve Smelser ? / Andy Cary and Paul Paonessa, 1989
Manly Bulges   John Ficker, 1987
Won't Get Fooled Again   Rich Shoup, 1/87
Chet's Arete   Andy Cary and Paul Paonessa, ??
S & M   Steve Smelser and Tony Mazzei, 11/87

Fatal Attraction Steve Smelser and Tony Mazzei, 11/87
Okay With Gaye Peter Hogan, Jan Holdeman, John Mchugh, 1987
Fu Man Chew John Ficker and John Mchugh, 2/87
Rawhide John Ficker and John Mchugh, 2/87
Somebody Get Me A Weiner Jan Holdeman and John Mchugh, 1987
Juicy Fruit, My Favorite John Mchugh and Jan Holdeman, 10/87
Scent Of Skunk Brad Mattingly, Pat Putnam, 12/87

Mcdowell Mountains

Lost Wall

Hanging Mantle Bob Barling, Jim Erwin, 1981
Lost and Found Bob Barling, Dave Brady, 1981
No Easy Four Bob Barling, Dave Brady, 1981
Sweet 'n Low Mike Long, Rand Black, 1982
Zig Zag Mike Long, Rand Black, 1982
Half N' Half Neil Sugarman & ?, 1982
Born Ready For A Thrill Jason Sandidge, Jim Zahn, 1986
Looks Like 5.6! Jason Sandidge, Sherry Duncan, 1986
Life In The Air Age Chris Dunn, 6/88

Fort McDowell

Flipper's Testicle Stretch Paul Paonessa, Bill Biederman, 1986
Sandidgehark Variation Paul Paonessa, K.C. Baum, 1986
Almost Whitney Bill Biederman, Mike Taylor, Paul Paonessa 1986

Tom's Thumb

Slip 'n Slide Glen Dickinson, Dan Loden, 1980
Venturi Highway Gary Youngblood, Matt Ashcraft, and Randy Plank, 5/88
Barbeque Chips and Beer Phil Falcone and Ted Olsen, 3/86
Water Drawn From An Ancient Well Paul Paonessa, Kevin Stevensm 1986
Treiber's Deception Larry Treiber, Becky Treiber, Bill Sewrey, Tom Kreuser, 1967
                        FFA Lance and Dane Daugherty, Larry Treiber, 1968
Men At Work Variation Jim Waugh, Frank Valendo, 1984
Hot Line Jeff Splitberger, John Charles, 1972 FFA Pete Noebels, Dennis Abbink, 1979
Powell Variation Eric Powell, Greg Byrd, 1973
Look But Don't Touch Jim Waugh, John Dargis, 1979
Hard Drivin' John Ficker, Jim Waugh, 1981
Ubangy Lips Jim Waugh, Dave Black, 1978
Pretty Girls Make Graves Jim Waugh, Andy Dannerbeck, 1986
Sacred Datura Direct (Original) Larry Treiber, Barbara Zinn, 1974
                        (Direct) Jim Waugh, John Ficker, 1980
Sucubus Dennis Abbink, Larry Treiber, 1976
Deep Freeze Larry Treiber, Dave Hodson, Terry Price, 1976 FFA Stan Mish, Jim Waugh, 1978
Garbanzo Bean Larry Treiber, Chuck Graf, Bob Watts, Phil Martineau, 1973
Garbanzo Bean Direct Jason Sandidge, William Coburn, and Jim Guadnola, 1993
Kreuser's Route Tom Kreuser, Don Weaver, 1965
Great Compromise Herb North Jr., Chip Norton, 1979
The Settlement Larry Treiber, Bill Sewrey, Don Witt, 1967 FFA Larry Treiber, Barbara Zinn, 1974
Face First Jason Sandidge, John Ficker, 1985
West Corner Dick Hart, Bill McMorris, 1948
Experiment In Terror (Second Pitch) 1985 Jason Sandidge, Mike Cook
                        (Third Pitch) 1965 Bill Sewrey, Don Weaver, Dick Chambers
                        FFA (Third Pitch) 1974 Larry Treiber, Barbara Zinn
Waubo Jason Sandidge, William Coburn, 1992

West Face Direct Jason Sandidge, Jim Zahn, 1986
Fatman's Delight Bill Sewrey, Larry Treiber, Dane Daugherty, Joe Theobald, 1966

The Rist

Yee Haa Jason Sandidge, Mark Haley, Clayton Van Nimwegen, 11/88
Last Line Of Defense Jim Zahn, Chris Pomeroy, Mark Haley, Clayton Van Nimwegen, 11/88
Overtime Chris Pomeroy, Jim Zahn, 11/88

Parking Lot Wall

Crossroads Jason Sandidge, Sherry Duncan, 1986
Overpass Jason Sandidge, Sherry Duncan, 1986

Gardener's Wall

Child Of Troubled Times Tom Mcmillan, Chris Raypole, 1985
Facer's Choice Chuck Hill, Jason Sandidge, 1984
Southeast Arete Jim Zahn, Kay Zahn, Jason Sandidge, 1986
First Impressions Jason Sandidge, Chuck Hill, 1984
The Phantom Unknown
Crime Of The Century Variation Jason Sandidge, Dave Gunn, 1984
Gobs Of Knobs Larry Treiber, Bruce Grubbs, 1977
Kreuser`s Chimney Direct (First Pitch) 1965 Tom Kreuser, Dave Olson
                               (Second Pitch) 1977 Bruce Grubbs, Larry Treiber, Bill Sewrey
Phantom Of The Opera Jason Sandidge, Jim Zahn, Chuck Hill, 1984
Renaissance Direct (First Pitch) Larry Treiber, Bruce Grubbs, Bill Sewrey, 1977
                     (Second Pitch) Chuck Hill, Eric Johnson, 1983
Parental Guidance Variation Jim Zahn, Chuck Hill, Jason Sandidge, 1984
Fearless Leader (First Pitch) Chuck Hill, Jason Sandidge, 1984
               (Second Pitch) Chuck Hill, Dave Gunn, 1984
Hanging Gardens Lance and Dane Daugherty, Larry Treiber, Joe Theobald, 1965
                 FFA Joe Theobald, Glen Kappel, Jon Biemer, 1971
Brusin' and Cruisin' Pete Noebels, Dennis Abbink, Larry Treiber, 1975
Lickety Split Larry Treiber, Dave Hodson, 1975
For Cryin' Out Loud Chuck Hill, Mike Cook, Jason Sandidge, 1984
Gravity Jim Waugh, Kalvan Swanky, 1979
Black Streak Jason Sandidge, Jim Zahn, 1986
Dog Fight Giggle Jason Sandidge, Jim Zahn, Chuck Hill, 1986
Seam-In' Jason Sandidge, Jim Zahn, 1986
Easy Chair Phil Falcone, Ted Olsen, and James Graves, 6/86

Glass Dome

Hand-Some Jim Zahn, Mike Long, 1983
Ariba-Dirt-Cheap Jason Sandidge, John Ficker, 1983
The White Line Mike Long, Rand Black, 1983
Ladies In Waiting Mike Long, Eric Child, ?
Feminine Protection Chris Bastek, Jason Sandidge, 1993
Thin Air Mike Long, Rand Black, 1983
Smooth Sailing Rand Black, Mike Long, 1983
Destination Unknown Mike Long, Rand Black, Neil Sugarman, 1983
Hot Shoe Ted Olsen, Phil Falcone, and James Graves, 6/86

Goat Hill

Cloven Hoof Jan Holdeman and Paul Paonessa, 12/91
Nice Yard Jan Holdeman and Paul Paonessa, 12/91

Morrell's Wall Parking Lot

Xerxes Scott Aldinger, Al Muto, 11/90
Back To The Wall Glen Dickinson, Cindy Zarlengo, 1984
Seven-Up John Ficker, Glen Dickinson, 1984
Lost John Ficker, Glen Dickinson, 1984
Firstlee John Ficker, Lee Ficker, 1984
Forced Entry John Ficker, Glen Dickinson, 1984
Pinky John Ficker, Glen Dickinson, 1984
Dinky Scott Aldinger, Al Muto, 11/90
Lightning Scott Aldinger, Wade Vincent, Al Muto, 10/90
Thunderbolt Al Muto, Wade Vincent, Scott Aldinger, 10/90
Lunar Landing Scott Aldinger, Wade Vincent, Al Muto, 10/90
Squeeze Box Greg Opland, (Rope Solo) 10/95
Phoenix Greg Opland, (Rope Solo) 10/95
Sphinctre Boy Ted Olsen and Richie Eastman, 7/92
Girlie Man Richie Eastman And Ted Olsen, 8/92
Another Piece Of Meat Ted Olsen and Richie Eastman, 8/92
Brain Fart Richie Eastman And Ted Olsen, 8/92
Slickophobia Ted Olsen And Richie Eastman, 10/92
Fairies In Tights Phil Falcone and James Graves, 12/86
Under Pressure Phil Falcone and Ted Olsen, 2/87

Morrell's Wall

Seduction Production Jeffrey Jones, Eric Logan, 1986
Waste Eep (Way Steep, Waist Deep) Mike Cook, Gary Perkins, 1985
Tumbling Dice Glen Dickinson, Jim Zahn, John Ficker, 1982
Crack A Smile Jason Sandidge, John Ficker, 1984
Mission Impossible Jason Sandidge, John Ficker, 1984
Rest In Peace (R.I.P.) John Ficker, Jason Sandidge, 1984
It's Your Party (Aka Wade's Got Wood) Scott Aldinger and Al Muto, 9/92
Eat Shit and Die (E.S.A.D.) John Ficker, Jason Sandidge
Home Of The Brave Steve Smelser, John Ficker, Jason Sandidge, 1985
Dead On Arrival (D.O.A.) John Ficker (Red Point), 1986
Halloweenie Jim Zahn, John Ficker, 1983
White-On George Thielman, Jason Sandidge, John Ficker, 1984
Side-Tracked John Ficker, Glen Dickinson, 1982
Space Cadets John Ficker, Glen Dickinson, 1982
Space Shuffle Jay Anderson, Chris Pomeroy, 11/88
Beat Feet Bill Ellis, Tom Taber, 1969 FFA 1981 Jim Waugh, John Ficker, Jim Zahn, 1981
Jungle Gym Jim Waugh, Frank Valendo, 1984
Two Bill Ellis, Tom Taber, 1969
Sinbad Jim Zahn, John Ficker, 1984
Dale Low Memorial Route FA Ted Olsen, Phil Falcone and Jay Clark, 1/86
Gargoyle Jim Zahn, John Ficker, 1983
Leave It To Beaver Direct (First Pitch) John Dargis, Jim Waugh, 1977
　　　　　　　　　　　　(Second Pitch) 1969 Bill Ellis, Tom Taber, 1969
　　　　　　　　　　　　FFA (Second Pitch) 1981 Jim Zahn, John Ficker, Jim Waugh, 1981
　　　　　　　　　　　　(Third Pitch) 1981 Jim Waugh, Jim Zahn, John Ficker, 1981
Eddie Haskell Variation John Ficker, Glen Dickinson, 1982
Mutt (First Pitch) John Dargis, Jim Waugh, 1976
　　　(Second Pitch) John Ficker, Glen Dickinson, 1982
Jeff (First Pitch) Jim Waugh, John Dargis, 1976
　　　(Second Pitch) Glen Dickinson, John Ficker, 1982
Harpoon A Troon Rick Hlava, Jeff Jones, Andy Vejnoska, 1986
Epacondilitis Noel Aronov and Mike Taylor, 3/90

Sven Slab

Energizer   Dale Low & Ted Olsen, 11/81
Gripple Variation   Chuck Hill, Jason Sandidge., 1984
Hawk   Dale Low & Ted Olsen, 11/81
Cold Fingers   Dale Low & Ted Olsen, 12/84
Arrowhead   Ted Olsen and Dale Low, 12/81
One For The Road   (First Pitch) Ted Olsen Or Bob Puryear, 1981
                                (Second Pitch) Phil Falcone and Ted Olsen, 10/85
Half Moon   Phil Falcone and Ted Olsen (Solo), 10/85
The Chute   Ted Olsen & Dale Low, 12/81
Mousetrap   Mike Lawson, Brent Roberts, 1978
Mousetracks   Damon Williams, Bob Puryear, 1981
Over The Hill   Jim Waugh, 1985
Black Death   Bob Puryear, Larry Braten, 1985
Cakewalk   Dan Dingle, Alex Mcguffie, 1978
Ego Trip   Rick Hlava, Calvin Hahn, 1985
I Sinkso   John Tattersall and Scott Davidson, 6/88
Quaker Oats   Stan Mish, Terry Price, 1976
Changes In Longitude   Alex Mcguffie, Brent Roberts, Mike Lawson, Dan Dingle, Maxie Mcguffie, 1978
Dark Passage   Neil Sugarman, Darius Azin, 1983
Changes In Attitude   Chris Bastek and Terry Merrill, March 1990
Peaches & Cream   Terry Price, Stan Mish, 1976
Changes In Latitude   Jim Waugh, John Dargis, Dylan Williams, 1981
Nit Nat   Jim Waugh, Dylan Williams, 1981
Hippity Hop   Jim Waugh, John Dargis, Dylan Williams, 1981

Knob Hill

F.C. 9797   John Tattersall, Rich Beaudoin, 4/88
Freudian Slip   Matt Hudson and Leo Bunuel, 8/91
Last Light   Peter Hogan and Paul Paonessa, 1/88
Blue Light   Blue Stringer Et Al., ?
Dyo's Route   Dyo Coles, 1988
Piggys Conch Shell   Paul Paonessa, Bill Dacier, Tim Standing, and J. Wilson, 10/89
Lord Of The Flies   Peter Hogan, Jan Holdeman, Paul Paonessa, and Dyo Coles, 1/88
Thrasher   Terry Merrill and Steve Powers, 1989
Brown Nose   Terry Merrill and Chris Bastek, 1989

Sven Towers

Fly By   Jan Holdeman and Paul Paonessa, 1/92
Just Fine   Jan Holdeman and Candace Luther, 12/91
Feel The Creep   Jan Holdeman, Paul Paonessa, and Eric Ramsey, 1/92
Coloring Book   John Ficker and Glen Dickinson (Left Gully Exit)
                          Paul Paonessa and Jan Holdeman, 1/92 (Face Above Roof).
Leaping Rabbit   Paul Paonessa, Leslie Waxman, and Jan Holdeman, 1/92
Unknown   FA Unknown.
Cary'd Away   Paul Paonessa, Steve Woodard, and Jan Holdeman, 1/92

Granite Ballroom – Ballroom

Delusions Of Grandeur   Noel Aronov, 2/92
Uneventful   Jeffrey Jones, Rick Hlava, 1986
Boston Bee Strangler   Chris Raypole, Dave Gunn, 1984
Logan's Run   Jeffrey Jones, Eric Logan, 1986
Piano Man   Jeffrey Jones, Rick Hlava, 1984

Granite Ballroom – Noah's Ark

Wattle 'n Daub Jeffrey Jones, Jim Roberts, 1986
Beam Me Up Scotty Jeffrey Jones, Ian Wickson, 1986
Schmidty's Route Ian Wickson, Steve Schmidt, and Bill Lefevre, July 1992
Keen Jan Holdeman and Paul Paonessa, 12/91
Burnt Offerings Paul Paonessa and Jan Holdeman, 12/91

Granite Ballroom – Rosetta Stone

Face Value Jan Holdeman, Anita Madrechesia, and Michael Nevels, 12/91
Obscure Origin Jan Holdeman and Anita Madrechesia, 12/91
Brazilian Tenant Farmers Paul Paonessa and Jan Holdeman, 12/91
The Cipher Jan Holdeman and Amy Moorhead, 12/91

Hog Heaven

John's Bag John Ficker, Jason Sandidge, John Mitchell, 1983
Sand's Bag Jason Sandidge, John Mitchell, John Ficker, 1983
Chalk Bag John Ficker, George Thielman, 1983
Triple "J" Direct Jim Zahn, Jason Sandidge, John Ficker, 1983
Static Cling John Ficker, Mike Cook, Jason Sandidge, 1983
George Of The Jungle George Thielman, Ken Akers, 1983
Pissed Off John Mitchell, Jason Sandidge, John Ficker, 1983
High On The Hog Steve Smelser, Bill Blosser, 12/88
Bony Fingers Steve Smelser, Perry Tetters, Larry Braten, 12/88
Sudden Impact John Ficker, Jason Sandidge, 1983
Shiver Me Timbers Jason Sandidge, John Ficker, Jim Zahn, 1983
Slime Slit Jason Sandidge, John Ficker, 1983
Domestic Longhair Terry Merrill and Chris Bastek, 1991
Little Dickens John Ficker, Jason Sandidge, John Mitchell, 1983
Dust-Proof Roof Jeff Szoke, John Ficker, 1983
Goof-Proof Roof John Ficker, Jason Sandidge, 1983
Fool-Proof Roof Jason Sandidge, John Ficker, 1983
Wired Wizard Steve Haire, John Conklin, Steve Schultz, 1984
'57 Pan Head Jason Sandidge, John Ficker, 1983
A.M.C. (Arizona Mouseketeering Club) John Ficker, Jason Sandidge, 1983
Thumbnail John Ficker, Jason Sandidge, 1983

Fist Grease Boulder

Numb Nuts Jim Zahn, Jason Sandidge, John Ficker, 1983
Fist Grease Jason Sandidge, John Ficker (1 Fall, Hang) / 1984 Jim Waugh (1 Fall)
Impending Doom Jim Zahn, Jason Sandidge, John Ficker, 1983
Freezer Burn Jason Sandidge, John Mitchell, 1983

Pinnacle Peak

Knob Wall

Double Digit Dilemma Jim Zahn. John Ficker, 1981
Inflation Jim Zahn. John Ficker ,1981
Famous Last Words Unknown

Lower East Wall

Any Time Around Chris Bastek, Mike Kelley, and Steve Agaciewski, Jan. 1991
Second Time Around Unknown
All The Right Moves Variation Neil Sugarman, 1986

Bookend Unknown
Leftovers Glen Dickinson & ?, 1983
Dispute Joe Theobald & ?
         FFA Lance & Dane Dougherty, Larry Treiber, Joe Theobald, Ron Potter, 1968
Lizard's Lip Dane & Lance Daugherty   FFA Dane & Lance Daugherty
         5.6 Var Dane & Lance Daugherty, Joe Theobald, Amc Members, 1968
The Groin Lance & Dane Daugherty. Jim Matteson, 1967
         FFA Larry Treiber, Chuck Parker, 1972
Wheat Thin FA Unknown FFA Jim Waugh. John Dargis, 1980
The Last Detail Jim Waugh. John Dargis, 1978
The Brown Jam John Byrd. Doug Rickard, 1972
Drop, Plop, Fly Or Die Jason Fletcher and Matt Heinbeck, 7/89
Layback Rex Lambert. Bill Ellis, 1967
         FFA Larry Treiber. Pat Copeland. Gale West, 1968
Hangover Lance & Dane Daugherty. Jim Matteson, 1967
         FFA Larry Treiber. Pete Noebels, 1974
On Golden Path Jim Waugh. Jason Sandidge, 1982
         Variation (Left) Unknown
Hidden Chimneys Lance & Dane Daugherty. Jim Matteson, 1967
         FFA 1973 Jon Biemer. Glenn Short, 1973
         Variation Jon Biemer. Glenn Short, 1973
No Mercy Jason Sandidge. Jim Waugh, 1982
Mad Man's Traverse (Right To Left) Lance & Dane Daugherty, 1968
         FFA (Left To Right) Steve Byrd. Jim Hunter, 1973
Down & Out In Phoenix Chuck Hill, 1986

Satan's Slab

Satan's Slab Lance & Dane Daugherty. Larry Treiber, 1967
White Warlock Chuck Parker. Larry Treiber. Bill Betcher, 1972
Devil's Disciple Mark Brown (Free Solo), 1973
Pasta Man Frank Valendo. Jim Waugh, 1983

AMC Boulder

Reunion Ted Olsen & Dale Low, 11/84
Varicose Arizona Mountaineering Club Members
Rurpture John Ficker, Ken Akers, Glen Dickinson, 1981
Mickey Mantle Arizona Mountaineering Club Members
         (Face Start Was Originally Done By John Ficker and Glen Dickinson)
Diamond Back Crack Richard Shoup and Chris Pomeroy, 1986
Up In Smoke Jay Anderson, James Duval, Steve Smelser, 1986
Delayed Flight Chuck Hill. Scherry Duncan, 1984
Scar Wars Steve Smelser. Brian Mcshane. Tom Kays, 1985
         FFA Steve Smelser. Jay Anderson. James Duval, 1986
Look Sharp Doug Fletcher, Jan Holdeman, 1985

Loafer's Choice Slab

Loafer's Choice John Ficker, Jim Zahn. Jim Waugh. Glen Dickinson, 1979
Dead Meat John Ficker. Steve Smelser, 1982
         Variations John Ficker, 1982

The Wedge

Hiliter Lance & Dane Daugherty, 1967
Redemption Lance & Dane Daugherty, 1968
Naked Edge Larry Treiber, 1974

Y-Crack Boulder

Y-Crack Pete Noebels. Dennis Abbink. Larry Treiber, 1977
Short But Sweet Ajax Greene & ? (Free Solo)
Send It Scott Aldinger & Greg Opland, 2/94
Jam On Jam Steve White, Tink Golamb, Bill Heer, 1983
Corona Club Phil Falcone and Ted Olsen, 8/87
Turtle Piss Steve Haire, Steve Shultz, 1984
Timed Release Jan Holdeman, John Mchugh, 1986
Chockstones On My Mind Doug Smucker. Noel Aronov, 1986
Short But Nasty Scott Aldinger and Greg Opland, 2/94
Tasha's Tower Noel Aronov. Doug Smucker, 1986
Unknown 5.Hard Unknown

Cactus Flower East

Anarchist's Delight Tim Bombaci, Chet Wade, and Fernando Schrader, 1/88
Worm Al Muto, Wade Vincent, Scott Aldinger, 2/90
Facist Pig Tim Bombaci, Chet Wade, Fernando Schrader 1/88
King Of Pain Chuck Hill, Mike Cook, 1985
Two Cams & Jam Chuck Hill, Pat Reineke, 1986
Banana Crack Unknown
Mystical Adventures Chuck Hill, Mike Cook, 1985
Black Sunday Chuck Hill, 1986
Fabulous Fables Jim Waugh, John Ficker, 1986
Live Oak Wade Vincent, Scott Aldinger, Al Muto, 2/90
Palo Verde Al Muto, Wade Vincent, Scott Aldinger, 2/90
Pomey Direct Pam Metzger, 1991
Cat Claw Al Muto, Scott Aldinger, Wade Vincent, 2/90
Pam's Jam Noel Aronov and Bart Garlotte, 9/86
Zenolith Jim Waugh, John Ficker, 1986
Political Asylum Tim Bombaci, Chet Wade, Fernando Schrader, 5/88
Banana Split Scott Aldinger, Wade Vincent, Al Muto, 2/90
Mixed Feelings Gary Youngblood. Noel Aronov. Jan Holdeman, 1986

Cactus Flower West

Cactus Flower Dana Hollister, Patty Hollister, 1977 FFA Chuck Parker. Dennis Abbink, 1978
Crumbled Freak Pat Putnam and Mike Covington, 12/87
You Can't Get There From Here Bob Jacobs, Shawn O'fallon. Ed Davis & Others, 1985
I Just Wanna Be In The Guidebook Ed Davis, Tom Mcmillan, Bob Jacobs, 1985
Arizona 7 Shawn O'fallon, Ed Davis, Bob Jacobs, 1985
Unnamed Paul Paonessa and Kc Baum, 2/87

Pinnacle Peak

Ass Trap Chuck Parker, Dana Hollister
Starting Point Chuck Parker, Dana Hollister
Mr. Creamjeans Dave Gunn, Chuck Hill, 1985
Birthday Party Dana Hollister. Chuck Parker. Pete Noebels, 1974
Pecker Party Chuck Hill, Jason Sandidge, Dave Gunn, 1985
Dried Oatmeal Pete Noebels, Chuck Parker, 1974
Boxer Chuck Parker, Misty Warsing, Kevin ?. Pete Noebels, 1974
Beegee Lance & Dane Daugherty, 1968 FFA Rick Sylvester and Chuck Parker, 1974
South Crack Ed George, Bill Mcmorris, 1947
Out On A Limb Larry Bratten, Steve Smelser, 1986
Flight 511 Jason Sandidge, 1986

Hades   Larry Treiber, Chuck Parker. Pete Noebels, 1976

Name It   Pete Noebels & ?, 1976

Fear Of Flying   FA (1st & 2nd Crux) Lance & Dane Daugherty, 1968
                      FFA (1st & 2nd Crux) Phil Armadas. Dave Black, Mark Force, 1977
                      FFA (Entire Route) Stan Mish, Dave Black, 1978

Powder Puff Direct   Stan Mish, Dave Black, Jim Waugh, 1978
                             (Direct Finish, Straight Above Fifth Bolt) Jim Waugh, Glenn Rink, 1979

Lesson In Discipline   Brad Smith, Eric Johnson, 1981

Sidewinder   Bob Box. Phil Martineau, 1970   FFA Pete Noebels, 1979

Feets Don't Fail Me Now Face   Stan Mish and Chuck Parker, 1979

Deliverance   Andy Embick, 1979

Deep Throat   Doug Rickard, Chuck Parker, 1973

Chug-A-Lug   (1st Pitch) 1973 Chuck Parker
               (2nd Pitch) 1975 Chuck Parker, Pete Noebels, Misty Warsing

Beer Route   Kachinas, 1948-49

Chutes and Ladders   Chuck Parker, Doug Rickard, 1973

Dungeons and Dragons (Aka Burnt Toast)   Jim Waugh, 1985

Lost Nuts   Dana Hollister. Monty Hollister, 1978   FFA Stan Mish. Jim Waugh, 1979

Deathwatch   Dane Daugherty, 1968   FFA Dave Black. Jim Waugh, 1979

Happy Robots   Chris Dunn, Janice Metzler Dunn, and Dave Houchin, 1/89

On My Own Damn Couch   Janice Metzler Dunn, Chris Dunn, and Dave Houchin, 1/89

Vanishing Point   (1st Pitch) John Williams, John Ficker, 1978
                   (2nd Pitch) Chuck Parker, Dana Hollister, Glenn Short, 1979

Baby Woolsey   Larry Bratten, Perry Teeters

Luna   Bill Paul

Sailin' Shoes   Unknown

My Daddy's A Hard Man   Perry Teeter and Mark Trainor, 1/93

Bear Route   (1st Pitch) Unknown
             (Complete) Jeff Splitgerber, John Charles, 1972

South Of Heaven   Bill Paul, ?

Never Never Land   Jim Waugh, John Dargis, 1979

South Gully   Jack Turnage, Bill Sewrey, 1965

Twenty-Eighth Day   (1st Pitch) Larry Treiber, Dana Hollister. Dennis Abbink, Pete Noebels, 1975
                    (Entire Route) Larry Treiber, 1975

Silhouette   Bob Blair, Tim Standing, Jay Abhus, Paul Paonessa, 1987

Shalayly Direct   (First Crux) Dave Black, Stan Mish, 1979
               (Entire Route) Jim Waugh, John Ficker, 1979

Thundering Hearts   Jim Waugh. Brad Smith. Eric Johnson, 1983

Beezlebub   Pete Noebels, Dana Hollister, 1977   FFA Stan Mish

Voluptuous Ham   Chuck Parker, 1973

Hamster Variation   Jim Waugh, Jim Zahnm 1985

Garbert's Chimney   Gary Garbert, 1965

The Feltzer   Jason Sandidge. Steve Brynne, Chuck Hill, 1985

Brown Out (Originally The Chancre)   Doug Rickard, Chuck Parker, 1973

Rastaman Vibration   Rick Donnelly, Rick Hlava, 1986

Good Vibrations   Rick Fritz (Rope Solo), 1977

Parallax View   Dave Hodson. Herb North Jr., Phil Armadas, 1976

Rossetti Rose   (Direct) Jim Waugh, Frank Valendo, 1983
            Jim Waugh, John Ficker, 1981

Spread-Em With Style Direct   (Original) John Williams, Jim Waugh, 1979
                              (Direct) Jim Waugh, Frank Valendo, 1983

Spiral Staircase   Jack Turnage. Bill Sewrey, 1965

Ezy Rider   Rick Fritz, Dana Hollister, Herb North Jr., 1976

Troon Mountain (Aka Windy Walks)

Penny Arcade

Centipede Glen Dickinson, Jim Waugh, Brad Smith, 1983
Missile Command John Ficker, Glen Dickinson, 1982
Pac Man (Comet Jeff Szoke, Glen Dickinson, John Ficker, 1982
Crazy Climber (Funnel) John Ficker, Glen Dickinson, 1982
Asteroids Jason Sandidge, Glen Dickinson, 1982
Battle Zone John Ficker, Jason Sandidge, 1983
Kong Jeff Szoke, Glen Dickinson, John Ficker, 1982

Sunshine Wall

Sunshine Glen Dickinson, Dan Loden, 1982
Two Easy Glen Dickinson, Cindy Zarlengo, 1982

RURP Rock

Fist Fight Mike Long, Glen Dickinson, ?
Tea Cups John Ficker, Jason Sandidge, Jim Zahn, 1982
Jelly Roll Jim Zahn, Jason Sandidge, John Ficker, 1982
Tender Vittles Jason Sandidge, Jim Zahn, Mike Long, John Ficker, 1982

The Gallery

Stiff Upper Lip Jason Sandidge, Jim Zahn, John Ficker, 1982
Hair Lip Jim Zahn, Jason Sandidge, John Ficker, 1982
Peanut Brittle Jason Sandidge (Free Solo), 1982
Peanuts Jason Sandidge, Mike Long, John Ficker, 1982
Popcorn John Ficker, Mike Long, Jason Sandidge, 1982
Snap, Crackle, & Pop Jason Sandidge, Mark Haley, 1982
Diamond Back Jim Waugh, John Ficker (Falls), 1982

The Tooth

Root Canal John Ficker, Mike Long, 1982
Party Line Jason Sandidge, John Ficker, Neil Sugarman, Mike Long, 1982
Cavity Mike Long, John Ficker, 1982

Ice Box

Thin Ice Jason Sandidge, Mike Long, John Ficker, 1982

Ray's Face Area Left

Cleavage Mike Long, Jim Zahn, John Ficker, 1982
Extra-Strength Tylenol John Ficker, Mike Long, Jim Zahn, Chris Raypole, 1982
Dual Identity Jim Zahn, John Ficker, Glen Dickinson, 1980
Basket Case Jim Zahn, Jason Sandidge, John Ficker, Glen Dickinson, 1982
Creep From The Deep John Ficker, Jason Sandidge, Jim Zahn, Glen Dickinson, 1982

Ray's Face Area Right

#1 Jim Zahn, John Ficker, 1980
Only The Strong Survive John Ficker, Jason Sandidge, 1982
Picture Window Route Dick Aleith, Jon Biemer, Ray Stauffer,. Oct. 1971
Acme Acres Jason Sandidge, John Ficker, 1984
Wimpetus Chris Raypole, Jim Waugh, 1985
Tip Trip Jim Waugh, Brad Smith, 1983

Change Up Jason Sandidge, John Ficker, 1982
#3 Jim Zahn, John Fickerj, 1980
Finger Delight Jason Sandidge, John Ficker, 1982
Added Security John Ficker, Jason Sandidge, 1982
Sundown Mike Long, Jason Sandidge, 1982
Pete John Ficker, Jim Zahn, 1980
Re-Pete Glen Dickinson, Jim Zahn, John Ficker, 1980
Combination Of The Two Jim Zahn, John Ficker, 1980
Crowbar John Ficker, Jim Zahn, 1980

White Bwana Boulder

A Bone For Bwana Jeffrey Jones, Jeff Wax, 1986
Call Me Bwana Jeff Wax, Jeffrey Jones, 1986

Tranquility Spire

Shaboomy Jim Zahn, Jason Sandidge, 1983
Sanity Route FA Lyle Huff, Jon Biemer, 1971
               FFA Jason Sandidge, Mike Long, 1983
Insanity Variation Larry Treiber, 1972
Death Of Ethos Chris Dunn, Mike Lawson, and Gerald Guidroz, 1987
Resolution Dennis Mcmahon and Chris Dunn, 1/87

Marshall Good's Wall

Pasta Man's Ride Jim Waugh, Frank Valendo, 1984
Marshall Good's Ride Jim Waugh, Jim Zahn, 1980
Lateralito Bandito Frank Valendo, Jim Waugh, 1984
Mistaken Identity Jim Waugh, Bob Barling, 1981

Rhythm And Blues Boulder Area

Heavy Metal Jim Waugh, John Ficker, 1981
Rhythm and Blues Rick Fritz, 1978 - FFA Jim Waugh, Peter Noebels, 1980
Everybody and His Brother Bob Barling, Dylan Williams, Frank Valendo, 1981
My Indecision Bob Barling, Dylan Williams, 1981
Lost Indian Dylan Williams, Bob Barling, 1981
Two Foot Shuffle Jim Waugh, John Ficker, 1981
Beauty Jim Waugh, Peter Noebels (Free Solo), 1980
Beast Peter Noebels, Jim Waugh (Free Solo), 1980

Summit Boulder Area

North Crack Unknown
Happy Hooker Steve Smelser, John Ficker, Larry Braten, 2/88
By Hook Or By Crook Steve Smelser, John Ficker, Larry Braten, 2/88
Diaphragm Slip Dylan Williams, John Dargis, 1981

Southeast Rockpile

Warm and Windy John Williams, Hubert Green, 1978
Breakfast Of Champions Jim Waugh, John Dargis, 1977
Hangin Out Glen Dickinson, Dan Loden, 1980 - FFA Brad Smith, 1980
Shades Of Granite Jungle Jim Waugh, John Dargis, 1979
Dance Of The Swallows Pat Putnam, Michael Covington, 1/88
Pussyfoot Jim Waugh, John Ficker, Jim Zahn, 1979
Bombay Flake Rick Fritz, Dan Joder, 1976
Archway Jason Sandidge, Mike Long, 1982

Fruit Loops

Tunnel Vision Jim Waugh, John Dargis, 1977
Shallow Tallo John Dargis, Jim Waugh, 1977
So Long Mickey Mouse Jim Waugh, John Dargis, 1977

East Pinnacles

Desolate Sojourner Eric Johnson, Brad Smith, 1982
Graham Cracker Jim Zahn, John Ficker, 1982
Ginger Bread Jim Waugh, John Ficker, 1981
Ginger Snap Var. Jim Waugh, Kent Brock, 1981
Face Sandwich Jim Waugh, John Dargis, 1979
Lookin' For Trouble Chuck Hill Et Al., 1980
Pit Or Pendulum Jim Waugh, John Dargis, 1977
Thunder Roe John Dargis, Jim Waugh, 1977
Short and Sassy Jim Waugh, Jeri Masoner, 1977
Melena Brad Smith, Jim Zahn, Eric Johnson, 1981
What A Drag Mike Long, Jason Sandidge, Jim Zahn, John Ficker, 1982

Tapered Wall Area

Hand Job Jason Sandidge, Bob Barling, Jim Zahn, Mike Long, Dave Houchin, 1982
Joke Book Jason Sandidge, Mike Long, Jim Zahn, John Ficker, 1982
It Don't Get No Traddern' That Tim Schneider, Greg Opland, 1/94
Bar None Dave Houchin, Jim Zahn, 1982
Bee Direct Bob Barling, Jim Erwin, 1981
        Var (5.9) Jason Sandidge, Bob Barling, 1982
The Perch John Ficker, Mike Long, 1982
Transformation Jim Zahn, Jason Sandidge, John Ficker, 1982
Step In Line Jason Sandidge, Dave Houchin, Bob Barling, 1982
Skid Marks Jim Zahn, Mike Long, 1982
Goob's R'out Greg Opland and Tim Schneider, 1/94

April Fool's Wall

April Fool Jim Waugh, Vicki Wegman, 1981
May Day Jim Waugh, Frank Valendo, 1984

The Nose

Risky Business Jim Waugh, Frank Valendo, 1984
The Nose John Ficker, Glen Dickinson (First Pitch), 1980
        Jim Waugh, Frank Valendo (Entire Route), 1984

Corner Stone Area

Lead It, Or Leave It Jason Sandidge, John Ficker, Jim Zahn. 1983
Corner Stone John Ficker, Glen Dickinson, 1981
Truth Or Consequences John Ficker, Jason Sandidge, 1983

White Tank Mountains

Waterfall Area Left

Easy Ledges Bob Blair, Terry Gerber, 1974
Banana Peel Variation Bob Blair, Joe Schmidt, Glenn Rink, 1976
Z Crack Chris Raypole, Greg Elbert, and Gary Elbert, 4/91
Rusty Piton (Reported) Bob Blair and Jim Guadnola, 2/91

Wombat Indirect Bob Blair, Andy Younker, Jeff Dryer/Mike Winters, Dave Wargo, 1990-91
Staircase Bob Blair, Terry Gerberm 1974
Steps Joe Schmidt, 1966
Ramp Joe Schmidt, Glenn Rink, 1976
Romp Variation Joe Schmidt, Glenn Rink, 1976

Waterfall Area Right

Electrophilic Aromatic Substitution Bob Blair, 1976
Crunchy Frog Bob Blair and Jim Guadnola, 2/91
Sweet Dream Bob Blair, Andy Younker, and Jeff Dryer, 1/91
Leaping Lizards Bob Blair, Terry Gerber, Greg Horstman, 1974
Bob and Eric's Excellent Adventure Bob Blair and Eric Agaciewski 9/91
Warmup Bill Heer, 1975

War Wall

Gorilla Warfare Bob Blair, Jay Abbas, and Eric Agaciewski, 12/91
Blood Bath Joe Schmidt, Glenn Rink, 1976
Massacre Bob Blair, Joe Schmidt, Glenn Rink, 1976
Rape Bob Blair and Jim Guadnola, 2/91
Fright Flight (TR) Mike Winters and Dave Wargo, 10/91
              (Rappel Pro) Bob Blair, Eric Agaciewski, and Chris Mccue, 12/91
Green Beret Bob Blair, Eric Agaciewski, Jay Abbas, and David Chesnutt, 12/91

The Slab

You Name The Route Karl Bond, 3/91
Theraphy Bob Blair, Eric Agaciewski, Chris Mccue, 12/91

Triangle Boulder Area

Exit Stage Left Kent Brock, Bob Blair, Rick Heehs, 1980
Layback Unknown
Arpeggio Rick Heehs, Kent Brock, Bob Blair, 1980

Illusion Wall Area

Joe Schmidt Route Joe Schmidt, 1977
Memory Lane Bob Blair and Eric Agaciewski, 1/92
Illusion Bob Blair and Eric Agaciewski, 1/92

Witch Wall

Poison Apple Bob Blair, and Eric Agaciewski, 12/91
Mirror, Mirror Eric Agaciewski, Bob Blair, and Chris Mccue, 12/91
Sleeping Beauty Bob Blair, Eric Agaciewski, and Chris Bastek, 11/91

The White Wall

Red Dog Bob Blair and Jim Guadnola, 12/90
Scorpion's Last Dance Bob Blair and Jim Guadnola, 12/90
Timmie's 5.12 Route Tom Martin, and Bob Blair, 12/90
Serrated Edge Bob Blair and Jim Guadnola, 12/90

The Black Lagoon Wall

Black Lagoon Bob Blair and Eric Agaciewski, 12/91

Fall Factor Wall

Hangbelly Crack Bob Blair, Bill Heer, Steve Friend, 1975
Potent Pudding Bob Blair, Joe Schmidt, 1974
Milkrun John Dargis, Mike Hamilton, 1975
Cactus Candy Bob Blair, Joe Schmidt, 1974
Snorfy Elaticor Bob Blair, Joe Schmidt, 1975
Turkey Traverse Variation Bob Blair, Joe Schmidt, 1975
The Jaws Of Rockomatic Kent Brock, Bob Blair, 1980
Attila The Hun Bob Blair, Glenn Rink, 1979
Sarazin Bob Blair and Eric Agaciewski, 10/91
Owlshit Crack Dale Steward, Joe Schmidt, Bob Blair, 1975
Fritz Fell Here Variation Rick Fritz, Chuck Rhoades, 1978

Odds-N-Ends

Lookout Mountain

Loose Layback Marty Karabin and Chris Bastek, 8/93
The Gnome Marty Karabin and Chris Bastek, 6/93
I Love Loosie Marty Karabin and Chris Bastek, 6/93
Junkyard Dog Paul Paonessa and Chuck Johnson, 10/86
Speed Freak Marty Karabin and Chris Bastek, 5/93
When Lester Comes Out To Play Marty Karabin and Chris Bastek, 6/93
Little Miss Dangerous Marty Karabin and Chris Bastek, 5/93
Too Loose To Goose Marty Karabin and Chris Bastek, 5/93
Unnamed Marty Karabin and Chris Bastek, 6/93
Falling Stars Marty Karabin and Chris Bastek, 6/93
The Contender Marty Karabin and Chris Bastek, 8/93
Double Feature Marty Karabin and Chris Bastek, 6/93
Unknown #1 Unknown, 80's?
Devil In Disguise Marty Karabin and Chris Bastek, 9/93
Totally Trad Marty Karabin and Chris Bastek, 9/93
Unknown #2 Unknown, 80's?
Scoobie Doobie Paul Paonessa and Chuck Johnson, 10/86
Pushin' Your Luck Marty Karabin and Chris Bastek, 9/93

CROWN KING AREA

Fool's Gold Wall

Steel Monkey (TR) Greg Opland and Tim Schneider, 12/91
                 (Lead) Greg Opland and Al Muto, 4/92
Flakey Bats On Crack Tim Schneider and Al Muto, 11/91
Scaryzona Tim Schneider, Al Muto, 11/91
Tim and Al's Grunge Band Al Muto and Tim Schneider, 11/91

Castle Rock

Whillan's Bloodbath Chris Beal and Bruce Grubbs, 1974
Last Will & Testament Bruce Grubbs and Chris Beal, 1974
Twenty Tiny Fingers Chris Beal and Bruce Grubbs, 1974
The Dreaded South Stack Bruce Grubbs and Chris Beal, 1974

EAGLETAIL MOUNTAINS AREA

Courthouse Rock

Standard Route FA Unknown

Eagletail Peak Area

Eagletail Peak (Aka North Feather) FA Ben Pedrick, Ray Garner, Ed George, and Dick Hart, April 1949
FFA 1977 Larry Treiber, Bruce Grubbs, and Chris Beal, 1977
Middle Feather Larry Treiber, Bruce Grubbs, and Chris Beal, 1977
South Feather Bruce Grubbs, Chris Beal, and Larry Treiber, 1977
Justice Of The Peace Larrytreiber and Bruce Grubbs, 1977

Four Peaks

The Lady Bug Chuck Graf, Bob Graf, and Bruce Grubbs, 1969
Bugeye Variation Greg Opland and Scott Aldinger, 8/95
The Far Side Gary Youngblood and Karl Erikson, 6/87

Brushy Basin

Zuma Chris Dunn and Dave Houchin, 2/82
Valentine Dave Houchin and Chris Dunn, 2/14/82
Pebbles and Bam Bam Chris Dunn, Janice Metzler Dunn and Jimi Duval, 1988
Zenolith Steve Smelser and Dave Houchin, 1981
Unnamed FA Unknown
Sinbad Dave Houchin and Chris Dunn, 1982

Picket Post Mountain

The Picket Post Bill Forrest and Gary Garbert, 1965
Hudson Route Matt Hudson and Clayton Van Nimwegen, 2/90

Yarnell Wall

Wide Glide Los Banditos, 1979
Languish Los Banditos, 1979
L.B.'s Panhead Los Banditos, 1979
Mish Mash Los Banditos, 1979
Mish Mash - Variation Los Banditos, 1979
The Sultan Los Banditos, 1979
The Knucklehead Los Banditos, 1980

Vulture Peak

The Vulture Bill Sewery and Larry Treiber, 10/67
The Talon Traverse Bill Sewery and Larry Treiber, 1967-1969

The first move of **Treiber's Deception** on Tom's Thumb is quite a stretch!

INDEX

Access: It's everybody's concern

THE ACCESS FUND, a national, non-profit climbers' organization, is working to keep you climbing. The Access Fund helps preserve access and protect the environment by providing funds for land acquisitions and climber support facilities, financing scientific studies, publishing educational materials promoting low-impact climbing, and providing start-up money, legal counsel and other resources to local climbers' coalitions.

the ACCESS FUND

Climbers can help preserve access by being responsible users of climbing areas. Here are some practical ways to support climbing:

- **COMMIT YOURSELF TO "LEAVING NO TRACE."** Pick up litter around campgrounds and the crags. Let your actions inspire others.

- **DISPOSE OF HUMAN WASTE PROPERLY.** Use toilets whenever possible. If none are available, choose a spot at least 50 meters from any water source. Dig a hole 6 inches (15 cm) deep, and bury your waste in it. *Always pack out toilet paper* in a "Zip-Lock"-type bag.

- **UTILIZE EXISTING TRAILS.** Avoid cutting switchbacks and trampling vegetation.

- **USE DISCRETION WHEN PLACING BOLTS AND OTHER "FIXED" PROTECTION.** Camouflage all anchors with rock-colored paint. Use chains for rappel stations, or leave rock-colored webbing.

- **RESPECT RESTRICTIONS THAT PROTECT NATURAL RESOURCES AND CULTURAL ARTIFACTS** . Appropriate restrictions can include prohibition of climbing around Indian rock art, pioneer inscriptions, and on certain formations during raptor nesting season. Power drills are illegal in wilderness areas. *Never chisel or sculpt holds in rock on public lands, unless it is expressly allowed* – no other practice so seriously threatens our sport.

- **PARK IN DESIGNATED AREAS,** not in undeveloped, vegetated areas. Carpool to the crags!

- **MAINTAIN A LOW PROFILE.** Other people have the same right to undisturbed enjoyment of natural areas as do you.

- **RESPECT PRIVATE PROPERTY.** Don't trespass in order to climb.

- **JOIN OR FORM A GROUP TO DEAL WITH ACCESS ISSUES IN YOUR AREA.** Consider clean-ups, trail building or maintenance, or other "goodwill" projects.

- **JOIN THE ACCESS FUND.** To become a member, *simply make a donation (tax-deductible) of any amount.* Only by working together can we preserve the diverse American climbing experience.

The Access Fund. Preserving America's diverse climbing resources.
The Access Fund • P.O. Box 17010 • Boulder, CO 80308